HARCOURT ART EVERYWHERE

Teacher Edition

AUTHORS

Jacqueline Chanda
Kristen Pederson Marstaller

CONSULTANTS

Katherina Danko-McGhee
María Teresa García-Pedroche

Harcourt
SCHOOL PUBLISHERS

Orlando   Austin   New York   San Diego   Toronto   London

Visit *The Learning Site!*
www.harcourtschool.com

ISBN 0-15-336457-2
     0-15-342015-4

2 3 4 5 6 7 8 9 10   030   13 12 11 10 09 08 07 06 05

Authors

Jacqueline Chanda

Chair, Division of Art Education and Art History, School of Visual Arts, University of North Texas; Co-Director, North Texas Institute for Educators on the Visual Arts

Research contributions: thematic instruction, literacy through art, art history

Kristen Pederson Marstaller

Instructional Coordinator of Fine Arts, Austin Independent School District; President, Texas Art Education Association, 2003–2005

Research contributions: teacher preparation, classroom management, creative expression

CONSULTANTS

Katherina Danko-McGhee

Early Childhood Art Education Coordinator, University of Toledo, Art Department—Center for the Visual Arts; Early Childhood Consultant, Toledo Museum of Art

Research contributions: aesthetic preferences of young children, museum studies

María Teresa García-Pedroche

Head of Family Programs and Community Outreach, Dallas Museum of Art; Visual Artist

Research contributions: school–home and community connections, museum studies, art and culture

How to Use
Art Everywhere

Art Everywhere is a comprehensive program that teaches the elements of art, the principles of design, and other art concepts. Thirty lessons and twelve cross-curricular features are organized into six thematic units designed to help students think critically about art and the world around them.

Plan

Use the **Planning Guide** and **Artist's Workshops Preview** to identify lesson objectives and plan production activities. Gather resources from a variety of options:

- Art Prints
- Teacher Resource Book
- Artist's Workshop Activities: English and Spanish
- Art Transparencies

Electronic Art Gallery CD-ROM, Intermediate

Visit *The Learning Site*
www.harcourtschool.com

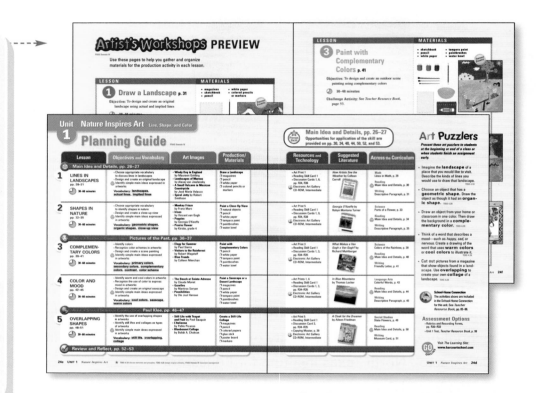

Provide Instruction

Teach the **elements of art,** the **principles of design,** and other **art concepts** through a variety of well-known and culturally diverse art images as well as student artworks. Encourage students' creativity and problem-solving skills through **Artist's Workshop** activities.

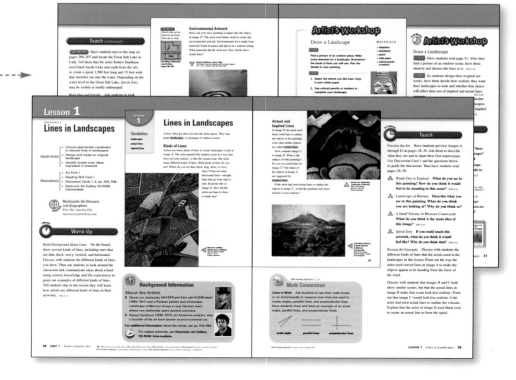

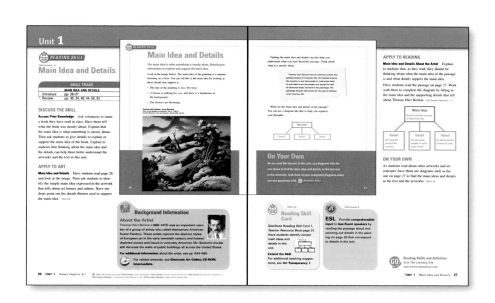

Support Reading

At the beginning of each unit, introduce a key **Reading Skill** that students will apply to artworks and to text throughout the unit.

Make Connections

Make **meaningful cross-curricular connections** between art and other disciplines, including reading/literature, social studies, math, and science.

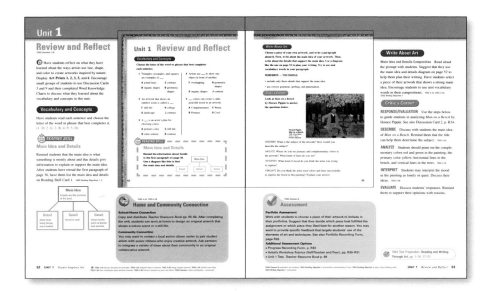

Review and Extend

Assess students' understanding of unit concepts with **Review and Reflect**. Extend the learning with additional **reading and writing** activities and opportunities for **response/evaluation**.

CONTENTS

Dear Young Artist . . . . **xiii**

Keeping a Sketchbook . . . . **xvi**

Visiting a Museum . . . . **xviii**

Reading Your Textbook . . . . **xx**

Elements and Principles . . . . **xxiv**

Unit 1   Nature Inspires Art 24a
Line, Shape, and Color

ART PRINTS **24b**

UNIT PLANNING GUIDE **24c**

ARTIST'S WORKSHOPS PREVIEW **24e**

INTRODUCING THE UNIT **24**

READING SKILL   **Main Idea and Details** **26**

LESSON 1   **Lines in Landscapes** **28**
Focus: Line
LANDSCAPE DRAWING

LESSON 2   **Shapes in Nature** **32**
Focus: Shape
CLOSE-UP VIEW PAINTING

ART ↔ SCIENCE CONNECTION   **PICTURES OF THE PAST** **36**
ART AND NATURE

LESSON 3   **Color Schemes** **38**
Focus: Color
COMPLEMENTARY COLORS PAINTING

LESSON 4   **Color and Mood** **42**
Focus: Color
SEASCAPE OR DESERT LANDSCAPE PAINTING

ART ↔ SOCIAL STUDIES CONNECTION   **Paul Klee** **46**
ARTIST BIOGRAPHY

LESSON 5   **Overlapping Shapes** **48**
Focus: Shape and Color
STILL-LIFE COLLAGE

REVIEW AND REFLECT **52**

Unit 2 Moments in Time 54a
Value, Texture, and Emphasis

ART PRINTS **54b**

UNIT PLANNING GUIDE **54c**

ARTIST'S WORKSHOPS PREVIEW **54e**

INTRODUCING THE UNIT **54**

READING SKILL | **Fact and Opinion** **56**

LESSON 6 | **Color and Value** **58**
Focus: Color and Value
MONOCHROMATIC PAINTING

LESSON 7 | **Natural Textures** **62**
Focus: Texture and Value
TEXTURE COLLAGE

ART ↔ SCIENCE CONNECTION | **EROSION** **66**
ART AND NATURE

LESSON 8 | **Light and Color** **68**
Focus: Value and Color
OUTDOOR SCENE PAINTING

LESSON 9 | **Values of Black and White** **72**
Focus: Value and Texture
CHARCOAL STILL LIFE

ART ↔ SOCIAL STUDIES CONNECTION | Henri Matisse **76**
ARTIST BIOGRAPHY

LESSON 10 | **Emphasis** **78**
Focus: Emphasis
PASTEL DRAWING

REVIEW AND REFLECT **82**

Unit 3   Proportion, Rhythm, and Form

Unit 3   People in Art 84a
Proportion, Rhythm, and Form

ART PRINTS 84b

UNIT PLANNING GUIDE 84c

ARTIST'S WORKSHOPS PREVIEW 84e

INTRODUCING THE UNIT 84

READING SKILL   **Narrative Elements** 86

LESSON 11   **Proportion in Portraits** 88
Focus: Proportion
PORTRAIT DRAWING

LESSON 12   **Abstract Portraits** 92
Focus: Shape and Proportion
ABSTRACT PORTRAIT

ART ↔ SOCIAL STUDIES CONNECTION   **Portraits in Time** 96
ART AND CULTURE

LESSON 13   **Figures in Motion** 98
Focus: Rhythm
PANEL DRAWING

LESSON 14   **Relief Sculpture** 102
Focus: Form
RELIEF SCULPTURE

ART ↔ SOCIAL STUDIES CONNECTION   **Marisol Escobar** 106
ARTIST BIOGRAPHY

LESSON 15   **Sculpture in History** 108
Focus: Form
SOAP SCULPTURE

REVIEW AND REFLECT 112

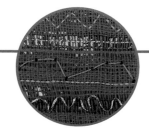
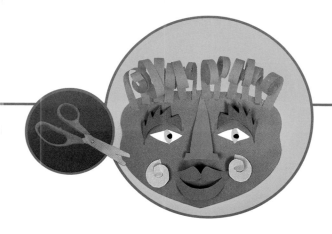

Unit 4   Art Reflects Culture 114a
Pattern and Balance

ART PRINTS **114b**

UNIT PLANNING GUIDE **114c**

ARTIST'S WORKSHOPS PREVIEW **114e**

INTRODUCING THE UNIT **114**

READING SKILL   **Compare and Contrast** **116**

LESSON 16   **Fiber Art** **118**
Focus: Pattern
REVERSE WEAVING

LESSON 17   **Balance in Masks** **122**
Focus: Balance
MASK

ART ↔ SOCIAL STUDIES CONNECTION   Amedeo Modigliani **126**
ARTIST BIOGRAPHY

LESSON 18   **Paper Art** **128**
Focus: Pattern and Balance
PAPER CUTTING

LESSON 19   **Folk Art** **132**
Focus: Balance
FOLK ART PAINTING

ART ↔ SOCIAL STUDIES CONNECTION   COWHANDS IN ART **136**
ART AND CULTURE

LESSON 20   **Symbols in Art** **138**
Focus: Balance
SYMBOLIC ART PRINT

REVIEW AND REFLECT **142**

Unit 5 The Artist's Environment.... 144a

Space, Movement, and Unity

ART PRINTS 144b

UNIT PLANNING GUIDE 144c

ARTIST'S WORKSHOPS PREVIEW 144e

INTRODUCING THE UNIT 144

Focus Skill

READING SKILL **Summarize and Paraphrase** 146

LESSON 21 **Depth and Distance** 148
Focus: Space
OUTDOOR SCENE DRAWING

LESSON 22 **Perspective Techniques** 152
Focus: Space and Color
LINEAR PERSPECTIVE DRAWING

ART ↔ SOCIAL STUDIES CONNECTION MISSION ARCHITECTURE 156
ART AND CULTURE

LESSON 23 **Garden Design** 158
Focus: Movement and Unity
PARK DESIGN

LESSON 24 **Architectural Balance** 162
Focus: Balance and Unity
BUILDING DESIGN

ART ↔ SOCIAL STUDIES CONNECTION I.M.Pei 166
ARTIST BIOGRAPHY

LESSON 25 **Outdoor Murals** 168
Focus: Movement and Unity
CLASS MURAL

REVIEW AND REFLECT 172

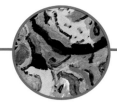

Unit 6   Stretch Your Imagination .. 174a
Variety

ART PRINTS 174b

UNIT PLANNING GUIDE 174c

ARTIST'S WORKSHOPS PREVIEW 174e

INTRODUCING THE UNIT 174

READING SKILL   **Author's Purpose** 176

LESSON 26   **Abstract Expressionism** 178
Focus: Unity and Variety
ACTION PAINTING

LESSON 27   **Surrealism** 182
Focus: Emphasis and Variety
SURREALIST PAINTING

ART ↔ SOCIAL STUDIES   Maya Lin 186
CONNECTION
ARTIST BIOGRAPHY

LESSON 28   **Constructions** 188
Focus: Variety
FOUND OBJECT CONSTRUCTION

LESSON 29   **Pop Art** 192
Focus: Variety
POP ART COLLAGE

ART ↔ SCIENCE   Vehicle Design 196
CONNECTION
CAREERS IN ART

LESSON 30   **Computer Art** 198
Focus: Variety
COMPUTER-GENERATED ART

REVIEW AND REFLECT 202

RESOURCES

Student Art Exhibitions **204**

Using the Student Handbook **R2**

Media and Techniques **R15**

Meeting Individual Needs **R24**

Assessment Options **R28**

Discussion Cards **R34**

Materials **R39**

Free and Inexpensive Materials **R41**

Alternative Planners
     Teaching by Media **R42**
     Teaching by Elements and Principles **R43**

Encyclopedia of Artists and Art History **R44**

Scope and Sequence **R66**

Index **R70**

Correlations **R76**

EVERYWHERE

AUTHORS

Jacqueline Chanda

Kristen Pederson Marstaller

CONSULTANTS

Katherina Danko-McGhee

María Teresa García-Pedroche

Harcourt
SCHOOL PUBLISHERS

Orlando   Austin   New York   San Diego   Toronto   London

Visit *The Learning Site!*
www.harcourtschool.com

Dear Young Artist,

What does the word *artist* mean to you? You may
think of an artist as only a person who draws or paints.
However, photographers, weavers, and sculptors are
also artists. Do you think of yourself as an artist?

In this book, you will see art from all over the world
and from many different time periods. As you learn
about these artworks and the artists who created them,
you will design and create your own artworks. You will
paint a landscape, draw a portrait, and even carve a
sculpture. Along the way, you may discover a new
artist—you!

Sincerely,

The Authors

CONTENTS

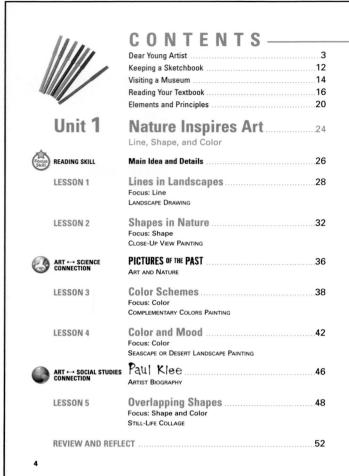

Dear Young Artist 3
Keeping a Sketchbook 12
Visiting a Museum 14
Reading Your Textbook 16
Elements and Principles 20

Unit 1   Nature Inspires Art 24
Line, Shape, and Color

READING SKILL   **Main Idea and Details** 26

LESSON 1   **Lines in Landscapes** 28
Focus: Line
LANDSCAPE DRAWING

LESSON 2   **Shapes in Nature** 32
Focus: Shape
CLOSE-UP VIEW PAINTING

ART ↔ SCIENCE CONNECTION   **PICTURES OF THE PAST** 36
ART AND NATURE

LESSON 3   **Color Schemes** 38
Focus: Color
COMPLEMENTARY COLORS PAINTING

LESSON 4   **Color and Mood** 42
Focus: Color
SEASCAPE OR DESERT LANDSCAPE PAINTING

ART ↔ SOCIAL STUDIES CONNECTION   **Paul Klee** 46
ARTIST BIOGRAPHY

LESSON 5   **Overlapping Shapes** 48
Focus: Shape and Color
STILL-LIFE COLLAGE

REVIEW AND REFLECT 52

Unit 2   Moments in Time 54
Value, Texture, and Emphasis

READING SKILL   **Fact and Opinion** 56

LESSON 6   **Color and Value** 58
Focus: Color and Value
MONOCHROMATIC PAINTING

LESSON 7   **Natural Textures** 62
Focus: Texture and Value
TEXTURE COLLAGE

ART ↔ SCIENCE CONNECTION   **EROSION** 66
ART AND NATURE

LESSON 8   **Light and Color** 68
Focus: Value and Color
OUTDOOR SCENE PAINTING

LESSON 9   **Values of Black and White** 72
Focus: Value and Texture
CHARCOAL STILL LIFE

ART ↔ SOCIAL STUDIES CONNECTION   **Henri Matisse** 76
ARTIST BIOGRAPHY

LESSON 10   **Emphasis** 78
Focus: Emphasis
PASTEL DRAWING

REVIEW AND REFLECT 82

Unit 3   People in Art 84
Proportion, Rhythm, and Form

READING SKILL   **Narrative Elements** 86

LESSON 11   **Proportion in Portraits** 88
Focus: Proportion
PORTRAIT DRAWING

LESSON 12   **Abstract Portraits** 92
Focus: Shape and Proportion
ABSTRACT PORTRAIT

ART ↔ SOCIAL STUDIES CONNECTION   **Portraits in Time** 96
ART AND CULTURE

LESSON 13   **Figures in Motion** 98
Focus: Rhythm
PANEL DRAWING

LESSON 14   **Relief Sculpture** 102
Focus: Form
RELIEF SCULPTURE

ART ↔ SOCIAL STUDIES CONNECTION   **Marisol Escobar** 106
ARTIST BIOGRAPHY

LESSON 15   **Sculpture in History** 108
Focus: Form
SOAP SCULPTURE

REVIEW AND REFLECT 112

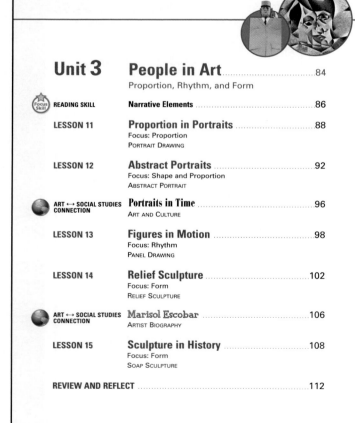

Unit 4   Art Reflects Culture 114
Pattern and Balance

READING SKILL   **Compare and Contrast** 116

LESSON 16   **Fiber Art** 118
Focus: Pattern
REVERSE WEAVING

LESSON 17   **Balance in Masks** 122
Focus: Balance
PAPER MASK

ART ↔ SOCIAL STUDIES CONNECTION   **Amedeo Modigliani** 126
ARTIST BIOGRAPHY

LESSON 18   **Paper Art** 128
Focus: Pattern and Balance
PAPER CUTTING

LESSON 19   **Folk Art** 132
Focus: Balance
FOLK ART PAINTING

ART ↔ SOCIAL STUDIES CONNECTION   **COWHANDS IN ART** 136
ART AND CULTURE

LESSON 20   **Symbols in Art** 138
Focus: Balance
SYMBOLIC ART PRINT

REVIEW AND REFLECT 142

Unit 5   The Artist's Environment ...144
Space, Movement, and Unity

READING SKILL   **Summarize and Paraphrase** ...146

LESSON 21   **Depth and Distance** ...148
Focus: Space
OUTDOOR SCENE DRAWING

LESSON 22   **Perspective Techniques** ...152
Focus: Space and Color
LINEAR PERSPECTIVE DRAWING

ART ↔ SOCIAL STUDIES CONNECTION   MISSION ARCHITECTURE ...156
ART AND CULTURE

LESSON 23   **Garden Design** ...158
Focus: Movement and Unity
PARK DESIGN

LESSON 24   **Architectural Balance** ...162
Focus: Balance and Unity
BUILDING DESIGN

ART ↔ SOCIAL STUDIES CONNECTION   I. M. Pei ...166
ARTIST BIOGRAPHY

LESSON 25   **Outdoor Murals** ...168
Focus: Movement and Unity
CLASS MURAL

REVIEW AND REFLECT ...172

8

Unit 6   Stretch Your Imagination ...174
Variety

READING SKILL   **Author's Purpose** ...176

LESSON 26   **Abstract Expressionism** ...178
Focus: Unity and Variety
ACTION PAINTING

LESSON 27   **Surrealism** ...182
Focus: Emphasis and Variety
SURREALIST PAINTING

ART ↔ SOCIAL STUDIES CONNECTION   Maya Lin ...186
ARTIST BIOGRAPHY

LESSON 28   **Constructions** ...188
Focus: Variety
FOUND OBJECT CONSTRUCTION

LESSON 29   **Pop Art** ...192
Focus: Variety
POP ART COLLAGE

ART ↔ SCIENCE CONNECTION   Vehicle Design ...196
CAREERS IN ART

LESSON 30   **Computer Art** ...198
Focus: Variety
COMPUTER-GENERATED ART

REVIEW AND REFLECT ...202

Student Handbook ...204
Maps of Museums and Art Sites ...206
Art Safety ...210
Art Techniques ...212
Elements and Principles ...228
Gallery of Artists ...240
Glossary ...254
Art History Time Line ...262
Index of Artists and Artworks ...264
Index ...267

9

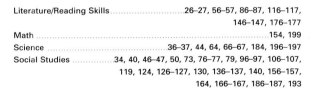

AT A GLANCE

Art Production

Collage ...71, 65, 195
Computer-Generated Art ...201
Construction/Assemblage ...191
Drawing ...31, 75, 81, 91, 95, 101, 151, 155, 161, 165
Painting ...35, 41, 45, 61, 71, 135, 171, 181, 185
Paper Folding/Cutting ...125, 131
Photographic Imagery ...51, 161, 195
Printmaking ...141
Sculpture ...105, 111
Weaving ...121

Elements and Principles

Balance ...122–125, 128–131, 132–135, 138–141, 159, 162–165
Color ...38–41, 42–45, 48–51, 58–61, 68–71, 152–155, 159, 183, 193–194, 198–199
Emphasis ...78–81, 182–185
Form ...102–105, 108–111
Line ...28–31, 62, 149, 153–154, 183, 193–194, 198
Movement ...158–161, 168–171
Pattern ...118–121, 128–131
Proportion ...88–91, 92–95
Rhythm ...98–101
Shape ...32–35, 48–51, 79, 92–95, 99, 183, 198–199
Space ...102–105, 148–151, 152–155
Texture ...62–65, 72–75, 160, 198, 200
Unity ...158–161, 162–165, 168–171, 178–181, 188–190, 192
Value ...58–61, 62–65, 68–71, 72–75, 78, 183, 200
Variety ...178–181, 182–185, 188–191, 192–195, 198–201

Cross-Curricular Connections

Literature/Reading Skills ...26–27, 56–57, 86–87, 116–117, 146–147, 176–177
Math ...154, 199
Science ...36–37, 44, 64, 66–67, 184, 196–197
Social Studies ...34, 40, 46–47, 50, 73, 76–77, 79, 96–97, 106–107, 119, 124, 126–127, 130, 136–137, 140, 156–157, 164, 166–167, 186–187, 193

Media

Cardboard ...191
Charcoal Pencils ...75
Clay ...105
Colored Pencils/Markers ...31, 91, 125, 131, 155, 161, 165
Computer ...201
Crayons ...65, 101
Fiber ...121
Found Objects ...191
Oil Pastels ...81, 95, 151
Paper ...51, 65, 125, 131, 195
Photographic Imagery ...51, 161, 195
Poster Board ...51, 65
Soap ...111
Tempera Paints ...35, 41, 45, 61, 71, 125, 135, 141, 171, 181, 185, 191
Watercolors ...71

10

Keeping a Sketchbook

Introduce Sketchbooks Share with students an example of a sketchbook or journal that contains both sketches and written ideas. Explain that many artists use sketchbooks to plan and design artworks, to practice drawing parts of an artwork, to try new styles, or to help themselves remember their ideas.

Discuss Pages 12–13 Have students read pages 12–13. Then ask them to describe the unusual style in the self-portrait on page 12. Have students examine the artwork at the bottom of page 12, and ask them to compare the facial features in it to those of a human face. (The face, nose, and neck are elongated.) Share with students the information about Amedeo Modigliani below.

Share Ideas Draw students' attention to the drawings, pictures, and other objects in the sketchbook shown on page 13. Ask students what kinds of things they would like to draw and keep in sketchbooks of their own. Ask students where they might take their sketchbooks.

Keeping a Sketchbook

When you make sketches and keep them together, you are keeping an art sketchbook. You can carry your sketchbook with you. Use it to make notes about your ideas, to sketch things you see, or to sketch what you imagine.

The artist Amedeo Modigliani created artworks of himself and the people around him in an unusual style.

◄ Amedeo Modigliani,
Self-Portrait.

In this sketch, Modigliani drew lines and shapes that may have been a plan for a sculpture. He used his sketches as a guide to create his sculptures.

Amedeo Modigliani, ▶
Head of a Caryatid.

12

Background Information

About the Artist
Amedeo Modigliani (moh•deel•YAH•nee) (1884–1920) was an Italian painter and sculptor best known for his portraits. He was influenced by African art, and many of his artworks resemble African masks. Modigliani once sculpted eight stone heads resembling the forms found in African sculpture. However, the stone dust from sculpting affected his health, forcing him to give up sculpting and return to painting. Modigliani composed his portraits with elongated noses and necks and long, slender faces. Many of his friends, including well-known artists, posed for his portraits.

Using a sketchbook is a good way to plan a finished artwork. You can sketch the composition of a painting, rearrange the parts of a sculpture, or experiment with patterns in a design. You can also practice your drawing skills.

You may want to collect poems, pictures, and textures that interest you. You can tape or glue them into your sketchbook. These things may give you ideas for art projects. If you write notes and dates next to your entries, your sketchbook will be a valuable resource for many years to come.

13

MAKING A SKETCHBOOK

Model for students one way to make a sketchbook.

1. Staple a piece of construction paper to poster board or thin cardboard to create a pocket.

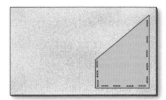

2. Staple a number of sheets of drawing paper to the poster board.

3. Make a cover, and use markers to decorate it.

USING A SKETCHBOOK

Encourage students to use their sketchbooks often. Share the following points about keeping and using a sketchbook.

- Imagine new ideas for art projects and sketch them in your sketchbook.

- Carry your sketchbook with you and sketch what you see.

- Use your sketchbook for projects in other subjects, such as recording weather patterns in science or getting ideas for your writing.

- Tape or glue pictures or examples of things you like onto the pages, or keep them in the pocket.

Student Self-Assessment

Have students make and keep several sketchbooks over the course of the school year. At the end of the year, they can look back at early sketchbooks and express ideas about their artworks and how they have grown as artists. See pages R30–R31 for assessment strategies.

Visiting a Museum

Access Prior Knowledge Have students share their experiences viewing art. Encourage them to talk about sculptures, murals, monuments, and other artworks in their community. Ask students to tell what kinds of art they like best and why. Then read page 14 with students.

Discuss Museum Features Help students brainstorm ways in which visiting a museum is different from viewing art in a book. You might use these ideas to get them started:

- You can see real artworks rather than photographs of them.
- You can look at sculptures from different sides.
- You can ask a docent, or museum guide, questions about the artworks.

Encourage volunteers to share their experiences visiting museums. Ask them where the museum was located and what they saw. Then tell students that the artworks shown in their *Student Editions* are located in museums around the world. Point out the museum names on pages 14 and 15, and read aloud the related Fast Facts.

LOCATE IT Have students turn to *Student Edition* page 24, and point out the Locate It logo at the bottom of the page. Explain to students that when they see this logo near an artwork, they can turn to the Maps of Museums and Art Sites on pages 206–209 to see where the artwork on that page came from or where it is now located.

Visiting a Museum

An art museum is a place where artworks are collected and displayed. You can find art museums in cities and towns all over the world.

When you visit a museum, remember to

- **Walk** slowly through the museum. Note the artworks that catch your eye.
- **Look** closely at the artworks, but don't touch them.
- **Think** about what each artist's message might be.
- **Listen** carefully to what the docent or guide tells you about the artworks.
- **Speak** quietly, but don't be afraid to ask questions.

▲ **The Parthenon**
Nashville, Tennessee

◄ **Guggenheim Museum**
New York, New York

 Fast Fact Visitors to the Guggenheim Museum walk down a continuous spiraling ramp to view the artworks.

Home and Community Connection

Visiting a Museum

Taking your class on a field trip to a museum in your region is a valuable way to enrich the art curriculum. Students can expand their ability to think critically about what they see by observing art and artifacts first-hand. Before your visit, talk with the museum education staff or with a docent. Prepare students for the visit by introducing the museum's major artists or exhibit themes.

Looking at Art

You may see artworks in museums, in books, or on websites. When you look at an artwork, you can follow these steps to better understand what you see:

- **DESCRIBE** Look closely at the artwork, and tell what you see. How would you describe the artwork to someone who has not seen it?

- **ANALYZE** Look at the way the artist organized the parts of the artwork. What part of it catches your eye first?

- **INTERPRET** Think about the idea or feeling the artist may be expressing in the artwork. Sometimes the title of an artwork can help you understand the artist's message.

- **EVALUATE** Use your observations about the artwork to form an opinion of it.

◀ **The Modern Art Museum of Fort Worth**
Fort Worth, Texas

 Fast Fact The Modern Art Museum of Fort Worth, chartered in 1892, is the oldest art museum in Texas.

15

Art Prints
Virtual Tour

If you are unable to arrange a museum visit, display the **Art Prints** to provide students with a similar experience. Refer to the backs of the **Art Prints** for discussion ideas.

For additional artworks, see **Electronic Art Gallery CD-ROM, Intermediate.**

ESL You can support students' **language acquisition** by using the additional teaching suggestions and resources in each lesson. See also Meeting Individual Needs, pages R24–R27, for ESL teaching strategies related to art education.

LOOKING AT ART

Discuss Art Criticism Tell students that art criticism is the process of describing the subject of an artwork and what the artwork means, and then forming an opinion about it. Explain to students that they should try to use art vocabulary to tell about the artworks they see. See also page R34 for Discussion Cards 1 and 2.

MODEL

Display **Art Print 1**. Tell students that it shows a painting by Edward Mitchell Bannister. Read the questions on *Student Edition* page 15 with students, and model the steps below, using the **Art Print**. Encourage students to share their own ideas for each step.

DESCRIBE Say: **This is a colorful painting of an outdoor scene. The sun is setting behind the clouds, and the moon is visible in the sky.**

ANALYZE Tell how the artist used the elements of art and the principles of design. Say: **The bright orange and yellow colors show the sunset. The dark colors in the clouds, farmhouse, and trees show that night is approaching.** Students will become increasingly successful with this step as their art vocabulary grows. For more information about the elements of art and the principles of design, see *Student Edition* pages 20–23 and 228–239.

INTERPRET Say: **The bright and dark colors work together to express the beauty of nature at sunset.**

EVALUATE Say: **I like this painting because it shows a familiar subject in a beautiful way. I think the artist was successful because he used diiferent colors to capture the effects of the setting sun.** Encourage students to explain their opinions of the painting.

Reading Your Textbook

Access Prior Knowledge About Types of Text
Display a fiction book that students are familiar with, and ask them to briefly describe what the book is about. Repeat with a familiar nonfiction book. Then use prompts like the ones below to help students distinguish between the kinds of text.

- Which book tells a story about made-up characters?
- Which book gives information about real people, things, events, or places?

Then discuss with students the genre of this book. (nonfiction; textbook; gives information)

Discuss Lesson Features
Tell students that the lessons in their art textbook have special features to help them locate and remember facts and ideas. Have students read pages 16–17. Then point out and discuss the text features:

- **title** (tells the main topic)
- **subheads** (tell the subtopics)
- **vocabulary** (important terms or concepts)
- **captions** (give the artist's name, the title of the artwork, materials used in the artwork, the dimensions of the artwork, the date the artwork was created, and its location.)

Reading Your Textbook

Knowing how to read your art textbook will help you remember and enjoy what you read. Each lesson contains nonfiction text about artists, artworks, art techniques, and art history. Remember that nonfiction texts give facts about real people, things, events, or places.

> The title tells the main topic of the lesson.

You can identify the most important ideas in each lesson by becoming familiar with the different features of your textbook. Look at this sample lesson from pages 48–51.

> Highlighted words are art vocabulary.

Lesson 5

Vocabulary
still life
overlapping
collage

Paul Gauguin,
Still Life with Teapot and Fruit,
1896, oil on canvas,
18½ in. x 26 in.,
Metropolitan Museum
of Art, New York,
New York.

Overlapping Shapes

Still Life
Image A is an example of a **still life**. In a still life, objects, including flowers and food, are arranged in interesting ways. Which objects in image A appear to be the closest to the viewer? Which ones appear to be the farthest away? The artist used **overlapping** to show that some objects are closer to the viewer than others. The objects in the back are partly covered by the objects in the front. The artist used overlapping to show that the teapot is in front of the flower. Where else did he use overlapping?

16

Captions next to each artwork give information such as the artist's name and the title of the artwork. Captions may also provide information about an artwork's date, materials, dimensions, and location. Subheads can provide clues about the ideas found in different sections of a lesson.

Captions give important information about each artwork.

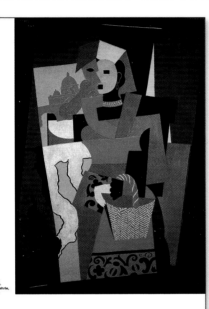

B Pablo Picasso,
L'Italienne,
1917, oil on canvas,
149.5 cm × 101.5 cm.
Foundation E.G. Buehrle,
Zurich, Switzerland.

Contrast

Now look at image B. What is the subject of this artwork? Point out some details in the painting that tell about the subject. Look at the colors and shapes in image B. How did the artist use them to show contrast? Find examples of overlapping in the painting. Which object is the closest to the viewer? Which one is the farthest away?

Subheads signal the beginning of a new section of text.

49

17

Reading Your Textbook

Have students turn to page 18, and point out the lesson features on the reduced student page 50:

- **Think Critically questions** (check students' understanding of lesson concepts)

- **Reading Skill logo** (indicates an important skill in reading and in viewing art)

- **Links** (additional information that may be related to a particular culture or to what students are learning in other subjects; may also show where an artwork is located)

Discuss Artist's Workshop Features Ask students to share their experiences with following directions from a book or manual. Tell students they were reading functional text, a kind of text that explains how to do something. Discuss with students why it is important to pay attention to the order of steps in functional texts. Then tell students that the Artist's Workshop activities in their *Student Edition* give directions for making an art project. Point out the features on the reduced student page 51:

- **materials list** (tells what materials are needed for the activity)

- **photographs** (show steps from the project)

- **tips** (give important information about techniques or safety)

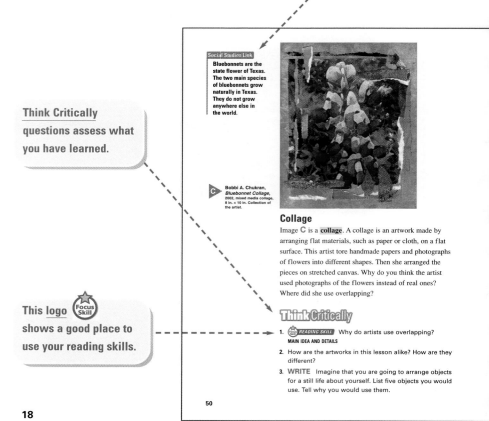

Other features of your textbook link artworks to related subject areas. Questions at the end of each lesson help you think about what you have learned.

Links give facts related to an artist or an artwork.

Think Critically questions assess what you have learned.

This logo shows a good place to use your reading skills.

Social Studies Link
Bluebonnets are the state flower of Texas. The two main species of bluebonnets grow naturally in Texas. They do not grow anywhere else in the world.

Bobbi A. Chukran, *Bluebonnet Collage*, 2002, mixed media collage, 8 in. × 10 in. Collection of the artist.

Collage
Image C is a **collage**. A collage is an artwork made by arranging flat materials, such as paper or cloth, on a flat surface. This artist tore handmade papers and photographs of flowers into different shapes. Then she arranged the pieces on stretched canvas. Why do you think the artist used photographs of the flowers instead of real ones? Where did she use overlapping?

Think Critically

1. *READING SKILL* Why do artists use overlapping? **MAIN IDEA AND DETAILS**

2. How are the artworks in this lesson alike? How are they different?

3. **WRITE** Imagine that you are going to arrange objects for a still life about yourself. List five objects you would use. Tell why you would use them.

50

18

You can find more resources in the Student Handbook:

- Maps of Museums and Art Sites, pp. 206–209
- Art Safety, pp. 210–211
- Art Techniques, pp. 212–227
- Elements and Principles, pp. 228–239
- Gallery of Artists, pp. 240–253
- Glossary, pp. 254–261
- Art History Time Line, pp. 262–263

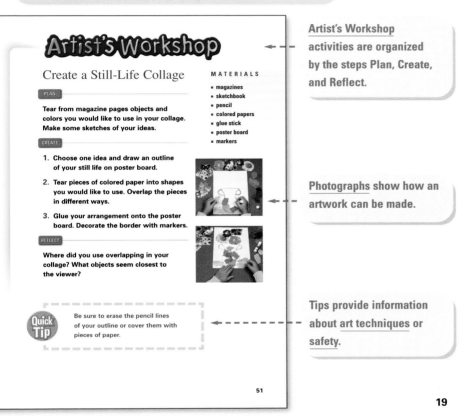

Artist's Workshop

Create a Still-Life Collage

PLAN

Tear from magazine pages objects and colors you would like to use in your collage. Make some sketches of your ideas.

MATERIALS
- magazines
- sketchbook
- pencil
- colored papers
- glue stick
- poster board
- markers

CREATE

1. Choose one idea and draw an outline of your still life on poster board.
2. Tear pieces of colored paper into shapes you would like to use. Overlap the pieces in different ways.
3. Glue your arrangement onto the poster board. Decorate the border with markers.

REFLECT

Where did you use overlapping in your collage? What objects seem closest to the viewer?

Quick Tip
Be sure to erase the pencil lines of your outline or cover them with pieces of paper.

Artist's Workshop activities are organized by the steps Plan, Create, and Reflect.

Photographs show how an artwork can be made.

Tips provide information about <u>art techniques</u> or <u>safety</u>.

51

19

Discuss Book Parts Tell students that their art textbook contains several resources to help them learn about art. Have them look at the list of resources on page 19.

As students look up each section in the back of their *Student Edition*, ask volunteers to tell what kinds of information each section gives.

- **Maps of Museums and Art Sites** (location of artworks shown in the book)
- **Art Safety** (guidelines for using materials)
- **Art Techniques** (instructions for making different kinds of art)
- **Elements and Principles** (photographs showing examples of each of the art elements and design principles)
- **Gallery of Artists** (pictures of and biographical information about artists in the book)
- **Glossary** (definitions and pronunciations for vocabulary terms)
- **Art History Time Line** (examples of artworks from many different periods in art history)

Technology

Tell students that they will be able to find more information about artists and art techniques online. Discuss with students rules for Internet safety.

GO ONLINE Visit *The Learning Site* www.harcourtschool.com

ESL Help students identify the parts of their book by **giving simple commands** and asking students to respond by pointing to the correct part of the page or section of the book. Then ask **yes/no questions** about the book parts.

Elements of Art

Access Prior Knowledge Play a game with students in which they invent and solve riddles about classroom objects. Use art elements such as shape, color, and texture in a riddle to get them started. For example, "I am long and rectangular. I can be brown, red, blue, or yellow. I feel smooth. I may be used to find length or width or to draw straight lines. What am I?" (ruler) Tell students to use sensory knowledge to communicate ideas about school objects in their riddles. Ask students to describe how an object looks, feels, smells, or sounds in their riddle clues. Explain to students that they will learn more about ways of observing art and objects in the world around them. TEKS 4.1A

Discuss Pages 20–21 Have students read pages 20–21, and discuss how the elements of art are shown in the photographs. Then have students identify lines, shapes, and colors in the classroom. Tell students that they will learn more about these elements of art throughout the year.

Elements and Principles

Elements of Art

The **elements of art** are the basic parts of an artwork. You can use them to describe art and to plan and create your own artworks. As you look at these photographs, think about other places where you have seen the elements of art.

SHAPE ▲

an object that has height and width

COLOR ▲

what we see when light is reflected off objects

LINE ▲

a mark that begins at one point and continues for a certain distance

20

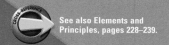
See also Elements and
Principles, pages 228–239.

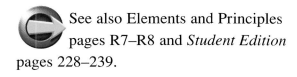
See also Elements and Principles
pages R7–R8 and *Student Edition*
pages 228–239.

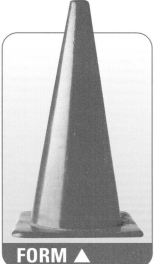

FORM ▲

an object that has height,
width, and depth

TEXTURE ▲

the way a surface looks or feels

SPACE ▲

the area around, between,
or within objects

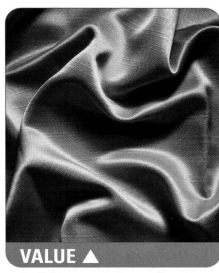

VALUE ▲

the lightness or darkness of a color

21

Principles of Design

Discuss Pages 22–23 Have students read the top of page 22. Discuss how the principles of design are shown in the photographs. For example, read the definition of *pattern*, and have students point out the repeated shapes and colors in the photograph. Ask students to describe the patterns in their clothing or in other places around the classroom. Tell students that they will learn more about the principles of design as they look at and create artworks.

Principles of Design

Artists use the **principles of design** to arrange art elements in artworks. Look for the elements of art in these photographs. Think about how they are arranged and the effect this creates in each image.

VARIETY ▲

the effect created by the use of different elements in an artwork to add interest

EMPHASIS ▲

importance given to one part of an artwork

MOVEMENT ▲

the way the viewer's eyes travel from one element to another in an artwork

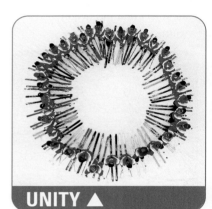

UNITY ▲

a sense that an artwork is complete and that its parts work together

22

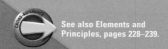 See also Elements and Principles, pages 228–239.

PROPORTION ▲

a sense that objects are the correct size in comparison to each other

PATTERN ▲

a design made with repeated lines, shapes, or colors

RHYTHM ▲

the visual beat created by the regular repeated elements in an artwork

BALANCE ▲

the steady feeling created by the equal weight of elements on both sides

23

See also Elements and Principles pages R7–R8 and *Student Edition* pages 228–239.

Picture File

Have students contribute to a classroom picture file with images they find in magazines and catalogs. Create labeled folders for each of the elements of art and the principles of design. You may also want to create folders for common subjects of artworks, such as portraits and landscapes, for students to use as a reference for their own artworks.

Unit 1

Line, Shape, and Color

Nature Inspires Art

The beauty of the natural world provides inspiration for many artists. In this unit, students will learn how artists use line, shape, and color to depict natural objects and scenes.

Resources

- Unit 1 Art Prints (1–3)
- Additional Art Prints (5, 6)
- Art Transparencies 1–3
- Test Preparation: Reading and Writing Through Art, pp. 1–16, 17–21
- Artist's Workshop Activities: English and Spanish, pp. 1–10
- Encyclopedia of Artists and Art History, pp. R44–R65
- Picture Cards Collection, card 55

Using the Art Prints

- Discussion Cards, pp. R34–R38
- Teaching suggestions, backs of Art Prints
- Art Print Teaching Suggestions: Spanish

Teacher Resource Book

- Vocabulary Cards in English and Spanish, pp. 7–10
- Reading Skill Card 1, p. 31
- Copying Masters, pp. 38, 39
- Challenge Activities, pp. 51–55
- School-Home Connection: English/Spanish, pp. 85–86
- Unit 1 Test, p. 99

Technology Resources

 Electronic Art Gallery CD-ROM, Intermediate

Picture Card Bank CD-ROM

 Visit *The Learning Site* www.harcourtschool.com

- Multimedia Art Glossary
- Multimedia Biographies
- Reading Skills and Activities

Art Prints for This Unit

ART PRINT 1

Untitled (Sunset with Quarter Moon and Farmhouse)
by Edward Mitchell Bannister

ART PRINT 2

Senecio (Head of a Man)
by Paul Klee

ART PRINT 3

Sheep
by Franz Marc

ART PRINT 5

Still Life of Summer Flowers
by Rachel Ruysch

ART PRINT 6

The Large Red Interior
by Henri Matisse

Unit 1

Nature Inspires Art — Line, Shape, and Color

Planning Guide

PDAS Domain IV

Lesson	Objectives and Vocabulary	Art Images	Production/Materials
Focus Skill — Main Idea and Details, pp. 26–27			
1 **LINES IN LANDSCAPES** pp. 28–31 — 30–60 minutes	• Choose appropriate vocabulary to discuss lines in landscapes • Design and create an original landscape (Focus Skill) Identify simple main ideas expressed in artworks **Vocabulary: landscapes, actual lines, implied lines**	• **Windy Day in England** by Maureen Golding • **Landscape of Murnau** by Alexej von Jawlensky • **A Small Volcano in Mexican Countryside** by José María Velasco • **Spiral Jetty** by Robert Smithson	**Draw a Landscape** ❑ magazines ❑ pencil ❑ white paper ❑ colored pencils or markers
2 **SHAPES IN NATURE** pp. 32–35 — 30–60 minutes	• Choose appropriate vocabulary to identify shapes in nature • Design and create a close-up view (Focus Skill) Identify simple main ideas expressed in artworks **Vocabulary: geometric shapes, organic shapes, close-up view**	• **Monkey Frieze** by Franz Marc • **Irises** by Vincent van Gogh • **Poppies** by Georgia O'Keeffe • **Prairie Flower** by Kirstie, grade 4	**Paint a Close-Up View** ❑ natural objects ❑ pencil ❑ white paper ❑ tempera paint ❑ paintbrushes ❑ water bowl
Art ↔ Science Connection: Pictures of the Past, pp. 36–37			
3 **COMPLEMENTARY COLORS** pp. 38–41 — 30–60 minutes	• Identify colors • Recognize color schemes in artworks • Design and create a scene painting (Focus Skill) Identify simple main ideas expressed in artworks **Vocabulary: primary colors, secondary colors, complementary colors, contrast, color scheme**	• **Elegy for Summer** by Paul Sierra • **Visitors to the Rainforest** by Robert Wagstaff • **Blue Fronds** by Colleen Meechan	**Paint with Complementary Colors** ❑ pencil ❑ white paper ❑ tempera paint ❑ paintbrushes ❑ water bowl
4 **COLOR AND MOOD** pp. 42–45 — 30–60 minutes	• Identify warm and cool colors in artworks • Recognize the use of color to express mood in artworks • Design and create an original seascape (Focus Skill) Identify simple main ideas expressed in artworks **Vocabulary: cool colors, seascape, warm colors**	• **The Beach at Sainte-Adresse** by Claude Monet • **Gazelles** by Matiros Sarian • **Possibilities** by Ole Juul Hansen	**Paint a Seascape or a Desert Landscape** ❑ magazines ❑ pencil ❑ white paper ❑ tempera paint ❑ paintbrushes ❑ water bowl
Art ↔ Social Studies Connection: Paul Klee, pp. 46–47			
5 **OVERLAPPING SHAPES** pp. 48–51 — 30–60 minutes	• Recognize the use of overlapping shapes in artworks • Identify still lifes and collages as types of artworks (Focus Skill) Identify simple main ideas expressed in artworks **Vocabulary: still life, overlapping, collage**	• **Still Life with Teapot and Fruit** by Paul Gauguin • **L'Italienne** by Pablo Picasso • **Bluebonnet Collage** by Bobbi A. Chukran	**Create a Still-Life Collage** ❑ magazines ❑ pencil ❑ colored papers ❑ glue stick ❑ poster board ❑ markers
Review and Reflect, pp. 52–53			

★ TEKS 4.1B discuss elements and principles; TEKS 4.2B design original artworks; PDAS Domain IV classroom management

Main Idea and Details, pp. 26–27

Focus Skill

Opportunities for application of the skill are provided on pp. 30, 34, 40, 44, 50, 52, and 53.

Art Puzzlers

Present these art puzzlers to students at the beginning or end of a class or when students finish an assignment early.

Resources and Technology	Suggested Literature	Across the Curriculum
• Art Print 1 • Reading Skill Card 1 • Discussion Cards 1, 6, pp. R34, R36 Electronic Art Gallery CD-ROM, Intermediate	*How Artists See the Weather* by Colleen Carroll 	**Math** Lines in Math, p. 29 **Reading** Main Idea and Details, p. 30 **Writing** Descriptive Paragraph, p. 31
• Art Print 5 • Reading Skill Card 1 • Discussion Cards 1, 9, pp. R34, R38 Electronic Art Gallery CD-ROM, Intermediate	*Georgia O'Keeffe* by Robyn Montana Turner	**Science** Parts of a Flower, p. 33 **Reading** Main Idea and Details, p. 34 **Writing** Descriptive Paragraph, p. 35
• Art Print 3 • Reading Skill Card 1 • Discussion Cards 1, 3, pp. R34–R35 Electronic Art Gallery CD-ROM, Intermediate	*What Makes a Van Gogh a Van Gogh?* by Richard Muhlberger	**Science** Colors of the Rainbow, p. 39 **Reading** Main Idea and Details, p. 40 **Writing** Friendly Letter, p. 41
• Art Prints 1, 6 • Reading Skill Card 1 • Discussion Cards 1, 3, pp. R34–R35 Electronic Art Gallery CD-ROM, Intermediate	*In Blue Mountains* by Thomas Locker 	**Language Arts** Colorful Words, p. 43 **Reading** Main Idea and Details, p. 44 **Writing** Descriptive Paragraph, p. 45
• Art Print 5 • Reading Skill Card 1 • Discussion Cards 1, 3, pp. R34–R35 • Copying Master, p. 39 Electronic Art Gallery CD-ROM, Intermediate	*A Cloak for the Dreamer* by Aileen Friedman 	**Social Studies** State Flowers, p. 49 **Reading** Main Idea and Details, p. 50 **Writing** Museum Card, p. 51

- Imagine the **landscape** of a place that you would like to visit. Describe the kinds of lines you would use to draw that landscape. **TEKS 4.1B**

- Choose an object that has a **geometric shape.** Draw the object as though it had an **organic shape.** TEKS 4.2B

- Draw an object from your home or classroom in one color. Then draw the background in a **complementary color.** TEKS 4.2B

- Think of a word that describes a mood—such as *happy, sad,* or *nervous.* Create a drawing of the word that uses **warm colors** or **cool colors** to illustrate it. **TEKS 4.2B**

- Cut out pictures from a magazine that show objects found in a landscape. Use **overlapping** to create your own **collage** of a landscape. TEKS 4.2B

 School-Home Connection
The activities above are included in the School-Home Connection for this unit. See *Teacher Resource Book,* pp. 85–86.

Assessment Options

- Rubrics and Recording Forms, pp. R30–R33
- Unit 1 Test, *Teacher Resource Book,* p. 99

 Visit *The Learning Site:*
www.harcourtschool.com

Artist's Workshops PREVIEW

Use these pages to help you gather and organize materials for the production activity in each lesson.

LESSON	MATERIALS

1 Draw a Landscape p. 31

Objective: To design and create an original landscape using actual and implied lines

 30–40 minutes

Challenge Activity: See *Teacher Resource Book*, page 51.

- magazines
- sketchbook
- pencil
- white paper
- colored pencils or markers

FINISHED EXAMPLE

LESSON

2 Paint a Close-Up View p. 35

Objective: To design and create a close-up view of an object using organic and geometric shapes

 30–40 minutes

Challenge Activity: See *Teacher Resource Book*, page 52.

- natural objects such as plants or fruit
- sketchbook
- pencil
- white paper
- tempera paint
- paintbrushes
- water bowl

FINISHED EXAMPLE

 For safety information, see Art Safety, p. R4, or the Art Safety Poster.

 For information on media and techniques, see pp. R15–R23.

③ Paint with Complementary Colors p. 41

- sketchbook
- pencil
- white paper
- tempera paint
- paintbrushes
- water bowl

Objective: To design and create an outdoor scene painting using complementary colors

🕐 **30–40 minutes**

Challenge Activity: See *Teacher Resource Book*, page 53.

LESSON

④ Paint a Seascape or a Desert Landscape p. 45

- magazines
- sketchbook
- pencil
- white paper
- tempera paint
- paintbrushes
- water bowl

Objective: To design and create an original seascape or desert landscape, using color to express a particular mood

🕐 **30–40 minutes**

Challenge Activity: See *Teacher Resource Book*, page 54.

LESSON

⑤ Create a Still-Life Collage p. 51

- magazines
- sketchbook
- pencil
- colored papers
- glue stick
- poster board
- markers

Objective: To design and create an original collage, using overlapping shapes and colors to create contrast

🕐 **30–40 minutes**

Challenge Activity: See *Teacher Resource Book*, page 55.

PDAS Domains I, II

Nature Inspires Art

PREVIEW THE UNIT

Tell students that in this unit they will view and create artworks that have been inspired by nature. Invite students to preview this unit by reading the lesson titles and examining the art images.

STEP INTO THE ART

Have students examine the painting on pages 24 and 25 and describe what they see. Then read page 25 with students, and discuss their answers to the questions.

- **Where in the scene would you go first?** Discuss an activity such as walking along the water's edge or sitting on one of the large rocks to watch the reflection of the sun.

- **What sounds would you hear?** Suggest to students the sound of the wind rustling in the trees or the sound of birds chirping.

- **What would you see on the ground?** Have students point out the boulders, grass, or rocks.

- **Would you enjoy being in this scene? Why or why not?** Have students communicate ideas about self, using sensory knowledge to describe how they would feel in this solitary natural setting. TEKS 4.1A

SHARE BACKGROUND INFORMATION

Tell students that Loch Long is a lake in Scotland. The word *loch* means "lake."

 See **Using the Maps of Museums and Art Sites**, p. R2.

Robert S. Duncanson, *Loch Long,*
1867, oil on canvas, 17.7 cm × 30.3 cm.

LOCATE IT

This painting can be found at the Smithsonian American Art Museum in Washington, D.C.

See Maps of Museums and Art Sites, pages 206–209.

Washington, D.C.

24

 Background Information

About the Artist
Robert Scott Duncanson (1821?–1872) studied painting in Scotland when he was 16 years old. He later became famous for his paintings of landscapes of different parts of the world.

For additional information about Robert Scott Duncanson, see the Encyclopedia of Artists and Art History, pp. R44–R65, and the Gallery of Artists, *Student Edition* pp. 240–253.

For related artworks, see **Electronic Art Gallery CD-ROM, Intermediate.**

Unit 1 — Line, Shape, and Color

Nature
Inspires Art

Step into the Art

Imagine that you could step into the scene in this painting. Where in the scene would you go first? What sounds would you hear? What would you see on the ground? Would you enjoy being in this scene? Why or why not?

ABOUT THE ARTIST

See Gallery of Artists, pages 240–253.

Unit Vocabulary

landscapes	primary colors	cool colors
actual lines	secondary colors	seascape
implied lines	complementary colors	warm colors
geometric shapes		still life
organic shapes	contrast	overlapping
close-up view	color scheme	collage

GO ONLINE Multimedia Art Glossary
Visit *The Learning Site*
www.harcourtschool.com

25

Language Arts Connection

Students may create a chart like the one below to identify familiar and unfamiliar vocabulary terms. Encourage them to add information to their charts as they work through this unit.

WORD KNOWLEDGE CHART		
I know this term.	I have seen this term before.	I have never seen this term.

Unit Vocabulary

Read aloud the terms with students, and use the Word Knowledge Chart below to assess and discuss their prior knowledge.

landscapes paintings of outdoor scenes

actual lines lines that clearly outline objects

implied lines lines that are suggested rather than drawn

geometric shapes shapes such as triangles or circles, made of straight lines and sharp corners or regular curves

organic shapes shapes made of curved, irregular lines

close-up view a detailed view of an object or part of an object

primary colors the colors red, yellow, and blue that are the basis for the other colors on the color wheel

secondary colors the colors orange, green, and violet, each created by combining two primary colors

complementary colors colors that are opposite each other on the color wheel

contrast a sharp difference between two things, making one or both stand out

color scheme an artist's plan for choosing color for an artwork

cool colors the colors blue, green, and violet

seascape an outdoor scene that shows the sea and sky

warm colors the colors red, yellow, and orange

still life an artwork that shows objects arranged together in an interesting way

overlapping a technique in which some objects partly cover other objects

collage an artwork made by gluing materials, such as paper or cloth, onto a flat surface

Vocabulary Resources

- Vocabulary Cards in English and Spanish: *Teacher Resource Book,* pp. 7–10
- Student Edition Glossary, pp. 254–261

GO ONLINE Multimedia Art Glossary
Visit *The Learning Site*
www.harcourtschool.com

READING SKILL

PDAS Domains I, II

Main Idea and Details

SKILL TRACE	
MAIN IDEA AND DETAILS	
Introduce	pp. 26–27
Review	pp. 30, 34, 40, 44, 50, 52

DISCUSS THE SKILL

Access Prior Knowledge Ask volunteers to name a book they have read in class. Have them tell what the book was mostly about. Explain that the main idea is what something is mostly about. Then ask students to give details to explain or support the main idea of the book. Explain to students that thinking about the main idea and the details can help them better understand the artworks and the text in this unit.

APPLY TO ART

Main Idea and Details Have students read page 26 and look at the image. Then ask students to identify the simple main idea expressed in the artwork that tells about art history and culture. Have students point out the details Benton used to support the main idea. TEKS 4.3A

READING SKILL

Main Idea and Details

The *main idea* is what something is mostly about. *Details* give information to explain and support the main idea.

Look at the image below. The main idea of the painting is a summer morning on a farm. You can tell this is the main idea by looking at these details that support it.

- The title of the painting is *June Morning*.
- A farmer is milking his cow, and there is a barn in the background.
- The flowers are blooming.

Thomas Hart Benton, *June Morning*,
1945, oil and tempera on masonite, $41\frac{7}{8}$ in. × $48\frac{1}{6}$ in.
Cummer Museum of Art and Gardens, Jacksonville, Florida.

26

Background Information

About the Artist

Thomas Hart Benton (1889–1975) was an important member of a group of artists who called themselves American Scene Painters. These artists rejected the abstract styles of European art in the early twentieth century and instead depicted scenes and issues in everyday American life. Benton's murals still decorate the walls of public buildings all across the United States.

For additional information about the artist, see pp. R44–R65.

  For related artworks, see **Electronic Art Gallery CD-ROM, Intermediate.**

★ **TEKS 4.3A** identify main ideas; **PDAS Domain I** active participation; **PDAS Domain II** learner-centered instruction; **PDAS Domain IV** classroom management;
TAKS Reading Objective 1 demonstrate understanding of texts; **TAKS Reading Objective 4** apply critical-thinking skills

Finding the main idea and details can also help you understand what you read. Read this passage. Think about what it is mostly about.

Thomas Hart Benton was an American artist who painted scenes of American life. He traveled around the country to see how people in rural areas lived. He got ideas from the people and scenes he saw. He sketched these scenes for his paintings. His paintings became well known for the way he showed rural American life.

What are the main idea and details in the passage? You can use a diagram like this to help you organize your thoughts.

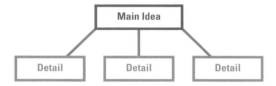

On Your Own

As you read the lessons in this unit, use diagrams like the one above to find the main idea and details in the text and in the artworks. Look back at your completed diagrams when you see questions with *READING SKILL* .

APPLY TO READING

Main Idea and Details About the Artist Explain to students that, as they read, they should be thinking about what the main idea of the passage is and what details support the main idea.

Have students read the passage on page 27. Work with them to complete the diagram by filling in the main idea and the supporting details that tell about Thomas Hart Benton. TAKS Reading Objectives 1, 4

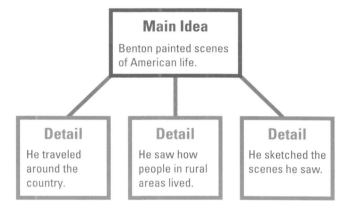

ON YOUR OWN

As students read about other artworks and art concepts, have them use diagrams such as the one on page 27 to find the main ideas and details in the text and the artworks. TEKS 4.3A

TEKS 4.3A

Reading Skill Card

Distribute Reading Skill Card 1, *Teacher Resource Book* page 31. Have students identify simple main ideas and details in this unit.

Extend the Skill
For additional teaching suggestions, see **Art Transparency 1.**

PDAS Domain IV

ESL Provide **comprehensible input** to **less-fluent speakers** by reading the passage aloud and pointing out details in the painting on page 26 that correspond to details in the text.

Reading Skills and Activities
Visit *The Learning Site*
www.harcourtschool.com

Lesson 1

Lines in Landscapes

OBJECTIVES
- Choose appropriate vocabulary to discuss lines in landscapes
- Design and create an original landscape
- Identify simple main ideas expressed in artworks

RESOURCES
- Art Print 1
- Reading Skill Card 1
- Discussion Cards 1, 6, pp. R34, R36
- Electronic Art Gallery CD-ROM, Intermediate

GO ONLINE

Multimedia Art Glossary and Biographies
Visit *The Learning Site*
www.harcourtschool.com

5 Minutes

Warm-Up

Build Background About Lines On the board, draw several kinds of lines, including ones that are thin, thick, wavy, vertical, and horizontal. Discuss with students the different kinds of lines you drew. Then ask students to look around the classroom and communicate ideas about school using sensory knowledge and life experiences to point out examples of different kinds of lines. Tell students that in this lesson they will learn how artists use different kinds of lines in their artworks. TEKS 4.1A

Lesson 1

Vocabulary
landscapes
actual lines
implied lines

Lines in Landscapes

Artists often get ideas for artwork from nature. They may paint **landscapes**, or paintings of outdoor scenes.

Kinds of Lines

Artists use many kinds of lines to create landscapes. Look at image **A**. The artist painted this outdoor scene in a way that does not look realistic, or like the actual scene. She used many different kinds of lines. What kinds of lines do you see? Where do you see thin, thick, long, short, or wavy lines? Point out some horizontal lines—straight lines that go from side to side. Read the title of image **A**. How did the artist use lines to show a windy day?

A Maureen Golding, *Windy Day in England*, 1991, gouache on paper, $12\frac{1}{2}$ in. × 16 in. Private collection.

Background Information

About the Artists
B Alexej von Jawlensky (ah·LEKS·yee fohn yah·VLEHN·skee) (1864–1941) was a Russian painter and printmaker. *Landscape of Murnau* shows a rural German town where von Jawlensky spent several summers.

D Robert Smithson (1938–1973), an American sculptor, was a founder of the art form known as environmental art.

For additional information about the artists, see pp. R44–R65.

 For related artworks, see **Electronic Art Gallery CD-ROM, Intermediate.**

★ TEKS **4.1A** communicate ideas; TEKS **4.3A** identify main ideas; **PDAS Domain I** active participation; **PDAS Domain II** learner-centered instruction; **TAKS Reading Objective 1** demonstrate understanding of texts; **TAKS Reading Objective 3** use a variety of strategies; *(continued)*

Actual and Implied Lines

In image **B** the artist used thick, bold lines to outline the objects in his painting. Lines that outline objects are called **actual lines**.

Now compare image **C** to image **B**. What is the subject of both paintings? Do you see actual lines in image **C**? The edges of the objects in image **C** are suggested by **implied lines**.

If the artist had used actual lines to outline the objects in image **C**, would the painting look more realistic or less realistic?

 Alexej von Jawlensky, *Landscape of Murnau,* 1912, oil on canvas, 48.05 cm × 53.5 cm. Private collection.

 José María Velasco, *A Small Volcano in Mexican Countryside,* 1887, oil on canvas. Narodni Galerie, Prague, Czech Republic.

29

Math Connection

TAKS Reading Objectives 1, 3, 4

Lines in Math Ask students to use their math books or an encyclopedia to research how lines are used to create angles, parallel lines, and perpendicular lines. Have students draw and label an example of an acute angle, parallel lines, and perpendicular lines.

acute angle   parallel lines   perpendicular lines

Teach

10-15 Minutes

Preview the Art   Have students preview images A through D on pages 28–30. Ask them to describe what they see and to share their first impressions. Use Discussion Card 1 and the questions below to guide the discussion. Then have students read pages 28–30.

 Windy Day in England   **What do you see in this painting? How do you think it would feel to be standing in this scene?** TEKS 4.1A

 Landscape of Murnau   **Describe what you see in this painting. What do you think you are looking at? Why do you think so?**

 A Small Volcano in Mexican Countryside **What do you think is the main idea of this image?** TEKS 4.3A

 Spiral Jetty   **If you could touch this artwork, what do you think it would feel like? Why do you think that?** TEKS 4.1A

Discuss Art Concepts   Discuss with students the different kinds of lines that the artists used in the landscapes in this lesson. Point out the way the artist used curved lines in image A to make the objects appear to be bending from the force of the wind.

Discuss with students that images B and C both show similar scenes, but that the actual lines in image B make that scene look less realistic. Point out that image C would look less realistic if the artist had used actual lines to outline the volcano. Explain that the artist of image D used black rock to create an actual line to form the spiral.

TAKS Reading Objective 4 apply critical-thinking skills

LESSON 1 *Lines in Landscapes* **29**

Teach (continued)

LOCATE IT Have students turn to the map on pages 206–207 and locate the Great Salt Lake in Utah. Tell them that the artist Robert Smithson used black basalt rocks and earth from the site to create a spiral 1,500 feet long and 15 feet wide that stretches out into the water. Depending on the water level in the Great Salt Lake, *Spiral Jetty* may be visible or totally submerged.

Main Idea and Details Ask students to look at images A, B, and C. Discuss with them

- the main idea of each painting.

- the details that support or explain each main idea. TEKS 4.3A

Then ask students to select an artwork in this lesson and interpret the ideas in it. TEKS 4.4B

Think Critically

Use the questions below to check students' understanding of lesson concepts.

1. **READING SKILL** **What kinds of lines can artists use in landscapes?** (Possible response: Artists can use thin, thick, long, short, wavy, or horizontal lines. They can use actual or implied lines.) **MAIN IDEA AND DETAILS** TEKS 4.1B

2. **If you were drawing a realistic landscape, would you use more implied lines or more actual lines?** (Possible response: implied lines, because there are more implied lines in real settings) **PERCEPTION/AESTHETICS** TEKS 4.1B

3. **WRITE** **Think of a place where you would like to create an environmental artwork. Describe the artwork you would create.**
   DESCRIPTIVE TAKS Writing Objective 1

LOCATE IT
Spiral Jetty can be found in the Great Salt Lake in Utah.

Great Salt Lake
UTAH

See Maps of Museums and Art Sites, pages 206–209.

Environmental Artwork

Have you ever seen anything in nature like the object in image **D**? The artist used nature itself to create this environmental artwork. Environmental art is made from materials found in nature and placed in a natural setting. What materials did the artist use? How did he show actual lines?

D Robert Smithson, *Spiral Jetty,*
1970, black rock, salt crystals, earth, red water (algae),
3 ft. × 15 ft. × 1500 ft. Great Salt Lake, Utah.

Think Critically

1. **READING SKILL** What kinds of lines can artists use in landscapes? **MAIN IDEA AND DETAILS**

2. If you were drawing a realistic landscape, would you use more implied lines or more actual lines?

3. **WRITE** Think of a place where you would like to create an environmental artwork. Describe the artwork you would create.

30

TEKS 4.1A

Art Print 1

Display **Art Print 1** and distribute Discussion Card 6: *Landscapes* to help students discuss lesson concepts. Have students use sensory knowledge and life experiences to communicate ideas about the geographical features of landscapes in their community.

ART PRINT 1

Untitled (Sunset with Quarter Moon and Farmhouse)
by Edward Mitchell Bannister

⭐ TEKS 4.1A communicate ideas; TEKS 4.1B discuss elements and principles; TEKS 4.2B design original artworks; TEKS 4.3A identify main ideas; TEKS 4.4A form conclusions about personal artworks; TEKS 4.4B interpret artworks by peers and others; PDAS Domain III evaluation and feedback; *(continued)*

Artist's Workshop

Draw a Landscape

MATERIALS

- magazines
- sketchbook
- pencil
- white paper
- colored pencils or markers

PLAN

Find a picture of an outdoor place. Make some sketches for a landscape. Brainstorm the kinds of lines you will use. Plan the details in your painting.

CREATE

1. Select the sketch you like best. Copy it onto white paper.
2. Use colored pencils or markers to complete your landscape.
3. Include a variety of lines in your drawing.

REFLECT

What kinds of lines did you use in your landscape? Did you use more implied lines or more actual lines?

Quick Tip
As you brainstorm kinds of lines, draw them on a scrap of paper. Choose from these lines to draw your landscape.

31

PDAS Domain IV

Activity Options

Quick Activity Have students sketch a landscape in pencil.

Early Finishers Have students add lines to their landscapes to show a change in the weather.

Challenge See *Teacher Resource Book*, p. 51.

PDAS Domain IV

ESL Assist students with **vocabulary development** by having them practice identifying different kinds of lines in their own artworks and in the artworks in this lesson.

Challenge Invite students to research how and why Robert Smithson created *Spiral Jetty* and report their findings.

Artist's Workshop
30-40 Minutes

Draw a Landscape

PLAN Have students read page 31. After they find a picture of an outdoor scene, have them identify and discuss the lines in it. TEKS 4.1B

CREATE As students design their original art-works, have them decide how realistic they want their landscapes to look and whether that choice will affect their use of implied and actual lines. TEKS 4.2B

REFLECT Have students use appropriate vocabulary to discuss the use of line in their landscapes. Ask them to describe their intent in using implied and actual lines. **SELF-EVALUATION** TEKS 4.1B, TEKS 4.4A

Wrap-Up
5-10 Minutes

Informal Assessment PDAS Domain III

- **How did learning about the kinds of lines artists use help you draw your landscape?** (Responses will vary.) **EVALUATION/CRITICISM**

- **What is the main idea of your landscape drawing? What details did you include to support the main idea?** (Responses will vary.) **MAIN IDEA AND DETAILS** TEKS 4.3A, TEKS 4.4A

Extend Through Writing
TEKS 4.1A; TAKS Writing Objective 1

DESCRIPTIVE PARAGRAPH Have students write a paragraph describing a visit to the landscape in their drawings. Students should communicate ideas about self using life experiences and sensory knowledge.

Recommended Reading

How Artists See the Weather by Colleen Carroll. Abbeville Kids, 1996. AVERAGE

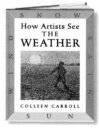

Lesson 2

PDAS Domains I, II
Shapes in Nature

OBJECTIVES
- Choose appropriate vocabulary to identify shapes in nature
- Design and create a close-up view
- Identify simple main ideas expressed in artworks

RESOURCES
- Art Print 5
- Reading Skill Card 1
- Discussion Cards 1, 9, pp. R34, R38
- Picture Card 55
- Electronic Art Gallery CD-ROM, Intermediate

Multimedia Art Glossary and Biographies
Visit *The Learning Site*
www.harcourtschool.com

5 Minutes

Warm-Up

Build Background About Shapes On the board, draw several shapes, including circles, triangles, rectangles, and squares. Ask students to name each shape. Then have students communicate ideas about school using sensory knowledge and life experiences to find classroom objects that have those shapes. Then draw on the board some irregular shapes, and ask students to describe them. Tell students that in this lesson they will learn how artists use various shapes in their artworks. TEKS 4.1A

Lesson 2

Shapes in Nature

Vocabulary
geometric shapes
organic shapes
close-up view

Some artists paint full landscapes of natural scenes. Other artists focus on certain natural objects as subjects for their artworks. Look at images **A** and **B**. What do you see in each painting?

Shapes

Each artist used different shapes to show his subject. Find the triangles in image **A**. Artists use lines with regular borders to paint **geometric shapes** such as triangles and circles. **Organic shapes** are made up of curved, irregular lines. Look at image **B**. Do you see more organic shapes or more geometric shapes in this painting?

 Franz Marc, *Monkey Frieze,*
1911, oil on canvas, 76 cm × 134.5 cm.
Hamburger Kunsthalle, Hamburg, Germany.

32

Background Information

About the Artists
A The German painter Franz Marc (1880–1916) tried to paint animals not as people saw them, but as he thought the animals themselves felt about their lives.

C Georgia O'Keeffe (1887–1986) decided to become an artist when she was only 12. She became one of the most famous female artists in the history of western art.

For additional information on the artists, see pp. R44–R65.

 For related artworks, see **Electronic Art Gallery CD-ROM, Intermediate.**

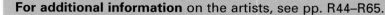 TEKS 4.1A communicate ideas; TEKS 4.1B discuss elements and principles; TEKS 4.2C produce artworks; PDAS Domain I active participation; PDAS Domain II learner-centered instruction; TAKS Reading Objective 1 demonstrate understanding of texts; (continued)

 Vincent van Gogh, *Irises*, 1889, oil on canvas, 71.1 cm × 93 cm. J. Paul Getty Museum, Los Angeles, California.

Natural Scenes

Look at the leaves in image **B**. Notice how the artist painted most of the leaves bending in the same direction. Did the artist use actual lines or implied lines to paint them? Follow the direction of the lines. Where do the lines lead your eyes?

The artist used diagonal, or slanted, lines to create the sense that the leaves and flowers are moving. What would image **B** look like if all the lines were vertical, or straight up and down? Point out the diagonal lines in image **A**. In which direction do they lead your eyes?

33

Teach
10-15 Minutes

Preview the Art Have students preview images A through D on pages 32–34. Ask them to describe what they see and carefully examine the shapes in each image. Use Discussion Card 1 and the questions below to guide the discussion. Then have students read pages 32–34.

A *Monkey Frieze* **What do you think is happening in this painting?**

B *Irises* **What kind of weather does this painting show?**

C *Poppies* **What details can you see in this painting?**

D *Prairie Flower* **How is this flower like the ones in image C? How is it different?**

Discuss Art Concepts Discuss with students the differences between geometric and organic shapes. In image A, students should point out the triangular shape of the mountain. Point out that the artist of image B used organic shapes for the flowers. He also used diagonal actual lines to make the flowers seem to be moving. Ask students to choose appropriate vocabulary to describe the organic shapes they find in the details in images C and D. TEKS 4.1B

TEKS 4.2C; TAKS Reading Objectives 1, 3, 4

Science Connection

Parts of a Flower Have students use an encyclopedia or their science textbook to research the parts of a flower. Have students invent ways to produce a drawing of the flower using a variety of art media. Students should label the parts of their drawing.

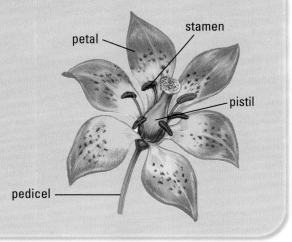

petal — stamen — pistil — pedicel

Teach (continued)

Cultural Link   Have students find New Mexico on the map on pages 206–207. Tell students that Georgia O'Keeffe was inspired by the desert landscapes and clear skies of New Mexico.

Main Idea and Details   Ask students to look at images A–D and identify the simple main idea expressed in each artwork. Then have students name details that support each main idea.   TEKS 4.3A

Think Critically

Use the questions below to check students' understanding of lesson concepts.

1. **FOCUS Skill** *READING SKILL*   **What kinds of shapes are most often found in nature?** (organic shapes) **MAIN IDEA AND DETAILS**

2. **What is the difference between geometric shapes and organic shapes?** (Geometric shapes, such as triangles, rectangles, and squares, include straight lines and sharp corners. Organic shapes are made up of curved, irregular lines.) **PERCEPTION/AESTHETICS**   TEKS 4.1B

3. **WRITE**   **Think about a nature scene you would like to paint. Tell how you would use shapes to show objects in your scene.**
EXPOSITORY   TAKS Writing Objective 1

Close-Up View

Look at images **C** and **D**. What is the subject of these images? Look back at the subject in image **B**. Compare it to image **C**. In image **B** the artist showed a large group of flowers. He painted them from far away. In image **C** the artist showed a **close-up view** of only two flowers. Painting a close-up view of a subject allows the viewer to see its details. Describe the shapes you see in images **C** and **D**.

 Georgia O'Keeffe, *Poppies,* 1950, oil on canvas, 36 in. × 30 in. Milwaukee Art Museum, Milwaukee, Wisconsin.

 Kirstie, grade 4, *Prairie Flower.*

Think Critically

1. *READING SKILL*   What kinds of shapes are most often found in nature? **MAIN IDEA AND DETAILS**

2. What is the difference between geometric shapes and organic shapes?

3. **WRITE**   Think about a nature scene you would like to paint. Tell how you would use shapes to show objects in your scene.

Art Print 5

Display **Art Print 5** and distribute Discussion Card 9: *Art Criticism* to students. Have them discuss lesson concepts such as shapes and close-up views as they view the artwork.

ART PRINT 5

Still Life of Summer Flowers
by Rachel Ruysch

★ TEKS 4.1B discuss elements and principles; TEKS 4.2B design original artworks; TEKS 4.3A identify main ideas; TEKS 4.4A form conclusions about personal artworks; TEKS 4.4B interpret artworks by peers and others; PDAS Domain III evaluation and feedback; PDAS Domain IV classroom management; *(continued)*

Artist's Workshop

Paint a Close-Up View

PLAN

Choose an object with an interesting close-up view. Make some sketches of the object from different angles. Look closely at the shapes that make up the object. Decide whether they are organic shapes or geometric shapes.

CREATE

1. Choose the sketch that shows the close-up view best.

2. Draw the object as large as possible on white paper. Try to fill the page.

3. Lightly outline each shape in pencil.

4. Choose your colors and paint the shapes.

REFLECT

Point out the different kinds of shapes you used.

MATERIALS

- natural objects, such as plants or fruit
- sketchbook
- pencil
- white paper
- tempera paint
- paintbrushes
- water bowl

Quick Tip Make the shapes in your close-up view stand out by outlining them in black marker.

35

Artist's Workshop

Paint a Close-Up View

PLAN Have students read the activity steps on page 35 and think about natural objects with interesting close-up views, such as flowers, pinecones, or seashells.

CREATE As students design their original artworks, have them look back at images C and D to note the shapes the artists used. TEKS 4.2B

REFLECT After students have pointed out examples of the shapes they used in their drawings, ask them to describe the intent of their paintings by explaining what they found most interesting about the object they chose to paint and how they showed that in their painting. **SELF-EVALUATION** TEKS 4.4A

5-10 Minutes

Wrap-Up

Informal Assessment PDAS Domain III

- **Would it be more interesting to view your object from far away or close up? Why?** (Responses will vary.) **PERSONAL RESPONSE**

- **What details support the main idea of your painting?** (Responses will vary.) **MAIN IDEA AND DETAILS**

Extend Through Writing
TEKS 4.4B; TAKS Writing Objective 1

DESCRIPTIVE PARAGRAPH Have students trade drawings with a partner and write a paragraph interpreting ideas in their peer's artwork by describing the close-up view they see.

Recommended Reading

Georgia O'Keeffe by Robyn Montana Turner. Little, Brown, 1991. CHALLENGING

PDAS Domain IV

Activity Options

Quick Activity Have students sketch a close-up view of the object they chose.

Early Finishers Have students draw a faraway view of the object they chose and then compare the two views.

Challenge See *Teacher Resource Book*, p. 52.

PDAS Domain IV

ESL Use **visuals** to support **comprehensible input** for flower names. Display *Picture Cards Collection*, card 55 for students to discuss and use as a reference.

See also *Picture Card Bank* CD-ROM, Category: Plants.

flower

PDAS Domains I, II

PICTURES OF THE PAST

ART AND THE ENVIRONMENT

DISCUSS THE IMAGES

Have students read pages 36–37.

- Encourage students to describe what they see in image A and image B. Ask students what they already know about fossils. Tell them that the word *fossil* comes from a Latin word meaning "to dig," because most fossils are discovered by digging.

- Discuss with students the objects Georgia O'Keeffe showed in image C. Point out that evidence of both the present, represented by the flowers, and the past, represented by the animal skull, can be found in the desert. Ask students to use life experiences to communicate ideas about how they could show evidence of both the past and the present in an artwork about their community. TEKS 4.1A

- Encourage students to discuss the way images A, B, and C all show pictures of the past—they give us a glimpse of what animals and plants of long ago looked like.

- For additional information about Georgia O'Keeffe, see pages R44–R65.

ART ⟷ SCIENCE CONNECTION

PICTURES OF THE PAST

How do both nature and artists show us pictures of the past?

A Mazon Creek fossil: shrimp-like animal.

B Mazon Creek fossil: plant frond.

Fossils are like pictures of the past. They show us how living things once looked. Many fossils can be found in rock. When a plant or an animal dies, the soft parts soon decay, or rot away. However, the harder parts may become buried over time. Parts that are saved like this are fossils.

Look at the fossil in image **A**. Does it look like any kind of animal you have seen before? This animal from the past was like a shrimp. What else do you notice about this fossil? Now look at the fossil in image **B**. Point out the stem and leaves.

Just as nature shows us images of the past, artists also show us images. Their images are from their own lives or the world around them. They capture a moment in time, whether real or imagined, and they save it for the future.

36

Background Information

Mazon Creek fossils are found in an area that stretches across four counties in northeast Illinois. Long ago, this area was a mixture of swamps and shallow bays. Many animals and plants lived there. As they died, their remains sank to the bottom of the bays, where they were buried by the mud washing in from the rivers. Chemicals in the water helped preserve many of those plants and animals as the fossils we see today.

Mazon Creek area
ILLINOIS

★ TEKS 4.1A communicate ideas; TEKS 4.2A integrate ideas in artworks; TEKS 4.4B interpret artworks by peers and others; PDAS Domain I active participation; PDAS Domain II learner-centered instruction

Georgia O'Keeffe was a twentieth-century artist who captured the beauty of nature in her paintings. In image **C**, O'Keeffe contrasts the bones of an animal with flowers and the desert sky. Why do you think she found beauty in these objects? How do images **A**, **B**, and **C** show us pictures of the past?

 Georgia O'Keeffe, *Summer Days*,
1936, Oil on canvas, 36 in. x 30 in.
Whitney Museum of American Art,
New York, New York.

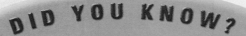

Suppose you were painting a picture for someone in the future. What would you want him or her to know about you or your world?

DID YOU KNOW?

Scientists who study fossils are called paleontologists. They learn from fossils what plants or animals were like, what they ate, and how they died. This information is important to understand what happened on Earth in the past.

37

Social Studies Connection

Petrified Forests Tell students that the western United States contains forests that seem to have turned to stone. Over time, minerals have replaced the wood fibers in the trees, giving them the appearance of stone.
For additional cross-curricular suggestions, see Art Transparency 2.

TEKS 4.4B
Student Art Show

Portfolios and Exhibitions Periodically during this unit, have students create a display or exhibition of their portfolios or other finished artworks. Ask students to interpret the moods and ideas they see in peers' portfolios. See *Teacher Edition* page 204 for planning and preparing a student art show.

DID YOU KNOW?

Use the facts below to discuss paleontologists with students.

- Paleontologists are scientists who use skills and information from many fields, including math, history, and geography, to reconstruct how the Earth's history might have been.

- Paleontologists' findings have led to new information about the geology of the Earth, including the locations of oil and natural gas deposits.

THINK ABOUT ART

Suppose you were painting a picture for someone in the future. What would you want him or her to know about you or your world?
(Responses will vary.) **PERSONAL RESPONSE**

ARTIST'S EYE ACTIVITY

Re-create a Summer Day Have students look again at image C and interpret the ideas in this artwork. Ask students to talk about why they think the artist chose the objects and the arrangement in her painting. Then ask students to discuss the objects they would include in a painting titled *Summer Days*. Have students integrate a variety of ideas about life events and community in a sketch for their painting. TEKS 4.2A

Lesson 3

Complementary Colors

OBJECTIVES

- Identify primary, secondary, and complementary colors in artworks
- Recognize the use of color schemes in artworks
- Design and create an outdoor scene painting
- Identify simple main ideas expressed in artworks

RESOURCES

- Art Print 3
- Reading Skill Card 1
- Discussion Cards 1, 3, pp. R34, R35
- Electronic Art Gallery CD-ROM, Intermediate

Multimedia Art Glossary and Biographies
Visit *The Learning Site*
www.harcourtschool.com

5 Minutes

Warm-Up

Build Background About Color Discuss with students pairs of colors or other color combinations that they find pleasing *and* those they dislike. Have students communicate ideas about self using sensory knowledge to tell why some colors seem to go together and others do not. Tell students that in this lesson they will learn about an artist's plan for choosing colors for an artwork. TEKS 4.1A

Lesson 3

Vocabulary

primary colors
secondary colors
complementary colors
contrast
color scheme

Color Schemes

Primary Colors

Red, blue, and yellow are **primary colors**. They are the most basic colors, because you cannot mix any other colors to get them. The primary colors are the building blocks for every color we see.

Find the primary colors on the color wheel on page 39. Then point out the primary colors in image **A**.

 Paul Sierra,
Elegy for Summer,
1995, oil on canvas,
80 in. × 60 in. Collection
of Mr. Rudy Elias.

38

 FYI

Background Information

About the Artists

B **Robert Wagstaff** was born and raised in Hawaii. Native Hawaiian plants and animals are often the subject of his works.

C **Colleen Meechan** most often paints landscapes inspired by the places where she has lived, including Hawaii and Florida.

For additional information about the artists, see pp. R44–R65.

For related artworks, see **Electronic Art Gallery CD-ROM, Intermediate.**

---

38 UNIT 1 *Nature Inspires Art*

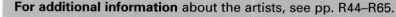 ★ **TEKS 4.1A** communicate ideas; **TEKS 4.1B** discuss elements and principles; **TEKS 4.4B** interpret artworks by peers and others; **PDAS Domain I** active participation; **PDAS Domain II** learner-centered instruction; **TAKS Reading Objective 1** demonstrate understanding of texts; *(continued)*

Secondary Colors

Secondary colors are created by mixing two primary colors together. For example, yellow and blue mixed together make green. Orange, green, and violet are secondary colors. What two primary colors mixed together make orange? What color do you get when you mix red and blue?

B Robert Wagstaff,
Visitors to the Rainforest,
2001, gouache on board,
12 in. x 18 in. Collection
of the artist.

Color Wheel

Complementary Colors

Colors such as red and green are opposite each other on the color wheel. They are called **complementary colors**. Complementary colors can be used together to create **contrast**, or a sharp difference between colors. Artists use contrast to guide a viewer's eyes toward certain parts of an artwork. Look at image **B**. What do you notice first? Which colors are complementary?

39

TAKS Reading Objectives 1, 3, 4

Science Connection

Colors of the Rainbow Ask students to use their science textbooks or an encyclopedia to research the relationship between the color wheel and a rainbow. Then have students draw a rainbow and label the colors in the correct order. (red, orange, yellow, green, blue, indigo, violet)

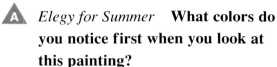

Teach

Preview the Art Have students preview images A through C on pages 38–40. Ask them to describe what they see. Use Discussion Card 1 and the questions below to guide the discussion. Then have students read pages 38–40.

A *Elegy for Summer* **What colors do you notice first when you look at this painting?**

B *Visitors to the Rainforest* **What details do you see that tell you about the setting of this painting?**

C *Blue Fronds* **What is the subject of this painting? Why do you think the artist chose the colors she did?** TEKS 4.4B

Discuss Art Concepts Have students look at the color wheel on page 39. Explain that it is a device for showing colors and their relationships to one another.

After volunteers point out the primary colors red, blue, and yellow on the color wheel, have them find the red shrubs and plants, the blue water, and the yellow reflections and plants in image A. Point out that in image B the red color of the cardinal and the green color of the leaves behind it create a sharp contrast.

In image C, have students choose appropriate vocabulary to discuss the use of complementary colors. Encourage students to express their opinions about the artist's use of a color scheme that is different from the real colors of her subject.
TEKS 4.1B

Teach (continued)

Social Studies Link Have students locate the state of Hawaii on the map on pages 206–207 or on a globe. Discuss with them their prior knowledge of this state and of the kinds of plants that grow there, such as the palm tree shown in image C.

Main Idea and Details Ask students to choose one artwork in this lesson and identify

- the main idea of the artwork.

- the details that support, or show more about, the main idea.

Then ask students to tell which artwork in this lesson they thought had the most interesting details, and ask them to support their opinions.
TEKS 4.3A

Think Critically

Use the questions below to check students' understanding of lesson concepts.

1. (Focus Skill) **READING SKILL** **Why are primary colors important?** (They are the building blocks for all the colors we see.) **MAIN IDEA AND DETAILS**

2. **Why might an artist paint an object in colors not usually seen in nature?** (Possible response: to show a different color scheme or to show how he or she feels about the subject) **PERCEPTION/AESTHETICS**

3. **WRITE** **Think of a place you know well. Then write a paragraph telling how you would paint it in unusual colors.** **DESCRIPTIVE**
TAKS Writing Objective 1

Colleen Meechan's paintings often focus on her home state, Hawaii.

HAWAII

PACIFIC OCEAN

Color Schemes

A **color scheme** is an artist's plan for choosing colors for an artwork. An artist might use a complementary color scheme to show contrast. Look at image **C**. Does the palm tree look realistic? Why or why not? In image **C**, the artist used colors that are not normally seen in nature. What do you think of the colors she chose?

C Colleen Meechan, *Blue Fronds*, 2001, acrylic on canvas, 42 in. × 48 in. Collection of the artist.

Think Critically

1. (Focus Skill) **READING SKILL** Why are primary colors important? **MAIN IDEA AND DETAILS**

2. Why might an artist paint an object in colors not usually seen in nature?

3. **WRITE** Think of a place you know well. Then write a paragraph telling how you would paint it in unusual colors.

40

Art Print 3

Display **Art Print 3** and distribute Discussion Card 3: *Elements of Art* to help students discuss the use of color in the artwork.

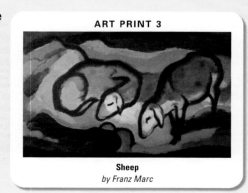

ART PRINT 3

Sheep
by Franz Marc

★ **TEKS 4.2B** design original artworks; **TEKS 4.3A** identify main ideas; **TEKS 4.4A** form conclusions about personal artworks; **PDAS Domain III** evaluation and feedback; **PDAS Domain IV** classroom management; **TAKS Writing Objective 1** composition; **TAKS Writing Objective 3** organization

Artist's Workshop

Paint with Complementary Colors

MATERIALS

- sketchbook
- pencil
- white paper
- tempera paint
- paintbrushes
- water bowl

PLAN

Think of an outdoor scene you would like to paint using complementary colors. Make a sketch of the scene. Then choose pairs of complementary colors to use in your painting.

CREATE

1. Using your sketch as a guide, draw the scene on white paper.

2. Paint your scene. Use complementary colors next to each other to show contrast.

REFLECT

Point out how you used complementary colors. Explain how you decided where to use contrast in your scene.

 Quick Tip
To keep your colors bright, remember to rinse your brush very well before using a new color.

41

 Activity Options

Quick Activity Have students paint swashes of complementary color pairs and note the contrast they create.

Early Finishers Have students add another pair of complementary colors to their paintings.

Challenge See *Teacher Resource Book*, p. 53.

ESL Have students use *Teacher Resource Book* page 38 to create their own color wheel and label the primary and secondary colors in both English and their first language. Students may use it to name the colors in their paintings.

Paint with Complementary Colors

30-40 Minutes

PLAN Have students read the activity steps on page 41. After students have finished their sketches, suggest that they refer to the color wheel on page 39 to choose pairs of complementary colors to use in their scenes.

CREATE As students design their original artworks, have them revisit the paintings on pages 38–40 to note the use of complementary colors. TEKS 4.2B

REFLECT Ask students to share the reasons for their color choices and their use of contrast.
SELF-EVALUATION TEKS 4.4A

5-10 Minutes

Wrap-Up

Informal Assessment PDAS Domain III

- **How did looking at the images in this lesson help you plan your painting?** (Responses will vary.) **EVALUATION/CRITICISM**

- **What is the main idea of your painting? What details support or explain the main idea?** (Responses will vary.) **MAIN IDEA AND DETAILS**
TEKS 4.3A

Extend Through Writing TAKS Writing Objectives 1, 3

FRIENDLY LETTER Have students each write a letter to a friend or family member in which they tell about a visit to the nature scenes they painted. Remind them to use the correct format for a friendly letter.

Recommended Reading

What Makes a Van Gogh a Van Gogh? by Richard Muhlberger. The Metropolitan Museum of Art/Viking, 2002. CHALLENGING

Lesson 4

PDAS Domains I, II

Color and Mood

OBJECTIVES

- Identify warm and cool colors in artworks
- Recognize the use of color to express mood in artworks
- Design and create an original seascape or desert landscape
- Identify simple main ideas expressed in artworks

RESOURCES

- Art Prints 1, 6
- Reading Skill Card 1
- Discussion Cards 1, 3, pp. R34–R35
- Electronic Art Gallery CD-ROM, Intermediate

Multimedia Art Glossary and Biographies
Visit *The Learning Site*
www.harcourtschool.com

5 Minutes

Warm-Up

Build Background Display **Art Print 6**, a colorful painting of a room by Henri Matisse. Ask volunteers to point out the different colors the artist used in the painting. Ask students what kind of feeling they get from this painting and why they think they get that feeling. Tell students that in this lesson they will learn how artists choose certain colors to create a mood, or feeling, in an artwork.

Lesson 4

Color and Mood

Vocabulary

cool colors

seascape

warm colors

Cool Colors

Artists may choose certain colors to create a mood, or feeling, in their artworks. Look at image **A**. What kind of mood did the artist create in this painting? What colors did the artist use? Blue, green, and violet are **cool colors**. They create a calm, peaceful mood.

Image **A** is a **seascape**. A seascape shows the sea, the sky, and sometimes the land. Why do you think seascapes are usually painted with cool colors?

 Claude Monet, *The Beach at Sainte-Adresse*, 1867, oil on canvas, 75.8 cm × 102.5 cm. The Art Institute of Chicago, Chicago, Illinois.

Background Information

About the Artists

A Claude Monet (KLOHD moh•NAY) (1840–1926) led the Impressionist movement in France. In fact, it took its name from Monet's painting, *Impression, Sunrise*.

B Matiros Sarian (1880–1972) felt that the artist in him came alive when, as a child, he listened to his parents' stories about their homeland, Armenia.

For additional information about the artists, see pp. R44–R65.

For related artworks, see **Electronic Art Gallery CD-ROM, Intermediate.**

Warm Colors

Look at image . What kind of mood did the artist create in this painting? Image B was painted with mostly **warm colors**. Warm colors create a mood of warmth and energy. Red, yellow, and orange are warm colors. Compare the mood in image B with the mood in image A. What is the setting of image B? Why do you think the artist chose warm colors for this painting?

 Matiros Sarian, *Gazelles,*
1926, oil on wood. Tretyakov Gallery,
Moscow, Russia.

43

 10-15 Minutes

Teach

Preview the Art Have students preview images A through C on pages 42–44. Ask them to name details that they find interesting in the artworks. Use Discussion Card 1 and the questions below to guide the discussion. Then have students read pages 42–44.

A *The Beach at Sainte-Adresse* **What do you think is the main idea of this painting?**
TEKS 4.3A

B *Gazelles* **Name the colors you see in this painting.**

C *Possibilities* **What do you think is happening in this painting?**

Discuss Art Concepts Point out to students that the artist of image B used warm colors to help viewers feel the heat of the sun and the sand. Then discuss with students the way the cool colors in image A create a calm mood.

Have students point out the warm and cool colors in image C. Ask students to interpret the moods in the artwork—how the energetic mood of the orange area contrasts with the calm mood beyond the door. TEKS 4.4B

Language Arts Connection

Colorful Words Discuss with students the connections between color and mood in the English language. Ask students the meanings of the expressions "I'm feeling blue" and "I'm green with envy." Discuss the moods or traits that these words commonly connote: *blue* (sad), *red* (angry), *yellow* (cowardly), *green* (new at something or jealous). Encourage students to identify colors for other moods or traits and to use color words in descriptive sentences.

Teach (continued)

Science Link   Ask volunteers to take a poll to find their classmates' top three color choices and top three ice-cream choices. Encourage students to graph the results and discuss their findings.

Main Idea and Details   Ask students to look at the artworks in this lesson and identify

- the main idea of each artwork.

- the details that support the main idea in each artwork.

Then ask students to tell which painting in this lesson they thought had the clearest main idea to interpret and how the details in it helped them interpret the main idea.   TEKS 4.3A, TEKS 4.4B

Think Critically

Use the questions below to check students' understanding of lesson concepts.

1. **READING SKILL**   **How would you use color to express a peaceful mood?** (Possible response: by using cool colors such as blue and green)   **MAIN IDEA AND DETAILS**   TEKS 4.1B

2. **When might an artist use warm colors to paint a seascape?** (Possible response: to show a seascape in bright sunlight or at sunset when the sky is red and orange)   **PERCEPTION/AESTHETICS**   TEKS 4.1B

3. **WRITE**   **Imagine you are the man in image C. Write a paragraph describing the changes you feel as you move across the scene.**   **NARRATIVE**   TAKS Writing Objective 1

 Ole Juul Hansen, *Possibilities*, 2002, crayon and watercolor on paper, 20 cm × 12.5 cm. Collection of the artist.

Science Link

Seeing color is an experience, just as tasting ice cream and hearing a song are experiences. No two people experience taste and sound in the same way. No two people experience color in exactly the same way, either.

Color and Contrast

Look closely at image **C**. Describe the scene. What colors did the artist use? Sometimes artists use both warm and cool colors to contrast different moods. What two moods did the artist contrast in image **C**?

Think Critically

1. **READING SKILL** How would you use color to express a peaceful mood? **MAIN IDEA AND DETAILS**

2. When might an artist use warm colors to paint a seascape?

3. **WRITE** Imagine you are the man in image **C**. Write a paragraph describing the changes you feel as you move across the scene.

44

Art Print 1

Display **Art Print 1** and distribute Discussion Card 3: *Elements of Art* to help students discuss the use of color in the artwork.

ART PRINT 1

Untitled (Sunset with Quarter Moon and Farmhouse)
by Edward Mitchell Bannister

★ TEKS 4.1B discuss elements and principles; TEKS 4.2B design original artworks; TEKS 4.3A identify main ideas; TEKS 4.4A form conclusions about personal artworks; TEKS 4.4B interpret artworks by peers and others; PDAS Domain III evaluation and feedback; PDAS Domain IV classroom management; *(continued)*

Artist's Workshop

Paint a Seascape or a Desert Landscape

MATERIALS
- magazines
- sketchbook
- pencil
- white paper
- tempera paint
- paintbrushes
- water bowl

PLAN

Look through magazines for pictures of seascapes and desert landscapes. Choose either one to draw. Then write a list of words to describe that kind of place. Sketch a couple of ideas based on your list of words.

CREATE

1. Select the sketch you like best, and copy it onto white paper.

2. Decide what mood you want to create. Choose warm colors or cool colors.

3. Paint your seascape or desert landscape.

REFLECT

How did you use color to create a feeling or mood? How did your list of words help you plan your painting?

Quick Tip
After your painting is dry, you may want to add details with pastels.

45

PDAS Domain IV

Activity Options

Quick Activity Have students paint a picture of a simple object using either cool colors or warm colors.

Early Finishers Have students redraw their scenes and paint them in the opposite color schemes.

Challenge See *Teacher Resource Book*, p. 54.

PDAS Domain IV

ESL Model using color words to form sentences with **idiomatic expressions**. For example, *The new worker is green because he's never done this before. When I get really angry, I see red!* Have students **develop oral language** by practicing the use of idioms in conversation.

30-40 Minutes
Artist's Workshop

Paint a Seascape or a Desert Landscape

PLAN Have students read the activity steps on page 45. Provide students with magazines containing photographs of various landscapes. Help students generate a list of adjectives describing the scene they chose.

CREATE As students design their original art-works, have them look back at the artworks in this lesson to decide what mood to show. TEKS 4.2B

REFLECT Have students form conclusions about the mood in their personal artwork, based on the color scheme they chose. **SELF-EVALUATION** TEKS 4.4A

5-10 Minutes
Wrap-Up

Informal Assessment PDAS Domain III

- **Which artwork in this lesson most influenced how you chose colors for your painting?** (Responses will vary.)
  EVALUATION/CRITICISM

- **What is the main idea of your painting? What details help support the main idea?**
  (Responses will vary.) **MAIN IDEA AND DETAILS**
  TEKS 4.3A

Extend Through Writing
TEKS 4.4A; TAKS Writing Objective 1

DESCRIPTIVE PARAGRAPH Have students write a paragraph describing their painting and the mood they created.

Recommended Reading

In Blue Mountains by Thomas Locker. Bell Pond Books, 2000. AVERAGE

PDAS Domains I, II

Paul Klee

ARTIST BIOGRAPHY

DISCUSS THE IMAGES

Have students read pages 46 and 47.

- Have students discuss what they see in image A and name some of the objects they would normally see in a landscape, such as the trees, fields, and maybe a mountain peak.

- Have students compare and contrast image A with the realistic landscape from a different cultural setting on pages 24–25. Point out that both paintings are landscapes. Have students identify natural objects, such as trees and rocks, in the realistic landscape. Then point out that Paul Klee used actual lines, unrealistic colors, and geometric shapes in image A to create a landscape that is not realistic. **TEKS 4.3B**

- After students view image B, have them compare it to image A as well as to **Art Print 2** in terms of color and shape. Ask students to interpret the ideas and moods in this sample portfolio of Paul Klee's work. **TEKS 4.1B, TEKS 4.4B**

Why might two artists paint a landscape in different ways?

Paul Klee (KLAY) was born in Switzerland in 1879. As a boy, Klee drew landscapes and comic sketches. His parents felt he had artistic talent and sent him to art school.

Before Klee was born, most artists painted in a realistic style. They made the people and objects in their paintings look real. Klee wanted to do something different. He developed a style that showed his feelings. He used bold lines, simple shapes, and bright colors.

 Paul Klee, *Moving Landscape,* 1920, oil on canvas, 31.5 cm x 49.5 cm. Private collection.

Background Information

The artworks of **Paul Klee** (KLAY) (1879–1940) are filled with connections to dreams, music, and poetry. During a trip to Tunisia, Klee was so impressed by the intense light and color he saw there that he began to paint vividly colored squares. The artwork on **Art Print 2**, *Senecio (Head of a Man)*, shows this style.

For additional information about Paul Klee and the Blue Rider group, see pp. R44–R65.

 For related artworks, see **Electronic Art Gallery CD-ROM, Intermediate.**

⭐ **TEKS 4.1B** discuss elements and principles; **TEKS 4.2C** produce artworks; **TEKS 4.3B** compare and contrast artworks; **TEKS 4.4B** interpret artworks by peers and others; **PDAS Domain I** active participation; **PDAS Domain II** learner-centered instruction; *(continued)*

B Paul Klee, *The Goldfish*, 1925, oil and watercolor on paper and board, 49.6 cm x 69.2 cm. Hamburger Kunsthalle, Hamburg, Germany.

Look at Klee's landscape painting in image **A**. Compare it to the landscape painting on pages 24–25. How are they different? What kinds of lines and shapes did Klee use in image **A**? Now look at image **B**. How would you describe the colors Klee used?

Think About Art

Many of Klee's subjects came from nature. How do you see this idea in images **A** and **B**?

 Multimedia Biographies
Visit *The Learning Site*
www.harcourtschool.com

 DID YOU KNOW?

Paul Klee was part of a group that called itself the Blue Rider. The group included painters, writers, poets, and composers of music. Blue Rider painters were known for their use of bright, exciting colors. The influence of the Blue Rider group can be seen in the work of some later artists.

47

DID YOU KNOW?

Use the facts below to discuss Paul Klee and the Blue Rider group with students.

- Klee and the other members of the Blue Rider group believed that art should represent ideas more than realistic objects.

- Klee especially valued children's artwork because he felt it showed pure creativity.

Think About Art

Many of Klee's subjects came from nature. How do you see this idea in images A and B?
(Possible response: The subjects of both paintings are things from nature—a landscape and a fish.)
PERCEPTION/AESTHETICS TEKS 4.4B

ARTIST'S EYE ACTIVITY

Drawing in Klee's Style Have students look back at the close-up views they painted in Lesson 2. Ask students to invent ways to produce artworks using a variety of materials to redraw their subjects in Paul Klee's style. Students should use heavy, actual lines, geometric shapes, and unrealistic colors. Ask students to compare their two drawings.
TEKS 4.2C

 **Multimedia Biographies**
Visit *The Learning Site*
www.harcourtschool.com

 TAKS Reading Objectives 1, 3, 4

Social Studies Connection

Switzerland Have students research Switzerland, Paul Klee's birthplace. Ask them to list facts about the country's geography, languages spoken, and major products.
For additional cross-curricular suggestions, see Art Transparency 3.

TEKS 4.4B

View an Artist's Work

Portfolios and Exhibitions Arrange for students to visit a museum, gallery, or other location to view original artworks in an artist's portfolio or exhibition. Students should interpret ideas and moods in the artworks, portfolios, and exhibitions they see.

TAKS Reading Objective 1 demonstrate understanding of texts; TAKS Reading Objective 3 use a variety of strategies; TAKS Reading Objective 4 apply critical-thinking skills

UNIT 1 *Paul Klee* **47**

Lesson 5

PDAS Domains I, II
Overlapping Shapes

OBJECTIVES

- Recognize the use of overlapping shapes in artworks
- Identify still lifes and collages as types of artworks
- Design and create an original collage
- Identify simple main ideas expressed in artworks

RESOURCES

- Art Print 5
- Reading Skill Card 1
- Discussion Cards 1, 3, pp. R34–R35
- Electronic Art Gallery CD-ROM, Intermediate

Multimedia Art Glossary and Biographies
Visit *The Learning Site*
www.harcourtschool.com

5 Minutes

Warm-Up

Build Background Draw a solid triangle and a solid circle on the board. Then draw the circle overlapping the triangle. Ask students which shape appears to be closer to them. Tell students that in this lesson they will learn why artists overlap shapes and colors.

Lesson 5

Vocabulary

still life
overlapping
collage

Overlapping Shapes

Still Life

Image **A** is an example of a **still life**. In a still life, objects, including flowers and food, are arranged in interesting ways. Which objects in image **A** appear to be the closest to the viewer? Which ones appear to be the farthest away?

The artist used **overlapping** to show that some objects are closer to the viewer than others. The objects in the back are partly covered by the objects in the front. The artist used overlapping to show that the teapot is in front of the flower. Where else did he use overlapping?

 A Paul Gauguin, *Still Life with Teapot and Fruit,* 1896, oil on canvas, 18¾ in. × 26 in. Metropolitan Museum of Art, New York, New York.

 Background Information

About the Artists

A The French artist **Paul Gauguin** (goh•GAN) (1848–1903) sailed to the South Seas in 1891 to escape European civilization. He lived there for most of his remaining years.

C Bobbi A. Chukran (1956–) is a contemporary folk artist whose artworks are strongly inspired by her memories of growing up in a small Texas town.

For additional information about the artists, see pp. R44–R65.

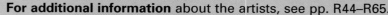 For related artworks, see **Electronic Art Gallery CD-ROM, Intermediate.**

 TEKS 4.1B discuss elements and principles; PDAS Domain I active participation; PDAS Domain II learner-centered instruction; TAKS Reading Objective 1 demonstrate understanding of texts; TAKS Reading Objective 3 use a variety of strategies; (*continued*)

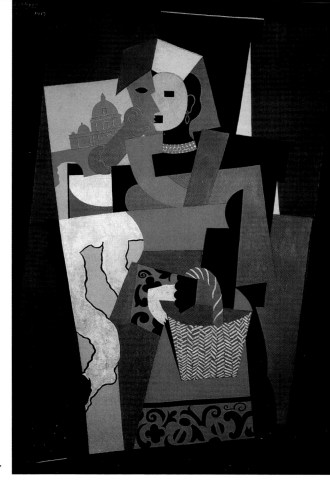

 Pablo Picasso,
L'Italienne,
1917, oil on canvas,
149.5 cm × 101.5 cm.
Foundation E.G. Buehrle,
Zurich, Switzerland.

Contrast

Now look at image **B**. What is the subject of this artwork?
Point out some details in the painting that tell about the
subject. Look at the colors and shapes in image **B**. How
did the artist use them to show contrast? Find examples of
overlapping in the painting. Which object is the closest to
the viewer? Which one is the farthest away?

49

 TAKS Reading Objectives 1, 3, 4

Social Studies Connection

State Flowers Have students turn to
the map on pages 206–207 and select
three states from different parts of the
country, not including their home state.
Then have students research the state
flower of each state they chose. Students
should sketch each flower and label it
with its name and its state's name.

**Bluebonnets,
Texas state flower**

 10-15 Minutes

Teach

Preview the Art Have students preview images A
through C on pages 48–50. Ask them to describe
what they see and to look for examples of overlapping shapes. Use Discussion Card 1 and the
questions below to guide the discussion. Then
have students read pages 48–50.

A *Still Life with Tea Pot and Fruit*
**What objects do you see in this still life?
Describe their colors and shapes.** TEKS 4.1B

B *L'Italienne* **What can you see in this
painting? What do you think the subject
of the painting is doing?**

C *Bluebonnet Collage* **How is this
artwork different from a photograph
of bluebonnets?**

Discuss Art Concepts Have students look at
image A. Point out that the spoon, part of the
cloth, and a large piece of fruit appear closest to
the viewer. Students should note that the yellow
flowers appear to be farthest from the viewer.
Help students conclude that overlapping shows
that one object is in front of another.

In image B, help students point out the woman's
head and torso, clothing, arm, and basket. Help
students see that the basket is closest to the viewer
and that the building is farthest away. Students
should identify and choose appropriate vocabulary
to describe the geometric shapes and the complementary colors red and green in the painting.
TEKS 4.1B

Point out how the overlapping photographs in
image C make the flowers look realistic.

LESSON 5 *Overlapping Shapes* **49**

Teach (continued)

Social Studies Link Ask students to find the names of the state tree and the state bird of Texas. (the pecan and the mockingbird)

Main Idea and Details Ask students to look at image B and identify what they think the main idea of the artwork is. Have them name some details to support the main idea. Ask them why they think the artist chose to show a person in such an unrealistic way. Then ask students to share and explain their opinions of image B.
TEKS 4.3A, TEKS 4.4B

Think Critically

Use the questions below to check students' understanding of lesson concepts.

1. **Focus Skill** **READING SKILL** **Why do artists use overlapping?** (to make some objects appear to be closer to the viewer and others appear to be farther away) **MAIN IDEA AND DETAILS**

2. **How are the artworks in this lesson alike? How are they different?** (Possible response: They all show overlapping. Two are still lifes; one is not. One is a collage; the others are not.)
COMPARE AND CONTRAST TEKS 4.3B

3. **WRITE** **Imagine that you are going to arrange objects for a still life about yourself. List five objects you would use. Tell why you would use them.** EXPOSITORY
TEKS 4.1A; TAKS Writing Objective 1

Social Studies Link
Bluebonnets are the state flower of Texas. The two main species of bluebonnets grow naturally in Texas. They do not grow anywhere else in the world.

C Bobbi A. Chukran, *Bluebonnet Collage,* 2002, mixed media collage, 8 in. × 10 in. Collection of the artist.

Collage

Image **C** is a **collage**. A collage is an artwork made by arranging flat materials, such as paper or cloth, on a flat surface. This artist tore handmade papers and photographs of flowers into different shapes. Then she arranged the pieces on stretched canvas. Why do you think the artist used photographs of the flowers instead of real ones? Where did she use overlapping?

Think Critically

1. **Focus Skill** **READING SKILL** Why do artists use overlapping? **MAIN IDEA AND DETAILS**

2. How are the artworks in this lesson alike? How are they different?

3. **WRITE** Imagine that you are going to arrange objects for a still life about yourself. List five objects you would use. Tell why you would use them.

50

Art Print 5

Display **Art Print 5** and distribute Discussion Card 3: *Elements of Art* to help students discuss overlapping shapes in the artwork.

ART PRINT 5

Still Life of Summer Flowers
by Rachel Ruysch

★ TEKS 4.1A communicate ideas; TEKS 4.2A integrate ideas in artworks; TEKS 4.2B design original artworks; TEKS 4.3A identify main ideas; TEKS 4.3B compare and contrast artworks; TEKS 4.4A form conclusions about personal artworks; TEKS 4.4B interpret artworks by peers and others; (*continued*)

Artist's Workshop

Create a Still-Life Collage

MATERIALS
- magazines
- sketchbook
- pencil
- colored papers
- glue stick
- poster board
- markers

PLAN

Tear from magazine pages objects and colors you would like to use in your collage. Make some sketches of your ideas.

CREATE

1. Choose one idea and draw an outline of your still life on poster board.

2. Tear pieces of colored paper into shapes you would like to use. Overlap the pieces in different ways.

3. Glue your arrangement onto the poster board. Decorate the border with markers.

REFLECT

Where did you use overlapping in your collage? What objects seem closest to the viewer?

Quick Tip
Be sure to erase the pencil lines of your outline or cover them with pieces of paper.

51

 30-40 Minutes

Artist's Workshop

Create a Still-Life Collage

PLAN After students have read the activity steps on page 51, provide them with magazines they can cut apart for their collages.

CREATE Have students integrate a variety of ideas about self as they design their original artworks. They should experiment with different arrangements before they glue their collage down.
TEKS 4.2A, TEKS 4.2B

REFLECT Have students describe the intent in their personal artworks by telling about the objects they used and describing their significance. Have them point out where they used overlapping.
SELF-EVALUATION TEKS 4.4A

5-10 Minutes

Wrap-Up

Informal Assessment PDAS Domain III

- **What does your collage tell about you?**
  (Responses will vary.) **PERSONAL RESPONSE** TEKS 4.4A

- **Would you prefer to paint a still life or make a collage of a still life? Explain why.**
  (Responses will vary.) **PERSONAL RESPONSE**

Extend Through Writing TAKS Writing Objective 6

MUSEUM CARD Have each student write a museum card to accompany their finished collage. See *Teacher Resource Book* page 39. Students should proofread their cards carefully.

Recommended Reading

A Cloak for the Dreamer by Aileen Friedman. Scholastic, 1994. CHALLENGING

 PDAS Domain IV

Activity Options

Quick Activity Have students sketch a group of objects to show overlapping.

Early Finishers Have students glue their collages onto a larger sheet of poster board and decorate the border.

Challenge See *Teacher Resource Book*, p. 55.

 PDAS Domain IV **MEETING INDIVIDUAL NEEDS**

ESL
Have students **build vocabulary** by working with an English-fluent partner to name the objects in their collages.

Special Needs
Students with vision impairments can use felt shapes and pre-cut pieces of paper to make their collages.

PDAS Domain III evaluation and feedback; PDAS Domain IV classroom management; TAKS Writing Objective 1 composition; TAKS Writing Objective 6 proofreading

LESSON 5 *Overlapping Shapes* 51

Unit 1

Review and Reflect

PDAS Domains I, III

 Have students reflect on what they have learned about the ways artists use line, shape, and color to create artworks inspired by nature. Display **Art Prints 1, 2, 3, 5,** and **6.** Encourage small groups of students to use Discussion Cards 3 and 9 and their completed Word Knowledge Charts to discuss what they learned about the vocabulary and concepts in this unit.

Vocabulary and Concepts

Have students read each sentence and choose the letter of the word or phrase that best completes it. (1. D; 2. G; 3. B; 4. F; 5. D)

Focus Skill — READING SKILL

Main Idea and Details

Remind students that the main idea is what something is mostly about and that details give information to explain or support the main idea. After students have reread the first paragraph of page 36, have them list the main idea and details on Reading Skill Card 1. **TAKS Reading Objectives 1, 4**

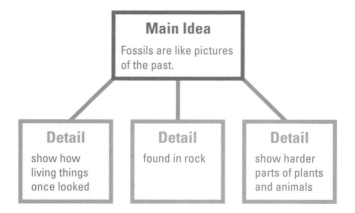

```
Main Idea
Fossils are like pictures
of the past.

Detail              Detail              Detail
show how            found in rock       show harder
living things                           parts of plants
once looked                             and animals
```

Unit 1 Review and Reflect

Vocabulary and Concepts

Choose the letter of the word or phrase that best completes each sentence.

1 Triangles, rectangles, and squares are examples of ___.

  A actual lines   **C** contrast

  B organic shapes   **D** geometric shapes

2 An artwork that shows an outdoor scene is called a ___.

  F still life   **H** collage

  G landscape   **J** contrast

3 A ___ is an artist's plan for choosing colors.

  A primary color   **C** still life

  B color scheme   **D** contrast

4 Artists use ___ to show one object in front of another.

  F overlapping   **H** geometric shapes

  G organic shapes   **J** contrast

5 ___ colors can create a calm, peaceful mood in an artwork.

  A Complementary   **C** Warm

  B Primary   **D** Cool

Focus Skill — READING SKILL

Main Idea and Details

Reread the information about fossils in the first paragraph on page 36. Use a diagram like this to find the main idea and details.

```
Main Idea

Detail    Detail    Detail
```

52

TEKS 4.2A, TEKS 4.2B

Home and Community Connection

School-Home Connection

Copy and distribute *Teacher Resource Book* pp. 85–86. After completing the unit, students can work at home to design an original artwork that shows a nature scene or a still life.

Community Connection

You may want to contact a local senior citizen center to pair student artists with senior citizens who enjoy creative artwork. Ask partners to integrate a variety of ideas about their community in an original collaborative artwork.

★ TEKS 4.1B discuss elements and principles; **TEKS 4.2A** integrate ideas in artworks; **TEKS 4.2B** design original artworks; **TEKS 4.3A** identify main ideas; **TEKS 4.4A** form conclusions about personal artworks; **TEKS 4.4B** interpret artworks by peers and others; **PDAS Domain I** active participation; *(continued)*

Write About Art

Choose a piece of your own artwork, and write a paragraph about it. First, write about the main idea of your artwork. Then, write about the details that support the main idea. Use a diagram like the one on page 52 to plan your writing. Try to use unit vocabulary words in your paragraph.

REMEMBER — YOU SHOULD

- include only those details that support the main idea.
- use correct grammar, spelling, and punctuation.

Critic's Corner

Look at *Man on a Bench* by Horace Pippin to answer the questions below.

Horace Pippin,
Man on a Bench,
1946, oil on fabric,
13 in. × 18 in.
Private collection.

DESCRIBE What is the subject of the artwork? How would you describe the subject?

ANALYZE Where do you see primary and complementary colors in the artwork? What kinds of lines do you see?

INTERPRET What kind of mood do you think the artist was trying to express?

EVALUATE Do you think the artist used colors and lines successfully to express the mood in this painting? Explain your answer.

53

PDAS Domain III

Assessment

Portfolio Assessment

Work with students to choose a piece of their artwork to include in their portfolios. Suggest that they decide which piece best fulfilled the assignment or which piece they liked best for another reason. You may want to provide specific feedback that targets students' use of the elements of art and techniques. See also Portfolio Recording Form, page R32.

Additional Assessment Options

- Progress Recording Form, p. R33
- Artist's Workshop Rubrics (Self/Teacher and Peer), pp. R30–R31
- Unit 1 Test, *Teacher Resource Book* p. 99

Write About Art

Main Idea and Details Composition Read aloud the prompt with students. Suggest that they use the main idea and details diagram on page 52 to help them plan their writing. Have students select a piece of their artwork that shows a strong main idea. Encourage students to use unit vocabulary words in their compositions. TEKS 4.3A, TEKS 4.4A; TAKS Writing Objective 1

Critic's Corner

RESPONSE/EVALUATION Use the steps below to guide students in analyzing *Man on a Bench* by Horace Pippin. See also Discussion Card 2, p. R34.

DESCRIBE Discuss with students the main idea of *Man on a Bench*. Remind them that the title can help them determine the subject. TEKS 4.3A

ANALYZE Students should point out the complementary colors red and green in the painting, the primary color yellow, horizontal lines in the bench, and vertical lines in the trees. TEKS 4.1B

INTERPRET Students may interpret the mood in the painting as lonely or quiet. Discuss their ideas. TEKS 4.4B

EVALUATE Discuss students' responses. Remind them to support their opinions with reasons.

 TAKS Test Preparation: **Reading and Writing Through Art,** pp. 1–16, 17–21

Unit 2

Value, Texture, and Emphasis

Moments in Time

Artists create artworks that preserve a moment in time. They may capture an event, a mood, or even the way light and shadow appear. In this unit students will learn how artists use value and emphasis to capture one moment in time.

Resources

- Unit 2 Art Prints (4–6)
- Additional Art Prints (1, 16)
- Art Transparencies 4–6
- Test Preparation: Reading and Writing Through Art, pp. 22–26
- Artist's Workshop Activities: English and Spanish, pp. 11–20
- Encyclopedia of Artists and Art History, pp. R44–R65
- Picture Cards Collection cards 10, 29, 48, 56, 58, 74, 75, 81, 85, 124

Using the Art Prints

- Discussion Cards, pp. R34–R38
- Teaching suggestions, backs of Art Prints
- Art Print Teaching Suggestions: Spanish

Teacher Resource Book

- Vocabulary Cards in English and Spanish, pp. 11–14
- Reading Skill Card 2, p. 32
- Challenge Activities, pp. 56–60
- School-Home Connection: English/Spanish, pp. 87–88
- Unit 2 Test, p. 100

Technology Resources

 Electronic Art Gallery CD-ROM, Intermediate
Picture Card Bank CD-ROM

 Visit *The Learning Site*
www.harcourtschool.com

- Multimedia Art Glossary
- Multimedia Biographies
- Reading Skills and Activities

Art Prints for This Unit

ART PRINT 6

The Large Red Interior
by Henri Matisse

ART PRINT 5

Still Life of Summer Flowers
by Rachel Ruysch

ART PRINT 1

Untitled (Sunset with Quarter Moon and Farmhouse)
by Edward Mitchell Bannister

ART PRINT 4

The Bathers
by Pierre-Auguste Renoir

ART PRINT 16

The Profile of Time
by Salvador Dalí

Lesson	Objectives and Vocabulary	Art Images	Production/Materials
Fact and Opinion, pp. 56–57			
6 COLOR AND VALUE pp. 58–61 30–60 minutes	• Choose appropriate vocabulary to discuss the use of value in artworks • Design and create an original monochromatic painting • Recognize facts and opinions in artworks **Vocabulary: dominant color, value, tints, shades, monochromatic**	• **Kathy's Bowl** by Meredith Brooks Abbott • **The Banks of the Bièvre near Bicêtre** by Henri Rousseau • **Homage to the Square/Red Series, Untitled III** by Josef Albers	**Create a Monochromatic Painting** ❏ pencil ❏ white paper ❏ tempera paint ❏ paintbrushes ❏ water bowl ❏ paper plates
7 NATURAL TEXTURES pp. 62–65 30–60 minutes	• Choose appropriate vocabulary to discuss texture in artworks • Design and create an original collage that has texture • Recognize facts and opinions in artworks **Vocabulary: tactile texture, visual texture, fiber**	• **Flowering Tree** by Chris Kenny • **Velvet Cat I** by Isy Ochoa • **Elysian Fields** by Memphis Wood	**Create Texture in a Collage** ❏ textured objects ❏ tissue paper ❏ crayons ❏ scissors; glue ❏ poster board ❏ yarn or string
Art ↔ Science Connection: Erosion, pp. 66–67			
8 LIGHT AND COLOR pp. 68–71 30–60 minutes	• Choose appropriate vocabulary to discuss the use of light and color in artworks • Design and create an original outdoor scene • Recognize and use statements of fact and opinion about artworks **Vocabulary: Impressionism, *plein air*, impasto**	• **Rouen Cathedral, Impression of Morning** by Claude Monet • **Rouen Cathedral, Bright Sun** by Claude Monet • **The Butterfly Hunt** by Berthe Morisot • **Children at the Beach** by Joaquín Sorolla y Bastida	**Paint an Outdoor Scene** ❏ magazines ❏ pencil ❏ white paper ❏ tempera paint or watercolors ❏ paintbrushes ❏ water bowl
9 VALUES OF BLACK AND WHITE pp. 72–75 30–60 minutes	• Choose appropriate vocabulary to discuss the use of value in artworks • Design and create an original charcoal drawing • Recognize and use statements of fact and opinion about artworks **Vocabulary: gray scale, blending**	• **Dance of the Corn Lilies** by Bruce Barnbaum • **Dewdrop** by M. C. Escher • **Untitled** by Matthew, grade 4	**Draw a Charcoal Still Life** ❏ classroom objects ❏ pencil ❏ white paper ❏ charcoal pencil ❏ tissue ❏ eraser
Art ↔ Social Studies Connection: Henri Matisse, pp. 76–77			
10 EMPHASIS pp. 78–81 30–60 minutes	• Choose appropriate vocabulary to discuss the use of emphasis in artworks • Design and create an original pastel drawing • Recognize and use statements of fact and opinion about artworks **Vocabulary: emphasis, three-dimensional, assemblage**	• **Palm Tree in Mauritania** by Raymond Depardon • **Portrait of Gordon Parks** by Johanna Fiore • **A Bigger Splash** by David Hockney • **Toward the Blue Peninsula** by Joseph Cornell	**Create a Pastel Drawing** ❏ magazines ❏ pencil ❏ white paper ❏ oil pastels
Review and Reflect, pp. 82–83			

Fact and Opinion, pp. 56–57

Opportunities for application of the skill are provided on pp. 60, 64, 70, 74, 80, 82, and 83.

Resources and Technology	Suggested Literature	Across the Curriculum
• Art Prints 1, 6 • Reading Skill Card 2 • Discussion Cards 1, 3, pp. R34–R35 • Electronic Art Gallery CD-ROM, Intermediate	*How Artists Use Color* by Paul Flux	**Social Studies** Natural Dyes, p. 59 **Reading** Fact and Opinion, p. 60 **Writing** Descriptive Paragraph, p. 61
• Art Print 16 • Reading Skill Card 2 • Discussion Cards 1, 3, pp. R34–R35 • Electronic Art Gallery CD-ROM, Intermediate	*How Artists Use Pattern and Texture* by Paul Flux	**Language Arts** Texture Categories, p. 63 **Reading** Fact and Opinion, p. 64 **Writing** Descriptive Paragraph, p. 65
• Art Prints 1, 4 • Reading Skill Card 2 • Discussion Cards 1, 7, pp. R34, R37 • Electronic Art Gallery CD-ROM, Intermediate	*What Makes a Monet a Monet?* by Richard Muhlberger 	**Social Studies** Research Impressionist Artists, p. 69 **Reading** Fact and Opinion, p. 70 **Writing** Friendly Letter, p. 71
• Art Print 5 • Reading Skill Card 2 • Discussion Cards 1, 3 pp. R34–R35 • Electronic Art Gallery CD-ROM, Intermediate	*Jumanji* by Chris Van Allsburg 	**Social Studies** Ansel Adams, p. 73 **Reading** Fact and Opinion, p. 74 **Writing** List, p. 75
• Art Print 5 • Reading Skill Card 2 • Discussion Cards 1, 4, pp. R34–R35 • Electronic Art Gallery CD-ROM, Intermediate	*The Art Room* by Susan Vande Griek 	**Social Studies** Mauritania, p. 79 **Reading** Fact and Opinion, p. 80 **Writing** Story, p. 81

Art Puzzlers

Present these art puzzlers to students at the beginning or end of a class or when students finish an assignment early.

- Choose a color you would like to use in a **monochromatic** artwork. Explain your choice and what you might draw with it. TEKS 4.1B

- Draw an object in your home or classroom in a way that shows its **visual texture.** TEKS 4.2B

- Draw two pictures of the same room. Paint each a different **color,** showing different times of day. TEKS 4.2B

- Create your own **gray scale.** Make a dark mark on a piece of paper with a pencil. Then rub a tissue over the mark to smudge it.

- Cut out a shape from a piece of construction paper. Create **emphasis** by gluing the shape to a background that has a complementary color. TEKS 4.2B

School-Home Connection
The activities above are included in the School-Home Connection for this unit. See *Teacher Resource Book,* pp. 87–88.

Assessment Options

- Rubrics and Recording Forms, pp. R30–R33
- Unit 2 Test, *Teacher Resource Book,* p. 100

Visit *The Learning Site:*
www.harcourtschool.com

Artist's Workshops PREVIEW

Use these pages to help you gather and organize materials for the production activity in each lesson.

LESSON	MATERIALS

6 Create a Monochromatic Painting p. 61

Objective: To use tints and shades to design and create an original monochromatic painting

 30–40 minutes

Challenge Activity: See *Teacher Resource Book,* p. 56.

MATERIALS

- pencil
- sketchbook
- white paper
- tempera paint
- paintbrushes
- water bowl
- paper plates

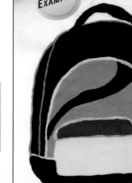

FINISHED EXAMPLES

LESSON

7 Create Texture in a Collage p. 65

Objective: To design and create an original collage with tactile and visual texture

 30–40 minutes

Challenge Activity: See *Teacher Resource Book,* p. 57.

- objects with different textures
- tissue paper
- crayons
- scissors
- glue
- poster board
- yarn or string

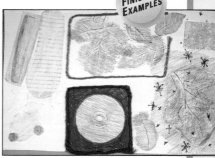

FINISHED EXAMPLES

 Safety Tips For safety information, see Art Safety, p. R4, or the Art Safety Poster.

 Quick Tip For information on media and techniques, see pp. R15–R23.

LESSON	MATERIALS

Paint an Outdoor Scene p. 71

- magazines
- pencil
- sketchbook
- white paper
- tempera paint or watercolors
- paintbrushes
- water bowl

FINISHED EXAMPLES

Objective: To use value and color to design and create an original outdoor scene

 30–40 minutes

Challenge Activity: See *Teacher Resource Book,* p. 58.

LESSON

9 Draw a Charcoal Still Life p. 75

- classroom objects
- pencil
- sketchbook
- white paper
- charcoal pencil
- tissue
- eraser

FINISHED EXAMPLES

Objective: To use value and blending to design and create an original charcoal drawing

 30–40 minutes

Challenge Activity: See *Teacher Resource Book,* p. 59.

LESSON

10 Create a Pastel Drawing p. 81

- magazines
- pencil
- sketchbook
- white paper
- oil pastels

FINISHED EXAMPLES

Objective: To use emphasis to design and create an original pastel drawing

 30–40 minutes

Challenge Activity: See *Teacher Resource Book,* p. 60.

Unit 2

PDAS Domains I, II

Moments in Time

PREVIEW THE UNIT

Tell students that in this unit they will view and create artworks that preserve a moment in time— they may capture an event or show the way light is reflected on surfaces. Invite students to preview this unit by reading the lesson titles and examining the art images.

STEP INTO THE ART

Have students examine the painting on pages 54 and 55 and describe what they see using sensory knowledge. Then read page 55 with students, and discuss their answers to the questions. TEKS 4.1A

- **What would the weather be like?** Students may conclude from the way the people in the painting are dressed that the weather is hot or balmy.

- **What would the air smell like?** Suggest the scents of grasses, other plants, and water.

- **What sounds would you hear?** Point out that the scene suggests quiet sounds such as people talking and water lapping in the wake of the boat.

- **How would the water feel?** Students may suggest that the water may be warm because people are swimming in it.

- **Would you go for a swim?** Encourage students to give reasons for their responses.

SHARE BACKGROUND INFORMATION

This painting depicts a group of workers relaxing by the Seine River near Paris, France.

 See **Using the Maps of Museums and Art Sites**, p. R2.

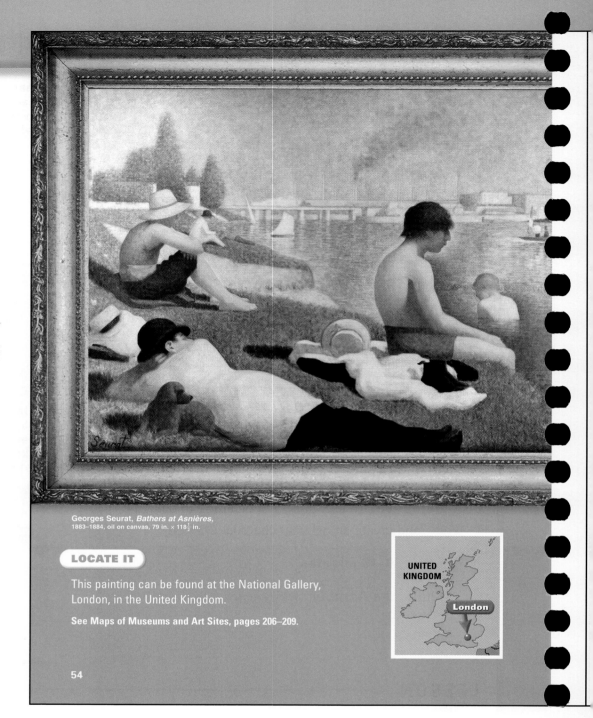

Georges Seurat, *Bathers at Asnières*,
1883–1884, oil on canvas, 79 in. × 118½ in.

This painting can be found at the National Gallery, London, in the United Kingdom.

See Maps of Museums and Art Sites, pages 206–209.

UNITED KINGDOM

London

54

Background Information

About the Artist

Georges Seurat (suh•RAH) (1859–1891) prepared for painting *Bathers at Asnières* by drawing many small sketches outdoors during the summer of 1883.

For additional information about Georges Seurat, see the Encyclopedia of Artists and Art History, pages R44–R65, and the Gallery of Artists, *Student Edition* pages 240–253.

For related artworks, see **Electronic Art Gallery CD-ROM, Intermediate.**

Unit 2
Value, Texture, and Emphasis

Moments in Time

Step into the Art

Imagine you could step into the scene in this painting. What would the weather be like? What would the air smell like? What sounds would you hear? How would the water feel? Would you go for a swim?

ABOUT THE ARTIST

See Gallery of Artists, pages 240–253.

Unit Vocabulary

dominant color	tactile texture	gray scale
value	visual texture	blending
tints	fiber	emphasis
shades	Impressionism	three-dimensional
monochromatic	*plein air*	assemblage
	impasto	

 Multimedia Art Glossary
Visit *The Learning Site*
www.harcourtschool.com

55

Language Arts Connection

Students may create a chart like the one below to identify familiar and unfamiliar vocabulary terms. Encourage them to add information to their charts as they work through this unit.

WORD KNOWLEDGE CHART		
I know this term.	I have seen this term before.	I have never seen this term.

Read aloud the terms with students, and use the Word Knowledge Chart below to assess and discuss their prior knowledge.

dominant color the color a viewer sees most in an artwork

value the lightness or darkness of a color

tint a lighter value of a color created by mixing white with the color

shade a darker value of a color created by mixing black with the color

monochromatic a group of values of one color

tactile texture the way the surface of a real object feels when you touch it

visual texture the appearance of texture on a drawn or painted surface

fiber a material such as cloth, yarn, or thread

Impressionism an art movement of the late nineteenth century in which artists painted the way light and color looked at a certain moment in time

plein air the practice of painting outdoors; from the French for *open air*

impasto a technique of painting that creates a bumpy surface by using thick brushstrokes

gray scale the range of values from pure black to pure white

blending mixing or smudging areas in an artwork to create gradual value changes

emphasis the special importance given to one part of an artwork

three-dimensional having height, width, and depth

assemblage a sculpture made from various objects and materials

Vocabulary Resources

- Vocabulary Cards in English and Spanish: *Teacher Resource Book,* pp. 11–14
- Student Edition Glossary, pp. 254–261

 **Multimedia Art Glossary**
Visit *The Learning Site*
www.harcourtschool.com

Focus Skill *READING SKILL*

PDAS Domains I, II

Fact and Opinion

SKILL TRACE	
FACT AND OPINION	
Introduce	pp. 56–57
Review	pp. 60, 64, 70, 74, 80, 82

DISCUSS THE SKILL

Access Prior Knowledge   Discuss the day's weather with students. Include facts about the temperature and weather conditions. Then offer an opinion about the weather, such as the way your mood is affected by it. Explain to students that a fact is a statement that can be proved and an opinion is a statement that expresses someone's thoughts or feelings. Encourage students to give one fact about the weather and to offer their opinions about it.

APPLY TO ART

Fact and Opinion   Ask students to read page 56 and look at the image. Have volunteers point out details that support the facts in the painting. Encourage them to give additional facts about the scene in the painting. Then discuss with students the artist's possible opinion. Ask students to offer their own opinions about what the artist may be expressing in the scene. TEKS 4.4B

Focus Skill *READING SKILL*

Fact and Opinion

A *fact* is a statement that can be proved. An *opinion* is a statement that expresses someone's thoughts or feelings.

Artists can show facts and opinions in their artworks. Look at the image below. The artist showed these facts in his painting:

- The weather is cold.
- Two cowhands and two horses are near a fence.
- There are no other people or animals in the scene.

Read the title of the painting. The artist may be expressing the opinion that it is sad that the cowhands' way of life is changing.

Frederic S. Remington, *The Fall of the Cowboy,*
1895, oil on canvas, 25 in. × 35$\frac{1}{8}$ in. Amon Carter Museum, Fort Worth, Texas.

56

 Background Information

About the Artist

Frederic S. Remington (1861–1909) was an American painter, sculptor, illustrator, and writer whose most famous works depicted the end of the frontier life of the American West. *The Fall of the Cowboy* is an example of the subject matter that Remington showed again and again in his career.

For additional information about Frederic S. Remington, see pp. R44–R65.

 For related artworks, see **Electronic Art Gallery CD-ROM, Intermediate.**

Knowing the difference between facts and opinions can help you understand what you read. Read the passage below. Think about which statements are facts and which are opinions.

> Frederic S. Remington was born on October 4, 1861, in Canton, New York. He went to school and then moved west and became a cowhand. He spent much of his life traveling through the western part of America, and he often drew or painted what he saw. It is important to study Remington's work to truly understand life in the American West. Remington's paintings and sculptures of the American West are the most interesting and beautiful in the world.

List the facts and opinions from the passage. You can use a chart like this one.

Facts	Opinions

On Your Own

As you read the lessons in this unit, use charts to keep track of facts and opinions in the text and in the artworks. Look back at your charts when you see questions with *READING SKILL* .

57

APPLY TO READING

Facts and Opinions About the Artist   Explain to students that as they read, they should look for facts, or statements that can be proved. They should also look for opinions, or statements that express someone's thoughts or feelings.

Have students read the passage on page 57. Work with them to complete the chart to list facts and opinions about Frederic S. Remington.
TAKS Reading Objective 4

Facts	Opinions
Frederic Remington was born on October 4, 1861, in Canton, New York.	It is important to study Remington's work to understand life in the American West.
He moved west and became a cowhand.	Remington's artworks are the most interesting and beautiful in the world.
He spent much of his life traveling through the American West.	

ON YOUR OWN

As students read the lessons in this unit, have them use charts such as the one on page 57 to keep track of facts and opinions in the text and in the artworks.

TAKS Reading Objective 4

Reading Skill Card

Distribute Reading Skill Card 2, *Teacher Resource Book* page 32. Have students identify facts and opinions in this unit.

Extend the Skill
For additional teaching suggestions, see **Art Transparency 4**.

PDAS Domain IV

ESL   Pair students with English-fluent peers to read the passage on page 57 together. Then have partners work together to **paraphrase** the passage and discuss the facts and opinions in it. Have partners complete their charts together.

Reading Skills and Activities
Visit *The Learning Site*
www.harcourtschool.com

Lesson 6

Color and Value

OBJECTIVES
- Choose appropriate vocabulary to discuss the use of value in artworks
- Design and create an original monochromatic painting
- Recognize facts and opinions in artworks

RESOURCES
- Art Prints 1, 6
- Reading Skill Card 2
- Discussion Cards 1, 3, pp. R34–R35
- Electronic Art Gallery CD-ROM, Intermediate

Multimedia Art Glossary and Biographies
Visit *The Learning Site*
www.harcourtschool.com

5 Minutes

Warm-Up

Build Background Display **Art Print 6**, and ask students what color they notice first. (red) Point out that artists carefully select the colors they will use in an artwork. Sometimes an artist decides to paint most of an artwork in one color, as Henri Matisse did in *The Large Red Interior*, to create a mood or feeling. Ask students to interpret the mood in this original artwork by Matisse. TEKS 4.4B

Lesson 6

Color and Value

Dominant Color

Look at the still-life painting in image **A**. What objects do you see? What color do you notice first? The color you see most in an artwork is the **dominant color**. The artist of image **A** used mostly the color red to create a dominant color scheme.

Vocabulary
- dominant color
- value
- tints
- shades
- monochromatic

 Meredith Brooks Abbott, *Kathy's Bowl*,
1993, oil on linen, 11 in. × 14 in. Private collection.

Background Information

About the Artists

A Meredith Brooks Abbott (1938–) is a contemporary American painter of still lifes, portraits, and landscapes.

C Josef Albers's (1888–1976) book on color, *Interaction of Color*, has been translated into eight languages and is a major tool in art education throughout the world.

For more information about the artists, see pp. R44–R65.

 For related artworks, see the **Electronic Art Gallery CD-ROM, Intermediate.**

★ TEKS 4.1B discuss elements and principles; TEKS 4.3A identify main ideas; TEKS 4.4B interpret artworks by peers and others; **PDAS Domain I** active participation; **PDAS Domain II** learner-centered instruction; **TAKS Reading Objective 1** demonstrate understanding of texts; *(continued)*

B Henri Rousseau,
The Banks of the Bièvre near Bicêtre,
1904, oil on canvas, 21 in. × 18 in.
The Metropolitan Museum of Art,
New York, New York.

Color and Mood

Now look at image **B**. What is the dominant color in this painting? Is it a warm color or a cool color? What kind of mood, or feeling, do you think the artist was trying to express in this painting? Compare image **A** to image **B**. Do you get a different feeling from image **A** than you do from image **B**? Why do you think this is so?

shades   tints

Value

Value is the lightness or darkness of a color. Artists can make lighter values, or **tints**, by mixing white with a color. They can make darker values, or **shades**, by mixing black with a color. The diagram above shows some tints and shades of green. Find these tints and shades in image **B**. Look at the way the artist used value to show shadows. Where do you see tints and shades of red in image **A**?

LOCATE IT

The painting in image **B** is located in the Metropolitan Museum of Art in New York, New York.

NEW YORK

New York City

See Maps of Museums and Art Sites, pages 206–209.

59

TAKS Reading Objectives 1, 3, 4

Social Studies Connection

Natural Dyes   Ask students to use the encyclopedia, magazine articles, or online resources to research sources of natural dyes used to color clothing and other materials before science introduced synthetic dyes. Have students report their findings to the class.

⏱ 10-15 Minutes

Teach

Preview the Art   Have students preview images A through C on pages 58–60. Ask them to describe what they see and to share their impressions of the effect of color on each image. Use Discussion Card 1 and the questions below to guide the discussion. Then have students read pages 58–60.

 Kathy's Bowl   **What is your opinion of this still life?**

 The Banks of the Bièvre near Bicêtre   **How would you describe this place to someone who hasn't seen it?**

 Homage to the Square/Red Series, Untitled III **What do you think is the main idea of this painting? Why do you think that?** TEKS 4.3A

Discuss Art Concepts   With students, compare the dominant colors in image A and image B. In image A, the dominant color—red—gives viewers a feeling of warmth and energy; in image B, the dominant color—green—creates a calm and peaceful mood. Students should recognize that red is a warm color and green is a cool color.

Discuss with students the way the artist used tints of green to show areas in the sunlight and shades to show areas of shadow. Have students choose appropriate vocabulary to discuss value by pointing out the tints and shades of red in image A that depict shadows on the fruit. Point out that shades of grayish-white show folds in the cloth.
TEKS 4.1B

Discuss with students the way the artist of image C used increasingly lighter values of red toward the center of the image. Have students use what they have learned about warm colors to describe the mood they get from image C. (lively, excited)

LOCATE IT   Have students turn to the map on pages 206–207 to locate New York City in the state of New York.

Teach (continued)

Fact and Opinion   Ask students to look at image A and tell

- a fact about the subject.

- what they think the artist's opinion of the subject was.   TEKS 4.4B

Then invite volunteers to tell which color scheme in the artworks in this lesson they thought was most effective and why.

Think Critically

Use the questions below to check students' understanding of lesson concepts.

1. **(Focus Skill) READING SKILL   State one fact about image C. What is your opinion of this painting?** (Possible responses: It shows squares; it has a red, monochromatic color scheme. Opinions will vary.)   **FACT AND OPINION**

2. **What is the difference between a dominant color scheme and a monochromatic color scheme?** (Dominant color is the color you see most in an artwork. A monochromatic color scheme includes values of one color.)
   PERCEPTION/AESTHETICS   TEKS 4.1B

3. **WRITE   Write a paragraph telling what it would be like to walk through the scene in image B. Describe the mood of the scene.**
   DESCRIPTIVE   TEKS 4.4B; TAKS Writing Objective 1

Monochromatic Color Scheme

Image C shows an example of a monochromatic color scheme. Look at the word *monochromatic*. *Mono* means "one," and *chrome* means "color." A **monochromatic** color scheme shows a group of values of one color. In image C, where did the artist use different values of the color he chose? What kind of mood do you get from image C?

> **C** Josef Albers,
> *Homage to the Square/Red Series, Untitled III,*
> 1968, oil on masonite, 32 in. × 32 in. Norman Simon Museum, Pasadena, California.

Think Critically

1. **(Focus Skill) READING SKILL   State one fact about image C. What is your opinion of this painting? FACT AND OPINION**

2. What is the difference between a dominant color scheme and a monochromatic color scheme?

3. **WRITE**   Write a paragraph telling what it would be like to walk through the scene in image B. Describe the mood of the scene.

60

TEKS 4.1B

Art Print 1

Display **Art Print 1** and distribute Discussion Card 3: *Elements of Art* to students. Have them discuss color and value in the painting.

ART PRINT 1

Untitled (Sunset with Quarter Moon and Farmhouse)
by Edward Mitchell Bannister

---

60   UNIT 2   *Moments in Time*   ★ **TEKS 4.1B** discuss elements and principles; **TEKS 4.2B** design original artworks; **TEKS 4.2C** produce artworks; **TEKS 4.4A** form conclusions about personal artworks; **TEKS 4.4B** interpret artworks by peers and others; **PDAS Domain III** evaluation and feedback; **PDAS Domain IV** classroom management; **TAKS Writing Objective 1** composition

Artist's Workshop

Create a Monochromatic Painting

PLAN

Think of an object you would like to paint. Make some sketches of your object. Choose one color to use.

CREATE

1. Copy your best sketch onto white paper.

2. On a paper plate, mix tints and shades of the color you chose. Decide where you want to use these values in your painting.

3. Paint your object. Use as many tints and shades as you can.

REFLECT

Point out the tints and shades you used in your painting.

MATERIALS

- pencil
- sketchbook
- white paper
- tempera paint
- paintbrushes
- water bowl
- paper plates

Quick Tip You can include pure white and pure black in a monochromatic painting.

61

Create a Monochromatic Painting

PLAN Have students read the activity steps on page 61. Provide a variety of objects for students to sketch.

CREATE As students design their original artwork, have them invent ways to produce them using a variety of art media and materials by experimenting with mixing several tints and shades of the color they chose. TEKS 4.2B, TEKS 4.2C

REFLECT Have students form conclusions about their paintings based on the values they chose.
SELF-EVALUATION TEKS 4.4A

5-10 Minutes — Wrap-Up

Informal Assessment PDAS Domain III

- **Describe the mood of your artwork. How would the mood change if you used a different color?** (Responses will vary.)
PERCEPTION/AESTHETICS TEKS 4.4A

- **Give one fact and one opinion about your painting.** (Responses will vary.) FACT AND OPINION
TEKS 4.4A

Extend Through Writing TEKS 4.4B; TAKS Writing Objective 1

DESCRIPTIVE PARAGRAPH Have students write a paragraph describing a peer's monochromatic painting and interpreting the mood and ideas in it. Encourage students to use unit vocabulary in their descriptions.

Recommended Reading

How Artists Use Color by Paul Flux. Heinemann, 2001.
AVERAGE

PDAS Domain IV

Activity Options

Quick Activity Have students practice mixing tints and shades of one color.

Early Finishers Have students mount their paintings on a larger sheet of mat board.

Challenge See *Teacher Resource Book*, p. 56.

PDAS Domain IV

ESL **Model the steps** in the activity as you read them aloud to students. Support **oral language development** by asking students to describe each step in their own words.

Lesson 7

Natural Textures

OBJECTIVES
- Choose appropriate vocabulary to discuss texture in artworks
- Design and create an original collage that has texture
- Recognize fact and opinion in artworks

RESOURCES
- Art Print 16
- Reading Skill Card 2
- Discussion Cards 1, 3, pp. R34–R35
- Electronic Art Gallery CD-ROM, Intermediate

GO ONLINE
Multimedia Art Glossary and Biographies
Visit *The Learning Site*
www.harcourtschool.com

5 Minutes

Warm-Up

Build Background Gather some objects with different textures, and ask students to touch them and describe what they feel like. Possible objects include a rock (rough), a sheet of paper (smooth), and a cotton ball or cloth (soft). Tell students that in this lesson they will learn how artists show texture in paintings. TEKS 4.1A

Lesson 7

Natural Textures

Vocabulary
tactile texture
visual texture
fiber

Tactile Texture and Visual Texture

Have you ever touched the bark of a tree? How would you describe what you felt? The surface of a real object has **tactile texture**. This is what the object feels like when you touch it. Look at image **A**. The artist has used line, color, and value to create visual texture. **Visual texture** shows the appearance of texture on a drawn or painted surface. How would you describe the texture you see in image **A**?

A Chris Kenny, *Flowering Tree*, 1992, oil on canvas, 152 cm × 122 cm. Private collection.

62

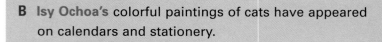
FYI Background Information

About the Artists

B **Isy Ochoa's** colorful paintings of cats have appeared on calendars and stationery.

C **Memphis Wood** taught art for many years in Jacksonville, Florida. She is best known for her colorful weavings.

For more information about the artists, see pp. R44–R65.

 For related artworks, see **Electronic Art Gallery CD-ROM, Intermediate.**

★ TEKS 4.1A communicate ideas; TEKS 4.1B discuss elements and principles; TEKS 4.3B compare and contrast artworks; PDAS Domain I active participation; PDAS Domain II learner-centered instruction

Value and Texture

The artist used value in image **A** to show a rough texture. Notice the way shades were used to show deep grooves in the bark of the tree.

Now describe the visual texture in image **B**. How is it different from the visual texture in image **A**? Notice how the artist used tints and shades to show a smooth, silky texture. What does the title of image **B** tell you about the cat's texture?

 Isy Ochoa, *Velvet Cat I*, 1996, oil on canvas, 30 cm × 30 cm. Private collection.

63

Language Arts Connection

Texture Categories Write on the board the words *rough*, *smooth*, *furry*, and *bristly* as the headings of four columns. Ask students to work in pairs to brainstorm objects that have those textures. Have partners list as many objects as they can and then share their lists with other pairs of students.

bristly

furry

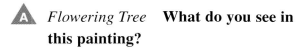

Preview the Art Have students preview images A through C on pages 62–64. Ask them to describe each one. Use Discussion Card 1 and the questions below to guide the discussion. Then have students read pages 62–64.

A *Flowering Tree* **What do you see in this painting?**

B *Velvet Cat I* **What is the subject of this painting? If you could touch it, what do you think it would feel like?**

C *Elysian Fields* **What do you think this artwork is made of?**

Discuss Art Concepts Discuss with students the differences between tactile texture and visual texture. Have students communicate ideas about self using sensory knowledge and life experiences to compare and contrast the rough visual texture in image A and the soft, velvety visual texture in image B. TEKS 4.1A, TEKS 4.3B

Help students form conclusions about the way artists use value to show texture by pointing out the shades in the tree trunk in image A and the tints in the cat's fur in image B. Ask students to choose appropriate vocabulary, such as *rough*, *bristly*, or *bumpy*, to describe the texture of the fibers used in image C. TEKS 4.1B

Teach (continued)

Science Link Have partners use two sheets of paper—one smooth and one crumpled—to compare and contrast the values and textures they see.

Fact and Opinion Ask students to look at image A and tell

- two facts about the subject.
- what they think the artist's opinion of the subject was. TEKS 4.4B

Then invite volunteers to point out details and give reasons to support their responses.

Think Critically

Use the questions below to check students' understanding of lesson concepts.

1. (Focus Skill) **READING SKILL** **How do you think the artist of image B feels about cats? Explain your answer using details from the painting.** (Possible response: She probably likes them, because the cat in the painting has beautiful fur and looks friendly.) **FACT AND OPINION** TEKS 4.4B

2. **Explain how artists use value to create visual texture.** (Possible response: Artists use tints and shades to show contrast in objects that have rough textures. Shades can show details such as deep grooves in an object.) **PERCEPTION/AESTHETICS** TEKS 4.1B

3. **WRITE** **Choose an object in your classroom to describe in a riddle. Write clues that describe the object's texture. Ask a classmate to read your riddle and to guess the object you chose. DESCRIPTIVE** TEKS 4.1A, TEKS 4.1B

Think about the smooth surface of a piece of notebook paper. A smooth surface reflects light evenly. Now think about crumpling that piece of notebook paper to give it a rough surface. A rough surface reflects the light unevenly, creating more dark values. The way light is reflected by a surface shows values and textures.

Fibers Create Texture

Describe the artwork in image C. This artwork was made with different kinds of fibers. A **fiber** is thread or a similar material, such as yarn or string. What do you think the tactile texture of the artwork in image C is like?

 Memphis Wood, *Elysian Fields,* 1978, mixed fibers, 96 in. × 88 in. (each panel 96 in. × 27½ in.) Jacksonville Museum of Modern Art, Jacksonville, Florida.

Think Critically

1. (Focus Skill) **READING SKILL** How do you think the artist of image B feels about cats? Explain your answer using details from the painting. **FACT AND OPINION**

2. Explain how artists use value to create visual texture.

3. **WRITE** Choose an object in your classroom to describe in a riddle. Write clues that describe the object's texture. Ask a classmate to read your riddle and to guess the object you chose.

64

TEKS 4.1B

Art Print 16

Display **Art Print 16** and distribute Discussion Card 3: *Elements of Art* to help students discuss texture in the artwork.

ART PRINT 16

The Profile of Time by Salvador Dalí

Artist's Workshop

Create Texture in a Collage

PLAN

Find objects with different textures, such as a feather, a sponge, a group of toothpicks, or the sole of a shoe.

CREATE

1. Use different colors of crayons to do a rubbing of each object on tissue paper.

2. Cut out your rubbings and decide how you want to arrange them in a collage.

3. Glue the rubbings onto a piece of poster board.

REFLECT

What kinds of visual textures are in your collage?

MATERIALS

- objects with different textures
- tissue paper
- crayons
- scissors
- glue
- poster board
- yarn or string

Quick Tip
You may want to add tactile texture to your collage by gluing yarn or string onto it in an interesting design.

65

Artist's Workshop

30-40 Minutes

Create Texture in a Collage

PLAN Have students read the activity steps on page 65. Provide students with as many textures as possible.

CREATE Students should invent ways to produce their collages using a variety of objects with textures that would make the most interesting rubbings. Ask students to experiment with the arrangement of their rubbings before deciding on a final design. TEKS 4.2B, TEKS 4.2C

REFLECT Have students interpret the ideas in a peer's collage and try to guess what object each rubbing was made from. SELF-EVALUATION TEKS 4.4B

Wrap-Up
5-10 Minutes

Informal Assessment PDAS Domain III

- **Do you prefer creating a collage or a painting? Give reasons to support your opinion.** (Responses will vary.) PERSONAL RESPONSE

- **What is one statement of fact about your collage? What is one opinion? Give reasons to support your opinion.** (Responses will vary.) FACT AND OPINION TEKS 4.4A

Extend Through Writing   TEKS 4.1B; TAKS Writing Objective 1

DESCRIPTIVE PARAGRAPH Have students choose appropriate vocabulary to discuss texture in a paragraph describing a classmate's collage.

Recommended Reading

How Artists Use Pattern and Texture by Paul Flux. Heinemann, 2001.
AVERAGE

Activity Options
PDAS Domain IV

Quick Activity Have students do a crayon rubbing of a single object's texture.

Early Finishers Have students create additional rubbings and then add details to turn the rubbings into animal figures.

Challenge See *Teacher Resource Book*, p. 57.

PDAS Domain IV

ESL Use **visuals** to support **comprehensible input** for animal textures. Display *Picture Cards Collection*, cards 74 and 75 for students to discuss and reference.

See also *Picture Card Bank* **CD-ROM**, Category: Animals

lion

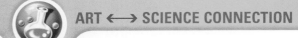
PDAS Domains I, II

EROSION

ART AND NATURE

DISCUSS THE IMAGES

Have students read pages 66–67.

- Encourage students to discuss what they see in image A. Students might suggest that Wave Rock looks like a giant ocean wave. Discuss with students the texture of Wave Rock—smooth, hard rock with deep grooves—and its colors—from gold to dark brown.

- Discuss the effects of erosion on the landform shown in image B. Explain that this sandstone rock formation was created by the rising and falling of the sea over time. The salt water cut deep grooves into the sandstone. Students may choose vocabulary such as *gouged*, *carved*, or *rough* to discuss the texture of the landform.
TEKS 4.1B

 ART ←→ SCIENCE CONNECTION

EROSION

What kinds of textures do you see and feel around you? How might textures change over time?

Think about the textures found in nature. The textures of some landforms and rocks have been made by a process called erosion. Erosion is the wearing away of rock and other materials by wind and moving water.

Image **A** shows one example of erosion. Wave Rock is about 50 feet high. How do you think it got its name? For millions of years, water carrying minerals such as iron ran down over the rock, cutting lines into it. The minerals also added streaks of color to the rock. What kind of texture do you think Wave Rock has? What colors can you see in it?

A Wave Rock, Western Australia.

Background Information

A **Wave Rock**, in Western Australia, is an overhanging wall on the north side of Hyden Rock, a large granite formation. Have students turn to the map on pages 208–209 to locate Wave Rock.

B **Torrey Pines State Reserve**, in San Diego, California, is a popular destination for hikers, cyclists, artists, photographers, and nature lovers. Hiking trails wind through terraces cut out of sandstone rock formations. Viewing platforms built right above the sea provide areas for watching dolphins as well as the yearly migration of whales.

 For related artworks, see **Electronic Art Gallery CD-ROM, Intermediate.**

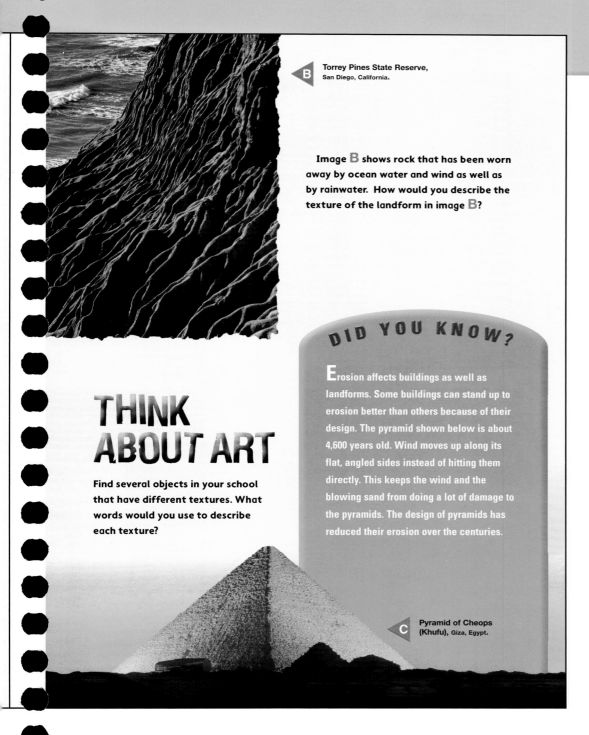

Image **B** shows rock that has been worn away by ocean water and wind as well as by rainwater. How would you describe the texture of the landform in image **B**?

THINK ABOUT ART

Find several objects in your school that have different textures. What words would you use to describe each texture?

DID YOU KNOW?

Erosion affects buildings as well as landforms. Some buildings can stand up to erosion better than others because of their design. The pyramid shown below is about 4,600 years old. Wind moves up along its flat, angled sides instead of hitting them directly. This keeps the wind and the blowing sand from doing a lot of damage to the pyramids. The design of pyramids has reduced their erosion over the centuries.

C Pyramid of Cheops (Khufu), Giza, Egypt.

Social Studies Connection

Building the Pyramids Explain that how the pyramids were built has long been debated. Many historians believe the stones were hauled up ramps using ropes.

For additional cross-curricular suggestions, see Art Transparency 5.

TEKS 4.4B

Student Art Show

Portfolios and Exhibitions Have students display finished artworks. Ask students to interpret ideas in peers' original artworks, portfolios, and exhibitions. See *Teacher Edition* page 204 for information on planning and preparing a student art exhibition.

DID YOU KNOW?

Use the facts below to discuss the Great Pyramid with students.

- The Great Pyramid, on the Giza plateau in Egypt, is the only one of the seven wonders of the ancient world still standing today.

- Five thousand years ago, Giza, on the west bank of the Nile River, became the site for the burial tombs of the pharaohs, the kings of the Fourth Dynasty of Egypt's Old Kingdom.

- Researchers believe that the builders of the pyramids might have been inspired by natural landforms that existed in the desert.

- Over 2 million blocks of stone were used to build the Great Pyramid. The heaviest blocks weigh approximately 40–60 tons.

- **LOCATE IT** Have students turn to the map on pp. 208–209 to locate Giza, Egypt.

THINK ABOUT ART

Find several objects in your school that have different textures. What words would you use to describe each texture? (Responses will vary.)
PERSONAL RESPONSE TEKS 4.1A, TEKS 4.1B

ARTIST'S EYE ACTIVITY

Rock Climb Invite groups of students to look again at image A or B. Then have students imagine what it would be like to climb either of these landforms. Ask students to communicate their ideas using life experiences and sensory knowledge. Then have them invent ways to explore the photographic imagery by using a variety of art media and materials to sketch the view that they might see once they reached the top of the landform. TEKS 4.1A, TEKS 4.2B

Lesson 8

PDAS Domains I, II

Light and Color

OBJECTIVES
- Choose appropriate vocabulary to discuss the use of light and color in artworks
- Design and create an original outdoor scene
- Recognize and use statements of fact and opinion about artworks

RESOURCES
- Art Prints 1, 4
- Reading Skill Card 2
- Discussion Cards 1, 7, pp. R34, R37
- Electronic Art Gallery CD-ROM, Intermediate

Multimedia Art Glossary and Biographies
Visit *The Learning Site*
www.harcourtschool.com

5 Minutes

Warm-Up

Build Background Display **Art Print 1** and ask volunteers to describe what they can tell about the subject of the painting as well as the setting. Ask students how the artist's use of color gives them clues to the time of day in the painting. Explain that in this lesson students will learn about artists who were more interested in light and color than they were in the exact details of their subjects.

Lesson 8

Light and Color

Vocabulary

Impressionism

plein air

impasto

Impressionism

The same building is shown in both image **A** and image **B**. How are the two paintings alike? How are they different? Read the title of each painting. How did the artist use color to show two different times of day?

These artworks were painted in the late nineteenth century in a style called **Impressionism**. The Impressionists were not interested in painting exact details. They wanted to show the way light and color looked at a certain moment in time. How do you think the artist of images **A** and **B** would show the building at sunset?

 Claude Monet, *Rouen Cathedral, Impression of Morning,* 1894, oil on canvas, 0.91 m × 0.63 m. Musée d'Orsay, Paris, France.

 Claude Monet, *Rouen Cathedral, Bright Sun,* 1894, oil on canvas, 0.91 m × 0.63 m. Musée d'Orsay, Paris, France.

Background Information

About the Artists

A Claude Monet (KLOHD moh•NAY) (1840–1926) often painted the same scene again and again in order to catch all its variations of light, shadow, and season.

C French painter Berthe Morisot's (behrt moh•ree•zoh) (1841–1895) paintings depict women and children in everyday domestic scenes.

For additional information about the artists, see pp. R44–R65.

 For related artworks, see **Electronic Art Gallery CD-ROM, Intermediate.**

★ **TEKS 4.1A** communicate ideas; **TEKS 4.1B** discuss elements and principles; **TEKS 4.3A** identify main ideas; **PDAS Domain I** active participation; **PDAS Domain II** learner-centered instruction; **TAKS Reading Objective 1** demonstrate understanding of texts; *(continued)*

 Berthe Morisot, *The Butterfly Hunt,*
1874, oil on canvas, 22 in. × 18 in.
Musée d'Orsay, Paris, France.

Outdoor Painters

The Impressionists often painted outdoors. Outdoor painting is called ***plein air*** (PLAYN AIR), which is French for "open air." Artists had usually painted outdoor scenes indoors, from memory. The Impressionists painted from real life instead. They painted very quickly to capture an impression of their subjects. Look at the painting in image C, and read the title. Why do you think the artist had to paint this subject very quickly?

LOCATE IT

Images A, B, and C can be found in the Musée d'Orsay, a museum in Paris, France.

Paris

FRANCE

See Maps of Museums and Art Sites, pages 206–209.

69

 TEKS 4.3A, TAKS Reading Objectives 1, 3, 4

Social Studies Connection

Research Impressionist Artists Share with students the information on Impressionism on pages R44–R65. Then encourage students to use art books, encyclopedias, or online resources to find additional information about the Impressionist movement in art. Direct students' searches toward finding information about the subjects and techniques used by Impressionist artists. Ask students to identify simple main ideas that tell about history and culture in the artworks they find.

Preview the Art Have students preview images A through D on pages 68–70. Ask them to describe what they see. Use Discussion Card 1 and the questions below to guide the discussion. Then have students read pages 68–70.

 Rouen Cathedral, Impression of Morning **How would you describe the subject of this painting?**

 Rouen Cathedral, Bright Sun **What is one difference between this painting and the one in image A?**

 The Butterfly Hunt **What is happening in this painting? How can you tell?** TEKS 4.3A

 Children at the Beach **Imagine you are in this scene. What might you hear and smell? How might you feel?** TEKS 4.1A

Discuss Art Concepts Have students point out that images A and B both show the same view of the building, but the artist used more yellow in image B to show bright sunlight. Students should choose appropriate vocabulary to discuss the color schemes in each image. TEKS 4.1B

Discuss with students that in order to capture the people's and butterflies' movements in image C, the artist had to paint very quickly. In image D, students should point out the light values in the clothing and the water, and the dark values in the shadow and the water. Discuss with students that the girl's long shadow in image D may indicate either early morning or late afternoon.

LOCATE IT Have students turn to the map on pages 208–209 to locate Paris, France, the site of the Musée d'Orsay.

Fact and Opinion   Ask students to choose one artwork in this lesson and give

- one fact about it.

- one opinion they think the artist had about the subject of the artwork.

Then ask students to give reasons to support the fact and the opinion they cited.   TEKS 4.4B

Think Critically

Use the questions below to check students' understanding of lesson concepts.

1. (Focus Skill) **READING SKILL**   **Do you think a painting of an outdoor scene would look more interesting if it were painted outdoors or from memory indoors?** (Possible response: outdoors, because the artist would see exactly how sunlight is reflected, instead of having to imagine or remember it)   FACT AND OPINION

2. **How did the artist of image D use value to create the appearance of waves?** (Possible response: The artist used both tints and shades to make the waves seem as if they are moving.)   PERCEPTION/AESTHETICS   TEKS 4.1B

3. **WRITE**   **Write a description of image D. Tell what you might see, hear, smell, and feel if you were standing next to the girl with the hat.**   DESCRIPTIVE   TEKS 4.1A; TAKS Writing Objective 1

 Joaquín Sorolla y Bastida, *Children at the Beach,* 1910, oil on canvas, 46½ in. × 72⅞ in. Museo del Prado, Madrid, Spain.

Everyday Themes

Look at image **D**. What do you see? The Impressionist painter captured a moment in his subjects' lives. Impressionism often focused on people doing ordinary things they enjoyed. Notice the thick brushstrokes in this painting. This technique, known as **impasto** (im•PAS•toh), gave the painting a bumpy tactile texture. Where do you see light and dark values? What time of day do you think he showed?

Think Critically

1. (Focus Skill) **READING SKILL**   Do you think a painting of an outdoor scene would look more interesting if it were painted outdoors or from memory indoors? FACT AND OPINION

2. How did the artist of image **D** use value to create the appearance of waves?

3. **WRITE**   Write a description of image **D**. Tell what you might see, hear, smell, and feel if you were standing next to the girl with the hat.

70

TEKS 4.1A

Art Print 4

Display **Art Print 4** and distribute to students Discussion Card 7: *Stories.* Have them communicate ideas about a family outing using sensory knowledge and life experiences and compare them to what they see in the painting.

ART PRINT 4

The Bathers
by Pierre-Auguste Renoir

★   TEKS 4.1A communicate ideas; TEKS 4.1B discuss elements and principles; TEKS 4.2B design original artworks; TEKS 4.2C produce artworks; TEKS 4.4A form conclusions about personal artworks; TEKS 4.4B interpret artworks by peers and others; PDAS Domain III evaluation and feedback; *(continued)*

Artist's Workshop

Paint an Outdoor Scene

PLAN

Find a picture in a magazine of an outdoor place you like. Notice the time of day in the picture. Make some quick sketches of the place, but don't be concerned with drawing the details.

CREATE

1. Using your sketches as a guide, paint your outdoor scene.

2. Use color in your painting to show the time of day. Use light values to show sunlight and dark values to show shadows.

REFLECT

How did you use value and color in your painting?

MATERIALS

- magazines
- pencil
- sketchbook
- white paper
- tempera paint or watercolors
- paintbrushes
- water bowl

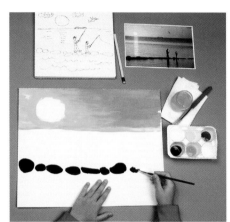

 Quick Tip Try to use quick brushstrokes as the Impressionists did.

71

Artist's Workshop
30-40 Minutes

Paint an Outdoor Scene

PLAN Have students read the activity steps on page 71. Provide students with magazine pictures of outdoor scenes. Help students determine the time of day shown in the scenes they choose.

CREATE Have students invent ways to explore the photographic imagery in the magazine picture, as they design their artworks, using a variety of art media and materials. Students should experiment with shades of color to indicate shadows, as appropriate, in their paintings. TEKS 4.2B, TEKS 4.2C

REFLECT Have students form conclusions about the time of day they showed in their scenes by explaining their use of value and color.
SELF-EVALUATION TEKS 4.1B, TEKS 4.4A

Wrap-Up
5-10 Minutes

Informal Assessment PDAS Domain III

- **How is your painting like an Impressionist painting? How is it different?** (Responses will vary.) EVALUATION/CRITICISM

- **Give a fact about the subject of your painting. Then tell your opinion about it.** (Responses will vary.) FACT AND OPINION

Extend Through Writing
TAKS Writing Objective 1

FRIENDLY LETTER Have students write a letter inviting a friend to visit their outdoor scene.

Recommended Reading

What Makes a Monet a Monet? by Richard Muhlberger. The Metropolitan Museum of Art/Viking, 2002. CHALLENGING

PDAS Domain IV

Activity Options

Quick Activity Have students use colored pencils to draw an object at a specific time of day, using values to show light and shadows.

Early Finishers Have students paint the same outdoor scene at a different time of day.

Challenge See *Teacher Resource Book*, p. 58.

PDAS Domain IV

MEETING INDIVIDUAL NEEDS

ESL Use **visuals** to support **comprehensible input** for outdoor place terms. Display *Picture Cards Collection*, cards 10, 48, 58, 81, and 85 for students to discuss and reference.

beach

See also *Picture Card Bank CD-ROM*, Category: Places People Go.

Lesson 9

PDAS Domains I, II

Values of Black and White

OBJECTIVES
- Choose appropriate vocabulary to discuss the use of value in artworks
- Design and create an original charcoal drawing
- Recognize and use statements of fact and opinion about artworks

RESOURCES
- Art Print 5
- Reading Skill Card 2
- Discussion Cards 1, 3, pp. R34–R35
- Electronic Art Gallery CD-ROM, Intermediate

Multimedia Art Glossary and Biographies
Visit *The Learning Site*
www.harcourtschool.com

Warm-Up

5 Minutes

Build Background Ask students to imagine what the world would be like if they saw everything in black and white. Ask students to communicate ideas about school using sensory knowledge and life experiences by describing a colorful classroom object such as a globe in only black, white, and gray. Then explain that when artists use only black, white, and gray in their artworks, the contrast between the values is especially obvious. Tell students that in this lesson they will learn about how artists use black, white, and gray in artworks. TEKS 4.1A

Lesson 9

Vocabulary
gray scale
blending

Values of Black and White

Value is the lightness or darkness of a color. When only black, white, and gray are used in an artwork, the contrast between values is especially obvious.

Gray Scale

Look at the gray scale below. A **gray scale** shows the gradual changes in value from pure black to pure white. In image **A**, point out the darkest and lightest values you can see. How would you describe the texture of image **A**?

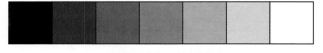

 Bruce Barnbaum, *Dance of the Corn Lilies*, 1991, photograph.

72

 Background Information

About the Artist

B M. C. Escher (ESH•er) (1898–1972) was a Dutch artist known for his detailed, intricate visual puzzles. Escher created images such as circular waterfalls and endless staircases.

For additional information about M. C. Escher, see pp. R44–R65.

For related artworks, see **Electronic Art Gallery CD-ROM, Intermediate.**

TEKS 4.1A communicate ideas; TEKS 4.1B discuss elements and principles; TEKS 4.3C identify roles in art; PDAS Domain I active participation; PDAS Domain II learner-centered instruction; TAKS Reading Objective 1 demonstrate understanding of texts; TAKS Reading Objective 3 use a variety of strategies; *(continued)*

 M. C. Escher, *Dewdrop,*
1946, mezzotint, 18 cm × 24.5 cm.
Cordon Art B. V., Baarn, Holland.

Value and Texture

What is the subject of the artwork in image **B**? Notice
the way the artist used value to show texture. Describe
the visual texture of the leaf. Now look at the dewdrop.
What do you think makes the dewdrop look wet?

Social Studies Link

Image **B** shows a
mezzotint. It was
made by applying
paper to a surface
that was carved and
then coated with ink.
Before the invention
of photography,
mezzotints enabled
people to see copies
of famous paintings.
Today only a few
artists use this
printing method.

73

TEKS 4.3C; TAKS Reading Objectives 1, 3, 4

Social Studies Connection

Ansel Adams Tell students that American
photographer Ansel Adams (1902–1984)
was well known for his black-and-white
photographs of dramatic landscapes of the
American West. Have students research
Adams's artwork to identify its role in
American society.

For additional information about Ansel Adams,
see pp. R44–R65.

10-15 Minutes

Teach

Preview the Art Have students preview images A
through C on pages 72–74. Ask them to describe
what they see. Use Discussion Card 1 and the
questions below to guide the discussion. Then
have students read pages 72–74.

A *Dance of the Corn Lilies* **How does the
title of the painting help you figure out
what you are looking at?**

 Dewdrop **What can you see in this
painting? If you could touch the real
subject of this image, what would it
feel like?**

 Untitled **What objects are shown in
this still life?**

Discuss Art Concepts Discuss the gray scale with
students. Ask them to point out value differences
in image A and describe the visual texture of the
corn lilies as smooth but having shallow ridges.
TEKS 4.1B

Turn to image B, and discuss the leathery texture
of the leaf. Point out that the wetness of the dewdrop was created by actual lines as well as dark
and light values that seem to magnify the texture
of the leaf beneath the dewdrop.

Have students point out gradual value changes
in image C created by blending to show shadows.

Social Studies Link Tell students that mezzotints
produce very gradual changes in value.
Sometimes outlines have to be added around
objects to give them more definition.

Fact and Opinion   Ask students to look at image B. Have them discuss

- facts about the subject of the image.

- opinions about their artist's choice of subject.

Have students give reasons to support their opinions and interpret the ideas and moods in the artwork. TEKS 4.4B

Think Critically

Use the questions below to check students' understanding of lesson concepts.

1. (Focus Skill) *READING SKILL* **Look at the title of image A. Is this a good title? Why or why not?** (Possible response: It's a good title because the corn lilies appear to be moving and swirling about as though they are dancing.) **FACT AND OPINION**

2. **What is a gray scale?** (A gray scale shows the changes in value from pure black to pure white.) **PERCEPTION/AESTHETICS**

3. **WRITE**   **Look at the objects in image C. If you wanted to create an artwork using these items, what type of artwork would you create? Describe your ideas.** **DESCRIPTIVE** TAKS Writing Objective 1

Value Changes

Look back at image **A**. Notice the sharp contrast in value from dark to light. Suppose an artist wanted to show gradual changes in value. The artist could use **blending**, or mixing, to create a smooth transition from dark to light. To blend the values in a charcoal drawing or in a painting, an artist can smudge darker areas to mix them with lighter areas. In image **C**, where do you find value changes?

Think Critically

1. (Focus Skill) *READING SKILL* Look at the title of image **A**. Is this a good title? Why or why not? **FACT AND OPINION**

2. What is a gray scale?

3. **WRITE**   Look at the objects in image **C**. If you wanted to create an artwork using these items, what type of artwork would you create? Describe your ideas.

 Matthew, grade 4, Untitled.

74

 **Art Print 5**

Display **Art Print 5** and Discussion Card 3: *Elements of Art* to help students discuss value and other lesson concepts in the painting.

ART PRINT 5

Still Life of Summer Flowers
by Rachel Ruysch

⭐ **TEKS 4.1B** discuss elements and principles; **TEKS 4.2B** design original artworks; **TEKS 4.4B** interpret artworks by peers and others; **PDAS Domain III** evaluation and feedback; **PDAS Domain IV** classroom management; **TAKS Writing Objective 1** composition

Artist's Workshop

Draw a Charcoal Still Life

MATERIALS
- classroom objects
- pencil
- sketchbook
- white paper
- charcoal pencil
- tissue
- eraser

PLAN

Choose a group of objects to draw. Arrange the objects in an interesting way. Make some sketches of your still life. Decide how you want to use value in your charcoal drawing.

CREATE

1. Use a charcoal pencil to copy your best sketch onto white paper.

2. Use a range of dark and light values to show textures and shadows in your still life.

3. Create gradual value changes by using a tissue to smudge, or blend, areas of your artwork.

REFLECT

How did you use value in your drawing? Where did you use blending?

Quick Tip
You can use an eraser to remove some of the charcoal to create contrast between areas.

75

PDAS Domain IV

Activity Options

Quick Activity Have students sketch one simple object in charcoal pencil.

Early Finishers Have students mount their still life on black construction paper and decorate the border.

Challenge See *Teacher Resource Book*, p. 59.

MEETING INDIVIDUAL NEEDS **PDAS Domain IV**

ESL Work with students to develop a list of **multiple-meaning words** in this lesson, such as *value*, *shade*, and *scale*. Discuss with students other meanings for these words, but make sure students understand the art vocabulary definition of each one.

Artist's Workshop

30-40 Minutes

Draw a Charcoal Still Life

PLAN Have students read the activity steps on page 75 and experiment with different arrangements of their objects.

CREATE As students design their original artworks, remind them to pay attention to the way the light falls on each object to help them decide where to use lighter and darker values. TEKS 4.2B

REFLECT Have students point out where they used blending in their drawing to create different values. SELF-EVALUATION

5-10 Minutes
Wrap-Up

Informal Assessment PDAS Domain III

- **What did you learn about value from the artwork in this lesson?** (Responses will vary.)
  EVALUATION/CRITICISM TEKS 4.1B

- **If you redrew your still life as a monochromatic drawing, what color would you choose and why?** (Responses will vary.)
  PERCEPTION/AESTHETICS

Extend Through Writing   TAKS Writing Objective 1

LIST Have students write a list of objects and animals that are naturally black, white, gray, or any combination of those colors. Challenge students to brainstorm as many items as possible.

Recommended Reading

Jumanji by Chris Van Allsburg. Houghton Mifflin, 1981. AVERAGE

PDAS Domains I, II

Henri Matisse

ARTIST BIOGRAPHY

DISCUSS THE IMAGES

Have students read pages 76 and 77.

- Ask students to discuss what they see in image B and name some of the complementary color pairs such as the red and green leaves in the pattern on the curtain, or the blue dish on the orange table. TEKS 4.1B

- Display **Art Print 6** to show another of Matisse's interiors. Present to students the **Art Print** and the artworks on pages 76–77 as a portfolio of Matisse's work. Ask students to interpret the ideas and moods in this portfolio of paintings. Students should compare and contrast the objects and color schemes in each piece. TEKS 4.4B

- Tell students that Matisse believed that the arrangement of colors and shapes in an artwork was as important as the subject. Have students compare and contrast the painting in image B with the collage in image C. Students should note that the painting shows recognizable objects and the collage shows a design of lines and shapes. Point out that Matisse used bright colors in both artworks.

- Have students read the English title of image C and point out the perpendicular lines that form the two trapeze swings.

Henri Matisse

How does an artist explore the same idea in different kinds of art?

Henri Matisse, *Self-Portrait,* 1918, oil on canvas, 65 cm x 54 cm. Private collection.

Henri Matisse (ahn•REE mah•TEES) was born in France in 1869. He had no interest in art until he was twenty years old. Then his mother gave him a set of paints to keep him busy while he was sick. Soon after, Matisse began to work as an artist.

Look at image **B**. How would you describe the colors Matisse used in this painting? What kinds of textures did he show?

Matisse created many colorful paintings and sculptures, as well as illustrations for books. He also designed interiors of rooms and sets and costumes for ballets. In all of his art projects, color was the most important element. Matisse used color to express his positive feelings about his life and work.

 Background Information

Henri Matisse (ahn•REE mah•TEES) (1869–1954) was one of the most influential artists of the early 1900s. Human figures, still lifes, and interior scenes were among Matisse's favorite subjects. He once said that he had not stopped working, seven days a week, from morning to nightfall, for more than 50 years.

For additional information about Henri Matisse, see pp. R44–R65.

For related artworks, see **Electronic Art Gallery CD-ROM, Intermediate.**

★ TEKS 4.1A communicate ideas; TEKS 4.1B discuss elements and principles; TEKS 4.2A integrate ideas in artworks; TEKS 4.4B interpret artworks by peers and others; PDAS Domain I active participation; PDAS Domain II learner-centered instruction

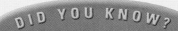

In 1905 a French art critic gave Matisse and some other French artists the name *the fauves* (FOHVZ). In French, *fauve* means "wild beast." The critic thought the colors these artists used were wild and bold. After that, Matisse and his fellow artists were called Fauvists.

 Henri Matisse,
Interior with Egyptian Curtain,
1948, oil on canvas, 116.2 cm x 84.1 cm.
Phillips Collection, Washington, D.C.

Near the end of his life, Matisse had health problems, but he did not stop working. When painting became too hard, he started small projects that he could work on in bed, such as collages. Look at image **C**. Matisse created this collage by using paper that he painted and then cut into different shapes.

 Henri Matisse,
The Trapeze Performers (Les Codomas),
1947, gouache on paper cutouts, 42 cm x 65 cm.
National Museum of Modern Art, Georges
Pompidou Center, Paris, France.

Think About Art

Look at the self-portrait of Matisse in image **A**. What do you see in this painting that might tell you something about Matisse?

 Multimedia Biographies
Visit *The Learning Site*
www.harcourtschool.com

77

Social Studies Connection

Family Traits Tell students that Matisse's grandson is a sculptor. Ask students to use life experiences to communicate ideas about family, including talents they share with relatives.

For additional cross-curricular suggestions, see Art Transparency 6.

Viewing an Artist's Work

Portfolios and Exhibitions Arrange for students to visit a museum or art gallery. Have students use the opportunity to examine artists' portfolios and exhibitions to interpret ideas and moods.

Use the facts below to discuss Henri Matisse and Fauvism with students.

- In 1905 Matisse and other Fauvist painters exhibited their artworks together in Paris, France. Their bold colors and patterns outraged French critics.

- After Matisse ended his association with the Fauvist painters in 1907, he never again belonged to a distinct movement or group of painters. He believed that an artist must avoid getting trapped by his own style or reputation.

- **For additional information** about Fauvism, see pages R44–R65.

Think About Art

Look at the self-portrait of Matisse in image A. What do you see in this painting that might tell you something about Matisse? (Possible response: He was a formal, serious man, since he was dressed in a suit and tie while creating his art.) **PERSONAL RESPONSE** TEKS 4.4B

ARTIST'S EYE ACTIVITY

Communicating Ideas About Self Invite students to imagine how Matisse decided what to include in his self-portrait. Then have students integrate a variety of ideas about self in a self-portrait that would help viewers understand something about them. Ask volunteers to share their ideas with classmates. TEKS 4.2A

 **Multimedia Biographies**
Visit *The Learning Site*
www.harcourtschool.com

Lesson 10

PDAS Domains I, II
Emphasis

OBJECTIVES
- Choose appropriate vocabulary to discuss the use of emphasis in artworks
- Design and create an original pastel drawing
- Recognize and use statements of fact and opinion about artworks

RESOURCES
- Art Print 5
- Reading Skill Card 2
- Discussion Cards 1, 4, pp. R34–R35
- Electronic Art Gallery CD-ROM, Intermediate

GO ONLINE Multimedia Art Glossary and Biographies
Visit *The Learning Site*
www.harcourtschool.com

5 Minutes

Warm-Up

Build Background Display **Art Print 5** and ask students what they notice first. Discuss the way the large pink flowers catch the viewer's eye first because their light color is in sharp contrast to the dark background. Explain that in this lesson students are going to learn how artists use different techniques in their artworks to grab the viewer's attention.

Lesson 10

Vocabulary
- emphasis
- three-dimensional
- assemblage

Emphasis

Artists create emphasis in an artwork to grab the viewer's attention. **Emphasis** is the special importance given to a part of an artwork. It is created by using the elements of art to make one or more parts of an artwork stand out.

A Raymond Depardon, *Palm Tree in Mauritania*, 1999, photograph.

Contrasting Values

Look at image **A**. How did the photographer create emphasis in this scene? The palm tree stands out because its dark value shows a contrast, or sharp difference, from the rest of the scene. Notice that the tree trunk is the only vertical line in the photograph. This also draws attention to the palm tree.

Now look at image **B**. What do you notice first? This artist used value to emphasize several areas in her artwork. Look at the light values in the moon, the wave, and the subject's hair. They stand out from the darker values in the sky, the water, and the subject's clothing.

B Johanna Fiore, *Portrait of Gordon Parks*, 1997, photograph.

FYI
Background Information

About the Artists
C **David Hockney's** (1937–) paintings have often been inspired by Los Angeles, California, where he lives and works.

D Many of **Joseph Cornell's** (1903–1972) artworks contain objects such as seashells and broken glass.

For additional information about the artists, see pp. R44–R65.

 For related artworks, see **Electronic Art Gallery CD-ROM, Intermediate.**

★ TEKS 4.1A communicate ideas; TEKS 4.1B discuss elements and principles; TEKS 4.4B interpret artworks by peers and others; PDAS Domain I active participation; PDAS Domain II learner-centered instruction; TAKS Reading Objective 1 demonstrate understanding of texts; *(continued)*

David Hockney, *A Bigger Splash*, 1967, acrylic on canvas, 96 in. × 96 in. Tate Gallery, London, England.

Contrasting Shapes

In image C, what catches your eye first? Most of this scene is made up of geometric shapes. Notice the contrast created by the organic shapes and lines in the splash of water. Imagine this scene without the splash of water. What kind of feeling would it create? How does the splash change the mood of the painting?

Cultural Link

The portrait in image B is of Gordon Parks, a photographer who used his art to show the everyday lives of African Americans. Parks won many awards for his accomplishments.

79

TAKS Reading Objectives 1, 3, 4

Social Studies Connection

Mauritania Encourage interested students to use encyclopedias or online resources to research the African country of Mauritania. They should look for facts about climate, geography, plants, animals, and major products. Have students give a brief presentation to classmates describing their findings and have them point out Mauritania on a world map or globe.

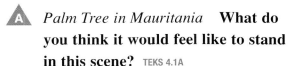

Teach

10-15 Minutes

Preview the Art Have students preview images A through D on pages 78–80. Ask them to describe what they see and to share what caught their attention first in each one. Use Discussion Card 1 and the questions below to guide the discussion. Then have students read pages 78–80.

A *Palm Tree in Mauritania* **What do you think it would feel like to stand in this scene?** TEKS 4.1A

B *Portrait of Gordon Parks* **Describe the subject of this photograph. What can you tell about this man?**

C *A Bigger Splash* **What do you think happened just before the artist painted this image?**

D *Toward the Blue Peninsula* **How would you describe this artwork?**

Discuss Art Concepts Have students point out the areas of contrast in image A and image B. Have them discuss the ways the photographers emphasized the subject, the shapes, and the values in each image.

Have students interpret the mood created by the splash in image C. Discuss the startling interruption to the calm scene. Then have students choose appropriate vocabulary to discuss the emphasis created by the bright blue square in image D. TEKS 4.1B, TEKS 4.4B

Cultural Link Tell students that the photographer Gordon Parks wrote several books, including *The Learning Tree*, a popular novel about an African American teenager in Kansas in the 1920s. The book was later made into a film.

Teach (continued)

Fact and Opinion Ask students to look again at image B. Have them discuss

- one or two facts about this photograph.
- what they think was the photographer's opinion of her subject.

Ask students to support their responses with details from the photograph. TEKS 4.4B

Think Critically

Use the questions below to check students' understanding of lesson concepts.

1. **(Focus Skill) READING SKILL State one fact and one opinion about the painting in image C.** (Possible facts: There are two palm trees in the picture. The house is orange and yellow. The roof of the house is flat. The diving board is yellow. Opinions will vary.) **FACT AND OPINION**

2. **What kind of color scheme could you use to create emphasis in an artwork?** (Possible response: A complementary color scheme, with contrasting colors.) **PERCEPTION/AESTHETICS** TEKS 4.1B

3. **WRITE Tell why you think the artist of image D named his artwork *Toward the Blue Peninsula*.** EXPOSITORY TEKS 4.4B; TAKS Writing Objective 1

Emphasis in Three-Dimensional Art

Artists create emphasis in three-dimensional art just as they do in a two-dimensional painting or photograph. **Three-dimensional** artworks have height, width, and depth. Image **D** is a three-dimensional artwork called an assemblage. An **assemblage** is an artwork made from a variety of materials, such as paper and wood. How would you describe the textures in this artwork? Where do you see emphasis in image **D**?

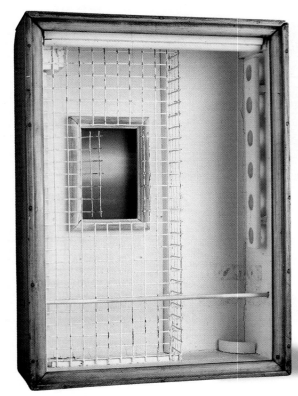

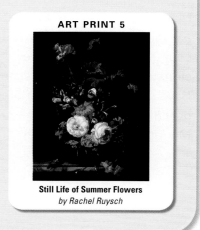

Think Critically

1. **(Focus Skill) READING SKILL** State one fact and one opinion about the painting in image **C**. **FACT AND OPINION**

2. What kind of color scheme could you use to create emphasis in an artwork?

3. **WRITE** Tell why you think the artist of image **D** named his artwork *Toward the Blue Peninsula*.

D Joseph Cornell, *Toward the Blue Peninsula*, 1951–1952, mixed media, 10⅝ in. × 14¹⁵⁄₁₆ in. × 3¹⁵⁄₁₆ in. Collection of Daniel Varenne, Geneva, Switzerland.

80

TEKS 4.1B

Art Print 5

Display **Art Print 5** and distribute to students Discussion Card 4: *Principles of Design.* Have students use what they learned about emphasis in this lesson to discuss the artwork.

ART PRINT 5

Still Life of Summer Flowers by Rachel Ruysch

★ TEKS 4.1B discuss elements and principles; TEKS 4.2A integrate ideas in artworks; TEKS 4.2B design original artworks; TEKS 4.2C produce artworks; TEKS 4.4A form conclusions about personal artworks; TEKS 4.4B interpret artworks by peers and others; PDAS Domain III evaluation and feedback; *(continued)*

Artist's Workshop

Create a Pastel Drawing

PLAN

Choose a magazine photograph of a subject you like. Make sketches of your subject.

CREATE

1. Choose your best sketch, and draw it on white paper.

2. Decide how you want to use emphasis in your drawing. You could contrast values, shapes, colors, or textures.

3. Use oil pastels to complete your drawing.

REFLECT

What do you want viewers to notice first in your drawing? How did you create emphasis?

MATERIALS

- magazines
- pencil
- sketchbook
- white paper
- oil pastels

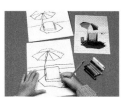

Quick Tip

You may add something surprising to your drawing, such as the splash in image C on page 79, to create emphasis.

81

Artist's Workshop

30-40 Minutes

Create a Pastel Drawing

PLAN Have students read the activity steps on page 81. Provide them with magazines or catalogs from which to choose their photographs.

CREATE Have students integrate a variety of ideas about self as they design their drawings. Students should invent ways to explore photographic imagery, using pastels or other art media and materials. TEKS 4.2A, TEKS 4.2B, TEKS 4.2C

REFLECT Have students describe the intent of their drawings and discuss their use of emphasis.
SELF-EVALUATION TEKS 4.1B, TEKS 4.4A

5-10 Minutes

Wrap-Up

Informal Assessment PDAS Domain III

- **What is a statement of fact about your drawing? What is a statement of opinion?** (Responses will vary.) FACT AND OPINION

- **Describe how a classmate showed emphasis in his or her pastel drawing.** (Responses will vary.) RESPONSE/EVALUATION TEKS 4.1B

Extend Through Writing
TAKS Writing Objectives 1, 6

STORY Have students write a brief story telling what made the splash in image C and what will happen next. Ask students to proofread their work.

Recommended Reading

The Art Room
by Susan Vande Griek.
Groundwood, 2002.
EASY

PDAS Domain IV

Activity Options

Quick Activity Have students find examples of emphasis in magazine photographs.

Early Finishers Have students draw the same scene in black and white, emphasizing the same objects.

Challenge See *Teacher Resource Book*, p. 60.

PDAS Domain IV

ESL Use **visuals** to support **comprehensible input** for examples of emphasis. Display *Picture Cards Collection*, cards 29, 56, and 124 for students to discuss and reference.

See also *Picture Card Bank* CD-ROM.

cloud

Unit 2

PDAS Domains I, III

Review and Reflect

 Have students reflect on what they have learned about the ways artists use value, texture, and emphasis to create artworks that capture a moment in time. Display **Art Prints 1, 4, 5, 6, and 16.** Encourage small groups of students to use Discussion Cards 3 and 4 on page R35, and their completed Word Knowledge Charts to discuss what they learned about the vocabulary and concepts in this unit.

Vocabulary and Concepts

Have students read each sentence and choose the letter of the word or phrase that best completes it. (1. D; 2. F; 3. D; 4. J; 5. B)

READING SKILL

Fact and Opinion

Remind students that a fact is a statement that can be proved and an opinion expresses some-one's thoughts or feelings. Before writing their paragraphs about the painting on pages 54–55, have students use the Fact-and-Opinion Chart on page 82 to plan their writing. TAKS Reading Objectives 1, 4; TAKS Writing Objective 1

Unit 2 Review and Reflect

Vocabulary and Concepts

Choose the letter of the word or phrase that best completes each sentence.

1 ___ is the lightness or darkness of a color.

  A Shade   **C** Impasto

  B Tint   **D** Value

2 ___ can be felt by touching.

  F Tactile texture   **H** Emphasis

  G Visual texture   **J** Value

3 A painting with ___ has a bumpy texture.

  A emphasis   **C** gray scale

  B dominant color   **D** impasto

4 A ___ shows values from black to white.

  F tactile texture   **H** blending

  G dominant color   **J** gray scale

5 Artists use ___ in an artwork to grab the viewer's attention.

  A texture   **C** value

  B emphasis   **D** impasto

READING SKILL

Fact and Opinion

Write a paragraph about the painting on pages 54–55. Include at least one fact and one opinion. Exchange papers with a partner. Read your partner's paragraph. Then use a chart like this one to list the facts and opinions your partner wrote.

Facts	Opinions

82

TEKS 4.2A, TEKS 4.2B, TEKS 4.4B

Home and Community Connection

School-Home Connection

Copy and distribute *Teacher Resource Book* pp. 87–88. After completing the unit, students can work at home to draw a picture that captures a moment in time. Students should integrate ideas about life events and family as they design their artwork.

Community Connection

You may want to contact a local professional photographer, and invite him or her to speak to students about a career in photography. Invite the photographer to bring his or her portfolio for students to examine and interpret the ideas in it. Have students prepare questions in advance to ask the photographer. **CAREER CONNECTION**

★ TEKS 4.1B discuss elements and principles; TEKS 4.2A integrate ideas in artworks; TEKS 4.2B design original artworks; TEKS 4.4A form conclusions about personal artworks; TEKS 4.4B interpret artworks by peers and others; PDAS Domain I active participation; PDAS Domain III evaluation and feedback; *(continued)*

Write About Art

Choose a piece of your artwork from this unit. Then write a paragraph that gives both facts and opinions about it. Use a chart like the one on page 82 to plan your writing.

REMEMBER — YOU SHOULD

- be able to prove the facts you write about.
- use correct spelling, punctuation, and grammar.
- try to use unit vocabulary words in your paragraph.

Critic's Corner

Look at *Basket of Bread* by Salvador Dalí to answer the questions below.

DESCRIBE What facts about the artwork can you state?

ANALYZE How would you describe the different textures in this artwork?

INTERPRET How do the colors and textures affect the mood in this artwork?

EVALUATE What is your opinion of the artist's choice of subject in this artwork? What do you think of the way he showed his subject?

Salvador Dalí, *Basket of Bread,*
1926, oil on wood panel, 12 in. × 12 in.
Dalí Museum, Reynolds Morse
Collection, St. Petersburg, Florida.

83

PDAS Domain III

Assessment

Portfolio Assessment

Work with students to choose a piece of their artwork to include in their portfolios. Suggest that they decide which piece best fulfilled the assignment or which piece they liked best for another reason. You may want to provide specific feedback that targets students' use of the elements of art and techniques. See also Portfolio Recording Form, page R32.

Additional Assessment Options

- Progress Recording Form, p. R33
- Artist's Workshop Rubrics (Self/Teacher and Peer), pp. R30–R31
- Unit 2 Test, *Teacher Resource Book* p. 100

Write About Art

Fact-and-Opinion Paragraph   Read aloud the prompt with students. Have them choose a piece of their own artwork through which they clearly expressed an opinion. Then have students use the Fact-and-Opinion Chart on page 82 to help them plan their paragraphs. Remind students to support their facts and explain their opinions. Have students make sure they use correct spelling, punctuation, and grammar.   TEKS 4.4A; TAKS Writing Objectives 1, 2, 4

Critic's Corner

RESPONSE/EVALUATION   Use the steps below to guide students in analyzing *Basket of Bread* by Salvador Dalí. See also Discussion Card 2, p. R34.

DESCRIBE   Discuss with students facts about *Basket of Bread*, such as: *The bread is in a basket and the basket is on a cloth.*

ANALYZE   Have students point out the woven texture in the basket, the rough texture of the bread crusts, and the soft texture of the cloth.   TEKS 4.1B

INTERPRET   Discuss with students the calm mood of the painting created by both the dull colors and the ordinary subject matter.

EVALUATE   Have students point out details in the artwork to support their opinions of it.

 TAKS Test Preparation: Reading and Writing Through Art, pp. 22–26

TAKS Reading Objective 1 demonstrate understanding of texts; **TAKS Reading Objective 4** apply critical-thinking skills;
TAKS Writing Objective 1 composition; **TAKS Writing Objective 2** conventions; **TAKS Writing Objective 4** sentence construction

UNIT 2   *Review and Reflect*   **83**

Unit 3

Proportion, Rhythm, and Form
People in Art

From earliest times, artists from all cultures have shown people in art. They have painted portraits or carved likenesses from wood or stone. In this unit students will learn some of the many ways in which artists portray people.

Resources

- Unit 3 Art Prints (7–9)
- Additional Art Prints (2, 11)
- Art Transparencies 7–9
- Test Preparation: Reading and Writing Through Art, pp. 27–47
- Artist's Workshop Activities: English and Spanish, pp. 21–30
- Encyclopedia of Artists and Art History, pp. R44–R65
- Picture Cards Collection, cards 6, 14, 23, 38, 40, 42, 45, 53, 57, 70, 82, 84, 100, 116, 117

Using the Art Prints

- Discussion Cards, pp. R34–R37
- Teaching suggestions, backs of Art Prints
- Art Print Teaching Suggestions: Spanish

Teacher Resource Book

- Vocabulary Cards in English and Spanish, pp. 15–18
- Reading Skill Card 3, p. 33
- Copying Master, p. 50
- Challenge Activities, pp. 61–65
- School-Home Connection: English/Spanish, pp. 89–90
- Unit 3 Test, p. 101

Technology Resources

 Electronic Art Gallery CD-ROM, Intermediate

Picture Card Bank CD-ROM

 Visit *The Learning Site*
www.harcourtschool.com

- Multimedia Art Glossary
- Multimedia Biographies
- Reading Skills and Activities

Art Prints for This Unit

ART PRINT 7

American Gothic
by Grant Wood

ART PRINT 8

The Family
by Marisol

ART PRINT 9

Limestone Bust of Queen Nefertiti
by Unknown Artist

ART PRINT 2

Senecio (Head of a Man)
by Paul Klee

ART PRINT 11

Jeanne Hebuterne with Hat
by Amedeo Modigliani

Lesson	Objectives and Vocabulary	Art Images	Production/Materials
Narrative Elements, pp. 86–87			
11 PROPORTION IN PORTRAITS pp. 88–91 ⏰ 30–60 minutes	• Choose appropriate vocabulary to discuss the use of proportion in portraits • Design and create an original portrait • Identify narrative elements in artworks **Vocabulary: portrait, facial proportions, self-portrait**	• **Young Man in Blue Suit** by Alice Kent Stoddard • **Portrait of Francesco I De'Medici** by Agnolo Bronzino • **Self-Portrait with Loose Hair** by Frida Kahlo	**Draw a Portrait** ❏ pencil ❏ sketchbook ❏ white paper ❏ colored pencils or markers
12 ABSTRACT PORTRAITS pp. 92–95 ⏰ 30–60 minutes	• Recognize distorted objects in abstract portraits • Design and create an original abstract portrait • Identify narrative elements in artworks **Vocabulary: abstract art, distortion, Cubism**	• **Mystical Head: Crow Wings (Mystischer Kopf: Rabenflügel)** by Alexej von Jawlensky • **Portrait of Picasso** by Juan Gris • **Woman Seated in an Armchair** by Pablo Picasso • **Untitled** by Anna, grade 4	**Create an Abstract Portrait** ❏ newspapers or magazines ❏ pencil ❏ sketchbook ❏ white paper ❏ oil pastels
Art ↔ Social Studies Connection: Portraits in Time, pp. 96–97			
13 FIGURES IN MOTION pp. 98–101 ⏰ 30–60 minutes	• Choose appropriate vocabulary to discuss rhythm in artworks • Design and create an original panel drawing • Identify narrative elements in artworks **Vocabulary: gesture drawing, rhythm**	• **Two Blue Dancers** by Edgar Degas • **Study of a Dancer (Etude de Danseuse)** by Edgar Degas • **The Bicycle Race** by Lyonel Feininger • **Child Who Runs on the Balcony** by Giacomo Balla	**Create a Panel Drawing** ❏ pencil ❏ sketchbook ❏ white paper ❏ crayons
14 RELIEF SCULPTURE pp. 102–105 ⏰ 30–60 minutes	• Choose appropriate vocabulary to discuss positive and negative space in artworks • Design and carve an original relief sculpture • Identify narrative elements in artworks **Vocabulary: relief sculpture, subtractive method, positive space, negative space**	• **Sacagawea coin** by Glenna Goodacre and Thomas Rogers • **Mount Rushmore National Memorial** by Gutzon Borglum • **Embarkation on Ship of Roman Troops** • **Head of Colossus of Ramses II** • **Moon Landing** by Mike O'Brien	**Carve a Relief Sculpture** ❏ pencil ❏ clay ❏ plastic knife ❏ sharpened pencil or paper clip ❏ craft stick
Art ↔ Social Studies Connection: Marisol Escobar, pp. 106–107			
15 SCULPTURE IN HISTORY pp. 108–111 ⏰ 30–60 minutes	• Choose appropriate vocabulary to identify and compare sculptures • Design and carve an original soap sculpture • Identify narrative elements in artworks **Vocabulary: form, terra-cotta**	• **Neron Child** • **Terra-Cotta Army Figure** • **The Rattlesnake** by Frederic Remington • **Man Ray** by Man Ray	**Carve a Soap Sculpture** ❏ magazines ❏ newsprint ❏ bar of soap ❏ toothpick ❏ plastic knife ❏ scrubber sponge
Review and Reflect, pp. 112–113			

★ **TEKS 4.2B** design original artworks; **TEKS 4.2C** produce artworks; **PDAS Domain IV** classroom management

Narrative Elements pp. 86–87

Focus Skill

Opportunities for application of the skill are provided on pp. 90, 94, 100, 104, 110, 112, and 113.

Resources and Technology	Suggested Literature	Across the Curriculum
• Art Print 7 • Reading Skill Card 3 • Discussion Cards 1, 5, pp. R34, R36 • Electronic Art Gallery CD-ROM, Intermediate	*The Young Artist* by Thomas Locker 	**Social Studies** Renaissance Clothing, p. 89 **Reading** Narrative Elements, p. 90 **Writing** Story, p. 91
• Art Prints 2, 11 • Reading Skill Card 3 • Discussion Cards 1, 8, pp. R34, R37 • Electronic Art Gallery CD-ROM, Intermediate	*Portraits* by Penny King and Clare Roundhill 	**Math** Geometry in Art, p. 93 **Reading** Narrative Elements, p. 94 **Writing** Compare-and-Contrast Composition, p. 95
• Art Print 8 • Reading Skill Card 3 • Discussion Cards 1, 7, pp. R34, R37 • Electronic Art Gallery CD-ROM, Intermediate	*What Makes a Degas a Degas?* by Richard Muhlberger 	**Music** Art-Inspired Music, p. 99 **Reading** Narrative Elements, p. 100 **Writing** Ad Poster, p. 101
• Art Print 9 • Reading Skill Card 3 • Discussion Cards 1, 5, pp. R34, R36 • Electronic Art Gallery CD-ROM, Intermediate	*Rushmore* by Lynn Curlee 	**Science** Physical Properties, p. 103 **Reading** Narrative Elements, p. 104 **Writing** Descriptive Paragraph, p. 105
• Art Prints 8, 9, 11 • Reading Skill Card 3 • Discussion Cards 1, 5, pp. R34, R36 • Electronic Art Gallery CD-ROM, Intermediate	*The Sculptor's Eye: Looking at Contemporary American Art* by Jan Greenberg and Sandra Jordan 	**Social Studies** State Statues, p. 109 **Reading** Narrative Elements, p. 110 **Writing** Narrative Story, p. 111

Art Puzzlers

Present these art puzzlers to students at the beginning or end of a class or when students finish an assignment early.

- Make a list of objects you would include in a **self-portrait** to reflect your personality.

- Cut several different geometric shapes from colored construction paper. Arrange them to create an **abstract portrait**.

- Draw a pattern of repeating shapes to create **rhythm**.

- Design your own coin. Draw an image or scene in a circle. Use a pencil to fill in the areas of **negative space**. TEKS 4.2B

- Think of a person you would like to make a **statue** of. Describe the person's pose in the statue.

School-Home Connection
The activities above can be included in the School-Home Connection for this unit. See *Teacher Resource Book* pp. 89–90.

Assessment Options

- Rubrics and Recording Forms, pp. R30–R33
- Unit 3 Test, *Teacher Resource Book,* p. 101

Visit *The Learning Site:*
www.harcourtschool.com

Artist's Workshops PREVIEW

Use these pages to help you gather and organize
materials for the production activity in each lesson.

LESSON	MATERIALS

11 Draw a Portrait p. 91

- pencil
- sketchbook
- white paper
- colored pencils or markers

Objective: To design and create an original portrait
using facial proportions

🕐 30–40 minutes

Challenge Activity: See *Teacher Resource Book*,
page 61.

FINISHED EXAMPLE

LESSON

12 Create an Abstract Portrait p. 95

- newspapers or magazines
- pencil
- sketchbook
- white paper
- oil pastels

Objective: To design and create an original
abstract portrait, using distortion to show
the subject's personality or emotions

🕐 30–40 minutes

Challenge Activity: See *Teacher Resource Book*,
page 62.

FINISHED EXAMPLE

 For safety information, see Art Safety, p. R4; or the Art Safety Poster.

 For information on media and techniques, see pp. R15–R23.

13 Create a Panel Drawing p. 101

- pencil
- sketchbook
- white paper
- crayons

Objective: To design and create an original panel drawing that shows an action

 30–40 minutes

Challenge Activity: See *Teacher Resource Book,* page 63.

FINISHED EXAMPLE

LESSON

14 Carve a Relief Sculpture p. 105

- pencil
- sketchbook
- clay
- plastic knife
- sharpened pencil or paper clip
- craft stick

Objective: To demonstrate understanding of positive space and negative space by designing and creating an original relief sculpture

 30–40 minutes

Challenge Activity: See *Teacher Resource Book,* page 64.

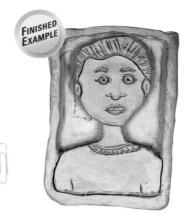
FINISHED EXAMPLE

LESSON

15 Carve a Soap Sculpture p. 111

- magazines or newspapers
- newsprint
- bar of soap
- toothpick or paper clip
- plastic knife
- scrubber sponge

Objective: To design and create an original soap sculpture using the subtractive method

 30–40 minutes

Challenge Activity: See *Teacher Resource Book,* page 65.

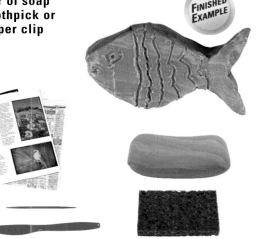
FINISHED EXAMPLE

Unit 3

PDAS Domains I, II

People in Art

PREVIEW THE UNIT

Tell students that in this unit they will view and create artworks that focus on people as their subjects. Invite students to preview this unit by reading the lesson titles and examining the art images.

STEP INTO THE ART

Have students examine the painting on pages 84 and 85 and describe what they see. Then read page 85 with students, and discuss their answers to the questions.

- **What do you think they [the children] would be talking about?** Students may suggest that the children might tell each other stories or talk about what they'd like to do next.

- **What kinds of games do you think they might play?** Discuss with students outdoor games such as hide-and-seek and tag.

- **What would you like to ask them?** Have students communicate ideas about self and family using sensory knowledge. Then ask them to think of questions that compare and contrast their lives and experiences with those of children from an earlier time. TEKS 4.1A

SHARE BACKGROUND INFORMATION

Beginning in 1867, Winslow Homer spent a decade painting a series of artworks that portrayed the traditional values of rural American life. His subjects were often girls and boys, either at play or relaxing in the sunshine. *Children on a Fence* is an example of one of these scenes.

 LOCATE IT See **Using the Maps of Museums and Art Sites,** p. R2.

Winslow Homer, *Children on a Fence*, 1874, watercolor over pencil on paper, 6 in. × 11 in.

 LOCATE IT

This painting can be found at the Williams College Museum of Art in Williamstown, Massachusetts.

See Maps of Museums and Art Sites, pages 206–209.

Williamstown

MASSACHUSETTS

84

FYI Background Information

About the Artist

Winslow Homer (1836–1910) is considered to be one of the greatest American painters of outdoor life. He is best known for his watercolors and his oil paintings of the sea. These paintings often show the dramatic power of nature.

For additional information about Winslow Homer, see the Encyclopedia of Artists and Art History, pp. R44–R65, and the Gallery of Artists, *Student Edition* pages 240–253.

For related artworks, see **Electronic Art Gallery CD-ROM, Intermediate.**

3

People in Art

Step into the Art

Imagine that you could step into this painting and join the children sitting on the fence. What do you think they would be talking about? What kinds of games do you think they might play? What would you like to ask them?

ABOUT THE ARTIST

See Gallery of Artists, pages 240–253.

Unit Vocabulary

portrait	Cubism	positive space
facial proportions	gesture drawing	negative space
self-portrait	rhythm	form
abstract art	relief sculpture	terra-cotta
distortion	subtractive method	

Multimedia Art Glossary
Visit *The Learning Site*
www.harcourtschool.com

85

Language Arts Connection

Students may create a chart like the one below to identify familiar and unfamiliar vocabulary terms. Encourage them to add information to their charts as they work through this unit.

WORD KNOWLEDGE CHART		
I know this term.	I have seen this term before.	I have never seen this term.

Unit Vocabulary

Read aloud the terms with students, and use the Word Knowledge Chart below to assess and discuss their prior knowledge.

portrait an artwork that shows what a person, a group of people, or an animal looks like

facial proportions the way the features of the human face, such as eyes, nose, and mouth, are related to each other in size and placement

self-portrait an artwork of a person made by himself or herself

abstract art art in which the details of real objects are simplified, distorted, or rearranged

distortion a technique used to change the way a subject looks by bending, stretching, or twisting its shape

Cubism a style of abstract art in which the artist may show more than one view of a subject at the same time

gesture drawing a sketch created with loose arm movements

rhythm the visual beat created by repeated lines, shapes, colors, or patterns

relief sculpture a three-dimensional artwork in which part of the image stands out from the background surface

subtractive method a sculpting method in which the artist cuts away, or subtracts, some of the original material

positive space the part of a three-dimensional artwork which has empty space around it

negative space the area in a three-dimensional artwork where material has been removed

form an object that has height, width, and depth

terra-cotta a type of reddish-brown clay that may be used in sculptures

Vocabulary Resources

- Vocabulary Cards in English and Spanish: *Teacher Resource Book*, pp. 15–18
- Student Edition Glossary, pp. 254–261

Multimedia Art Glossary
Visit *The Learning Site*
www.harcourtschool.com

Unit 3

Focus Skill READING SKILL
PDAS Domains I, II
Narrative Elements

SKILL TRACE	
NARRATIVE ELEMENTS	
Introduce	pp. 86–87
Review	pp. 90, 94, 100, 104, 110, 112

DISCUSS THE SKILL

Access Prior Knowledge   Display a book that students have read in class, and ask volunteers to describe the setting—where and when the story takes place—the characters, and the plot, or what happens in the story. Explain to students that artists may also tell stories in their artworks.

APPLY TO ART

Narrative Elements   Ask students to read page 86 and interpret ideas in the artwork. Have students discuss the characters, setting, and plot and then note any additional details. (Possible responses: Setting—The trees are full of ripe fruit, so it must be fall. Characters—There are five people and eight animals in the scene. Plot—Everyone looks busy.) TEKS 4.4B

Focus Skill READING SKILL
Narrative Elements

Narrative elements are the parts of a story. They include the characters, setting, and plot. The *characters* are the people or animals in the story. The *setting* is when and where the story takes place. The *plot* is what happens in the story.

Artists may tell stories in their artworks. Look at the image below.

- The **characters** are the people working on the farm, as well as the animals.
- The **setting** is a farm in the country, perhaps long ago.
- The **plot** is what is happening on the farm.

Look at what the characters are doing and at details in the setting to help you understand the story the artist is telling.

Anna Pugh, *A Day in the Country*, 1993, acrylic on board, 32 in. × 28 in. Private collection.

Background Information

About the Artist
Born in Wales during World War II, Anna Pugh is one of England's leading folk artists. Because one of her parents was a veterinarian and the other an avid gardener, Pugh grew up surrounded by animals and plants. Her colorful paintings reflect her love of animals, plants, and the countryside.

For additional information about the artist, see pp. R44–R65.

For related artworks, see **Electronic Art Gallery CD-ROM, Intermediate.**

★ TEKS 4.4B interpret artworks by peers and others; PDAS Domain I active participation; PDAS Domain II learner-centered instruction; PDAS Domain IV classroom management; TAKS Reading Objective 2 apply knowledge of literary elements

Knowing the characters, setting, and plot can also help you understand the stories you read. Read this passage. Think about the narrative elements.

"Now, Jack, be sure to get every one of those ripe apples before sundown," Dad said as he walked by with the wheelbarrow.

"Do you think Mom will win the pie contest at the fair again this year, Dad?" asked Jack.

"Of course she'll win! She's won every year for three years! But she'll need a lot of apples to make enough for the judges."

"I just hope there's some left over for us this year," Jack said. "Last year the judges ate everything."

Dad laughed. "Don't worry, Jack. It's a good crop this year. We'll be having pie after the fair for sure!"

What are the characters, setting, and plot? Use a story map like this one to help you.

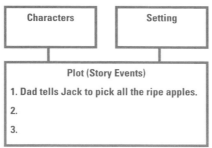

Characters	Setting

Plot (Story Events)

1. Dad tells Jack to pick all the ripe apples.
2.
3.

On Your Own

As you look at the artworks in this unit, use story maps to record narrative elements in the artworks. Look back at your completed story maps when you see questions with *READING SKILL* .

87

APPLY TO READING

Narrative Elements   Explain to students that, as they read the passage, they should be thinking about the characters, setting, and plot.

Have students read the passage on page 87. Work with them to complete the story map to determine the narrative elements in the passage.
TAKS Reading Objective 2

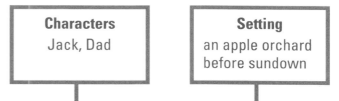

Characters	Setting
Jack, Dad	an apple orchard before sundown

Plot (Story Events)

1. Dad tells Jack to pick all the ripe apples.
2. Jack asks Dad if Mom's pie will win the contest.
3. Dad assures Jack that Mom will win and that they will have pie left over after the fair.

ON YOUR OWN

As students view the artworks in this unit, have them use story maps such as the one on page 87 to note the narrative elements in them.

TAKS Reading Objective 2

Reading Skill Card

Distribute Reading Skill Card 3, *Teacher Resource Book* page 33. Have students look for narrative elements in this unit.

Extend the Skill
For additional teaching suggestions, see **Art Transparency 7**.

PDAS Domain IV

ESL   For **language support,** pair students with English-fluent peers to **pantomime** the actions and read the dialogue of the characters in the passage on page 87. Then have students ask and answer questions that **demonstrate understanding** of the narrative elements in the passage. Have partners complete their story maps together.

 Reading Skills and Activities
Visit *The Learning Site*
www.harcourtschool.com

Lesson 11

PDAS Domains I, II

Proportion in Portraits

OBJECTIVES

- Choose appropriate vocabulary to discuss the use of proportion in portraits
- Design and create an original portrait
- Identify narrative elements in artworks

RESOURCES

- Art Print 7
- Reading Skill Card 3
- Discussion Cards 1, 5, pp. R34, R36
- Electronic Art Gallery CD-ROM, Intermediate

GO ONLINE

Multimedia Art Glossary and Biographies
Visit *The Learning Site*
www.harcourtschool.com

5 Minutes

Warm-Up

Build Background   Display **Art Print 7**, a painting by Grant Wood, and ask volunteers to describe what they see in the painting. Ask students to list details in the painting that give them clues about the subjects, such as their clothing and their facial expressions. Tell students that in this lesson they will learn how artists show what the subjects of their artworks are like. TEKS 4.4B

Lesson 11

Vocabulary
portrait
facial proportions
self-portrait

Proportion in Portraits

Images **A**, **B**, and **C** are portraits. A **portrait** is an artwork that shows a person, a group of people, or an animal. An artist creates a portrait to show how a subject looks or what a subject is like.

Personality in Portraits

A portrait often reflects the subject's personality. An artist may experiment with lines, shapes, or colors to express the feelings and character of the subject. What do you think the artist wanted to show about the man in image **A**?

 Alice Kent Stoddard, *Young Man in Blue Suit,* **about 1930, oil on canvas, 34 in. × 30 in. Collection of David David Gallery, Philadelphia, Pennsylvania.**

Background Information

About the Artists

B The portraits painted by Agnolo Bronzino (AHN•yoh•loh brawn•DZEE•noh) (1503–1572) reflected life in the world of Italian nobility.

C Many of Frida Kahlo's (FREE•dah KAH•loh) (1907–1954) paintings deal directly with physical struggles she endured after a disabling traffic accident.

For additional information about the artists, see pp. R44–R65.

 For related artworks, see the **Electronic Art Gallery CD-ROM, Intermediate.**

★ **TEKS 4.4B** interpret artworks by peers and others; **PDAS Domain I** active participation; **PDAS Domain II** learner-centered instruction; **TAKS Reading Objective 1** demonstrate understanding of texts; **TAKS Reading Objective 3** use a variety of strategies; **TAKS Reading Objective 4** apply critical-thinking skills

LOCATE IT

The portrait in image **B** can be found in Florence, Italy.

Florence

ITALY

See Maps of Museums and Art Sites, pages 206–209.

B Agnolo Bronzino, *Portrait of Francesco I De'Medici,* 1551, tempera on wood panel, 58.5 cm × 41.5 cm. Uffizi Gallery, Florence, Italy.

Facial Proportions

When an artist draws or paints a realistic portrait, he or she studies the subject's head, eyes, nose, and mouth. Then the artist shows the **facial proportions**, or how these features are related to each other in size and placement.

Notice the facial proportions in image **B**. Compare the boy's face with the diagram. The boy's eyes are about halfway between the top of his head and his chin. His nose is about halfway between his eyes and his chin, and his mouth is about halfway between his nose and his chin.

89

TAKS Reading Objectives 1, 3, 4

Social Studies Connection

Renaissance Clothing Encourage students to use the encyclopedia or online resources to learn how children dressed during the Renaissance. Have students narrow their search by selecting a particular country or city in Europe and looking at that place's history. Have students prepare a presentation with pictures and report their findings to the class.

Preview the Art Ask students to look at images A through C on pages 88–90. Encourage them to describe what they see and to share their first impressions. Use Discussion Card 1 and the questions below to guide the discussion. Then have students read pages 88–90.

 Young Man in Blue Suit **What do you think the subject of this painting is feeling? Why do you think that?**

 Portrait of Francesco I De'Medici **What are some of the details you can see in this portrait? What do the details tell you about the boy?**

 Self-Portrait with Loose Hair **Describe what you see in this portrait.**

Discuss Art Concepts Have students interpret moods and ideas in the artworks. Discuss with them that the artist of the portrait in image A showed her subject deep in thought through his pose and the serious look on his face.

In image B, point out the gilded details in the boy's clothing, which indicate that he is from a noble family. His expression and pose are stiff and formal. Discuss with students the facial proportions diagram on page 89, and have them examine the proportions in each of the images.

In image C, point out to students the serious, somewhat sad expression on the artist's face that reflects her emotions. Discuss the writing at the bottom of the painting, which means, "Here I painted myself, Frida Kahlo, with the image from my mirror. I am 37 years old and it is the month of July in 1947. I'm in Coyoacán, Mexico, the place where I was born." TEKS 4.4B

LOCATE IT Have students turn to the world map on pages 208–209 to locate Florence, Italy.

Narrative Elements   Ask students to look at images A, B, and C. Ask them to identify

• one detail about the person in each portrait.

• one detail about the setting of each portrait.

Then ask students to compare and contrast these artworks from a variety of cultural settings. Have students identify the simple main ideas in the images that tell about art history and culture.
TEKS 4.3A, TEKS 4.3B

Think Critically

Use the questions below to check students' understanding of lesson concepts.

1. **READING SKILL** **Imagine that the boy in image B is a character in a story. What do you think he is like?** (Responses will vary.) **NARRATIVE ELEMENTS** TEKS 4.4B

2. **What is the difference between a portrait and a self-portrait?** (A portrait is an artwork that shows a person, a group of people, or an animal. Self-portraits are portraits that artists create of themselves.) **PERCEPTION/AESTHETICS**

3. **WRITE**   **Describe how you would show yourself in a self-portrait. What would you be wearing? What else would you put in the painting that would say something about you?** **DESCRIPTIVE** TEKS 4.1A; TAKS Writing Objective 1

Self-Portraits

Self-portraits are portraits that artists create of themselves. Image **C** is a self-portrait by Mexican artist Frida Kahlo. Each of Kahlo's many self-portraits expressed something about her personality. Kahlo added details to reflect her emotions. What can you tell about the artist by the details she included?

Think Critically

1. **READING SKILL** Imagine that the boy in image **B** is a character in a story. What do you think he is like?
NARRATIVE ELEMENTS

2. What is the difference between a portrait and a self-portrait?

3. **WRITE** Describe how you would show yourself in a self-portrait. What would you be wearing? What else would you put in the painting that would say something about you?

C Frida Kahlo,
Self-Portrait with Loose Hair,
1947, oil on masonite, 24 in. × 17¾ in.
Private collection.

TEKS 4.3A, TEKS 4.3B

Art Print 7

Display **Art Print 7** and distribute to students Discussion Card 5: *Portraits.* Have students identify the simple main idea expressed in **Art Print 7** and then compare and contrast it with the other portraits in this lesson.

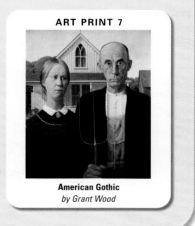

ART PRINT 7

American Gothic
by Grant Wood

Artist's Workshop

Draw a Portrait

PLAN

MATERIALS
- pencil
- sketchbook
- white paper
- colored pencils or markers

Choose a classmate you would like to draw. Observe your classmate's facial features closely. Lightly sketch what you see. Look at the diagram of human facial proportions on page 89 to help you.

CREATE

1. Use your sketch as a guide to draw the portrait. Think about the size and placement of each facial feature.

2. Use colored pencils or markers to add color and details to your drawing.

3. Show something in your portrait about your classmate's personality.

REFLECT

How did you use facial proportions? Point out the details in your portrait that show something about your classmate.

Quick Tip

To check the proportions of facial features on your portrait, lightly draw the lines you see in the diagram on page 89. Erase these lines before you add color to your portrait.

91

Artist's Workshop

30-40 Minutes

Draw a Portrait

PLAN Have students read the activity steps on page 91. Distribute *Teacher Resource Book* page 50 to help students with facial proportions. Review the diagram of human facial proportions with students, and tell them to try several quick sketches of a human face before beginning their sketch of a classmate.

CREATE Remind students to include a detail about their classmate's personality in their portrait. TEKS 4.2B

REFLECT Have students choose appropriate vocabulary to discuss proportion in their portraits. Then ask them to tell how they showed something about their classmate's personality. **SELF-EVALUATION** TEKS 4.1B, TEKS 4.4A

Wrap-Up

5-10 Minutes

Informal Assessment PDAS Domain III

- **How did looking at the portraits in this lesson help you create your own portrait?** (Responses will vary.) EVALUATION/CRITICISM

- **If the classmate in your portrait was a character in a story, what would the plot of the story be?** (Responses will vary.) NARRATIVE ELEMENTS TEKS 4.4A

Extend Through Writing TAKS Writing Objective 1

STORY Have students write a story about the subject of their portrait. Suggest to students that they use a story map to help them think about the character, setting, and plot of their story.

Recommended Reading

The Young Artist by Thomas Locker. Dial, 1989. AVERAGE

 PDAS Domain IV

Activity Options

Quick Activity Have students draw a pencil sketch of their classmate using correct facial proportions.

Early Finishers Have students add details to their portraits to tell something about the setting.

Challenge See *Teacher Resource Book*, p. 61.

 PDAS Domain IV

ESL Use **visuals** to support **comprehensible input** for facial features. Display *Picture Cards Collection,* cards 42, 45, 82, and 84 for children to discuss and reference.

See also *Picture Card Bank* CD-ROM, Category: My Body.

ear

Lesson 12

PDAS Domains I, II

Abstract Portraits

OBJECTIVES
- Recognize distorted objects in abstract portraits
- Design and create an original abstract portrait
- Identify narrative elements in artworks

RESOURCES
- Art Prints 2, 11
- Reading Skill Card 3
- Discussion Cards 1, 8, pp. R34, R37
- Electronic Art Gallery CD-ROM, Intermediate

GO ONLINE
Multimedia Art Glossary and Biographies
Visit *The Learning Site*
www.harcourtschool.com

5 Minutes

Warm-Up

Build Background   Display **Art Print 11**, a portrait by Amedeo Modigliani, and ask students to describe what they see. Ask volunteers to point out parts of the portrait that seem true to life, such as the woman's clothing. Then ask students to point out parts of the portrait that seem different from real life, such as the woman's elongated hand and facial proportions. Tell students that in this lesson they will see how some artists choose to show people in portraits in ways that look different from real life.

Lesson 12

Abstract Portraits

Vocabulary
- abstract art
- distortion
- Cubism

Look at the portrait in image **A**. Trace the subject's nose with your finger. How does it compare with a real person's nose? Artists may use line, shape, and color in unusual ways to create images that look different from real life. This kind of art is called **abstract art**. How can you tell that image **A** is an abstract portrait?

Geometric shapes are commonly used in abstract art. What geometric shapes do you see in images **A**, **B**, **C**, and **D**?

The way an artist uses line, shape, and color in an abstract portrait might show the emotions of the subject in a way that realistic art cannot. What kind of feeling do you get from image **A**? What do you think the subject's mood was?

Alexej von Jawlensky, *Mystical Head: Crow Wings (Mystischer Kopf: Rabenflügel)*, 1918, oil on paper laid down on card, 10 in. × 7⅝ in.

FYI

Background Information

About the Artists

B Juan Gris (GREES) painted *Portrait of Picasso* in the Cubist style as a tribute to his mentor and friend.

C Pablo Picasso (pih•KAHS•soh) and fellow artist Georges Braque developed the Cubist style in France around 1907.

For additional information about the artists and about Cubism, see pp. R44–R65.

For related artworks, see **Electronic Art Gallery CD-ROM, Intermediate.**

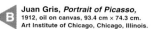
Juan Gris, *Portrait of Picasso*,
1912, oil on canvas, 93.4 cm × 74.3 cm.
Art Institute of Chicago, Chicago, Illinois.

Distortion and Cubism

Look again at image **A**. Think about the facial proportions.
Are the facial proportions in image **A** true to life? When
artists change the proportions from what a viewer might
expect, they are using **distortion**. Artists can distort the way
a subject looks by bending, stretching, or twisting parts of
the image. What parts of the face in image **A** are distorted?
How are they distorted?

Image **B** is an abstract portrait of the artist Pablo
Picasso, painted by the artist Juan Gris (GREES). Gris
admired Picasso's style of abstract painting, called **Cubism**.
Artists who painted in this style often showed more than
one view of a subject in the same image. Look closely at the
face of the subject in image **B**. Point out his eyes, nose, and
mouth. Can you see more than one view of the subject?

LOCATE IT

The portrait in
image B can be found
at the Art Institute of
Chicago in Chicago,
Illinois.

Chicago
ILLINOIS

See Maps of Museums
and Art Sites,
pages 206–209.

93

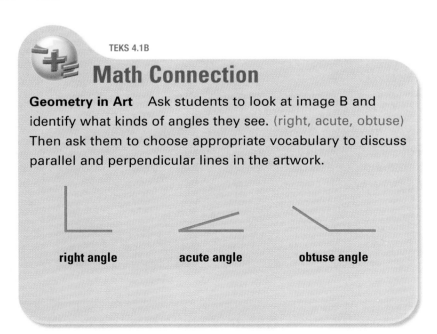

TEKS 4.1B

Math Connection

Geometry in Art Ask students to look at image B and
identify what kinds of angles they see. (right, acute, obtuse)
Then ask them to choose appropriate vocabulary to discuss
parallel and perpendicular lines in the artwork.

right angle   acute angle   obtuse angle

Preview the Art Invite students to preview
images A through D on pages 92–94. Ask them to
compare what they see to what they have learned
about facial proportions. Use Discussion Card 1
and the questions below to guide the discussion.
Then have students read pages 92–94.

A   *Mystical Head: Crow Wings*   **Do you
think the person in the portrait is young
or old? How can you tell?**

B   *Portrait of Picasso*   **How would you
describe the subject of this painting?
What is he wearing?**

C   *Woman Seated in an Armchair*   **What
makes this portrait different from others
you have seen?**

D   *Untitled*   **What is the first thing you notice
when you look at this painting? Why?**

Discuss Art Concepts Tell students that abstract
art was developed by artists who chose to express
themselves in nontraditional ways. Discuss with
students the unrealistic features of the portrait in
image A. Point out that the shapes of the subject's
eyes and mouth give her a sad expression.

Help students recognize the large eyes of the
woman in image A and the positions of the facial
features in image B as examples of distortion.

To reinforce students' understanding of Cubism,
have them cover the right side of Picasso's face in
image B to reveal his profile. Help students find
the front and side views of the face in image D.
TEKS 4.1B

LOCATE IT Have students turn to pages 206–207
to locate Chicago, Illinois. Tell students that the
Art Institute of Chicago was founded in 1866 and
houses over 300, 000 works of art, including 33
paintings by Claude Monet.

Teach (continued)

Narrative Elements Ask students to look at the abstract portrait in image D. Ask students to tell

- what the girl in the portrait might be like.

- what the setting of the portrait might be.

Then ask students to brainstorm plot events for a story that would include the subject and setting of the portrait in image D. TEKS 4.4B

Think Critically

Use the questions below to check students' understanding of lesson concepts.

1. (Focus Skill) *READING SKILL* **What is the subject of image B holding in his hand? What does it tell you about him?** (The subject is holding an artist's palette with paints on it. It tells you that he's an artist.) **NARRATIVE ELEMENTS** TEKS 4.4B

2. **How is image D like image A? How is it different?** (Possible response: Both are abstract portraits. Image D shows two views of the subject's face. Image A shows one view.) **PERCEPTION/AESTHETICS** TEKS 4.3B

3. **WRITE** **Write a paragraph explaining your opinion about whether artists should study the works of other artists.** **DESCRIPTIVE**
TAKS Writing Objective 1

Look at image **C**. Do you recognize any of the objects in the painting? Read the painting's title. Look for objects such as the armchair and the woman's arms.

Now look at image **D**. What does it have in common with image **B**? How many different views of the subject's face do you see?

Think Critically

1. (Focus Skill) *READING SKILL* What is the subject of image **B** holding in his hand? What does it tell you about him? **NARRATIVE ELEMENTS**

2. How is image **D** like image **A**? How is it different?

3. **WRITE** Write a paragraph explaining your opinion about whether artists should study the works of other artists.

D Anna, grade four, Untitled.

94

TEKS 4.3B

Art Print 2

Display **Art Print 2** and distribute to students Discussion Card 8: *Abstract Art*. Have them compare and contrast **Art Print 2** with the other abstract portraits in this lesson.

ART PRINT 2

Senecio (Head of a Man)
by Paul Klee

⭐ **TEKS 4.2B** design original artworks; **TEKS 4.2C** produce artworks; **TEKS 4.3B** compare and contrast artworks; **TEKS 4.4A** form conclusions about personal artworks; **TEKS 4.4B** interpret artworks by peers and others; **PDAS Domain III** evaluation and feedback; **PDAS Domain IV** classroom management; **TAKS Writing Objective 1** composition

Artist's Workshop

Create an Abstract Portrait

PLAN

Choose a photograph of a person from a newspaper or magazine. Make some sketches of your subject's face.

CREATE

1. Select the sketch you like best.

2. Use your sketch to experiment with distortion by using geometric shapes for facial features. You may want to change the sizes of some of your subject's features.

3. Use oil pastels to draw the abstract portrait. Use lines and colors to show what your subject's personality might be like.

REFLECT

How did you use distortion? What does your portrait show about your subject's personality or emotions?

Quick Tip
Remember that cool colors in a portrait might show a quiet personality. Warm colors might show a lively personality.

95

 Artist's Workshop

30-40 Minutes

Create an Abstract Portrait

PLAN After students have read the activity steps on page 95, have them look back at images B and D to note how the artists included two views of their subjects in each portrait.

CREATE Have students invent ways to explore the shapes in the photographic imagery, using a variety of art media and materials. Students may choose warm or cool colors to show something about their subject's personality. TEKS 4.2B, TEKS 4.2C

REFLECT Have students describe the intent of their artworks and tell what makes their portraits abstract. **SELF-EVALUATION** TEKS 4.4A

 Wrap-Up

5-10 Minutes

Informal Assessment   PDAS Domain III

- **Which abstract portrait in this lesson is yours most like? Describe the similarities.** (Responses will vary.) **EVALUATION/CRITICISM**

- **How can an abstract portrait tell viewers a story?** (Possible response: Shapes, colors, and details can give clues to the mood and personality of the subject.) **NARRATIVE ELEMENTS**

Extend Through Writing TAKS Writing Objective 1

COMPARE-AND-CONTRAST COMPOSITION   Have students write a composition comparing and contrasting their portraits with the magazine photograph they used as their subject.

Recommended Reading

Portraits
by Penny King and Clare Roundhill.
Crabtree, 1996.
AVERAGE

 PDAS Domain IV

Activity Options

Quick Activity   Have students draw a pencil sketch of a person's face, substituting geometric shapes for facial features.

Early Finishers   Have students add background details that tell something about their subjects.

Challenge   See *Teacher Resource Book*, p. 62.

 PDAS Domain IV

ESL   **Model** the activity steps to ensure understanding. Have students **read aloud** the steps with you to develop fluency. After students have completed their portraits, have them work with an English-fluent partner to discuss their use of distortion and other details.

ART ←→ SOCIAL STUDIES CONNECTION

PDAS Domains I, II

Portraits in Time

ART AND CULTURE

DISCUSS THE IMAGES

Have students read pages 96–97.

- Encourage students to discuss what they see in image A. Tell students that Diego Velázquez was a Spanish artist who became well known as the official painter for the king of Spain in the seventeenth century.

- Explain to students that because subjects of portraits had to sit for such long periods of time, artists often entertained them by bringing along musicians or other performers. Ask students why Princess Margarita might not have wanted to pose for a portrait. (It would take too long and bore her.) Have students communicate ideas about school portraits using life experiences. TEKS 4.1A

- Tell students that image B is a photograph of Sam Houston. Many images of Houston include a walking stick, which he used after an injury in the fight for Texas's independence. Houston's Indian blanket signified his pride at being associated with the Indians whom he lived with.

Portraits in Time

How is posing for a portrait today different from posing for a portrait long ago?

Before photography was invented, portraits were usually painted. The subjects of most portraits were important people. They would sit for the portraits in elaborate clothing for many hours at a time.

Image **A** helps us imagine what it was like to pose for a portrait long ago. The artist has cleverly shown not only the subjects of the portrait but also their viewpoints. Both King Philip IV and Queen Mariana of Spain are reflected in the mirror on the back wall of the room. What do they see as they pose for their portrait? Where do you see a self-portrait of the artist, Diego Velázquez?

 Diego Velázquez, *Las Meninas*, 1656, oil on canvas, 125 in. x 108¾ in. Museo del Prado, Madrid, Spain.

The young girl in the center of image **A** is Princess Margarita, the king and queen's daughter. Her maid seems to be encouraging her to pose for the painting. Why do you think the princess is unwilling to join her parents?

96

 Background Information

About the Artist

A *Las Meninas* is considered to be one of **Diego Velázquez's** (vay•LAHS•kes) (1599–1660) greatest paintings. Art historians have noted that the artist's presence in the painting seems to indicate Velázquez's pride in his artwork.

For additional information about the artist, see pp. R44–R65.

 For related artworks, see **Electronic Art Gallery CD-ROM, Intermediate.**

Image **B** is a photographic portrait of Sam Houston, the first and third president of the Republic of Texas. Having your portrait painted or photographed showed that you were important. Subjects often posed with objects that told something about them. Why do you think Sam Houston wanted to pose wearing a blanket and holding a walking stick?

Think About Art

Think of a famous person you would like to paint. What objects would you include in your painting that might tell something about that person? Explain your answer.

DID YOU KNOW?

The first successful kind of photograph, a daguerreotype (duh•GEH•roh•typ), was invented in the 1830s. Subjects of early photographs had to sit motionless for 3 to 15 minutes while chemicals in the camera were exposed to bright sunlight.

The daguerreotype below is of Frederick Douglass.

Portrait of Frederick Douglass, about 1850.

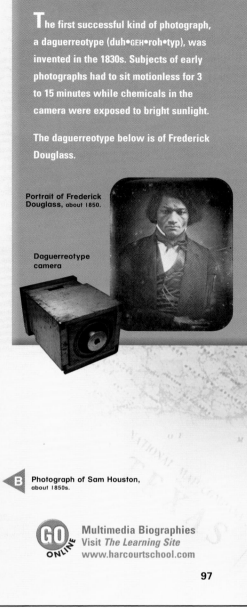

Daguerreotype camera

 Photograph of Sam Houston, about 1850s.

 Multimedia Biographies
Visit *The Learning Site*
www.harcourtschool.com

97

DID YOU KNOW?

Use the facts below to discuss photography with students.

- Long ago, heavy camera equipment made it necessary for most photographs to be taken in studios.

- Today, digital cameras store images on a tiny computer chip or on a memory card. The photographer can view, add to, and delete from stored color images on a small screen.

Think About Art

Think of a famous person you would like to paint. What objects would you include in your painting that might tell something about that person? Explain your answer. (Responses will vary.) PERSONAL RESPONSE

ARTIST'S EYE ACTIVITY

Re-create a Scene Invite groups of students to re-create the setting in image A. Have them study the position of each person and then position themselves in the same way. Ask students what they found most difficult about re-creating the composition.

 **Multimedia Biographies**
Visit *The Learning Site*
www.harcourtschool.com

TEKS 4.3C

Social Studies Connection

Presidential Portraits Have students identify the roles of portraits in American society. Tell them that the National Portrait Gallery displays portraits of all U.S. Presidents.

For additional cross-curricular suggestions, see Art Transparency 8.

TEKS 4.4B

Viewing an Artist's Work

Portfolios and Exhibitions Arrange for students to visit a museum. Have students examine artists' portfolios and exhibitions for details in the artworks that provide clues about the historical time and place in which the artist lived and worked, and to interpret ideas and moods in the artworks.

Lesson 13

PDAS Domains I, II

Figures in Motion

OBJECTIVES

- Choose appropriate vocabulary to discuss rhythm in artworks
- Design and create an original panel drawing
- Identify narrative elements in artworks

RESOURCES

- Art Print 8
- Reading Skill Card 3
- Discussion Cards 1, 7, pp. R34, R37
- Electronic Art Gallery CD-ROM, Intermediate

Multimedia Art Glossary and Biographies
Visit *The Learning Site*
www.harcourtschool.com

5 Minutes

Warm-Up

Build Background   Ask volunteers to pantomime different actions, such as throwing a baseball or painting a picture. Ask their classmates to use exact details to describe what each volunteer is doing. Then invite students to think about how an artist might be able to capture motion in an artwork. Explain that in this lesson, students will learn how artists create images of people in motion.

Lesson 13

Figures in Motion

Vocabulary

gesture drawing

rhythm

A Edgar Degas, *Two Blue Dancers,* about 1900, pastel on paper, 75 cm × 49 cm. Von der Heydt Museum, Wuppertal, Germany.

B Edgar Degas, *Study of a Dancer (Etude de Danseuse),* pastel and charcoal on paper, 12¾ in. × 8½ in.

Artists create portraits of people in still poses and of people in motion. What are the people in image **A** doing? How can you tell they are in motion?

Gesture Drawing

Before artists create a finished artwork, they draw a sketch. Image **B** shows a sketch that Edgar Degas (duh•GAH) made of a ballerina. One kind of sketch, a **gesture drawing**, is created by using loose arm movements. Why do you think an artist might use a gesture drawing to sketch a person in motion?

98

Background Information

About the Artists

A Edgar Degas (duh•GAH) (1834–1917) was best known for painting people in more informal poses than what was typically shown in traditional portraits.

C Besides being an accomplished painter, Lyonel Feininger (1871–1956) also worked as a musician, a professor, a cartoonist, and an author of children's books.

For additional information about the artists, see pp. R44–R65.

For related artworks, see **Electronic Art Gallery CD-ROM, Intermediate.**

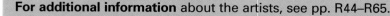

TEKS 4.1A communicate ideas; TEKS 4.1B discuss elements and principles; TEKS 4.4B interpret artworks by peers and others; PDAS Domain I active participation; PDAS Domain II learner-centered instruction; TAKS Reading Objective 1 demonstrate understanding of texts; TAKS Reading Objective 3 use a variety of strategies; *(continued)*

Rhythm

In music, when a sound is repeated, it creates a beat or rhythm. Artists create a visual beat or **rhythm** by repeating lines, shapes, or colors. Both artists and musicians may use rhythm to create a certain mood. Look at images **A** and **B**. How do the lines of the arms show rhythm?

Lyonel Feininger, the artist of image **C**, was trained as a violinist before he became an artist. How do you think his training as a musician may have helped him as an artist? How did he create rhythm in image **C**? What kind of feeling did he show?

LOCATE IT

The painting in image C can be found at the National Gallery of Art in Washington, D.C.

Washington, D.C.

See Maps of Museums and Art Sites, pages 206–209.

 Lyonel Feininger, *The Bicycle Race,*
1912, oil on canvas, 31⅝ in. × 39½ in.
National Gallery of Art, Washington, D.C.

99

Music Connection

TEKS 4.1A; TAKS Reading Objectives 1, 3, 4

Art-Inspired Music Have students work in pairs or small groups to brainstorm the kinds of music they think would be best suited to each of the images in this lesson. Encourage students to discuss their ideas with the music teacher and use sensory knowledge to communicate ideas about school musical performances. Then ask groups to describe the rhythm, genre, and volume level of the music they chose and, if possible, to play recordings of the music they selected.

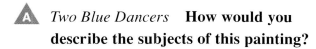

Teach

10-15 Minutes

Preview the Art Ask students to look at images A through D on pages 98–100. Have them describe what they see in each artwork. Use Discussion Card 1 and the questions below to guide the discussion. Then have students read pages 98–100.

A *Two Blue Dancers* **How would you describe the subjects of this painting?**

B *Study of a Dancer* **What is one difference between this artwork and the one in image A?**

C *The Bicycle Race* **If this painting had a different title, would you be able to tell what it showed? Why or why not?**

D *Child Who Runs on the Balcony* **What is happening in this painting?** TEKS 4.4B

Discuss Art Concepts Students should recognize that the subjects are dancing in images A and B, racing bicycles in image C, and running in image D.

Students should point out the repeated lines, shapes, and colors that create rhythm in each one. Discuss with students the way these elements are clues that the people are in motion. Point out that the softer, organic shapes and cool colors in image A create a sense of slow, graceful movement; the triangular shapes and the warm colors in image C reflect a feeling of high energy and rapid movement. Discuss with students the blurred effect created by the dots of color in image D that make the subject appear to run. TEKS 4.1B

LOCATE IT Ask students to turn to the map on pages 206–207 to locate Washington, D.C. Tell students that the artwork in image C can be found in the National Gallery's East Building, which houses its collection of 20th century art.

Teach (continued)

Narrative Elements Have students look back at image A and describe

- the characters in it.
- the setting.

Then ask students which artwork in this lesson they think best conveys a sense of energy and motion, and why they think so.

Think Critically

Use the questions below to check students' understanding of lesson concepts.

1. **(Focus Skill) *READING SKILL*** **What are the characters, setting, and plot in image C?** (Possible response: The characters are bicyclists. The setting is a road. The plot is about bicyclists in a bike race.) **NARRATIVE ELEMENTS** TEKS 4.4B

2. **How would you change the shapes in image C to show a different feeling?** (Possible response: More organic shapes might show a more peaceful feeling. Squares might show things standing still.) **PERCEPTION/AESTHETICS** TEKS 4.1B

3. **WRITE** **Look at image D. Write a story about why the child was running on the balcony.** **NARRATIVE** TAKS Writing Objective 1

Read the title of image **D**. Do you think this is a good title for the painting? Why or why not? How did the artist of image **D** use rhythm?

Think Critically

1. **(Focus Skill) *READING SKILL*** What are the characters, setting, and plot in image **C**? **NARRATIVE ELEMENTS**

2. How would you change the shapes in image **C** to show a different feeling?

3. **WRITE** Look at image **D**. Write a story about why the child was running on the balcony.

Giacomo Balla, *Child Who Runs on the Balcony,* 1912, oil on canvas, 127.5 cm × 127.5 cm. Civica Galleria d'Arte Moderna, Milan, Italy.

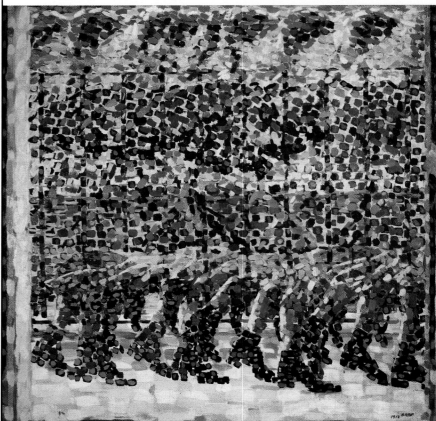

TEKS 4.1A

Art Print 8

Display **Art Print 8** and distribute to students Discussion Card 7: *Stories.* Have them discuss the narrative elements they see in this artwork. Then have students communicate ideas about their own families, using sensory knowledge and life experiences.

ART PRINT 8

The Family by Marisol

★ TEKS 4.1A communicate ideas; TEKS 4.1B discuss elements and principles; TEKS 4.2A integrate ideas in artworks; TEKS 4.2B design original artworks; TEKS 4.4A form conclusions about personal artworks; TEKS 4.4B interpret artworks by peers and others; PDAS Domain III evaluation and feedback; *(continued)*

Artist's Workshop

Create a Panel Drawing

MATERIALS
- pencil
- sketchbook
- white paper
- crayons

PLAN

Brainstorm a list of steps for performing an action, such as hitting a baseball. Then have a partner model the steps. Use simple lines and shapes to make gesture drawings of your partner.

CREATE

1. Fold a sheet of paper into three sections, or panels. Draw a vertical line along each fold to separate the sections.

2. Use your gesture drawings as a guide to draw your subject at the beginning, middle, and end of the action. Make a drawing in each panel.

3. Use crayons to add color and details to your panel drawing.

REFLECT

What kind of action did you show in your panel drawing? If you cut your panel drawing apart, could your partner put the panels back in order?

Quick Tip For help with drawing figures in motion, look back at page 98.

101

30-40 Minutes Artist's Workshop

Create a Panel Drawing

PLAN Have students read the activity steps on page 101.

CREATE Students should integrate a variety of ideas about life events into their drawings. As students design their artworks, remind them that repeating lines and shapes in their drawings will create rhythm. TEKS 4.2A, TEKS 4.2B

REFLECT Have students describe intent about their panel drawing and then pantomime the action they depicted. SELF-EVALUATION TEKS 4.4A

5-10 Minutes Wrap-Up

Informal Assessment PDAS Domain III

- **How do the lines, shapes, and colors you used in your drawing show rhythm?** (Responses will vary.) PERCEPTION/AESTHETICS TEKS 4.1B

- **If you were telling a story with your drawing, how would you describe the plot?** (Responses will vary.) NARRATIVE ELEMENTS TEKS 4.4A

Extend Through Writing
TEKS 4.1A; TAKS Writing Objective 1

AD POSTER Have students imagine that their artwork is a poster for a school event. Ask them to communicate ideas about school using sensory knowledge and life experiences in written text to go along with the art.

Recommended Reading

What Makes a Degas a Degas? by Richard Muhlberger. The Metropolitan Museum of Art/Viking, 2002. CHALLENGING

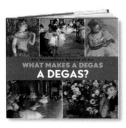

PDAS Domain IV

Activity Options

Quick Activity Create a gesture drawing of a classmate in motion.

Early Finishers Have students add at least two more panels to their drawing to show more of the action.

Challenge See *Teacher Resource Book*, p. 63.

PDAS Domain IV

MEETING INDIVIDUAL NEEDS

ESL Use **visuals** to support **comprehensible input** for action terms. Display *Picture Cards Collection*, cards 70, 100, and 116 for students to discuss and reference.

See also *Picture Card Bank* CD-ROM, Category: Places People Go.

jump

Lesson 14

PDAS Domains I, II

Relief Sculpture

OBJECTIVES
- Choose appropriate vocabulary to discuss positive and negative space in artworks
- Design and carve an original relief sculpture
- Identify narrative elements in artworks

RESOURCES
- Art Print 9
- Reading Skill Card 3
- Discussion Cards 1, 5, pp. R34, R36
- Electronic Art Gallery CD-ROM, Intermediate

GO ONLINE Multimedia Art Glossary and Biographies
Visit *The Learning Site*
www.harcourtschool.com

5 Minutes

Warm-Up

Build Background Have students examine and touch both sides of a coin and describe what they feel. Ask students to look closely at the face side. Discuss with them whether they think the face on the coin can be considered a portrait, and why or why not. Tell students that in this lesson, they will learn about portraits that are carved rather than painted.

Lesson 14

Relief Sculpture

Vocabulary
- relief sculpture
- subtractive method
- positive space
- negative space

Have you ever reached into your pocket and felt the raised surface of a coin? The people and symbols on our coins are shown as relief sculptures. A **relief sculpture** is an image that stands out from the background surface. Image **A** is a relief sculpture of Lewis and Clark's Native American guide, Sacagawea.

A Glenna Goodacre and Thomas Rogers, **Sacagawea coin,** designed in 1999.

Subtractive Method

To make relief sculptures, artists may carve a slab of material such as clay or marble. This process is called the **subtractive method** because the artist cuts away, or subtracts, some of the original material.

B Gutzon Borglum, *Mount Rushmore National Memorial,* 1927–1941, granite, 60 ft. high. Near Rapid City, South Dakota.

Background Information

Art History
A One of Sacagawea's descendants was a model for the coin.
B Ninety percent of Mount Rushmore was carved with dynamite. After each detonation, workers removed stone to within six inches of the finished surface. It took 14 years to complete the sculpture.
C Early Romans frequently decorated tombs with relief sculptures. The sculptures often depicted the deceased person with his or her family.

 For related artworks, see **Electronic Art Gallery CD-ROM, Intermediate.**

★ **TEKS 4.1A** communicate ideas; **TEKS 4.1B** discuss elements and principles; **TEKS 4.3B** compare and contrast artworks; **TEKS 4.3C** identify roles in art; **PDAS Domain I** active participation; **PDAS Domain II** learner-centered instruction; **TAKS Reading Objective 1** demonstrate understanding of texts;

Image **B** shows a huge relief sculpture on the side of a mountain. Gutzon Borglum created this sculpture of four United States Presidents—George Washington, Thomas Jefferson, Theodore Roosevelt, and Abraham Lincoln. Most sculptors use small, handheld tools for carving, but Borglum used dynamite and huge drills.

 Unknown artist, *Embarkation on Ship of Roman Troops*, (detail from Trajan's Column), about A.D. 106–113, marble. Rome, Italy.

Positive and Negative Space

Relief sculptures have both positive space and negative space. The raised areas make up the **positive space**. The **negative space** is where the artist cut away the original material to create the raised areas. Look at image **C**. What objects are shown in the positive space?

103

TEKS 4.1A; TAKS Reading Objectives 1, 3, 4

Science Connection

Physical Properties Encourage students to use their science textbooks or an encyclopedia to research the physical properties of several sculpting materials, such as sandstone, marble, and granite. Then have students use sensory knowledge and life experiences to communicate ideas about where these materials are found in their communities.

granite

marble

10-15 Minutes

Teach

Preview the Art Ask students to look at images A through E on pages 102–104. Have them describe what they see and name some details about each artwork. Use Discussion Card 1 and the following questions to guide the discussion. Then have students read pages 102–104.

A *Sacagawea coin* **How is this coin like others you have seen? How is it different? Who is pictured on the coin?**

B *Mount Rushmore National Memorial* **Which Presidents do you recognize?**

C *Embarkation on Ship of Roman Troops* **What do you think is happening in this scene?**

D *Head of Colossus of Ramses II* **Does this portrait remind you of any portraits you have seen before?** TEKS 4.3B

E *Moon Landing* **If you could touch this artwork, what do you think it would feel like?** TEKS 4.1A

Discuss Art Concepts Discuss with students the subtractive method and the resulting positive and negative space. Students should choose appropriate vocabulary to discuss the examples of positive space they see in the artworks: the face, letters, and numbers on the coin in image A; the Presidents' faces in image B; the men and part of the boat in image C; the subject's face and beard in image D; and the astronaut and ladder in image E. TEKS 4.1B

Then have students compare and contrast these artworks from a variety of cultural settings and identify the roles of those shown in image A, image B, and image E in American society.
TEKS 4.3B, TEKS 4.3C

Teach (continued)

LOCATE IT Have students turn to the map on pages 208–209 to locate Abu Simbel in Egypt. Tell them that the temple built at Abu Simbel, where the Colossus of Ramses II stands, was designed so that on two days out of the year, in February and October, the light of the morning sun would fill the entire interior of the structure.

Narrative Elements Ask students to look at image E. Have them identify

- the character in the sculpture.

- the setting of the sculpture.

Then ask students to discuss story events in the plot about the subject of this artwork.

Think Critically

Use the questions below to check students' understanding of lesson concepts.

1. **Focus Skill READING SKILL** **What is the setting of the scene in image C?** (Possible response: a ship long ago) **NARRATIVE ELEMENTS**

2. **Why is the process of carving called the subtractive method?** (The artist subtracts, or cuts away, some of the original material.) **PERCEPTION/AESTHETICS**

3. **WRITE** **Describe an event you would like to show in a relief sculpture.** **DESCRIPTIVE**
TAKS Writing Objective 1

LOCATE IT
The artwork in image D can be found in southern Egypt.

Abu Simbel
EGYPT

See Maps of Museums and Art Sites, pages 206–209.

Relief Sculptures in History

Throughout history, relief sculptures have been used to show leaders and to record historical or cultural events. Image **D** shows a relief sculpture of the ancient Egyptian ruler Ramses II. This sculpture was carved into a sandstone wall at the entrance of a temple in Egypt.

Image **E** shows a twentieth-century relief sculpture from the Texas State History Museum. It celebrates Neil Armstrong's historic first step on the moon. How did the sculptor of this artwork use positive and negative space?

 Mike O'Brien, *Moon Landing*, 2001, glass fiber reinforced concrete, 11 ft. × 16 ft. The Bob Bullock Texas State History Museum, Austin, Texas.

 Unknown artist, Head of Colossus of Ramses II, about 1250 B.C., sandstone. Abu Simbel, Egypt.

Think Critically

1. **Focus Skill READING SKILL** What is the setting of the scene in image **C**? **NARRATIVE ELEMENTS**

2. Why is the process of carving called the subtractive method?

3. **WRITE** Describe an event you would like to show in a relief sculpture.

TEKS 4.3A, TEKS 4.3B

Art Print 9

Display **Art Print 9** and distribute to students Discussion Card 5: *Portraits.* Have them compare and contrast the portrait in **Art Print 9** with the portraits in this lesson. Students should note the variety of cultural settings among the artworks. Have students use their understanding of art history and culture to identify simple main ideas expressed in the portraits.

ART PRINT 9

Limestone Bust of Queen Nefertiti
by Unknown Artist

★ TEKS 4.1B discuss elements and principles; TEKS 4.2B design original artworks; TEKS 4.2C produce artworks; TEKS 4.3A identify main ideas; TEKS 4.3B compare and contrast artworks; PDAS Domain III evaluation and feedback; PDAS Domain IV classroom management; TAKS Writing Objective 1 composition

Artist's Workshop

Carve a Relief Sculpture

PLAN

Choose a friend or classmate whose portrait you would like to create. Sketch a portrait of your friend's face.

CREATE

1. Flatten a slab of clay. Then trim the edges with a plastic knife to form a background for your relief sculpture.

2. Use a pencil point to carve the outline of your portrait. Use a craft stick or other carving tool to carve away clay to create negative space.

3. Use a pencil point or one end of an opened paper clip to carve details into the clay.

REFLECT

Point out the positive space and negative space in your relief sculpture.

MATERIALS

- pencil
- sketchbook
- clay
- plastic knife
- sharpened pencil or paper clip
- craft stick

 Safety Tips Use tools one at a time. Remember to point sharp objects away from your body.

105

 30-40 Minutes

Artist's Workshop

Carve a Relief Sculpture

PLAN Have students read the activity steps on page 105. Distribute *Teacher Resource Book* page 50 to help students with facial proportions.

CREATE Display the Art Safety poster, and have students read the Safety Tips on page 105 before beginning their relief sculptures. As students design their portraits, have them invent ways to produce their sculptures using a variety of art materials and carving tools. TEKS 4.2B, TEKS 4.2C

REFLECT Have students choose appropriate vocabulary to discuss their use of positive and negative space in their relief sculptures. SELF-EVALUATION TEKS 4.1B

5-10 Minutes

Wrap-Up

Informal Assessment PDAS Domain III

- **How did looking at the images in this lesson help you make your relief sculpture?** (Responses will vary.) EVALUATION/CRITICISM

- **What details could you add to your relief sculpture to tell something about your subject's personality?** (Responses will vary.) NARRATIVE ELEMENTS

Extend Through Writing TAKS Writing Objective 1

DESCRIPTIVE PARAGRAPH Have students write a paragraph describing their artwork, including the materials they used and the steps involved in the process.

Recommended Reading

Rushmore by Lynn Curlee. Scholastic, 1999. CHALLENGING

 PDAS Domain IV

Activity Options

Quick Activity Have students sketch a design for two sides of a coin.

Early Finishers Have students create a clay frame for their relief sculpture.

Challenge See *Teacher Resource Book*, p. 64.

 PDAS Domain IV

ESL Use **visuals** to support **comprehensible input** for 3-D objects. Display *Picture Cards Collection*, cards 6, 38, 57, and 117 for students to discuss and to point out positive space and negative space.

See also *Picture Card Bank* **CD-ROM.**

 astronaut

PDAS Domains I, II

Marisol Escobar

ARTIST BIOGRAPHY

DISCUSS THE IMAGES

Have students read pages 106 and 107.

- Invite students to talk about what they see in image A. Explain that the subject of the sculpture is a former president of France. Charles deGaulle led the French resistance against the Germans in World War II and later helped form France's current system of government.

- Display **Art Print 8** and explain to students that this is another sculpture by Marisol. Have students identify the simple main idea expressed in this group sculpture. TEKS 4.3A

- Tell students that one art critic compared Marisol to a toymaker. Ask students if they agree or disagree with the critic's observation, and why. Explain that many of Marisol's sculptures show her subjects in a light, humorous way. Ask students to interpret the ideas and moods in this portfolio of Marisol's work and discuss what they found humorous in the artwork. TEKS 4.4B

Marisol Escobar

How might an artist represent herself and others in an artwork?

As a young girl, Marisol Escobar dreamed of becoming an artist. She first studied art at the age of sixteen, hoping to become a painter. Encouraged by her father, she later studied in Paris and New York.

As Marisol studied art and met other artists, she learned about other ways of expressing herself, besides painting. She began to experiment with clay and wood carving, which she combined in her artwork.

Marisol, who decided to use just her first name, became known for her witty, large wooden figures. She painted the figures and attached everyday objects and pieces of her own clothing to them. She sometimes included plaster casts of her own face, hands, and feet. Marisol's artwork often expressed her feelings about herself and the world around her in a humorous way.

A Marisol, *President Charles DeGaulle*, 1967, wood, plaster, and mirror, 107¼ in. x 86¼ in. x 31⅞ in. Smithsonian American Art Museum, Washington, D.C.

106

Background Information

About the Artist

Marisol Escobar (mah•ree•SOHL es•koh•VAR) (1930–) uses carpentry tools—such as power saws and axes—along with traditional art materials to create her unique artwork. Besides her whimsical wooden figures, Marisol has also created life-size portrait figures, including those of President Lyndon B. Johnson, Queen Elizabeth II, and comedian Bob Hope.

For additional information about the artist, see pp. R44–R65.

For related artworks, see **Electronic Art Gallery CD-ROM, Intermediate.**

Marisol has created many sculptures of friends, world leaders, and famous artists. Look at images **A** and **B**. What objects in the sculptures surprise you? How do you think the artist feels about the subjects of these artworks?

DID YOU KNOW?

Marisol's sculpture *The Generals* shows George Washington and Simón Bolívar on a horse. This artwork contains a built-in phonograph that plays military music. Bolívar is known as the George Washington of South America. He led several revolutions against Spanish rule and became president of Colombia and of Peru.

B Marisol, *The Generals*, 1961–1962, wood and mixed media, 87 in. x 28 in. x 76 in. Albright-Knox Art Gallery, Buffalo, New York.

Think About Art

Think of a person you admire. If Marisol created a sculpture of that person, what objects might she include?

GO ONLINE Multimedia Biographies
Visit *The Learning Site*
www.harcourtschool.com

107

DID YOU KNOW?

Use the facts below to discuss George Washington (1732–1799) and Simón Bolívar (1783–1830) with students.

- When he was President, George Washington had his portrait painted by more than a dozen artists.

- The following South American countries honor Simón Bolívar as the leader who freed their nations from the rule of Spain: Venezuela, Colombia, Panama, Ecuador, Peru, and Bolivia.

Think About Art

Think of a person you admire. If Marisol were creating a sculpture of that person, what objects might the sculpture include?
(Responses will vary.) **PERSONAL RESPONSE**

ARTIST'S EYE ACTIVITY

Marisol-Style Sculptures   Ask students to brainstorm a list of common objects and forms they would use in a group sculpture that communicates ideas about their family using sensory knowledge and life experiences. Have students share their ideas with classmates.   TEKS 4.1A

 **Multimedia Biographies**
Visit *The Learning Site*
www.harcourtschool.com

Social Studies Connection

Marisol and Her Subjects   Tell students that Marisol created many artworks using people whom she admired as her subjects, including world leaders, public figures, and fellow artists.

For additional cross-curricular suggestions, see Art Transparency 9.

TEKS 4.4B
Student Art Show

Portfolios and Exhibitions
Periodically during this unit, help students create an exhibit of their finished artworks. Ask students to interpret ideas and moods in peers' portfolios and exhibitions. See *Teacher Edition* page 204 for ideas on planning and preparing a student art exhibition.

Lesson 15

Lesson 15

PDAS Domains I, II

Sculpture in History

OBJECTIVES
- Choose appropriate vocabulary to identify and compare sculpture
- Design and carve an original soap sculpture
- Identify narrative elements in artworks

RESOURCES
- Art Prints 8, 9, 11
- Reading Skill Card 3
- Discussion Cards 1, 5, pp. R34, R36
- Electronic Art Gallery CD-ROM, Intermediate

GO ONLINE Multimedia Art Glossary and Biographies
Visit *The Learning Site*
www.harcourtschool.com

5 Minutes

Warm-Up

Build Background Display **Art Prints 8** and **9**, and ask students to describe similarities and differences between the ancient and the modern sculpture. Point out the different materials used in each artwork, and ask students to discuss the effects the different materials have on the artwork. Explain that in this lesson students will learn about the different materials and techniques that artists from different cultures have used to create free-standing sculptures. TEKS 4.3B

Vocabulary

form

terra-cotta

Sculpture in History

A sculpture is an example of a **form**. A form is a three-dimensional shape. It has length, width, and height. One type of sculpture is a statue. A statue takes up positive space. It is surrounded on all sides by negative space.

Ancient Statues

Look at image **A**, which shows a statue of a boy. What does the boy's clothing tell you about when or where he lived? The ancient Greeks and Romans carved detailed statues, with lifelike proportions, out of marble. They used the subtractive method to shape blocks of marble into portraits of their leaders and other important people.

 Unknown artist, *Neron Child*, marble. The Louvre Museum, Paris, France.

108

 Background Information

About the Artists

C Frederic S. Remington's (1861–1909) popular sculptures were reproduced for sale to the public.

D Man Ray (1890–1976) created "rayographs" by placing objects on light-sensitive paper and developing the images like traditional photographs.

For additional information about the artists, see pp. R44–R65.

For related artworks, see **Electronic Art Gallery CD-ROM, Intermediate.**

★ TEKS 4.1A communicate ideas; TEKS 4.3B compare and contrast artworks; TEKS 4.3C identify roles of art; TEKS 4.4B interpret artworks by peers and others; PDAS Domain I active participation; PDAS Domain II learner-centered instruction; TAKS Reading Objective 1 demonstrate understanding of texts; *(continued)*

Image **B** shows a statue from ancient China. In the third century B.C., the first Chinese emperor wanted to be buried with an army of soldiers to protect him after he died. Thousands of statues like this one were sculpted in terra-cotta. **Terra-cotta** is a kind of reddish brown clay that sculptors shape with their hands and then bake until it hardens.

The Chinese statues have different designs on their uniforms and armor. These designs show each soldier's rank. The emperor's artists also sculpted horses, chariots, and weapons for the soldiers. Archaeologists are still uncovering this army of statues to learn more about this ancient Chinese civilization.

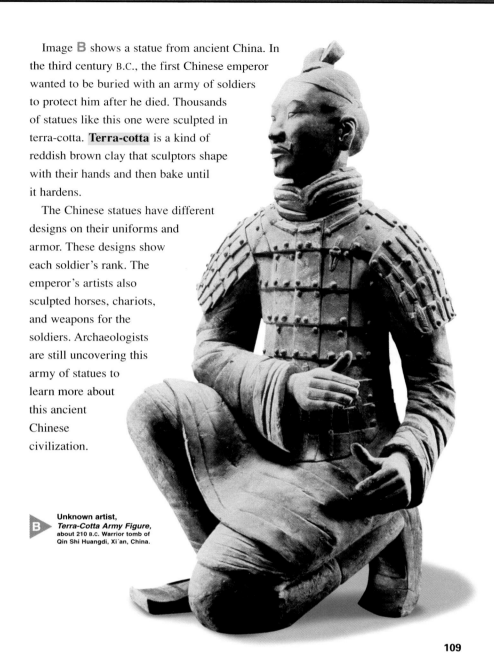

B Unknown artist,
Terra-Cotta Army Figure,
about 210 B.C. Warrior tomb of
Qin Shi Huangdi, Xi'an, China.

109

TEKS 4.3C; TAKS Reading Objectives 1, 3, 4

Social Studies Connection

State Statues   Tell students that Huntsville, Texas, is the home of the world's tallest statue of an American hero— Sam Houston. Sculpted by artist David Adickes from 1992 to 1994, the statue stands sixty-seven feet tall on a ten-foot-tall base. Ask students to use encyclopedias or online resources to research famous statues in their home states or communities, and the sculptors who made them. Have students identify the roles of statues such as these in American society and present their findings to their classmates.

10-15 Minutes

Teach

Preview the Art   Have students preview images A through D on pages 108–110. Ask them to talk about similarities among and differences between the artworks. Use Discussion Card 1 and the questions below to guide the discussion. Then have students read pages 108–110.

A *Neron Child*   **What do you think this boy is doing?**

B *Terra-Cotta Army Figure*   **What do the title and the subject's clothing tell you about him?**

C *The Rattlesnake*   **What is happening in this sculpture? If you were the person on the horse, how would you feel? Why?**   TEKS 4.1A

D *Man Ray*   **What is the first thing you notice in this artwork? Why?**

Discuss Art Concepts   Discuss with students the concept of form by having them compare shapes such as circles and squares with forms such as spheres and cubes, noting the three-dimensional quality of forms. Then have students compare and contrast the artworks in images A, B, and C, noting the variety of cultural settings.   TEKS 4.3B

Point out the robes the boy in image A is wearing and explain to students that this was the style of clothing typically worn in ancient Greece and Rome. Have students describe the statues' clothing in images B and C. Ask students to point out the details that identify the figure in image B as a warrior and the figure on horseback in image C as a cowhand.

Discuss with students the different materials used by the artists in images A, B, C, and D. Ask them which material—marble, terra-cotta, or bronze— they would prefer to use in a sculpture, and why.

Teach (continued)

LOCATE IT Have students turn to the map on pages 206–207 and locate Fort Worth, Texas. Tell students that the Amon Carter Museum is home to the largest collection of art by Frederic Remington in the world.

Narrative Elements Have students examine image D and use their imaginations to identify

- the character and setting in the artwork.
- what is happening in the artwork, as well as what might have happened just before and just after the scene.

Then ask students to interpret the ideas in each artwork in this lesson and identify the one they think tells the most interesting story, and why.
TEKS 4.4B

Think Critically

Use the questions below to check students' understanding of lesson concepts.

1. **READING SKILL** **What do you think the characters, setting, and plot are in image C?** (Possible responses: Setting: the American frontier in the nineteenth century; Characters: a cowboy and his horse; Plot: The horse is surprised by a rattlesnake on the trail.)
NARRATIVE ELEMENTS TEKS 4.4B

2. **What are some differences between the ancient and modern statues shown in this lesson?** (Possible response: The ancient statues were made from marble or clay. The modern ones are made of materials such as plexiglass.)
PERCEPTION/AESTHETICS TEKS 4.3B

3. **WRITE** **Write a short story about the statue in image B. Include characters, setting, and plot.** NARRATIVE TEKS 4.4B; TAKS Writing Objective 1

★ TEKS 4.2B design original artworks; TEKS 4.2C produce artworks; TEKS 4.3B compare and contrast artworks; TEKS 4.4A form conclusions about personal artworks; TEKS 4.4B interpret artworks by peers and others; PDAS Domain III evaluation and feedback; PDAS Domain IV classroom management; (continued)

LOCATE IT
The original version of the artwork in image **C** can be found at the Amon Carter Museum in Fort Worth, Texas.

See Maps of Museums and Art Sites, pages 206–209.

Modern Materials

Over time, sculptors began to use materials other than stone and clay for their art. The sculptures shown in images **C** and **D** were made in the twentieth century. They are made of bronze, a kind of metal.

Do the subjects of image **C** seem to be in motion? What parts of the sculpture give the sense that the subjects are moving?

C Frederic Remington, *The Rattlesnake*, 1905, bronze reproduction, 22⅝ in. × 13 in. Buffalo Bill Historical Center, Cody, Wyoming.

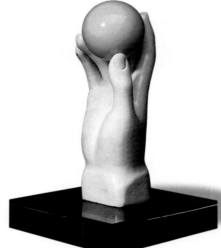

D Man Ray, *Man Ray*, 1971, painted bronze and plexiglass, 8 in. high without base.

Think Critically

1. **READING SKILL** What do you think the characters, setting, and plot are in image **C**? NARRATIVE ELEMENTS

2. What are some differences between the ancient and modern statues shown in this lesson?

3. **WRITE** Write a short story about the statue in image **B**. Include characters, setting, and plot.

110

TEKS 4.3B
Art Print 11

Display **Art Print 11** and distribute to students Discussion Card 5: *Portraits.* Have students compare this painted portrait to the artworks in this lesson.

ART PRINT 11

Jeanne Hebuterne with Hat
by Amedeo Modigliani

Artist's Workshop

Carve a Soap Sculpture

PLAN

Find a magazine or newspaper photograph of an animal you would like to sculpt.

CREATE

1. Place a bar of soap on a sheet of newsprint. Use a toothpick or the end of a paper clip to carve the outline of your animal on both sides of the soap.

2. Use a plastic knife to shave away the soap around the outline.

3. When you are finished, use a scrubber sponge to smooth the surface of the sculpture.

REFLECT

What kind of animal did you sculpt? How did you use the subtractive method?

MATERIALS

- magazines or newspapers
- newsprint
- bar of soap
- toothpick or paper clip
- plastic knife
- scrubber sponge

Quick Tip Try not to cut away big pieces of the soap all at once. Work slowly, carving a little at a time.

111

Artist's Workshop

30-40 Minutes

Create a Soap Sculpture

PLAN Have students read the activity steps on page 111. Encourage students to select an animal with simple lines and few details.

CREATE As they design and create their sculptures, tell students to experiment with a variety of carving tools and materials to invent ways to produce different effects. TEKS 4.2B, TEKS 4.2C

REFLECT Have students tell about the animal they carved and explain how they used the subtractive method in their sculptures. SELF-EVALUATION TEKS 4.4A

5-10 Minutes

Wrap-Up

Informal Assessment PDAS Domain III

- **Describe the setting in which your animal might live.** (Responses will vary.) NARRATIVE ELEMENTS

- **Compare the steps involved in painting a portrait and carving a sculpture. Which do you prefer to do? Why?** (Responses will vary.) EVALUATION/CRITICISM

Extend Through Writing

TAKS Writing Objectives 1, 5

NARRATIVE STORY Have students write a story about the animal they carved in its natural environment. Encourage them to use an interesting and imaginative plot in their stories.

Recommended Reading

The Sculptor's Eye: Looking at Contemporary American Art by Jan Greenberg and Sandra Jordan. Delacorte Press, 1993. CHALLENGING

Activity Options

PDAS Domain IV

Quick Activity Have students carve a simple design into a bar of soap.

Early Finishers Have students carve textures and other details into their animal sculptures.

Challenge See *Teacher Resource Book,* p. 65.

PDAS Domain IV

ESL Use **visuals** to support **comprehensible input** for animal names. Display *Picture Cards Collection*, cards 14, 23, 40, and 53 for students to discuss and reference.

See also *Picture Card Bank* CD-ROM, Category: Animals/Pets.

bird

PDAS Domain IV

Review and Reflect

 Have students reflect on what they have learned about the ways that artists use proportion, rhythm, and form to create artworks that portray people. Display **Art Prints 7, 8, 9, 2,** and **11.** Encourage small groups of students to use Discussion Cards 4, 5, and 7 and their completed Word Knowledge Charts to discuss what they learned about the vocabulary and concepts in this unit.

Vocabulary and Concepts

Have students read each sentence and choose the letter of the word or phrase that best completes it. (1. A; 2. G; 3. C; 4. G; 5. B)

READING SKILL

Narrative Elements

Have students write their stories and trade them with a classmate. Then ask them to complete a diagram like the one on page 112 to list the narrative elements in their classmate's story.
TAKS Writing Objectives 1, 3, 4

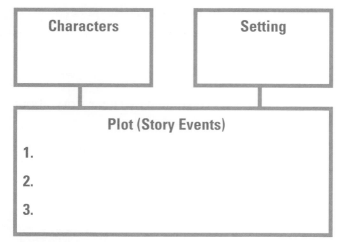

Unit 3 Review and Reflect

Vocabulary and Concepts

Choose the letter of the word or phrase that best completes each sentence.

1 Artworks that artists create of themselves are ___.

  A self-portraits   **C** patterns

  B portraits   **D** forms

2 ___ is a type of abstract art.

  F Terra-cotta   **H** Form

  G Cubism   **J** Rhythm

3 ___ is the visual beat created by repeated lines and shapes.

  A Abstract art   **C** Rhythm

  B Color   **D** Space

4 In a relief sculpture, the raised area is called ___ space.

  F abstract   **H** rhythm

  G positive   **J** negative

5 A ___ is a three-dimensional shape.

  A pattern   **C** distortion

  B form   **D** terra-cotta

READING SKILL

Narrative Elements

Select an artwork in this unit, and write a story about it. Trade stories with a partner. Use a diagram like this to record the narrative elements in your partner's story.

Characters		Setting

Plot (Story Events)
1.
2.
3.

112

 TEKS 4.1A, TEKS 4.2A, TEKS 4.4B

Home and Community Connection

School-Home Connection
Copy and distribute *Teacher Resource Book* pp. 89–90. After completing the unit, students can work at home to create a portrait of a family member. Students should communicate ideas about family, using sensory knowledge and life experiences, and then integrate a variety of ideas about their subject's personality into their artwork.

Community Connection
You may want to request permission from your city hall to hold an exhibition of students' artworks in a public place. During the exhibition, have students interpret the ideas and moods in their peers' artwork.

Write About Art

Choose a piece of your own artwork, and write a story about it.
Describe the characters, setting, and events in the plot. Use a
diagram like the one on page 112 to help you plan your writing.

REMEMBER — YOU SHOULD

- use descriptive words that make your story interesting.

- use correct grammar, spelling, and punctuation.

Critic's Corner

Look at *Golconda* by René Magritte to answer the questions below.

René Magritte, *Golconda*,
1953, oil on canvas, 31⅝ in. × 39¾ in.
Menil Foundation, Houston, Texas.

DESCRIBE What do you think are the characters, setting, and plot in
the artwork?

ANALYZE How has the artist created rhythm in this artwork?

INTERPRET What ideas do you think the artist expressed in this
artwork?

EVALUATE What is your opinion of the story this artwork tells?

113

PDAS Domain III

Assessment

Portfolio Assessment

Work with students to choose a piece of their artwork to include in their
portfolios. Suggest that they decide which piece best fulfilled the assignment or which piece they liked best for another reason. You may want to
provide specific feedback that targets students' use of elements, principles, and techniques. See also Portfolio Recording Form, p. R32.

Additional Assessment Options

- Progress Recording Form, p. R33
- Artist's Workshop Rubrics (Self/Teacher and Peer), pp. R30–R31
- Unit 3 Test, *Teacher Resource Book,* p. 101

Write About Art

Story Read aloud the prompt with students.
Suggest that students use the diagram on page 112
to help them plan their stories. Remind students
to use correct spelling, punctuation, and grammar
as they write their stories. Have students proofread their work. TAKS Writing Objectives 1, 2, 4, 6

Critic's Corner

RESPONSE/EVALUATION Use the steps below
to guide students in analyzing *Golconda* by René
Magritte (ruh•NAY ma•GREET). See also
Discussion Card 2, p. R34.

DESCRIBE Discuss with students the characters
(men in black suits and hats), the setting (building
with a red roof), and the plot (the men are floating
in the air) in the painting. TEKS 4.4B

ANALYZE Discuss with students the way the
repeated men and windows create rhythm.

INTERPRET Discuss students' responses as they
try to interpret the ideas in the artwork. TEKS 4.4B

EVALUATE Based on their observations, ask
students to present their opinions. Discuss with
students their ideas about the story that *Golconda*
may tell. TEKS 4.4B

TAKS Test Preparation: Reading and Writing
Through Art, pp. 27–47

Unit 4

Pattern and Balance
Art Reflects Culture

Artists from different cultures express their thoughts and feelings about the world in ways that have special meaning to them. They use a variety of materials and techniques to depict important ideas. In this unit, students will learn about artworks from many cultures, both past and present.

Resources

- Unit 4 Art Prints (10–12)
- Additional Art Prints (7, 9)
- Art Transparencies 10–12
- Test Preparation: Reading and Writing Through Art, pp. 48–52
- Artist's Workshop Activities: English and Spanish, pp. 31–40
- Encyclopedia of Artists and Art History, pp. R44–R65
- Picture Cards Collection, cards 41, 59, 87, 108, 109

Using the Art Prints

- Discussion Cards, pp. R34–R38
- Teaching suggestions, backs of Art Prints
- Art Print Teaching Suggestions: Spanish

Teacher Resource Book

- Vocabulary Cards in English and Spanish, pp. 19–22
- Reading Skill Card 4, p. 34
- Copying Masters, pp. 39, 40
- Challenge Activities, pp. 66–70
- School-Home Connection: English/Spanish, pp. 91–92
- Unit 4 Test, p. 102

Technology Resources

 Electronic Art Gallery CD-ROM, Intermediate
Picture Card Bank CD-ROM

 Visit *The Learning Site*
www.harcourtschool.com

- Multimedia Art Glossary
- Multimedia Biographies
- Reading Skills and Activities

Art Prints for This Unit

ART PRINT 10

Panamanian Cuna Mola with Iguanas and Birds
by Unknown Artist

ART PRINT 11

Jeanne Hebuterne with Hat
by Amedeo Modigliani

ART PRINT 12

Three Flags
by Jasper Johns

ART PRINT 7

American Gothic
by Grant Wood

ART PRINT 9

Limestone Bust of Queen Nefertiti
by Unknown Artist

Lesson	Objectives and Vocabulary	Art Images	Production/Materials

Focus Skill — Compare and Contrast, pp. 116–117

16 FIBER ART pp. 118–121 — 30–60 minutes	• Choose appropriate vocabulary to discuss pattern in artworks • Design and create an original reverse weaving • *Focus Skill* Compare and contrast artworks **Vocabulary: weaving, pattern, tapestry**	• **Navajo traditional shawl** • **Detail of African kente cloth** • **Chinese Emperor's Twelve Symbol Robe** • **Reverse Weaving** by Vicky, age 9	**Create a Reverse Weaving** ❏ 6 in. × 6 in. burlap pieces ❏ colored yarn ❏ ruler ❏ scissors
17 BALANCE IN MASKS pp. 122–125 — 30–60 minutes	• Choose appropriate vocabulary to identify balance in artworks • Design and create an original paper mask • *Focus Skill* Compare and contrast artworks **Vocabulary: vertical axis, symmetrical balance**	• **Aztec mask** • **African Kwele mask** • **Inuit finger masks** • **Paper sculpture mask** by Caleb, age 9	**Create a Paper Mask** ❏ poster board ❏ scissors ❏ markers or paint ❏ paintbrushes ❏ glue ❏ colored paper ❏ decorative materials

Art ↔ Social Studies Connection: **Amedeo Modigliani, pp. 126–127**

18 PAPER ART pp. 128–131 — 30–60 minutes	• Choose appropriate vocabulary to discuss balance in artworks • Recognize the use of visual weight to create balance in artworks • Design and create an original paper cutting • *Focus Skill* Compare and contrast artworks **Vocabulary: radial balance, asymmetrical balance, visual weight**	• **Window Flowers for New Year** • **Paper cutting in Polish traditional style** by Bernadine Jendrzejczak • **Flowery Words: Stories, Poems, Song, History, & Wisdom** by Carmen Lomas Garza	**Create a Paper Cutting** ❏ pencil ❏ white paper ❏ scissors ❏ colored pencils or markers
19 FOLK ART pp. 132–135 — 30–60 minutes	• Recognize folk art style in artworks • Choose appropriate vocabulary to discuss balance in artworks • Design and create an original folk art painting • *Focus Skill* Compare and contrast artworks **Vocabulary: folk art**	• **The Old Checkered House** by Grandma Moses • **Creole Dance** by Pedro Figari • **Bird Tree**	**Create a Folk Art Painting** ❏ pencil ❏ white paper ❏ tempera paint ❏ paintbrushes ❏ water bowl

Art ↔ Social Studies Connection: **Cowhands in Art, pp. 136–137**

20 SYMBOLS IN ART pp. 138–141 — 30–60 minutes	• Identify the use of symbols in artworks • Design and create an original print with a symbol • *Focus Skill* Compare and contrast artworks **Vocabulary: symbols**	• **The Fourth of July** by Frederick Childe Hassam • **The American Farm** by Warren Kimble • **George Washington** by Sante Graziani	**Create a Print** ❏ pencil ❏ foam tray ❏ tempera paint ❏ foam brush ❏ water bowl ❏ white or colored paper

✓ Review and Reflect, pp. 142–143

Compare and Contrast pp. 116–117

Focus Skill

Opportunities for application of the skill are provided on pp. 120, 124, 130, 134, 140, 142, and 143.

Resources and Technology	Suggested Literature	Across the Curriculum
• Art Print 10 • Reading Skill Card 4 • Discussion Cards 1, 4, pp. R34, R35 ⊘ Electronic Art Gallery CD-ROM, Intermediate	*The Chief's Blanket* by Michael Chanin 	**Social Studies** Navajo Art, p. 119 **Reading** Compare and Contrast, p. 120 **Writing** Museum Card, p. 121
• Art Print 9 • Reading Skill Card 4 • Discussion Cards 1, 4, pp. R34, R35 ⊘ Electronic Art Gallery CD-ROM, Intermediate	*Start with Art: Animals* by Sue Lacey 	**Social Studies** Inuit Life, p. 123 **Reading** Compare and Contrast, p. 124 **Writing** Story, p. 125
• Art Print 10 • Reading Skill Card 4 • Discussion Cards 1, 4, pp. R34, R35 • Color Wheel Poster ⊘ Electronic Art Gallery CD-ROM, Intermediate	*Butterflies for Kiri* by Cathryn Fallwell 	**Social Studies** Kirigami, p. 129 **Reading** Compare and Contrast, p. 130 **Writing** Descriptive Paragraph, p. 131
• Art Print 10 • Reading Skill Card 4 • Discussion Cards 1, 10, pp. R34, R38 ⊘ Electronic Art Gallery CD-ROM, Intermediate	*Can a Coal Scuttle Fly?* by Camay Calloway Murphy 	**Social Studies** Folk Music, p. 133 **Reading** Compare and Contrast, p. 134 **Writing** Story, p. 135
• Art Print 12 • Reading Skill Card 4 • Discussion Cards 1, 9, pp. R34, R38 ⊘ Electronic Art Gallery CD-ROM, Intermediate	*The Talking Cloth* by Rhonda Mitchell 	**Social Studies** Flags Around the World, p. 139 **Reading** Compare and Contrast, p. 140 **Writing** Poem, p. 141

Art Puzzlers

Present these art puzzlers to students at the beginning or end of a class or when students finish an assignment early.

• Think about what kinds of shapes and colors you'd like to see in a **pattern.** Cut out those shapes from construction paper to make a model of the pattern. TEKS 4.2C

• Find at least two objects that show **symmetrical balance.** Point out how they are balanced.

• Draw a design that shows **radial balance.** TEKS 4.2B

• Describe a cultural event in your community that you would like to show in a piece of **folk art.** Explain why you chose that event, and tell what materials you would use to create the artwork. TEKS 4.1A

• Think of a **symbol** you see around you every day. Draw the symbol and write a sentence about what it means. TEKS 4.2B

 School-Home Connection
The activities above are included in the School-Home Connection for this unit. See *Teacher Resource Book,* pp. 91–92.

Assessment Options

• Rubrics and Recording Forms, pp. R30–R33
• Unit 4 Test, *Teacher Resource Book,* p. 102

 Visit *The Learning Site:*
www.harcourtschool.com

Artist's Workshops PREVIEW

Use these pages to help you gather and organize materials for the production activity in each lesson.

LESSON	MATERIALS

16 Create a Reverse Weaving p. 121

- 6 in. × 6 in. burlap pieces
- colored yarn
- ruler
- scissors

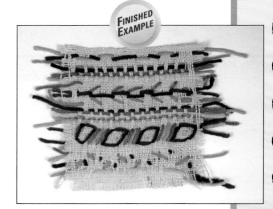

FINISHED EXAMPLE

Objective: To design and create an original reverse weaving that shows patterns

 30–40 minutes

Challenge Activity: See *Teacher Resource Book*, page 66.

LESSON

17 Create a Paper Mask p. 125

- pencil
- poster board
- scissors
- markers or paint
- paintbrushes
- glue
- colored paper
- decorative materials

FINISHED EXAMPLE

Objective: To design and create an original paper mask that shows symmetrical balance

 30–40 minutes

Challenge Activity: See *Teacher Resource Book*, page 67.

Safety Tips For safety information, see Art Safety, page R4, or the Art Safety Poster.

Quick Tip For information on media and techniques, see pp. R15–R23.

LESSON	MATERIALS

18 Create a Paper Cutting p. 131

Objective: To design and create an original paper cutting, using visual weight to create balance

 30–40 minutes

Challenge Activity: See *Teacher Resource Book,* page 68.

- pencil
- sketchbook
- white paper
- scissors
- colored pencils or markers

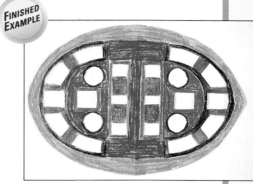

LESSON

19 Create a Folk Art Painting p. 135

Objective: To show symmetrical or asymmetrical balance in an original folk art painting

 30–40 minutes

Challenge Activity: See *Teacher Resource Book,* page 69.

- pencil
- sketchbook
- white paper
- tempera paint
- paintbrushes
- water bowl

LESSON

20 Create a Print p. 141

Objective: To design and create an original print with a symbol

 30–40 minutes

Challenge Activity: See *Teacher Resource Book,* page 70.

- pencil
- sketchbook
- foam tray
- tempera paint
- foam brush
- water bowl
- white or colored paper

PDAS Domains I, II

Art Reflects Culture

PREVIEW THE UNIT

Tell students that in this unit they will view artworks from many cultures. Invite students to preview this unit by reading the lesson titles and examining the art images.

STEP INTO THE ART

Have students examine the artwork on pages 114 and 115 and describe what they see. Then read page 115 with students, and discuss their answers to the questions about the subjects of the artworks.

- **What might they be talking about?** Students may suggest that the women are discussing the quilt or the man with the flowers.

- **What would you ask them?** Students may suggest asking questions about the quilt, the women's lives, or the setting of the artwork.

- **What would you say to Vincent van Gogh?** Remind students that they have seen artwork by van Gogh on page 33. Encourage them to think about why van Gogh is in the artwork.

SHARE BACKGROUND INFORMATION

Tell students that this artwork is a story quilt. It shows a group of historical African American women leaders, including Sojourner Truth, Rosa Parks, and Mary McLeod Bethune. Explain that the Dutch artist Vincent van Gogh, famous for his paintings of sunflowers, lived for a year in the south of France, in the town of Arles.

LOCATE IT See **Using the Maps of Museums and Art Sites,** p. R2.

Faith Ringgold, *The Sunflower Quilting Bee at Arles*, 1996, color lithograph, 22 in. × 30 in.

 LOCATE IT

This painting can be found at the Philadelphia Museum of Art in Philadelphia, Pennsylvania.

See Maps of Museums and Art Sites, pages 206–209.

PENNSYLVANIA

Philadelphia

114

Background Information

About the Artist

Faith Ringgold (1930–), best known for her quilts, which combine painting, fabric, and storytelling, is also an author of children's books. Her first published book, *Tar Beach*, is based on her story quilt of the same name.

For additional information about Faith Ringgold, see the Encyclopedia of Artists and Art History, pp. R44–R65, and the Gallery of Artists, *Student Edition* pp. 240–253.

 For related artworks, see **Electronic Art Gallery CD-ROM, Intermediate.**

Art Reflects Culture

Step into the Art

Imagine that you could step into this artwork and join the women holding the quilt. What might they be talking about? What would you ask them? The man on the right side of the image is the artist Vincent van Gogh. What would you say to him?

Unit Vocabulary

weaving	symmetrical balance	visual weight
pattern	radial balance	folk art
tapestry	asymmetrical balance	symbols
vertical axis		

ABOUT THE ARTIST

See Gallery of Artists, pages 240–253.

 Multimedia Art Glossary
Visit *The Learning Site*
www.harcourtschool.com

115

Unit Vocabulary

Read aloud the terms with students, and use the Word Knowledge Chart below to assess and discuss their prior knowledge.

weaving a cloth created from fibers that have been interlaced, or woven together

pattern a design made of repeated lines, shapes, or colors

tapestry a type of weaving that has colorful designs or scenes in it

vertical axis an invisible line that divides the left and right sides of an image

symmetrical balance a type of balance created when the left and right sides of an artwork match

radial balance a type of balance in which a pattern extends from the center of the artwork, like the spokes of a wheel

asymmetrical balance a type of balance achieved when two sides of an artwork are different but have equal visual weight

visual weight the emphasis given to each side of an artwork to create a sense of balance

folk art a style of art made by people who have had little formal training in art

symbol a picture or object that stands for an idea

Vocabulary Resources

- Vocabulary Cards in English and Spanish: *Teacher Resource Book,* pp. 19–22
- Student Edition Glossary, pp. 254–261

 Multimedia Art Glossary
Visit *The Learning Site*
www.harcourtschool.com

Language Arts Connection

Students may create a chart like the one below to identify familiar and unfamiliar vocabulary terms. Encourage them to add information to their charts as they work through this unit.

WORD KNOWLEDGE CHART		
I know this term.	I have seen this term before.	I have never seen this term.

Unit 4

Focus Skill **READING SKILL**

PDAS Domains I, II

Compare and Contrast

SKILL TRACE	
COMPARE AND CONTRAST	
Introduce	pp. 116–117
Review	pp. 120, 124, 130, 134, 140, 142

DISCUSS THE SKILL

Access Prior Knowledge   Display two classroom objects and ask students to tell how they are alike and how they are different. Explain that when you think about how things are alike, you compare them. When you think about how things are different, you contrast them. Tell students that comparing and contrasting artworks can help them better understand what they see.

APPLY TO ART

Compare and Contrast   Have students read page 116 and look at the images. Use the information on page 116 to have students compare and contrast the selected artworks from a variety of cultural settings. Students should point out that the two objects are different because they come from different locations, different cultures, and different time periods. TEKS 4.3B

Focus Skill **READING SKILL**

Compare and Contrast

When you think about how things are alike, you *compare*.
When you think about how things are different, you *contrast*.

Look at the objects shown below. They are **alike** in these ways:

- Both are pieces of clothing with long sleeves.
- Both have designs on them.

They are **different** in these ways:

- Image **A** has organic shapes in its design. Image **B** has geometric shapes in its design.
- Image **B** has fringe, and image **A** does not.

A Unknown artist, British herald's tunic, 1707–1714, silk, metallic thread, beads, back length 34 in. Philadelphia Museum of Art, Philadelphia, Pennsylvania.

B Unknown artist, Indian warrior's shirt, buckskin with beadwork and fringe, 30 in. vertical.

116

FYI **Background Information**

Art History

A A **tunic** is a coat with partially open sides. Tunics such as this one were worn in eighteenth-century England. The objects on this tunic include the three lions of England and the lion of Scotland next to the harp of Ireland. The objects are clues that this tunic was made some time after 1707, the year when the parliaments of England and Scotland were combined.

For related artworks, see **Electronic Art Gallery CD-ROM, Intermediate.**

★ TEKS 4.3B compare and contrast artworks; **PDAS Domain I** active participation; **PDAS Domain II** learner-centered instruction; **PDAS Domain IV** classroom management; **TAKS Reading Objective 1** demonstrate understanding of texts; **TAKS Reading Objective 4** apply critical-thinking skills

Comparing and contrasting can help you understand what you read. Read this passage to learn more about the clothing in images **A** and **B**.

Eighteenth-century British soldiers and royalty decorated their garments, or clothing, with specific designs so that others could recognize them quickly. The Plains Indians of North America decorated their clothing with colorful geometric shapes that told about their tribes. The British garments were made of silk. The Indians used animal hides and glass beads to make their garments.

Compare and contrast the two types of garments. You can use a Venn diagram like this to help you.

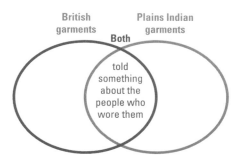

British garments — Both — Plains Indian garments

told something about the people who wore them

On Your Own

As you read the lessons in this unit, use Venn diagrams to compare and contrast information that you read and artworks that you see. Look back at your diagrams when you see questions with **READING SKILL**.

117

APPLY TO READING

Compare and Contrast Clothing Explain to students that as they read the passage, they should be thinking about how the two garments are alike and different.

Have students read the passage on page 117 and complete the Venn diagram to compare and contrast the two garments. TEKS 4.3B; TAKS Reading Objectives 1, 4

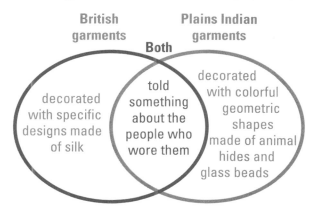

British garments — Both — Plains Indian garments

decorated with specific designs made of silk | told something about the people who wore them | decorated with colorful geometric shapes made of animal hides and glass beads

ON YOUR OWN

As students read about other artworks and art concepts in this unit, have them use a Venn diagram such as the one on page 117 to compare and contrast details in the text and the artworks.

TAKS Reading Objective 4

Reading Skill Card

Distribute Reading Skill Card 4, *Teacher Resource Book* page 34. Have students compare and contrast the artworks in this unit.

Extend the Skill
For additional teaching suggestions, see **Art Transparency 10.**

PDAS Domain IV

ESL Aid **oral language development** by helping students **paraphrase** the passage. Then use **visuals** to support **comprehensible input** for clothing terms. Display *Picture Cards Collection* cards 41, 59, 87, 108, and 109 for reference. See also *Picture Card Bank* **CD-ROM.**

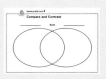

shirt

Reading Skills and Activities
Visit *The Learning Site*
www.harcourtschool.com

Lesson 16

PDAS Domains I, II
Fiber Art

OBJECTIVES
- Choose appropriate vocabulary to discuss pattern in artworks
- Design and create an original reverse weaving
- Compare and contrast artworks

RESOURCES
- Art Print 10
- Reading Skill Card 4
- Discussion Cards 1, 4, pp. R34–R35
- Electronic Art Gallery CD-ROM, Intermediate

GO ONLINE
Multimedia Art Glossary and Biographies
Visit *The Learning Site*
www.harcourtschool.com

5 Minutes

Warm-Up

Build Background Display **Art Print 10** and ask students to describe what they see. Explain that this image shows a mola, a fabric panel that forms part of a blouse. Molas are made and worn by the Cuna Indian women of Panama. Have students point out the images of lizards and birds in the fabric and discuss why these animals might have been used in the mola. Then ask students to communicate ideas about self using life experiences to discuss other fabric designs they have seen. Tell students that in this lesson they will learn about artworks from many different cultures. TEKS 4.1A

Lesson 16

Fiber Art

Vocabulary
weaving
pattern
tapestry

An artist can choose from a variety of materials to create an artwork. Some artworks are made of fiber. Fibers are interlaced, or woven together, to create a **weaving**, or cloth.

Patterns in Weavings

Look at the weavings in images **A** and **B**. What kinds of lines, shapes, and colors do you see in each one? When lines, shapes, or colors are repeated, they create a **pattern**. How are the patterns in images **A** and **B** alike? How are they different?

The kente cloth in image **B** was made in Africa. The word *kente* comes from the word *kenten*, which means "basket." Notice that the pattern in the cloth looks like the pattern in a basket.

 Unknown artist, Navajo traditional shawl, about 1850–1860, wool, 59 in. × 43 in. Collection of the Lowe Art Museum, The University of Miami, Coral Gables, Florida.

 Unknown artist, Detail of African kente cloth, about mid-1900s, woven silk. The British Museum, London, England.

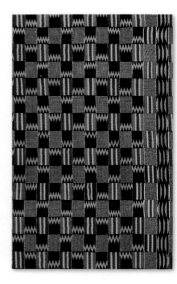

118

FYI

Background Information

Art History
A **The Navajo Indian tribe** learned how to build looms and weave fabrics from another tribe, the Hopi. The Navajo used geometric shapes, diamonds, and zigzags in their woven designs.

B **Kente cloth** is woven from silk, cotton, or rayon fibers to form geometric patterns.

C **The Ching dynasty,** established in 1636, was the last of the imperial dynasties of China. During the rule of the Ching emperors, handicraft industries, painting, printmaking, and porcelain manufacturing thrived.

 For related artworks, see **Electronic Art Gallery CD-ROM, Intermediate.**

★ TEKS 4.1A communicate ideas; TEKS 4.1B discuss elements and principles; TEKS 4.3C identify roles of art; PDAS Domain I active participation; PDAS Domain II learner-centered instruction; TAKS Reading Objective 1 demonstrate understanding of texts; *(continued)*

C ▶ Unknown artist,
**Chinese Emperor's
Twelve Symbol Robe,**
Ch'ing dynasty (1644–1911),
silk K'o-ssu tapestry weave,
58½ in. × 65 in. Collection
of the Lowe Art Museum,
The University of Miami,
Coral Gables, Florida.

The robe in image **C** is an example of tapestry from China. A **tapestry** is a type of weaving that has colorful designs or scenes in it. Many tapestries are heavy and are hung on walls. Some are used in clothing. How is this robe like other robes you have seen? How is it different?

Social Studies Link
Long ago, kente cloth, such as that shown in image **B**, was worn by kings and other powerful people in Ghana, Africa.

119

TEKS 4.3C; TAKS Reading Objectives 1, 3, 4

Social Studies Connection

Navajo Art Tell students that modern Navajo artists produce a wide range of objects, including blankets, clothing, rugs, jewelry, pottery, and sculpture. Have students research contemporary Navajo art and identify the roles of art like this in American society.

10-15 Minutes

Teach

Preview the Art Have students preview images A through D on pages 118–120. Ask them to describe what they see. Use Discussion Card 1 and the questions below to guide the discussion. Then have students read pages 118–120.

A *Navajo traditional shawl* **What first catches your attention when you look at this artwork?**

B *Detail of African kente cloth* **What do you think the fabric in this image might be used for?**

C *Chinese Emperor's Twelve Symbol Robe* **What are some of the details you see in this robe?**

D *Reverse Weaving* **If you could touch this artwork, what do you think it would feel like?**

Discuss Art Concepts As students compare the patterns in images A and B, they should choose appropriate vocabulary to discuss pattern in the artworks. Have them point out the pattern of zig-zags, straight and wavy lines, and diamond shapes in the weaving in image A. In image B, students should note the use of repeated rectangle shapes to create a basket pattern. TEKS 4.1B

Students may point out that the general shape of the robe in image C is similar to others they have seen, although the detailed patterns and animal designs make it different. Students should point out that both A and D show stripes and zigzags, although the colors in the two weavings are different.

Social Studies Link Have students turn to the map on pages 208–209 to locate Ghana, Africa. Explain that Ghana's arts also include dance, music, pottery, wood carvings, and jewelry.

Teach (continued)

Compare and Contrast Ask students to look at images A and C. Have them compare and contrast these artworks from a variety of cultural settings and discuss

- each object's purpose.

- the colors in each object.

- the patterns in each object. TEKS 4.1B, TEKS 4.3B

Then have students interpret ideas in these original artworks and tell which artwork they thought had the most interesting patterns and why. TEKS 4.4B

Think Critically

Use the questions below to check students' understanding of lesson concepts.

1. (Focus Skill) *READING SKILL* **How are the weavings in images A and D alike and different?**
   (Possible response: They are alike because they both have straight lines and zigzags. They have different colors.) **COMPARE AND CONTRAST**
   TEKS 4.1B, TEKS 4.3B

2. **Describe the patterns you see in image C.**
   (colorful, diagonal lines on the sleeves and the bottom section; dragons against a yellow background; dragons against a black background on the sleeves and around the neck)
   PERCEPTION/AESTHETICS TEKS 4.1B

3. **WRITE** **Write a paragraph describing a piece of clothing that is special to you. Include details about its color, pattern, or texture.** **DESCRIPTIVE** TEKS 4.1A; TAKS Writing Objective 1

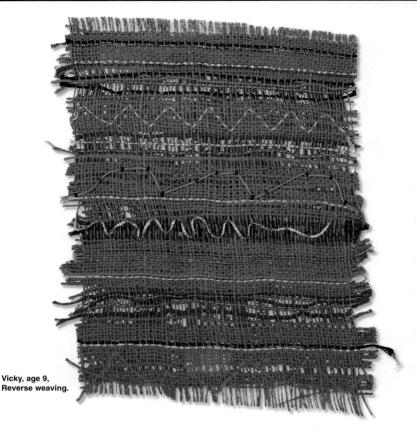

 Vicky, age 9,
Reverse weaving.

What kinds of patterns do you see in image **D**? Compare image **D** with image **B**. How are the weavings alike? How are they different?

Think Critically

1. (Focus Skill) *READING SKILL* How are the weavings in images **A** and **D** alike and different? **COMPARE AND CONTRAST**

2. Describe the patterns you see in image **C**.

3. **WRITE** Write a paragraph describing a piece of clothing that is special to you. Include details about its color, pattern, or texture.

120

TEKS 4.1B

Art Print 10

Display **Art Print 10** and distribute to students Discussion Card 4: *Principles of Design.* Have them choose appropriate vocabulary to discuss pattern in this artwork.

ART PRINT 10

Panamanian Cuna Mola with Iguanas and Birds
by Unknown Artist

★ TEKS 4.1A communicate ideas; TEKS 4.1B discuss elements and principles; TEKS 2.2B design original artworks; TEKS 4.2C produce artworks; TEKS 4.3B compare and contrast artworks; TEKS 4.4A form conclusions about personal artworks; TEKS 4.4B interpret artworks by peers and others; *(continued)*

Artist's Workshop

Create a Reverse Weaving

PLAN

Look at the reverse weaving in image **D**. Think about the colors and patterns you would like to use in your own reverse weaving.

CREATE

1. Pull some of the strands out of a piece of burlap, creating open areas.

2. Measure and cut several pieces of yarn about an inch or so longer than the width of the burlap. Weave the yarn in and out of the strands of burlap.

3. After weaving several pieces of yarn, pinch the pieces together to create a tighter weave.

REFLECT

Describe the pattern you created in your weaving.

MATERIALS

- 6 in. × 6 in. burlap pieces
- colored yarn
- ruler
- scissors

Quick Tip

Tape one end of the yarn to the tip of a craft stick. Use the craft stick like a needle to weave through the burlap.

121

 30-40 Minutes

Artist's Workshop

Create a Reverse Weaving

PLAN Have students read page 121. Ask them to sketch several patterns with lines and shapes before choosing one to use in their weaving.

CREATE As students design their original artworks, they should slowly pull strands from their burlap from one direction to create neat, even rows. Have students invent ways to produce their weavings using a variety of materials. TEKS 4.2B, TEKS 4.2C

REFLECT Have students describe the patterns in their weaving. Ask them to form conclusions about their artworks based on the patterns and colors they used. SELF-EVALUATION TEKS 4.1B, TEKS 4.4A

5-10 Minutes

Wrap-Up

Informal Assessment PDAS Domain III

- **How did viewing the artworks in this lesson help you design your reverse weaving?** (Responses will vary.) EVALUATION/CRITICISM TEKS 4.4A

- **How is your weaving like the one in image D? How is it different?** (Responses will vary.) COMPARE AND CONTRAST

Extend Through Writing TAKS Writing Objective 1

MUSEUM CARD Have students make a card for their artwork that includes its title, materials, and other information. See *Teacher Resource Book*, page 39.

Recommended Reading

The Chief's Blanket by Michael Chanin. H. J. Kramer, 1997. CHALLENGING

PDAS Domains I, II

Balance in Masks

OBJECTIVES
- Choose appropriate vocabulary to identify balance in artworks
- Design and create an original paper mask
- Compare and contrast artworks

RESOURCES
- Art Print 9
- Reading Skill Card 4
- Discussion Cards 1, 4, pp. R34–R35
- Electronic Art Gallery CD-ROM, Intermediate

Multimedia Art Glossary and Biographies
Visit *The Learning Site*
www.harcourtschool.com

5 Minutes

Warm-Up

Build Background About Masks Have students communicate ideas about school, family, and community using life experiences to discuss events or celebrations when they have worn a mask. Such occasions may include plays, costume parties, or family or community celebrations. Invite volunteers to describe the masks they have worn. Tell students that in this lesson they will learn about masks from cultures around the world.
TEKS 4.1A

Lesson 17

Vocabulary

vertical axis

symmetrical balance

Balance in Masks

Almost every culture in the world has created masks for special events and celebrations.

Symmetrical Balance

Image **A** shows a mask from the Aztec culture. Hundreds of years ago, the Aztecs ruled a large part of what is now central and southern Mexico.

Use your finger to trace a line down the middle of image **A**. This line is the **vertical axis** of the artwork. Compare the left side of the mask to the right side. The artist matched the lines and shapes on one side of the mask to those on the other side. Artworks with this kind of arrangement show **symmetrical balance**.

 Unknown artist, Aztec mask, about 1500, white jade, 10.5 cm × 14.5 cm × 4 cm. Peabody Museum, Harvard University, Cambridge, Massachusetts.

122

FYI

Background Information

Art History

A By 1500, the **Aztecs** had the most advanced civilization in North America. Their capital city, Tenochtitlán, stood on an island in a lake. Huge white palaces and decorated temples reflected the wealth and power of the Aztecs.

B The **Kwele** people live in the northern region of the Congo and in Gabon, Africa. This kind of mask is used in a social celebration that brings together the Kwele families living in the region.

 For related artworks, see **Electronic Art Gallery CD-ROM, Intermediate.**

★ TEKS 4.1A communicate ideas; TEKS 4.1B discuss elements and principles; TEKS 4.3B compare and contrast artworks; PDAS Domain I active participation; PDAS Domain II learner-centered instruction; TAKS Reading Objective 1 demonstrate understanding of texts; *(continued)*

Unknown artist,
African Kwele mask,
pigment on carved wood,
26 in. high. Western
Equatorial Africa.

Materials in Masks

Ancient mask makers used
materials such as tree bark, shells,
minerals, leather, metals, wood,
cornhusks, and feathers in their work.

Look at the African mask in image **B**. It was
carved from wood. The mask in image **A** was carved from
jade, a mineral that is usually green or white in color. Jade
was used by the Aztecs and other ancient peoples to make
jewelry and other decorative objects. How are the African
mask and the Aztec mask alike? How are they different?

123

TAKS Reading Objectives 1, 3, 4

Social Studies Connection

Inuit Life Have students
use an encyclopedia or
online resources to research
one aspect of the Inuit's
traditional way of life. Have
students present their findings in an oral report.

Preview the Art Have students preview images A
through D on pages 122–124. Ask them to describe
the faces they see in each one. Use Discussion
Card 1 and the questions below to guide the
discussion. Then have students read pages 122–124.

A *Aztec mask* **What are some details
you see on this mask?**

B *African Kwele mask* **What feeling do
you think this mask is expressing?
Why do you think that?**

C *Inuit finger masks* **What parts of the
human face do you see in these masks?
What parts are missing?**

D *Paper sculpture mask* **Where might
you see a mask like this?**

Discuss Art Concepts Remind students that the
woven patterns in the artworks on pages 118–120
showed symmetry. Tell students that artists of other
art forms such as masks also show symmetry in
their artwork. As students trace the vertical axis in
image A, have them point out the matching eyes,
ears, and jewelry on both sides of the mask.

Students should choose appropriate vocabulary to
discuss the symmetrical balance in the mask in
image B, and should point out the different materials in each mask. TEKS 4.1B

In image C, students should first find the vertical
axis in each mask and note the way the facial
features are balanced on either side. As they
compare the artworks in images C and D, students
should note the similar shapes of the eyes as well
as the symmetrical balance in each mask. As they
contrast the masks, they should point out the
different sizes of the masks as well as the materials,
colors, and details in each one. TEKS 4.1B, TEKS 4.3B

Social Studies Link Have students turn to pages 208–209, and help them locate the region where Inuit tribes are known to live—from Greenland across northern Canada and Alaska, and to eastern Siberia. Tell students that this region is under ice and snow for six to nine months a year.

Compare and Contrast Ask students to look at images A, B, C, and D, and compare and contrast the facial features in these artworks from a variety of cultural settings. Then ask students to identify the simple main ideas expressed in the artworks that tell about art history and culture. Encourage students to tell which mask they would like to wear and why. **TEKS 4.3A, TEKS 4.3B**

Think Critically

Use the questions below to check students' understanding of lesson concepts.

1. (Focus Skill) **READING SKILL** **How is the mask in image A different from a human face? How is it the same?** (It is different because it has objects on the cheeks and on the hair. It is the same because it has two eyes, a nose, and a mouth.) **COMPARE AND CONTRAST**

2. **Does the mask in image D show symmetrical balance? Why or why not?** (Yes, because the right and left sides match across the vertical axis.) **PERCEPTION/AESTHETICS** **TEKS 4.1B**

3. **WRITE** **Imagine a party where people might wear masks. Write a paragraph about the party and the kinds of masks you might see there.** **DESCRIPTIVE** **TAKS Writing Objective 1**

Social Studies Link
The name *Inuit* means "the people." Today, there are more than 100,000 Inuits living in a region that stretches from Greenland in the west to eastern Siberia.

 C Unknown artist, Inuit finger masks, 19th century, carved wood, $4\frac{1}{2}$ in. × $3\frac{1}{2}$ in. × $\frac{5}{8}$ in. The Detroit Institute of Arts, Detroit, Michigan.

Finger Masks

The masks in image **C** were not worn on the face. Inuit women wore one of these finger masks on each hand. They danced with their hands and kept their feet still. Do the masks in image **C** show symmetrical balance? How do you know?

Compare the masks in image **C** to the mask in image **D**. How are they alike? How are they different?

D Caleb, age 9, Paper sculpture mask.

Think Critically

1. (Focus Skill) **READING SKILL** How is the mask in image **A** different from a human face? How is it the same? **COMPARE AND CONTRAST**

2. Does the mask in image **D** show symmetrical balance? Why or why not?

3. **WRITE** Imagine a party where people might wear masks. Write a paragraph about the party and the kinds of masks you might see there.

124

TEKS 4.1B

Art Print 9

Display **Art Print 9** and distribute to students Discussion Card 4: *Principles of Design*. Ask students to choose appropriate vocabulary to discuss symmetrical balance in this artwork.

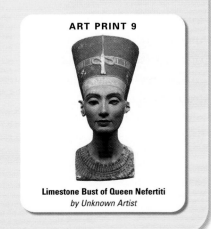

ART PRINT 9

Limestone Bust of Queen Nefertiti
by Unknown Artist

★ **TEKS 4.1B** discuss elements and principles; **TEKS 4.2B** design original artworks; **TEKS 4.2C** produce artworks; **TEKS 4.3A** identify main ideas; **TEKS 4.3B** compare and contrast artworks; **PDAS Domain III** evaluation and feedback; **PDAS Domain IV** classroom management; *(continued)*

Artist's Workshop

Create a Paper Mask

PLAN

Sketch some ideas for a mask you would like to make. Use lines, shapes, and colors to create symmetrical balance.

CREATE

1. Choose your best sketch, and draw the outline of your mask on poster board.

2. Cut out your mask. Cut holes for eyes and other facial features.

3. Add color and other details to your mask with markers or paint, colored paper, feathers, or beads.

REFLECT

How does your mask show symmetrical balance? What kinds of materials did you use, and why did you choose them?

MATERIALS

- pencil
- poster board
- scissors
- markers or paint
- paintbrushes
- glue
- colored paper
- decorative materials

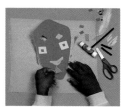

Safety Tips Carefully poke a hole in the center of the area you want to remove. Cut the outline of the facial feature from that center point.

125

Activity Options
PDAS Domain IV

Quick Activity Have students sketch a mask that shows symmetrical balance.

Early Finishers Have students add decorations to their mask.

Challenge See *Teacher Resource Book*, p. 67.

PDAS Domain IV

ESL Invite students to **share cultures** by talking about masks and celebrations from their own cultures. Reinforce **oral language development** by asking students to describe what the masks from their culture are made from and which celebrations they are used for.

Artist's Workshop
30-40 Minutes

Create a Paper Mask

PLAN Have students read the activity steps on page 125. Students may want to measure their sketches against their own faces to match the placement of eyes and other facial features.

CREATE As students design their original artworks, have them lightly sketch a vertical axis down the middle of their poster to make sure their design has symmetrical balance. Have students invent ways to produce their artworks using a variety of materials and art media. TEKS 4.2B, TEKS 4.2C

REFLECT Ask students to tell how their masks show symmetrical balance and discuss their choices of materials. **SELF-EVALUATION** TEKS 4.1B

Wrap-Up
5-10 Minutes

Informal Assessment PDAS Domain III

- **How would you describe the facial expression on your mask? What did you do to create that expression?** (Responses will vary.)
  PERSONAL RESPONSE

- **How is your mask like the one in image D? How is it different?** (Responses will vary.)
  COMPARE AND CONTRAST TEKS 4.3B

Extend Through Writing
TAKS Writing Objective 1

STORY Have students imagine their mask was used by an ancient civilization. Then ask them to write a story about the mask's origin and purpose.

Recommended Reading

Start with Art: Animals by Sue Lacey. Copper Beach, 1999. AVERAGE

PDAS Domains I, II

AMEDEO MODIGLIANI

ARTIST BIOGRAPHY

DISCUSS THE IMAGES

Have students read pages 126–127.

- Encourage students to describe what they see in image A. Tell students that despite the fact that Modigliani painted many portraits, this is his only self-portrait.

- 🖼 Display **Art Print 11** and talk about this portrait along with the other images on these pages. Have students note the different materials the artist used. (Art Print 11, image A, and image D are oil paintings; image B is a crayon sketch; and image C is a stone sculpture.) **Help** students recognize that despite the differences in these artworks, they show a similar use of distortion. Have students point out the elongated ovals of the faces and the long, thin noses and necks in each portrait. Then display **Art Print 7**, and have students compare the facial features in this painting to those in the artworks by Modigliani.

- Ask students to look back at the African mask on page 123. Then have them compare it to the sculpture in image C and note the similarities in the elongated shapes of the faces and noses, the narrow eyes, and the large foreheads.
TEKS 4.3B

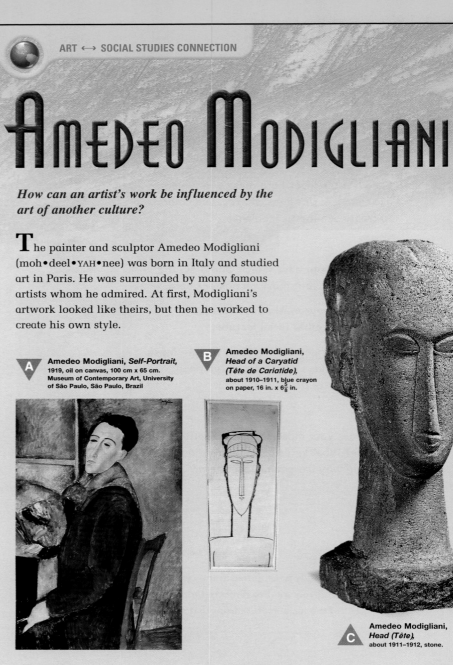

ART ⟷ SOCIAL STUDIES CONNECTION

AMEDEO MODIGLIANI

How can an artist's work be influenced by the art of another culture?

The painter and sculptor Amedeo Modigliani (moh•deel•YAH•nee) was born in Italy and studied art in Paris. He was surrounded by many famous artists whom he admired. At first, Modigliani's artwork looked like theirs, but then he worked to create his own style.

A Amedeo Modigliani, *Self-Portrait*, 1919, oil on canvas, 100 cm x 65 cm. Museum of Contemporary Art, University of São Paulo, São Paulo, Brazil

B Amedeo Modigliani, *Head of a Caryatid (Tête de Cariatide)*, about 1910–1911, blue crayon on paper, 16 in. x $6\frac{5}{8}$ in.

C Amedeo Modigliani, *Head (Tête)*, about 1911–1912, stone.

126

FYI Background Information

About the Artist

Italian painter and sculptor Amedeo Modigliani (moh•deel•YAH•nee) (1884–1920) incorporated into his work the elongated and simplified forms found in African sculpture. The influence of African art continued to be reflected throughout his career in his paintings, including his many portraits.

For additional information about Amedeo Modigliani, see pp. R44–R65.

 For related artworks, see **Electronic Art Gallery CD-ROM, Intermediate.**

Look at the self-portrait in image A. Compare it to the other images on these pages. How are images A, B, C, and D alike?

How would you describe the style of Modigliani's artwork? Look back at the African mask on page 123. How is it like Modigliani's work? How is it different?

Modigliani studied different styles and artworks from outside Europe. Many artists in Paris became interested in African art at this time. Modigliani combined ideas from African masks and sculpture with European styles of carving to create something new.

Amedeo Modigliani,
Jeanne Hebuterne,
1917–1918, oil on canvas,
18 in. x 11 in.

THINK ABOUT ART

Why do you think it is important to study art from other cultures?

DID YOU KNOW?

Many artists use their family members and friends as models for their artwork. Modigliani's friend, Jeanne, was the model for the portrait in image D. Modigliani also painted portraits of the artists Diego Rivera and Pablo Picasso.

GO ONLINE **Multimedia Biographies**
Visit *The Learning Site*
www.harcourtschool.com

127

DID YOU KNOW?

Use the facts below to talk about two well-known artists who were subjects of Modigliani's portraits between 1914 and 1916.

- Diego Rivera (1886–1957) was a famous Mexican painter who created enormous murals portraying the lives and history of the Mexican people.

- Pablo Picasso (1881–1973) was one of the best-known artists of the twentieth century. He was one of the first people Modigliani met when he arrived in Paris.

For additional information about these artists, see pp. R44–R65.

THINK ABOUT ART

Why do you think it is important to study art from other cultures? (Responses will vary.)
PERSONAL RESPONSE

ARTIST'S EYE ACTIVITY

Drawing in Modigliani's Style   Ask students to think about Modigliani's use of distortion in his portraits. Then ask students to work in pairs to design original artworks, quickly sketching a portrait of their partner in the style of Modigliani. Have students share their sketches and interpret moods in their peers' original artworks.
TEKS 4.2B, TEKS 4.4B

Social Studies Connection

At the Acropolis   Tell students that the sketch in image B refers to a caryatid (kar•ee•AT•ihd), or maiden. Statues of caryatids were used as columns in ancient Greek architecture.

For additional cross-curricular suggestions, see Art Transparency 11.

TEKS 4.4B
Viewing an Artist's Work

Portfolios and Exhibitions
Arrange for students to visit a museum or art gallery. Have students use the opportunity to examine artists' portfolios and exhibitions to interpret ideas and moods in the original artworks.

Multimedia Biographies
Visit *The Learning Site*
www.harcourtschool.com

Lesson 18

PDAS Domains I, II
Paper Art

OBJECTIVES
- Choose appropriate vocabulary to discuss balance in artworks
- Recognize the use of visual weight to create balance in artworks
- Design and create an original paper cutting
- Compare and contrast artworks

RESOURCES
- Art Print 10
- Reading Skill Card 4
- Discussion Cards 1, 4, pp. R34–R35
- Color Wheel Poster
- Electronic Art Gallery CD-ROM, Intermediate

GO ONLINE **Multimedia Art Glossary and Biographies**
Visit *The Learning Site*
www.harcourtschool.com

5 Minutes
Warm-Up

Build Background Display the **Color Wheel Poster,** and ask students if it shows balance. Point out the lines that come out of the center and that divide the wheel into equal parts. Help students recognize that no matter which way the wheel is turned, the parts remain equal and the wheel remains balanced. Then ask students to communicate ideas about self using life experiences to name objects that show the same kind of balance. (bicycle wheels, kaleidoscopes, etc.) Tell students that in this lesson they will learn how artists use lines, colors, and patterns to create different kinds of balance in paper artworks. TEKS 4.1A

Lesson 18

Paper Art

Vocabulary
- radial balance
- asymmetrical balance
- visual weight

The tradition of paper cutting came from ancient China. It is thought to have started about 206 B.C.—around the time that paper was invented. Eventually, the art of paper cutting spread to other parts of the world. Different cultures developed their own styles of paper cutting.

How did the artist of image **A** use shape to create symmetrical balance? What kinds of patterns do you see?

A Unknown artist, *Window Flowers for New Year,* about 1950, Chinese paper cutting, $8\frac{1}{2}$ in. × $4\frac{1}{2}$ in. Museum of International Folk Art/Museum of New Mexico, Santa Fe, New Mexico.

128

Background Information

About the Artist
C American painter, printmaker, and children's book author-illustrator **Carmen Lomas Garza** (1948–) grew up in a traditional Hispanic community in South Texas. She taught herself to draw by practicing every day, drawing whatever was in front of her. Today, her work is exhibited in galleries and museums around the world.

For additional information about Carmen Lomas Garza, see pp. R44–R65.

  For related artworks, see **Electronic Art Gallery CD-ROM, Intermediate.**

  TEKS 4.1A communicate ideas; TEKS 4.1B discuss elements and principles; **PDAS Domain I** active participation; **PDAS Domain II** learner-centered instruction; **TAKS Reading Objective 1** demonstrate understanding of texts; **TAKS Reading Objective 3** use a variety of strategies; *(continued)*

Bernadine Jendrzejczak,
**Paper cutting in Polish
traditional style,**
1998, cut paper on
white cardboard, 10 in.
Private collection.

Now look at image **B**. What shapes do you recognize? In Poland it has been a tradition to make cutouts like this as decorations for everyday use and for special occasions. The patterns are often inspired by nature. Describe how image **B** shows symmetrical balance.

Image **B** also shows **radial balance** because the same pattern radiates, or extends, from the center, like the spokes of a wheel. Put your finger on the center of image **B**. Then look at the way the pattern is repeated around the artwork.

129

TAKS Reading Objectives 1, 3, 4

Social Studies Connection

Kirigami Ask volunteers who are familiar with origami to share what they know about it. Tell students that kirigami is the ancient Japanese art of folding and cutting paper. Encourage students to use an encyclopedia or online resources to research both origami and kirigami and to show their classmates examples of each art form.

kirigami

origami

10-15 Minutes

Teach

Preview the Art Ask students to look at images A through C on pages 128–130. Ask them whether the artworks show balance and how they know. Use Discussion Card 1 and the questions below to guide the discussion. Then have students read pages 128–130.

 Window Flowers for New Year **Describe what you see in this artwork.**

 Paper cutting in Polish traditional style **What kinds of lines, colors, and shapes did the artist use in this artwork?**

 Flowery Words: Stories, Poems, Song, History & Wisdom **What kind of story might this artwork tell?**

Discuss Art Concepts As students view image A, have them talk about symmetrical balance by noting that the organic shapes of the flowers and the curved lines of the foliage match each other on both sides of the vertical axis.

Have students identify the symmetrical balance in image B by pointing out the matching lines, shapes, and colors of the flowers. To help students distinguish between symmetrical balance and radial balance, have them turn image B on its side and then upside down, so that they can see that the pattern continues to spread out from the center in the same way, all around the paper cutting.
TEKS 4.1B

Have students trace the vertical axis of image C and note that although the two sides do not match, they have equal visual weight.

Teach (continued)

Cultural Link The village of San Salvador Huixcolotla (weesh•ko•LO•tlah) in Puebla, Mexico, is best known for its *papel picado*. These traditional paper banners are strung together and used as decorations for festivals and celebrations of all kinds.

Compare and Contrast Ask students to look at the plants in images A and B. Have them compare and contrast these artworks from a variety of cultural settings by examining

- the colors used in the artworks.

- the lines and shapes used in the artworks.

Then ask students to discuss ways these artworks are similar to and different from paintings of flowers and plants. TEKS 4.1B, TEKS 4.3B

Think Critically

Use the questions below to check students' understanding of lesson concepts.

1. *READING SKILL* **Compare the three artworks in this lesson. How are they alike? How are they different?** (Possible responses: alike: are examples of paper cutting, show plants, have organic shapes and curved lines; different: have different colors, show different kinds of balance) **COMPARE AND CONTRAST** TEKS 4.3B

2. **How would you change image C to show symmetrical balance?** (Possible response: Copy it and place the two artworks side by side so that the figures face each other.) **PERCEPTION/AESTHETICS**

3. **WRITE** **Write a paragraph to explain how you think the title of image C relates to the artwork.** **EXPOSITORY** TEKS 4.4B; TAKS Writing Objective 1

Cultural Link

Image **C** shows an example of *papel picado*, which means "punched paper" in Spanish. In this traditional Mexican artwork, stacks of about fifty sheets of tissue paper are cut at one time with a small, sharp chisel. Designs might include people, animals, flowers, or words.

C Carmen Lomas Garza, *Flowery Words: Stories, Poems, Song, History & Wisdom,* 1993, white paper cutouts. Collection of the artist.

Trace the vertical axis in image **C**. This artwork shows **asymmetrical balance**. The artist arranged lines and shapes to show balance even though the artwork is not the same on both sides. Look at the woman's head in the lower right corner. Now look at the thick, curved line of the plant in the upper left corner. These two objects have the same **visual weight**, or importance, in the artwork. Artists use visual weight to create a sense of balance in their artworks.

Think Critically

1. *READING SKILL* Compare the three artworks in this lesson. How are they alike? How are they different? **COMPARE AND CONTRAST**

2. How would you change image **C** to show symmetrical balance?

3. **WRITE** Write a paragraph to explain how you think the title of image **C** relates to the artwork.

130

TEKS 4.1B

Art Print 10

Display **Art Print 10** and distribute to students Discussion Card 4: *Principles of Design.* Have students discuss the balance in this artwork.

ART PRINT 10

Panamanian Cuna Mola with Iguanas and Birds
by Unknown Artist

TEKS 4.1B discuss elements and principles; TEKS 4.2A integrate ideas in artworks; TEKS 4.2B design original artworks; TEKS 4.3B compare and contrast artworks; TEKS 4.4A form conclusions about personal artworks; TEKS 4.4B interpret artworks by peers and others; *(continued)*

Artist's Workshop

Create a Paper Cutting

PLAN

Think of a design you would like to show in a paper cutting. Sketch some of your ideas.

CREATE

1. Fold a sheet of paper in half. Draw half of your design so that it meets the fold of the paper. Make your drawing large enough to fill up the folded paper.

2. Cut out your design. Then open the paper.

3. Add color with colored pencils or markers to the side of your design that does not have pencil marks.

REFLECT

How would you describe your paper cutting? What kind of balance does your design show?

MATERIALS
- pencil
- sketchbook
- white paper
- scissors
- colored pencils or markers

Quick Tip Do not cut all the way through the fold of your paper.

131

Create a Paper Cutting

PLAN Have students read the activity steps on page 131. Then encourage students to practice cutting out the design before they work on the final artwork.

CREATE If students plan to use radial balance, you may want to distribute *Teacher Resource Book* page 40 for students to use in designing their original artworks. Have students integrate a variety of ideas about self, life events, and family in their artworks. TEKS 4.2A, TEKS 4.2B

REFLECT Ask students to form conclusions about their artworks and discuss what kind of balance they showed. **SELF-EVALUATION** TEKS 4.1B, TEKS 4.4A

5-10 Minutes

Wrap-Up

Informal Assessment PDAS Domain III

- **Describe the organic and geometric shapes you chose to use to design your paper cutting.** (Responses will vary.) PERCEPTION/AESTHETICS

- **How is your paper cutting like one of the artworks in this lesson? How is it different?** (Responses will vary.) COMPARE AND CONTRAST TEKS 4.3B

Extend Through Writing TEKS 4.4B; TAKS Writing Objectives 1, 6

DESCRIPTIVE PARAGRAPH Have students write a descriptive paragraph interpreting the ideas in a peer's paper cutting. Ask them to proofread their work.

Recommended Reading

Butterflies for Kiri by Cathryn Fallwell. Lee and Low, 2003. AVERAGE

PDAS Domain IV

Activity Options

Quick Activity Have students fold a sheet of white paper in half and cut out a few simple geometric or organic shapes.

Early Finishers Have students mount their paper cuttings on a sheet of colored construction paper.

Challenge See *Teacher Resource Book*, p. 68.

PDAS Domain IV

ESL To **build vocabulary**,
work with students to generate a list of verbs for the steps in this activity—such as *fold, cut, open*, and *color*. Have students **demonstrate comprehension** by reading each word aloud and **pantomiming** the action.

Lesson 19

Folk Art

PDAS Domains I, II

OBJECTIVES
- Recognize folk art style in artworks
- Choose appropriate vocabulary to discuss balance in artworks
- Design and create an original folk art painting
- Compare and contrast artworks

RESOURCES
- Art Print 10
- Reading Skill Card 4
- Discussion Cards 1, 10, pp. R34, R38
- Electronic Art Gallery CD-ROM, Intermediate

GO ONLINE Multimedia Art Glossary and Biographies
Visit *The Learning Site*
www.harcourtschool.com

5 Minutes

Warm-Up

 Build Background   Display **Art Print 10.** Explain to students that the artists who create the molas are not formally trained in art school. Crafting molas is a tradition unique to the Panamanian culture and handed down from generation to generation. Ask students to communicate ideas about family and community using life experiences to discuss any arts or crafts they know of from their own cultures and communities.   TEKS 4.1A

Lesson 19

Folk Art

Vocabulary
folk art

Look at the scene shown in image **A**. How would you describe it? Notice the objects on each side of the painting. The artist balanced the visual weight of the checkered house on the left side with the running horses and dog and the red barns on the right side. Does image **A** show symmetrical balance or asymmetrical balance?

 A Grandma Moses, *The Old Checkered House,* 1944, oil on pressed wood, 24 in. × 43 in. Seiji Togo Museum, Gekkoso, Japan.

132

 Background Information

About the Artists

A **Grandma Moses** (1860–1961) was born Anna Mary Robertson. She did not begin painting until she was in her seventies.

B **Pedro Figari** (1861–1938) was a distinguished Uruguayan painter, lawyer, journalist, and educator. His paintings often focused on the traditions and customs of Uruguay.

For additional information about the artists, see pp. R44–R65.

For related artworks, see **Electronic Art Gallery CD-ROM, Intermediate.**

★ TEKS 4.1A communicate ideas; TEKS 4.1B discuss elements and principles; TEKS 4.3A identify main ideas; TEKS 4.4B interpret artworks by peers and others; PDAS Domain I active participation; PDAS Domain II learner-centered instruction; TAKS Reading Objective 1 demonstrate understanding of texts; *(continued)*

Pedro Figari,
Creole Dance,
oil on board,
19.75 cm × 27.5 cm.

The style of the artwork shown in this lesson is called folk art. **Folk art** is created by people who have had little formal training in art. Folk artists often use art techniques that have been passed down through their families or cultures. Most folk artists use materials that are easy for them to find. For example, instead of painting on a canvas, a folk artist might paint on a piece of wood.

Some folk artists create art to help people remember part of their culture. Look at image **B**. What kind of event do you think the artist was trying to show? Now look at the colors and shapes the artist used to make certain parts of the artwork stand out. Does this painting show symmetrical balance or asymmetrical balance? Why do you think so?

133

TEKS 4.1A, TAKS Reading Objectives 1, 3, 4

Social Studies Connection

Folk Music   Share with students that folk music, like folk art, is often passed down from one generation to another. Have students work in groups to report on an example of folk music or traditional music from a culture they choose. Ask groups to interview family members or others within their communities to learn about the role that music has played in their cultures. Then have students communicate ideas about family and community using sensory knowledge. Invite students to share examples of the music they researched.

Teach

Preview the Art   Have students preview images A through C on pages 132–134. Ask them to discuss details that they find interesting in the artworks. Use Discussion Card 1 and the questions below to guide the discussion. Then have students read pages 132–134.

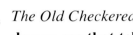 *The Old Checkered House*   **What details do you see that tell you about the setting of this painting?**

 Creole Dance   **How would you describe the mood in this artwork?** TEKS 4.4B

 Bird Tree   **What do you think is the main idea of this artwork?** TEKS 4.3A

Discuss Art Concepts   Discuss with students the farm scene in image A. Students should recognize the use of asymmetrical balance and point out the details noted on page 132.

After discussing folk art with students, have them point out that the bright colors and dancing figures in image B show a lively, festive scene. Students should note that image B shows asymmetrical balance—the figures on either side of the vertical axis have the same visual weight. Point out that the large rock on the left is balanced by the patch of blue sky on the right.   TEKS 4.1B

To help students determine what type of balance the artist used in image C, point out that the tree trunk provides a visible vertical axis. Students can then look at either side of the tree trunk and see that although the sizes, colors, and number of birds on each branch varies, the sculpture has asymmetrical balance, because each side of the tree has equal visual weight.

Teach (continued)

LOCATE IT Have students turn to pages 206–207 to locate Philadelphia, Pennsylvania. Tell students that Philadelphia is also home to many murals and large artworks in public spaces that celebrate the diversity of cultures found in that city.

Compare and Contrast Ask students to compare and contrast the artworks in this lesson that are from a variety of cultural settings and discuss

- the subjects of the artworks.

- the materials used in the artworks.

Then ask students to choose one artwork in this lesson and interpret the moods and ideas in it.
TEKS 4.3B, TEKS 4.4B

Think Critically

Use the questions below to check students' understanding of lesson concepts.

1. **(Focus Skill) READING SKILL** **Compare the settings in images A and B. How are they alike? How are they different?** (Possible response: Both paintings show people outdoors. In image A, the people are walking, riding horses, and traveling in a carriage. In image B, the people are dancing, sitting, and playing instruments.)
   COMPARE AND CONTRAST TEKS 4.3B

2. **Which objects have the most visual weight in image C?** (Possible responses: the large birds in the center of the sculpture and the base of the sculpture.) **PERCEPTION/AESTHETICS**

3. **WRITE** **Write a short story describing the events in image A.** **NARRATIVE**
   TAKS Writing Objective 1

LOCATE IT The artwork in image C can be found at the Philadelphia Museum of Art in Philadelphia, Pennsylvania.

PENNSYLVANIA

Philadelphia

See Maps of Museums and Art Sites, pages 206–209.

Look at image **C**. The artist created this sculpture from wood. How would you describe the kind of balance shown in this sculpture?

 Unknown artist, *Bird Tree*, about 1800–1830, painted hardwoods, wire, 17⅜ in. high. Philadelphia Museum of Art, Philadelphia, Pennsylvania.

Think Critically

1. **(Focus Skill) READING SKILL** Compare the settings in images **A** and **B**. How are they alike? How are they different?
   COMPARE AND CONTRAST

2. Which objects have the most visual weight in image **C**?

3. **WRITE** Write a short story describing the events in image **A**.

134

TEKS 4.1A

Art Print 10

Display **Art Print 10** and distribute to students Discussion Card 10: *Community Art*. Discuss with students how this artwork tells about the culture that the artist comes from. Have students communicate ideas about family and community by using sensory knowledge to describe traditional art forms they know well.

ART PRINT 10

Panamanian Cuna Mola with Iguanas and Birds
by Unknown Artist

★ TEKS 4.1A communicate ideas; TEKS 4.2A integrate ideas in artworks; TEKS 4.2B design original artworks; TEKS 4.3B compare and contrast artworks; TEKS 4.4A form conclusions about personal artworks; TEKS 4.4B interpret artworks by peers and others; *(continued)*

Artist's Workshop

Create a Folk Art Painting

MATERIALS
- pencil
- sketchbook
- white paper
- tempera paint
- paintbrushes
- water bowl

PLAN

Think of a tradition your family or community has that you would like to paint. Sketch some ideas. Think of ways to create asymmetrical balance in your painting.

CREATE

1. Choose your best sketch, and copy it onto white paper.

2. Before you begin to paint, make sure both sides of your drawing have the same visual weight.

3. Use tempera paint to finish your artwork.

REFLECT

What subject did you choose for your painting? How did you create asymmetrical balance?

Quick Tip
Remember that visual weight can be created with lines, shapes, or colors that make the artwork seem balanced.

135

 30-40 Minutes

Artist's Workshop

Create a Folk Art Painting

PLAN Have students read the activity steps on page 135.

CREATE Have students integrate a variety of ideas about life events, family, and community into their original artworks. As students design their paintings, remind them that in order to balance the visual weight in their painting, they must include details that draw the viewer's attention to both sides of the artwork. TEKS 4.2A, TEKS 4.2B

REFLECT Have students describe the intent of their artworks and point out how they created asymmetrical balance. SELF-EVALUATION TEKS 4.4A

 5-10 Minutes

Wrap-Up

Informal Assessment PDAS Domain III

- **How would you describe the mood of your painting? What colors, patterns, or details did you use to convey that mood?** TEKS 4.4A (Responses will vary.) EVALUATION/CRITICISM

- **Compare the subject of your painting to the subject of one of the images in this lesson. How are they alike? How are they different?** (Responses will vary.) COMPARE AND CONTRAST TEKS 4.3B

Extend Through Writing ✎ TAKS Writing Objective 1

STORY Have students write a short story about what is happening in their folk art painting.

Recommended Reading

Can a Coal Scuttle Fly? by Camay Calloway Murphy. Maryland Historical Society, 1996. AVERAGE

 PDAS Domain IV

Activity Options

Quick Activity Have students sketch a scene with asymmetrical balance.

Early Finishers Have students mount their paintings on construction paper or poster board and decorate the framed border with a pattern.

Challenge See *Teacher Resource Book*, p. 69.

 PDAS Domain IV

ESL

ESL Invite students to **share cultures** as they brainstorm traditions, events, or celebrations to use as the subject of their folk art paintings. You may want to create a list of words and phrases related to students' cultures and share them with the class.

PDAS Domains I, II

COWHANDS IN ART

ART AND CULTURE

DISCUSS THE IMAGES

Have students read pages 136 and 137.

- Have students discuss what they know about the tradition of cowhands in American history and identify the roles of art such as the images on pages 136 and 137 in American society. Then discuss the scene shown in image A. Have students turn to the map of the United States on pages 206–207. Explain to them that cowboys guided huge herds of cattle from Texas to as far north as Wyoming. The trails followed by cattle drives were very long, nearly a thousand miles, and getting a herd of cattle to a town with a railroad station at the end of the trail could take many months. **TEKS 4.3C**

- Discuss image B with students. Explain that the image shows a mural painted on one of the walls of the Cowgirl Museum. Ask students to describe what type of balance they see in the artwork. Point out the two women—one a cowhand, the other a Native American—on each side of the arch and the matching pattern behind each woman. **TEKS 4.1B**

- Encourage students to discuss what they know about rodeos. Explain that the five standard rodeo events are calf roping, bull riding, steer wrestling, saddle bronc-riding, and bareback bronc-riding. Point out that a *bronc*, or *bronco*, is an unbroken range horse. Tell students that young people compete in approximately 500 junior rodeos held each year.

ART ⟷ SOCIAL STUDIES CONNECTION

COWHANDS IN ART

How do artists help us remember the lifestyle of the American cowhand?

A W. Herbert Dunton, *Old Texas*, 1929, oil on canvas, 28 in. x 39 in. San Antonio Art League Museum, San Antonio, Texas.

Cowhands have a special place in American culture. Their long journeys guiding cattle from Texas into the Great Plains of the United States were full of challenges. Their adventures have inspired imaginations all over the world since the first cattle drives of the 1800s. Artists created images that introduced the rest of the world to the cowhand's way of life.

136

Background Information

About the Artist

A **W. Herbert Dunton** (1878–1936) was born on a farm in Maine. In 1896, he took a trip to Montana and developed an interest in the West. In 1914, Dunton moved from the East Coast to New Mexico and became a full-time artist. His nostalgia for frontier life can be seen in his paintings of the men and women who inhabited the nineteenth-century American West.

For additional information about W. Herbert Dunton, see pp. R44–R65.

For related artworks, see **Electronic Art Gallery CD-ROM, Intermediate.**

 Richard Haas, *Cowgirl Mural* on the east exterior wall of the National Cowgirl Museum and Hall of Fame, 2002, Artex paint over sealant and primer, 22 ft. x 36 ft. Fort Worth, Texas.

Today, cowhands still live and work in parts of the United States. Many things have changed, but one important part of the cowhand's life continues to thrill Americans—the rodeo.

Rodeos began in the 1800s so that cowhands could show off their skills in riding horses and roping cattle. Today, rodeo performers compete for prizes in front of cheering crowds. Just like the cowhands of the Old West, rodeo cowhands inspire artists.

THINK ABOUT ART

Why do you think the life of a cowhand was so inspiring to artists?

DID YOU KNOW?

The National Cowgirl Museum and Hall of Fame, in Fort Worth, Texas, honors the lives of women who represented the spirit of the American West. These women include Narcissa Prentiss Whitman, the first pioneer woman to cross the Rockies, and Georgia O'Keeffe, an artist who painted scenes of the American Southwest.

National Cowgirl Museum and Hall of Fame

137

DID YOU KNOW?

Use the facts below to talk about the National Cowgirl Museum, which opened in Fort Worth, Texas, in the spring of 2002.

- On display are more than 2,000 artifacts related to female ranchers, artists, and writers.

- Each year the museum adds four to six women to its Hall of Fame. Some of the women inducted into the Hall of Fame include Sacagawea, Dale Evans, and U.S. Supreme Court Justice Sandra Day O'Connor.

- The motto of the Cowgirl Hall of Fame came directly from the words of a cowgirl: "Saddle your own horse, do what has to get done, be responsible. And that really is the basis of the cowgirl spirit."

THINK ABOUT ART

Why do you think the life of a cowhand was so inspiring to artists? (Possible response: A cowhand's life was full of challenges and the possibility of adventure.) **PERSONAL RESPONSE**

ARTIST'S EYE ACTIVITY

Museum Advertisement Tell students that paintings of cowhands generally portrayed them involved in their day-to-day activities. Have students create a poster advertising the National Cowgirl Museum and Hall of Fame. As students design their original artworks, have them make sure their poster includes a picture of a traditional cowgirl at work. TEKS 4.2B

Social Studies Connection

Cowhand Clothes Tell students that the clothing worn by cowhands was important for their work. For example, hats protected their heads, and leather boots protected their feet.

For additional cross-curricular suggestions, see Art Transparency 12.

TEKS 4.4B

Student Art Show

Portfolios and Exhibitions Periodically during this unit, have students create a display of their portfolios and finished artworks. Ask students to interpret ideas and moods in peers' original artworks, portfolios, and the exhibit as a whole. See *Teacher Edition* page 204 for ideas on planning an exhibition.

Lesson 20

Symbols in Art

OBJECTIVES
- Identify the use of symbols in artworks
- Design and create an original print with a symbol
- Compare and contrast artworks

RESOURCES
- Art Print 12
- Reading Skill Card 4
- Discussion Cards 1, 9, pp. R34, R38
- Electronic Art Gallery CD-ROM, Intermediate

GO ONLINE

Multimedia Art Glossary and Biographies
Visit *The Learning Site*
www.harcourtschool.com

5 Minutes

Warm-Up

Build Background Display **Art Print 12,** which shows an artwork created by American artist Jasper Johns. Ask students to communicate ideas about self using life experiences to describe what kind of message they get from the artwork and why. Tell students that in this lesson they will learn how artists use familiar objects such as flags to communicate ideas and feelings through art.
TEKS 4.1A

Lesson 20

Vocabulary

symbols

Symbols in Art

Symbols are pictures or objects that stand for ideas. Artists may use symbols to communicate ideas and feelings through art. The artist of image **A** showed a Fourth of July celebration. What symbols did he use to express his feelings of patriotism? What kind of feeling do you get from image **A**?

 Frederick Childe Hassam, *The Fourth of July*, 1916, oil on canvas, 36 in. × 26 in.

138

 Background Information

About the Artists

A American painter and printmaker **Frederick Childe Hassam** (1859–1935) was greatly influenced by the Impressionists.

B American folk artist **Warren Kimble** has his studio in a 200-year-old Vermont barn.

C American painter and educator **Sante Graziani** (1920–) has painted several large murals in public buildings.

For additional information about the artists, see pp. R44–R65.

For related artworks, see **Electronic Art Gallery CD-ROM, Intermediate.**

★ TEKS 4.1A communicate ideas; TEKS 4.1B discuss elements and principles; TEKS 4.3C identify roles of art; PDAS Domain I active participation; PDAS Domain II learner-centered instruction; TAKS Reading Objective 1 demonstrate understanding of texts; *(continued)*

 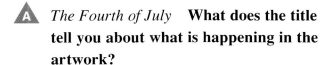

Different artists may convey the same message, such as patriotism, in different ways. Read the title of the painting in image **B**. The artist used his subject as a symbol. The American farm is a symbol of traditional rural life in the United States. How do you think the artist felt about rural life? What other symbols do you see in image **B**? Describe the patterns the artist created. How did he use these patterns as symbols?

B Warren Kimble,
The American Farm,
2000, acrylic on antique
wood, 16½ in. × 23 in.
Private collection.

139

Preview the Art　Have students preview images A through C on pages 138–140. Ask them to describe what they see and to point out familiar objects in the artworks. Use Discussion Card 1 and the questions below to guide the discussion. Then have students read pages 138–140.

A *The Fourth of July*　**What does the title tell you about what is happening in the artwork?**

B *The American Farm*　**What patterns do you see in this painting? Describe them.**
TEKS 4.1B

C *George Washington*　**What do the colors and shapes tell you about the subject of this painting?**

Discuss Art Concepts　Have students look at image A and note the symbols of patriotism shown in the repeated American flags. Ask students to identify the roles of artworks, such as the images in this lesson, in American society.
TEKS 4.3C

Discuss with students the way the artist of image B showed rural life to represent America. Students should note that the American flags on top of the barn and filling the sky are patriotic symbols.

Students should point out the colors red, white, and blue, the stars and stripes, and George Washington's portrait in image C. Discuss with students the artist's use of symmetrical balance in the artwork. Explain to students that this image would show radial balance only if the center circle also showed radial balance.　TEKS 4.1B

TAKS Reading Objectives 1, 3, 4

Social Studies Connection

Flags Around the World　Have students use a world map or globe to select two countries from different parts of the world. Then have students research the colors and symbols of the flag of each country. Students should sketch each flag and label it with the name of the country. Have students share in an oral report what they learned about the symbols used in each flag.

Teach (continued)

Social Studies Link Ask students to imagine they are going to create a neighborhood flag. Have them communicate ideas about community using sensory knowledge and life experiences as they decide what colors and objects should be included on the flag. TEKS 4.1A

Compare and Contrast Ask students to look at images A, B, and C. Have them compare and contrast

- the type of balance in each artwork.

- the use of patterns in the artworks.

Then ask students to tell which image in this lesson they thought best conveyed a patriotic feeling and why. TEKS 4.4B

Think Critically

Use the questions below to check students' understanding of lesson concepts.

1. **READING SKILL** **Compare and contrast the patterns you see in images A and B.** (Possible responses: Both paintings have the stars and stripes in the United States flag; the pattern is repeated more often in image A.) **COMPARE AND CONTRAST** TEKS 4.3B

2. **What other symbols can you think of that can give a message of patriotism or state pride?** (Possible response: an eagle, a state tree or flower) **PERSONAL RESPONSE**

3. **WRITE** **Look at image C. Write a paragraph describing what the symbols in this artwork mean to you.** EXPOSITORY TEKS 4.1A; TAKS Writing Objective 1

The artist of image **C** has put patriotic symbols together in a new way. What symbols do you recognize? What message do you think this artist is trying to convey? Does the artwork in image **C** show symmetrical balance or asymmetrical balance?

C Sante Graziani, *George Washington,* 1968, woodcut print, 12 in. × 12 in. Private collection.

Think Critically

1. **READING SKILL** Compare and contrast the patterns you see in images **A** and **B**. **COMPARE AND CONTRAST**

2. What other symbols can you think of that can give a message of patriotism or state pride?

3. **WRITE** Look at image **C**. Write a paragraph describing what the symbols in this artwork mean to you.

140

TEKS 4.3A, TEKS 4.4B

Art Print 12

Display **Art Print 12** and distribute to students Discussion Card 9: *Art Criticism.* Have students identify simple main ideas in the artwork and use its symbols to interpret the ideas and moods in it.

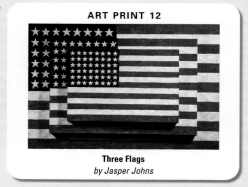

ART PRINT 12

Three Flags by Jasper Johns

★ TEKS 4.1A communicate ideas; TEKS 4.1B discuss elements and principles; TEKS 4.2A integrate ideas in artworks; TEKS 4.3A identify main ideas; TEKS 4.3B compare and contrast artworks; TEKS 4.4A form conclusions about personal artworks; TEKS 4.4B interpret artworks by peers and others; (continued)

Artist's Workshop

Create a Print

PLAN

Think of a design for a rubber stamp that shows symbols. Make some sketches.

CREATE

1. Choose your best sketch, and draw it lightly onto a foam tray. Carve your drawing into the foam by pressing with a dull pencil point.

2. Spread a thin layer of tempera paint evenly over the foam tray with a foam brush.

3. Lay a clean sheet of paper across the wet paint. Press gently and evenly on the paper with your fingers. Then carefully lift the paper off the tray.

REFLECT

What does the symbol in your print mean to you?

MATERIALS

- pencil
- sketchbook
- foam tray
- tempera paint
- foam brush
- water bowl
- white or colored paper

Quick Tip
You can use the foam tray again by rinsing off the paint. Apply another color of paint to the tray to make a different print.

141

PDAS Domain IV

Activity Options

Quick Activity Have students sketch a personal symbol.

Early Finishers Have students use another color to make an additional print of the same symbol.

Challenge See *Teacher Resource Book*, p. 70.

PDAS Domain IV

ESL Have students **build vocabulary** by talking about the symbols found on the flags of their home countries.

Challenge Have students create a set of universal symbols for classroom or school places and procedures.

30-40 Minutes

Artist's Workshop

Create a Print

PLAN After students have read the activity steps on page 141, brainstorm with them some common symbols, such as smiley faces, hearts, or stars.

CREATE Ask students to integrate a variety of ideas about self, life events, and family into their original artworks. Have them decide what kind of balance they will use to organize the symbols in their print. TEKS 4.1B, TEKS 4.2A

REFLECT Have students describe the intent in their personal artworks and form conclusions about the symbol they created. SELF-EVALUATION TEKS 4.4A

5-10 Minutes

Wrap-Up

Informal Assessment PDAS Domain III

- **Does your print have symmetrical or asymmetrical balance? Explain.** (Responses will vary.) PERCEPTION/AESTHETICS TEKS 4.1B

- **How is your print like the artwork in image C? How is it different?** (Responses will vary.) COMPARE AND CONTRAST TEKS 4.3B

Extend Through Writing TAKS Writing Objectives 1, 6

POEM Have students write a poem telling what the symbol in their print means to them. Remind students to proofread their writing.

Recommended Reading

The Talking Cloth by Rhonda Mitchell. Orchard, 1997. EASY

Unit 4

PDAS Domains I, III

Review and Reflect

 Have students reflect on what they have learned about artists' use of pattern and balance in artworks from different cultures. Display **Art Prints 10, 11, 12, 7,** and **9.** Encourage small groups of students to use Discussion Card 4 on page R35 and their completed Word Knowledge Charts to discuss what they learned about the vocabulary and concepts in this unit.

Vocabulary and Concepts

Have students read each sentence and choose the letter of the word or phrase that best completes it. (1. B; 2. J; 3. A; 4. H; 5. D)

READING SKILL
Compare and Contrast

Remind students that comparing and contrasting in art is like comparing and contrasting information in text—you look closely at two or more things and think about how they are alike and how they are different. As they reread the information on the artworks they have selected, encourage students to think about the subjects in the artworks they are comparing and contrasting, as well as the way the artists used patterns and balance. TEKS 4.3B; TAKS Reading Objective 4

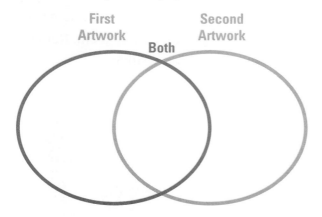

First Artwork   Second Artwork
Both

Unit 4   Review and Reflect

Vocabulary and Concepts

Choose the letter of the word or phrase that best completes each sentence.

1 Repeated lines, shapes, or colors create a ___.

  A weaving   **C** tapestry

  B pattern   **D** symbol

2 An artwork shows ___ when both sides are the same.

  F pattern   **H** asymmetrical balance

  G symbols   **J** symmetrical balance

3 An artwork shows ___ when the same patterns extend from its center.

  A radial balance   **C** depth

  B asymmetrical balance   **D** symbols

4 Artists may use ___ to create a sense of balance.

  F pattern   **H** visual weight

  G tapestry   **J** symbols

5 A ___ is a picture or object that stands for an idea.

  A pattern   **C** tapestry

  B weaving   **D** symbol

READING SKILL
Compare and Contrast

Select two artworks from different lessons in this unit, and reread the information about them. Use a Venn diagram to compare and contrast them.

Artwork 1   Both   Artwork 2

142

TEKS 4.1A, TEKS 4.2B, TEKS 4.2C, TEKS 4.4B

Home and Community Connection

School-Home Connection
Copy and distribute *Teacher Resource Book* pp. 91–92. After students complete the unit, have them communicate ideas about themselves and their families by using sensory knowledge and life experiences to sketch a textile design using a symbol that has meaning to them.

Community Connection
You may want to invite a local artist to visit your class to share his or her portfolio. Have students prepare for a question-and-answer session to help them interpret moods and ideas in the artist's portfolio.
CAREER CONNECTION

★ TEKS 4.1A communicate ideas; TEKS 4.1B discuss elements and principles; TEKS 4.2B design original artworks; TEKS 4.2C produce artworks; TEKS 4.3A identify main ideas; TEKS 4.3B compare and contrast artworks; TEKS 4.4A form conclusions about personal artworks; *(continued)*

Write About Art

Choose two pieces of your own artwork, and write a composition in which you compare and contrast them. Use a Venn diagram to plan your writing. Use unit vocabulary words to describe each artwork.

REMEMBER — YOU SHOULD

- write about the similarities in one paragraph and the differences in another.
- use correct grammar, spelling, and punctuation.

Critic's Corner

Look at *Four Seasons* by John Biggers to answer the questions below.

DESCRIBE What are the subjects in the artwork? How would you describe them? How are the figures in the artwork alike? How are they different?

John Biggers, *Four Seasons,*
1984, color lithograph, 24 in. × 32 in.
Private collection.

ANALYZE Does the artwork show symmetrical balance or asymmetrical balance?

INTERPRET What ideas do you think the artist was trying to express in this artwork?

EVALUATE What is your opinion of the way the artist showed the four seasons in this artwork?

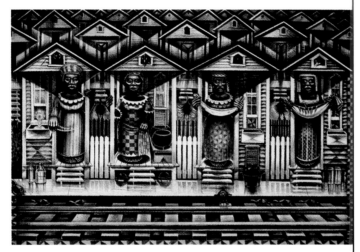

143

PDAS Domain III

Assessment

Portfolio Assessment

Work with students to choose a piece of their artwork to include in their portfolios. Suggest that they decide which piece best fulfilled the assignment or which piece they liked best for another reason. You may want to provide specific feedback that targets students' use of principles of design and techniques. See also Portfolio Recording Form, page R32.

Additional Assessment Options

- Progress Recording Form, p. R33
- Artist's Workshop Rubrics (Self/Teacher and Peer), pp. R30–R31
- Unit 4 Test, *Teacher Resource Book* p. 102

Write About Art

Compare-and-Contrast Composition Read aloud the writing prompt with students. Suggest that they think about their uses of pattern and balance in their artworks, as well as other elements and principles, as they plan their writing. Encourage students to use unit vocabulary words in their writing. TEKS 4.1B, TEKS 4.4A; TAKS Writing Objectives 1, 3, 4

Critic's Corner

RESPONSE/EVALUATION Use the steps below to guide students in analyzing *Four Seasons* by John Biggers. See also Discussion Card 2, p. R34.

DESCRIBE Students should note that the subjects, four women, are at work in four different seasons. The figures look alike but are wearing different dresses and are doing different jobs. TEKS 4.3A

ANALYZE Students should point out that the artwork shows symmetrical balance because the lines and shapes on either side of the vertical axis are very similar. TEKS 4.1B

INTERPRET Students may say that the artwork shows that each of the four seasons has equal importance. Discuss their ideas. TEKS 4.4B

EVALUATE Students should support their opinions with reasons.

 TAKS Test Preparation: Reading and Writing Through Art, pp. 48–52

TEKS 4.4B interpret artworks by peers and others; PDAS Domain I active participation; PDAS Domain III evaluation and feedback; TAKS Reading Objective 4 apply critical-thinking skills; TAKS Writing Objective 1 composition; TAKS Writing Objective 3 organization; TAKS Writing Objective 4 sentence construction

UNIT 4 *Review and Reflect* **143**

Unit 5

Space, Movement, and Unity

The Artist's Environment

Artists may draw inspiration from their environments, but sometimes they create new environments. In this unit, students will learn how artists create environments such as landscape paintings, architecture, garden designs, and murals.

Resources

- Unit 5 Art Prints (13–15)
- Additional Art Prints (4, 17)
- Art Transparencies 13–15
- Test Preparation: Reading and Writing Through Art, pp. 53–57
- Artist's Workshop Activities: English and Spanish, pp. 41–50
- Encyclopedia of Artists and Art History, pp. R44–R65
- Picture Cards Collection, cards 17, 26, 68, 81, 98, 103, 115, 121

Using the Art Prints

- Discussion Cards, pp. R34–R38
- Teaching suggestions, backs of Art Prints
- Art Print Teaching Suggestions: Spanish

Teacher Resource Book

- Vocabulary Word Cards in English and Spanish, pp. 23–26
- Reading Skill Card 5, p. 35
- Copying Masters, pp. 41, 46, 47
- Challenge Activities, pp. 71–75
- School-Home Connection: English/Spanish, pp. 93–94
- Unit 5 Test, p. 103

Technology Resources

 Electronic Art Gallery CD-ROM, Intermediate
Picture Card Bank CD-ROM

 Visit *The Learning Site*
www.harcourtschool.com

- Multimedia Art Glossary
- Multimedia Biographies
- Reading Skills and Activities

Art Prints for This Unit

ART PRINT 13

Bus Interior
by Richard Estes

ART PRINT 14

Pyramid du Louvre
by I. M. Pei

ART PRINT 15

The Alamo
by Unknown Architect

ART PRINT 17

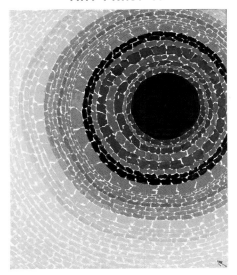

Eclipse
by Alma Woodsey Thomas

ART PRINT 4

The Bathers
by Pierre-Auguste Renoir

Lesson	Objectives and Vocabulary	Art Images	Production/ Materials

Focus Skill: Summarize and Paraphrase, pp. 146–147

Lesson	Objectives and Vocabulary	Art Images	Production/ Materials
21 **DEPTH AND DISTANCE** pp. 148–151 🕐 30–60 minutes	• Discuss the element of space in artworks • Design and create an original scene that shows depth • *(Focus Skill)* Summarize and paraphrase ideas in artworks **Vocabulary: space, depth, foreground, background, middle ground**	• **Marcoussis–Cows Grazing** by Jean Baptiste Camille Corot • **Café Terrace on the Place du Forum, Arles, At Night** by Vincent van Gogh • **The Discovery** by Jack Gunter	**Create Depth in a Scene** ❏ pencil ❏ sketchbook ❏ white paper ❏ oil pastels
22 **PERSPECTIVE TECHNIQUES** pp. 152–155 🕐 30–60 minutes	• Understand and identify the use of perspective in artworks • Draw a scene with linear perspective • *(Focus Skill)* Summarize and paraphrase ideas in artworks **Vocabulary: atmospheric perspective, horizon line, linear perspective, vanishing point**	• **Among the Sierra Nevada Mountains, California** by Albert Bierstadt • **Alfalfa Fields, Saint-Denis** by Georges Seurat • **Commuter Trains, Union Station** by Don Jacot	**Draw a Scene with Linear Perspective** ❏ pencil ❏ sketchbook ❏ white paper ❏ ruler ❏ colored pencils

Art ↔ Social Studies Connection: Mission Architecture, pp. 156–157

Lesson	Objectives and Vocabulary	Art Images	Production/ Materials
23 **GARDEN DESIGN** pp. 158–161 🕐 30–60 minutes	• Identify movement and unity in artworks • Create a design for a park • *(Focus Skill)* Summarize and paraphrase ideas in artworks **Vocabulary: movement, unity**	• **Garden at Villandry, France** • **Flower Conservatory, Golden Gate Park** • **Desert Pavilion at the Brooklyn Botanical Garden**	**Design a Park** ❏ pencil ❏ sketchbook ❏ colored pencils or markers ❏ magazines ❏ scissors ❏ glue
24 **ARCHITECTURAL BALANCE** pp. 162–165 🕐 30–60 minutes	• Choose appropriate vocabulary to discuss the use of balance in architecture • Design an original building • *(Focus Skill)* Summarize and paraphrase ideas in artworks **Vocabulary: architect**	• **Chase Building** Dallas, Texas • **City Hall** designed by Norman Foster • **Hotel Nice** Nice, France	**Design a Building** ❏ books or magazines ❏ pencil ❏ sketchbook ❏ white paper ❏ colored pencils or markers

Art ↔ Social Studies Connection: I. M. Pei, pp. 166–167

Lesson	Objectives and Vocabulary	Art Images	Production/ Materials
25 **OUTDOOR MURALS** pp. 168–171 🕐 30–60 minutes	• Identify the characteristics of murals • Design and create a class mural • *(Focus Skill)* Summarize and paraphrase ideas in artworks **Vocabulary: mural, trompe l'oeil**	• **Sunflower Mural on Fence** Cape Town, South Africa • **Common Threads** by Meg Fish Saligman • **Seven Point One (Siete Punto Uno)** by John Pugh	**Create a Class Mural** ❏ pencil ❏ sketchbook ❏ butcher paper ❏ tempera paint ❏ large and small paintbrushes ❏ water bowl

Review and Reflect, pp. 172–173

★ **TEKS 4.1A** communicate ideas; **TEKS 4.2B** design original artworks; **PDAS Domain IV** classroom management

Summarize and Paraphrase, pp. 146–147

Focus Skill

Opportunities for application of the skill are provided on pp. 150, 154, 160, 164, 170, 172, and 173.

Resources and Technology	Suggested Literature	Across the Curriculum
• Art Print 4 • Reading Skill Card 5 • Discussion Cards 1, 3, pp. R34, R35 • Electronic Art Gallery CD-ROM, Intermediate	*The First Starry Night* by Joan Shaddox Isom 	**Social Studies** A Visit to Arles, p. 149 **Reading** Summarize and Paraphrase, p. 150 **Writing** Postcard, p. 151
• Art Print 13 • Reading Skill Card 5 • Discussion Cards 1, 3, pp. R34, R35 • Electronic Art Gallery CD-ROM, Intermediate	*How Artists Use Perspective* by Paul Flux 	**Social Studies** Sierra Nevada, p. 153 **Reading** Summarize and Paraphrase, p. 154 **Writing** Short Story, p. 155
• Art Print 17 • Reading Skill Card 5 • Discussion Cards 1, 4, pp. R34, R35 • Electronic Art Gallery CD-ROM, Intermediate	*The Legend of the Indian Paintbrush* by Tomie dePaola 	**Science** Cactus Types, p. 159 **Reading** Summarize and Paraphrase, p. 160 **Writing** Diary Entry, p. 161
• Art Prints 14, 15 • Reading Skill Card 5 • Discussion Cards 1, 10, pp. R34, R38 • Electronic Art Gallery CD-ROM, Intermediate	*Going to the Getty* by J. Otto Seibold and Vivian Walsh 	**Social Studies** Architecture Throughout History, p. 163 **Reading** Summarize and Paraphrase, p. 164 **Writing** Travel Guide, p. 165
• Art Print 15 • Reading Skill Card 5 • Discussion Cards 1, 10, pp. R34, R38 • Electronic Art Gallery CD-ROM, Intermediate	*Diego* by Jonah Winter 	**Social Studies** Mural Search, p. 169 **Reading** Summarize and Paraphrase, p. 170 **Writing** News Story, p. 171

Art Puzzlers

Present these art puzzlers to students at the beginning or end of a class or when students finish an assignment early.

- Think about the space directly in front of you. If you were looking at it in a picture, what would be in the **foreground, middle ground**, and **background**?

- Look around your classroom. Choose a part of the room where you see an example of **linear perspective**, like a corner. Draw that part of the room. TEKS 4.2B

- Sketch a garden path that shows **movement.** TEKS 4.2B

- If you could meet the **architect** I. M. Pei, what questions would you ask him?

- Imagine a **mural** that showed special events in your family. Describe it. TEKS 4.1A

 School-Home Connection
The activities above are included in the School-Home Connection for this unit. See *Teacher Resource Book* pp. 93–94.

Assessment Options
- Rubrics and Recording Forms, pp. R30–R33
- Unit 5 Test, *Teacher Resource Book,* p. 103

 Visit *The Learning Site*
www.harcourtschool.com

Artist's Workshops PREVIEW

Use these pages to help you gather and organize
materials for the production activity in each lesson.

LESSON	MATERIALS

21 Create Depth in a Scene p. 151

- pencil
- sketchbook
- white paper
- oil pastels

FINISHED EXAMPLE

Objective: To design and create an original scene
that shows depth

 30–40 minutes

Challenge Activity: See *Teacher Resource Book*,
page 71.

LESSON

22 Draw a Scene with Linear Perspective

p. 155

- pencil
- sketchbook
- white paper
- ruler
- colored pencils

FINISHED EXAMPLE

Objective: To practice perspective techniques
by designing and creating an original scene
using linear perspective

 30–40 minutes

Challenge Activity: See *Teacher Resource Book*,
page 72.

 Safety Tips For safety information,
see Art Safety, p. R4,
or Art Safety Poster.

 Quick Tip For information on media and
techniques, see pp. R15–R23.

LESSON	MATERIALS

23 Design a Park p. 161

- pencil
- sketchbook
- colored pencils or markers
- magazines
- scissors
- glue

Objective: To create a design for a park, using the principles of movement and unity

🕐 **30–40 minutes**

Challenge Activity: See *Teacher Resource Book*, page 73.

24 Design a Building p. 165

- books or magazines
- pencil
- sketchbook
- white paper
- colored pencils or markers

Objective: To practice using the principle of balance by designing an original building

🕐 **30–40 minutes**

Challenge Activity: See *Teacher Resource Book*, page 74.

25 Create a Class Mural p. 171

- pencil
- sketchbook
- butcher paper
- tempera paint
- large and small paintbrushes
- water bowl

Objective: To incorporate a variety of ideas about school and community into a class mural

🕐 **30–40 minutes**

Challenge Activity: See *Teacher Resource Book*, page 75.

Unit 5

PDAS Domains I, II

The Artist's Environment

PREVIEW THE UNIT

Tell students that in this unit they will view artworks that were inspired by the artists' surroundings. Invite students to preview this unit by reading the lesson titles and examining the art images.

STEP INTO THE ART

Have students examine the painting on pages 144 and 145 and describe what they see. Then read page 145 with students, and discuss their answers to the questions.

- **Describe what you would hear and feel.** Students may list sensory details such as the patter of rain on the umbrellas, the clatter of carriage wheels and footsteps on the road and sidewalk, and the feel of cool, wet air. TEKS 4.1A

- **Which person would you talk to?** Discuss with students the reasons for their choices.

- **What would you say to that person?** Encourage students to role-play a conversation with the person they chose.

SHARE BACKGROUND INFORMATION

Tell students that this artwork is considered by many to be the artist's masterpiece. The setting is a busy intersection near a train station in Paris, France. The painting depicts the broad new boulevards and modern apartment buildings built in Paris in the 1850s and 1860s.

 See **Using the Maps of Museums and Art Sites,** p. R2.

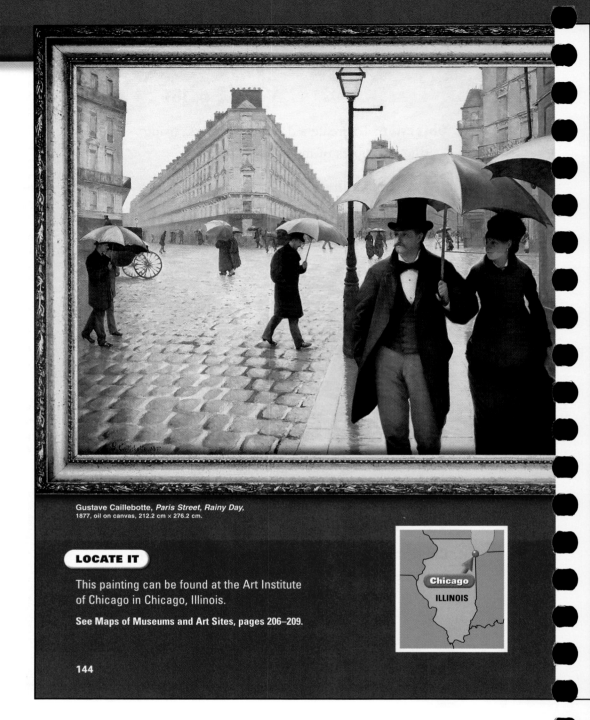

Gustave Caillebotte, *Paris Street, Rainy Day,* 1877, oil on canvas, 212.2 cm × 276.2 cm.

This painting can be found at the Art Institute of Chicago in Chicago, Illinois.

See Maps of Museums and Art Sites, pages 206–209.

Chicago
ILLINOIS

144

Background Information

About the Artist
Gustave Caillebotte (goos•TAHV ky•yuh•BAWT) (1848–1894) studied art in Paris, where he met Impressionist artists. Like them, Caillebotte is known for his use of vivid colors and natural light.

For additional information about the artist, see the Encyclopedia of Artists and Art History, pp. R44–R65, and the Gallery of Artists, *Student Edition* pp. 240–253.

For related artworks, see **Electronic Art Gallery CD-ROM, Intermediate.**

Unit 5 Space, Movement, and Unity

The Artist's Environment

Step into the Art

Imagine you could step into the scene in this painting. Describe what you would hear and feel. Which person would you talk to? What would you say to that person?

 ABOUT THE ARTIST

See Gallery of Artists, pages 240–253.

Unit Vocabulary

space	atmospheric perspective	movement
depth	horizon line	unity
foreground	linear perspective	architect
background		mural
middle ground	vanishing point	trompe l'oeil

 Multimedia Art Glossary
Visit *The Learning Site*
www.harcourtschool.com

145

Unit Vocabulary

Read aloud the terms with students, and use the Word Knowledge Chart below to assess and discuss their prior knowledge.

space the area around, between, and within objects

depth the appearance of space or distance in a two-dimensional artwork

foreground the part of an artwork that seems closest to the viewer

background the part of an artwork that seems farthest from the viewer

middle ground the part of an artwork that is between the foreground and the background

atmospheric perspective a technique used to create a sense of depth in a two-dimensional artwork by using dull colors and fuzzy edges in the background

horizon line a line that shows where the sky meets the land or the water

linear perspective a technique used to create a sense of depth in a two-dimensional artwork by making parallel lines meet at a vanishing point

vanishing point the point on the horizon line where parallel lines meet

movement the way a viewer's eyes travel from one element to another in an artwork

unity a sense that an artwork is complete

architect a person who designs buildings

mural a painting that is created on a wall or ceiling, indoors, or outdoors

trompe l'oeil a style of painting that seems to show a three-dimensional scene on a two-dimensional surface; from the French for "trick the eye"

Language Arts Connection

Students may create a chart like the one below to identify familiar and unfamiliar vocabulary terms. Encourage them to add information to their charts as they work through this unit.

WORD KNOWLEDGE CHART		
I know this term.	I have seen this term before.	I have never seen this term.

Vocabulary Resources

- Vocabulary Cards in English and Spanish: *Teacher Resource Book,* pp. 23–26
- Student Edition Glossary, pp. 254–261

 **Multimedia Art Glossary**
Visit *The Learning Site*
www.harcourtschool.com

Focus Skill READING SKILL

PDAS Domains I, II

Summarize and Paraphrase

SKILL TRACE	
SUMMARIZE AND PARAPHRASE	
Introduce	pp. 146–147
Review	pp. 150, 154, 160, 164, 170, 172, 173

DISCUSS THE SKILL

Access Prior Knowledge Ask volunteers to name topics they are studying in their social studies or science classes. Discuss with students what they do to help themselves understand complex information. Tell them that finding the main idea of a passage and retelling a passage in their own words are helpful skills that can also be used to understand artworks.

APPLY TO ART

Summarize and Paraphrase Have students read page 146 and look at the image. Then have them point out details in the painting that support the summarize and paraphrase statements. Help students conclude that they can summarize what is happening in the artwork in one or two sentences that tell the main idea and that they can paraphrase what is happening by retelling the main idea in their own words and by adding more detail.
TEKS 4.4B

Focus Skill READING SKILL

Summarize and Paraphrase

When you *summarize,* you tell only main ideas or important events. When you *paraphrase,* you use your own words to restate information or to retell a story. When you paraphrase, you give more details than when you summarize.

Look at the image below. You can **summarize** the image like this:

• People are enjoying an outdoor swimming pool in different ways.

You can **paraphrase** the image like this:

• Many people have come to the swimming pool to enjoy the day. Some are talking, some are resting, and others are looking at the water.

William James Glackens, *Outdoor Swimming Pool,*
oil on canvas, 18 in. x 24 in.

146

Background Information

About the Artist

For many years, William James Glackens (1870–1938) worked as an illustrator for newspapers and magazines. Later, he focused on painting. Many of his paintings were of city parks, street scenes, and other images of contemporary urban life.

For additional information about the artist, see pp. R44–R65.

For related artworks, see **Electronic Art Gallery CD-ROM, Intermediate.**

★ **TEKS 4.4B** interpret artworks by peers and others; **PDAS Domain I** active participation; **PDAS Domain II** learner-centered instruction; **PDAS Domain IV** classroom management; **TAKS Reading Objective 1** demonstrate understanding of texts; *(continued)*

To make sure that you understand what you read, you can summarize or paraphrase the text. Read this passage:

> Lara spent the whole day at the community swimming pool. She saw a lot of people there. Most of them were sunbathing at the edge of the pool, but a few people were getting ready to swim. A little boy and his mother sat on the ground, playing with some toys. Two women sat on a bench, talking and laughing. Everyone seemed to be enjoying the day.

Summarize the passage in two sentences. Then paraphrase the passage in a new paragraph. You can use a chart like this to help you.

Summary: Main Ideas Only
Lara spent the whole day at the pool. She saw a lot of people having fun in different ways.

Paraphrase: Main Ideas and Details in Your Own Words

On Your Own

As you read the lessons in this unit, use charts like the one above to summarize and paraphrase when you read information and view artworks. Look back at your charts when you see questions with *READING SKILL*.

147

APPLY TO READING

Summarize and Paraphrase the Passage   Explain to students that as they read the passage, they should be thinking about how to summarize the main idea in one or two sentences and then how to paraphrase by retelling the events in the passage in their own words.

Have students read the passage on page 147. Work with them to complete the chart to summarize and then paraphrase the passage.
TAKS Reading Objectives 1, 3, 4

Summary: Main Ideas Only
Lara spent the whole day at the pool. She saw a lot of people having fun in different ways.

Paraphrase: Main Ideas and Details in Your Own Words
Lara spent the day at the pool. She saw people sunbathing, swimming, and sitting on a bench talking. She saw a little boy and his mother playing with toys on the ground. Everyone seemed to be having a good time.

ON YOUR OWN

As students read about other artworks and art concepts, have them use a chart such as the one on page 147 to help them summarize and paraphrase the information in the artworks and the text.

TAKS Reading Objective 4

Reading Skill Card

Distribute Reading Skill Card 5, *Teacher Resource Book* page 35. Have students summarize and paraphrase the information in this unit.

Extend the Skill
For additional teaching suggestions, See **Art Transparency 13.**

PDAS Domain IV

ESL   To reinforce the difference between summarizing and paraphrasing, pair students with English-fluent peers and have them read the passage on page 147 together. Then have them work together to find details in the passage to use in their **paraphrase.**

Reading Skills and Activities
Visit *The Learning Site*
www.harcourtschool.com

Lesson 21

Depth and Distance

OBJECTIVES
- Choose appropriate vocabulary to discuss the element of space in artworks
- Identify and recognize the characteristics of depth in artworks
- Design and create an original scene that shows depth
- Summarize and paraphrase ideas in artworks

RESOURCES
- Art Print 4
- Reading Skill Card 5
- Discussion Cards 1, 3, pp. R34–R35
- Electronic Art Gallery CD-ROM, Intermediate

Multimedia Art Glossary and Biographies
Visit *The Learning Site*
www.harcourtschool.com

5 Minutes

Warm-Up

Build Background   Arrange three classroom objects, such as three chairs or three stools, at different distances from students. Help students generalize that the closer the object is to them, the larger it appears. Tell students that in this lesson they will learn how artists use different techniques to show distance in two-dimensional artworks.

Lesson 21

Depth and Distance

Vocabulary
- space
- depth
- foreground
- background
- middle ground

Space is the three-dimensional area around, between, and within objects. One way an artist can show space on a flat surface is to create the feeling of depth. **Depth** is the appearance of space or distance in an artwork. Artists use different techniques to show depth.

Foreground, Middle Ground, and Background

Look at image **A**. The artist created a feeling of depth by dividing the scene into parts. The part that seems closest to the viewer is called the **foreground**. The part that seems farthest from the viewer is called the **background**. The part that is between the foreground and the background is called the **middle ground**. What do you see in the foreground of image **A**? What do you see in the middle ground and background?

A Jean Baptiste Camille Corot, *Marcoussis—Cows Grazing*, 1845–1850, oil on canvas, 16¼ in. × 29⅝ in. Private Collection.

Background Information

Art History

A Jean Baptiste Camille Corot (1796–1875) preferred to work outdoors, sketching what he saw.

B During his lifetime, Vincent van Gogh (van GOH) (1853–1890) sold only one painting out of the hundreds he created. Today, van Gogh is considered one of the giants of modern art.

For additional information about the artist, see pp. R44–R65.

For related artworks, see **Electronic Art Gallery CD-ROM, Intermediate.**

TEKS 4.1A communicate ideas; TEKS 4.1B discuss elements and principles; PDAS Domain I active participation; PDAS Domain II learner-centered instruction; TAKS Reading Objective 1 demonstrate understanding of texts; *(continued)*

LOCATE IT

The artwork shown in image **B** can be found in the Netherlands.

THE NETHERLANDS

Otterlo

See Maps of Museums and Art Sites, pages 206–209.

Vincent van Gogh, *Café Terrace on the Place du Forum, Arles, At Night,* 1888, oil on canvas, 81 cm × 65.5 cm. Kröller-Müller Museum, Otterlo, the Netherlands.

Detail and Distance

Now look at the scene in image . What do you see in the foreground? The artist used thick, curved lines to paint the cobblestones in this part of the street. Notice how much less detail the artist used to paint the cobblestones in the background. Objects that have more detail seem to be closer to the viewer. Objects that have less detail seem to be farther away.

149

TAKS Reading Objectives 1, 3, 4

Social Studies Connection

A Visit to Arles   Explain to students that Arles was a prominent city in France long before Vincent van Gogh began painting there. Since ancient times, Arles has been a center of commerce and an outlet to the Mediterranean Sea. Have students find Arles on a map or globe. Ask them to imagine that they are travel agents planning a vacation for someone going to Arles. Encourage them to use encyclopedias or online resources to gather interesting facts about Arles, places tourists might want to visit, and things to do. Ask volunteers to prepare oral presentations for their classmates.

10-15 Minutes

Teach

Preview the Art   Invite students to preview images A through C on pages 148–150. Ask them to describe the details they see. Use Discussion Card 1 and the questions below to guide the discussion. Then have students read pages 148–150.

A *Marcoussis—Cows Grazing*   **How would you describe the setting in this painting?**

B *Café Terrace on the Place du Forum, Arles, At Night*   **What kinds of sounds do you think you would hear if you were in this scene?**   TEKS 4.1A

C *The Discovery*   **What does the title tell you about this painting?**

Discuss Art Concepts   Have students choose appropriate vocabulary to discuss the artist's use of space in the artwork in image A by pointing out the two cows grazing in the foreground, the group of cows in the middle ground, and the trees in the background.   TEKS 4.1B

In image B, students should point out the cobblestones in the foreground and note the loss of detail toward the background.

Discuss with students that the trees in the foreground in image C are much larger than those in the background. Point out that the artist showed the most detail on the trees in the foreground and used very little detail on the trees in the background.

LOCATE IT   Tell students that the subject of the painting in image B was a café in Arles, France. This café still exists today—it is now called Café Van Gogh.

Summarize and Paraphrase Ask students to look at image B. Have them write one or two sentences to summarize

- the setting shown in the painting.

- what might be happening in the painting.

Then have students use details to describe in their own words the setting and plot in the painting.
TEKS 4.4B

Think Critically

Use the questions below to check students' understanding of lesson concepts.

1. **READING SKILL** **Summarize what you think the artist's message is in image A.**
(Possible response: Cows grazing is a pleasant, peaceful sight.) **SUMMARIZE AND PARAPHRASE**
TEKS 4.3A, TEKS 4.4B

2. **How did the artist use size to show depth in image A?** (Possible response: The cows in the foreground are larger than the cows in the middle ground, so they seem to be closer to the viewer.) **PERCEPTION/AESTHETICS**

3. **WRITE** **Read the title of image C. Write a short story telling about the discovery.**
NARRATIVE TAKS Writing Objective 1

Size and Distance

What do you notice about the sizes of the trees in image **C**? Larger objects seem to be closer to the viewer. Smaller objects seem to be farther away. Compare the trees in the foreground to those in the background. How did the artist use detail to show distance?

C Jack Gunter, *The Discovery,*
2001, oil on canvas, 78 in. × 42 in.
Private collection.

Think Critically

1. **READING SKILL** Summarize what you think the artist's message is in image **A**. **SUMMARIZE AND PARAPHRASE**

2. How did the artist use size to show depth in image **A**?

3. **WRITE** Read the title of image **C**. Write a short story telling about the discovery.

150

TEKS 4.1B

Art Print 4

Display **Art Print 4** and distribute to students Discussion Card 3: *Elements of Art.* Have them discuss the art element of space and how the artist created a sense of depth in the artwork.

ART PRINT 4

The Bathers
by Pierre-Auguste Renoir

★ TEKS 4.1B discuss elements and principles; TEKS 4.2A integrate ideas in artworks; TEKS 4.2B design original artworks; TEKS 4.3A identify main ideas; TEKS 4.4A form conclusions about personal artworks; TEKS 4.4B interpret artworks by peers and others; *(continued)*

Artist's Workshop

Create Depth in a Scene

MATERIALS
- pencil
- sketchbook
- white paper
- oil pastels

PLAN

Think of an outdoor scene you would like to draw. Sketch some ideas. Think about how you can show depth in your scene by changing the sizes or details of the objects you draw.

CREATE

1. Choose your best sketch, and copy it onto white paper.
2. Use oil pastels to add color to your drawing.

REFLECT

How did you show depth in your drawing? What did you draw in the foreground, middle ground, and background?

Quick Tip
You may want to look through books and magazines for ideas for your drawing.

151

 Artist's Workshop

30-40 Minutes

Create Depth in a Scene

PLAN After students have read page 151, distribute *Teacher Resource Book*, page 46 to give them practice with the concepts.

CREATE Have students integrate a variety of ideas about community into their artworks to help them plan which objects will be in the foreground, middle ground, and background. TEKS 4.2A, TEKS 4.2B

REFLECT Have students explain how they created depth in their scenes and form conclusions about space in their artworks. SELF-EVALUATION TEKS 4.4A

Wrap-Up
5-10 Minutes

Informal Assessment PDAS Domain III

- **How did viewing the artworks in this lesson help you create depth in your artwork?**
(Responses will vary.) EVALUATION/CRITICISM TEKS 4.4B

- **Give a summary of your scene.** (Responses will vary.) SUMMARIZE AND PARAPHRASE TEKS 4.4A

Extend Through Writing TAKS Writing Objective 1

POSTCARD Ask students to imagine that their outdoor scene is the front of a postcard. Have them address the postcard to a friend and write a brief message describing the scene.

Recommended Reading

The First Starry Night by Joan Shaddox Isom. Whispering Coyote, 1997. AVERAGE

 PDAS Domain IV

Activity Options

Quick Activity Have students create depth in a pencil sketch of a scene.

Early Finishers Have students add more detail to their scenes.

Challenge See *Teacher Resource Book*, p. 71.

 PDAS Domain IV

ESL Use **visuals** to support **comprehensible input** for terms related to the outdoors. Display **Picture Cards Collection** cards 68, 81, and 98 for students to discuss and use as reference.

river

See also **Picture Card Bank CD-ROM**, Category: Places People Go.

PDAS Domains I, II
Perspective Techniques

OBJECTIVES
- Understand and identify the use of atmospheric perspective and linear perspective in artworks
- Design and create an original scene with linear perspective
- Summarize and paraphrase ideas in artworks

RESOURCES
- Art Print 13
- Reading Skill Card 5
- Discussion Cards 1, 3, pp. R34, R35
- Electronic Art Gallery CD-ROM, Intermediate

Multimedia Art Glossary and Biographies
Visit *The Learning Site*
www.harcourtschool.com

Warm-Up

Build Background   Display **Art Print 13,** a painting by Richard Estes, and ask students to describe what they see. Have students point out the part of the painting that appears closest to them and the part that appears farthest away. Ask them to compare the details in the foreground of the painting with the details in the background. Tell students that in this lesson they will learn more techniques artists use to create the feeling of depth in their artworks.

Lesson 22

Perspective Techniques

Lesson 22

Vocabulary
- atmospheric perspective
- horizon line
- linear perspective
- vanishing point

Atmospheric Perspective

Artists use different perspective techniques to create the feeling of depth and distance in flat artworks. Look at the background in image **A**. The artist used a technique called **atmospheric perspective** to create the feeling of great distance. He used dull colors and fuzzy edges to make objects seem to fade away in the distance.

 Albert Bierstadt, *Among the Sierra Nevada Mountains, California*, 1868, oil on canvas, 183 cm × 305 cm. National Museum of American Art, Washington, D.C.

152

Background Information

About the Artists

A American painter **Albert Bierstadt** (BEER•stat) (1830–1902) produced large paintings depicting the beauty of the American West.

B **Georges Seurat** (suh•RAH) (1859–1891) pioneered the use of pointillism—painting tiny dots of contrasting colors so close together that they seem to blend.

For additional information about the artist, see pp. R44–R65.

 For related artworks, see **Electronic Art Gallery CD-ROM, Intermediate.**

★ **TEKS 4.3A** identify main ideas; **PDAS Domain I** active participation; **PDAS Domain II** learner-centered instruction; **TAKS Reading Objective 1** demonstrate understanding of texts; **TAKS Reading Objective 3** use a variety of strategies; (*continued*)

Horizon Line

Find the place in image where the sky seems to meet the land. This is called the **horizon line**. In image B the horizon line appears high up in the scene. The artist was probably sitting down and looking up when he painted the artwork. Where do you think the horizon line would be if the artist had been standing as he painted?

Georges Seurat, *Alfalfa Fields, Saint-Denis*, 1885–1886, oil on canvas, 25¼ in. × 31⅞ in. National Gallery of Scotland, Edinburgh, Scotland.

153

TAKS Reading Objectives 1, 3, 4

Social Studies Connection

Sierra Nevada The subject in the painting in image A is the majestic Sierra Nevada mountain range in California. Have students work in pairs to find more facts about this mountain range in an encyclopedia or reference book. Ask students to list their findings and draw conclusions about why Albert Bierstadt found these mountains such a fascinating subject.

10-15 Minutes

Teach

Preview the Art Have students preview images A through C on pages 152–154. Ask them to describe details that show depth in each image. Use Discussion Card 1 and the questions below to guide the discussion. Then have students read pages 152–154.

A *Among the Sierra Nevada Mountains, California* **What do you think is the main idea expressed in this painting?**
TEKS 4.3A

B *Alfalfa Fields, Saint-Denis* **What time of day do you think is shown in this scene? Why do you think that?**

C *Commuter Trains, Union Station* **Describe what you see in this painting.**

Discuss Art Concepts Discuss with students the difference between the darker colors and crisper details in the foreground of image A and the duller colors and fuzzier details in the background.

In image B, help students understand that if the artist had been standing while he painted, the horizon line would be higher up in the scene.

In image C, have students point out the artist's use of linear perspective to show depth in the ceiling, in the train tracks, and on the side of each train.

Teach (continued)

Math Link Have students communicate ideas about school using sensory knowledge to identify examples of linear perspective in the classroom. Have them note the way the lines of the walls, floor, and ceiling appear to grow closer together in the distance. TEKS 4.1A

Summarize and Paraphrase Ask students to look back at image C. Then have them

- summarize the artwork by telling its main idea.

- describe the artwork in their own words.

Then ask students to discuss the difference between the summary and the description of the artwork. TEKS 4.3A

Think Critically

Use the questions below to check students' understanding of lesson concepts.

1. (Focus Skill) *READING SKILL* **Summarize the technique of linear perspective.** (To show depth, the artist draws parallel lines closer together in the distance until they meet at the vanishing point on the horizon line.) **SUMMARIZE AND PARAPHRASE**

2. **Why do artists use a vanishing point?** (to show depth) **PERCEPTION/AESTHETICS**

3. **WRITE** **Imagine you are riding one of the trains in image C. Write a paragraph telling where you are going and what you will do when you arrive.** **NARRATIVE** TAKS Writing Objective 1

Math Link

In the 1400s an Italian architect named Filippo Brunelleschi used mathematics to apply linear perspective to landscapes. He showed relationships among points, lines, and planes.

Linear Perspective

Imagine you are standing on the walkway in image **C** and looking into the distance. Does the walkway seem to get wider or narrower in the distance? The artist of image **C** used **linear perspective** to show depth. He made the lines of the walkway get closer together until they reached the horizon line. The point where these lines seem to meet the horizon line is called the **vanishing point**. Where else do you see lines that meet at a vanishing point?

C Don Jacot, *Commuter Trains, Union Station,* 1991, oil on linen, 36 in. × 48 in. Louis K. Meisel Gallery, New York, New York.

Think Critically

1. (Focus Skill) *READING SKILL* Summarize the technique of linear perspective. **SUMMARIZE AND PARAPHRASE**

2. Why do artists use a vanishing point?

3. **WRITE** Imagine you are riding one of the trains in image **C**. Write a paragraph telling where you are going and what you will do when you arrive.

154

TEKS 4.1B

Art Print 13

Display **Art Print 13** and distribute to students Discussion Card 3: *Elements of Art.* Ask students to choose appropriate vocabulary to discuss the art element of space and all of the perspective techniques used by the artist in the artwork.

ART PRINT 13

Bus Interior
by Richard Estes

---

154 **UNIT 5** *The Artist's Environment*

★ TEKS 4.1A communicate ideas; TEKS 4.1B discuss elements and principles; TEKS 4.2B design original artworks; TEKS 4.3A identify main ideas; TEKS 4.4A form conclusions about personal artworks; TEKS 4.4B interpret artworks by peers and others; *(continued)*

Artist's Workshop

Draw a Scene with Linear Perspective

MATERIALS
- pencil
- sketchbook
- white paper
- ruler
- colored pencils

PLAN

Brainstorm some ways to show linear perspective in a scene. You might show the lines in a road, a path, or train tracks come together at a vanishing point.

CREATE

1. Sketch your scene on white paper. Use a ruler to draw the lines to the vanishing point.

2. Experiment with the sizes of objects to create the feeling of depth in your drawing.

3. Finish your drawing with colored pencils.

REFLECT

How did you use linear perspective in your drawing? What other ways did you use to show depth?

Quick Tip
Think of drawing a large upside-down *V* for *vanishing point*.

155

Activity Options

Quick Activity Have students sketch a road or trail leading to a vanishing point.

Early Finishers Have students draw the scene from the opposite viewpoint—as though they are standing at the vanishing point— and compare their drawings.

Challenge See *Teacher Resource Book*, p. 72.

PDAS Domain IV

ESL Use **visuals** to support **comprehensible input** for examples of linear perspective. Display *Picture Cards Collection* cards 26, 115, and 121 for students to discuss and use for reference.

city

Artist's Workshop
30-40 Minutes

Draw a Scene with Linear Perspective

PLAN Have students read the activity steps on page 155. Then distribute *Teacher Resource Book* page 47 to give students an example of linear perspective.

CREATE Remind students that the vanishing point does not have to be in the center of the artwork. As students design their artwork, encourage them to try setting the vanishing point somewhere other than the center to create a unique composition. **TEKS 4.2B**

REFLECT Have students explain how they used linear perspective and other perspective techniques in their drawings. **SELF-EVALUATION** TEKS 4.4A

Wrap-Up
5-10 Minutes

Informal Assessment PDAS Domain III

- **Describe your use of color in your artwork.**
  (Responses will vary.) **PERCEPTION/AESTHETICS**
  TEKS 4.4A

- **Examine the artwork of one of your classmates and summarize the ideas in it.**
  (Responses will vary.) **SUMMARIZE AND PARAPHRASE**
  TEKS 4.3A, TEKS 4.4B

Extend Through Writing
TAKS Writing Objective 1

SHORT STORY Have students use the setting of their scenes to write a short story.

Recommended Reading

How Artists Use Perspective by Paul Flux. Heinemann, 2001. AVERAGE

PDAS Domains I, II

MISSION ARCHITECTURE

ART AND CULTURE

DISCUSS THE IMAGES

Have students read pages 156–157.

- Explain to students that the architectural designs of the Spanish missions in the American Southwest depended on the available materials and the expertise of the builders. Many missions were built of stone and lime mortar. Others were built of adobe and timber or adobe bricks.

- Explain that the mission in image A is an example of the Pueblo style of architecture. Point out the earthy colors of adobe, the flat roof, the rounded corners, the massive round-edged walls, the heavy timbers extending through the walls, and the simple, sunken window.

- Tell students that the mission in image B, completed in 1755, is an example of Spanish Colonial architecture. Most of the colorful geometric designs that once covered its surface have been worn away by time.

- Display **Art Print 15,** an image of the Alamo. This building in San Antonio, Texas, was originally built as part of a mission. Have students compare the two missions on these pages with the Alamo. One characteristic of all the missions was a belfry rising above the church in which bells were hung. The bells were generally rung at sunrise and noon. Have students point out the belfries in the structures on pages 156–157.

MISSION ARCHITECTURE

How can building styles show different ways of life?

In the late 1600s and early 1700s, the Spanish were eager to expand their territory in the New World. They began building settlements called missions in what are now Texas, New Mexico, and California.

The missions of the American Southwest were designed to meet the needs of the people who lived there. They were often surrounded by walls for protection. Inside the walls were houses, workplaces, a school, and a church. Outside the walls, the settlers raised crops and tended livestock. The missions were built to be self-sufficient. This means that everything the people needed was produced at the mission.

 San Francisco de Asis Mission, Taos, New Mexico.

 Background Information

Art History

In the seventeenth century, Spain colonized what is now the southwestern part of the United States, building settlements called missions to bring their ideas of religion and civilization to the people who lived in the area. The missions often became the center of ranching and farming communities, where crops such as corn, beans, melons, and many kinds of fruit were grown. Over time many of these mission communities grew into towns and cities, including what is today San Antonio, Texas.

For related artworks, see **Electronic Art Gallery CD-ROM, Intermediate.**

★ TEKS 4.2B design original artworks; TEKS 4.2C produce artworks; TEKS 4.4B interpret artworks by peers and others; PDAS Domain I active participation; PDAS Domain II learner-centered instruction

B Mission Nuestra Señora de la Concepción de Acuña, San Antonio, Texas.

Image **A** is a photograph of a mission built in New Mexico. The walls of the mission were built with adobe (uh•DOH•bee), a kind of brick made from mud and chopped straw. Adobe is often used in areas with hot, dry weather. An adobe building stays cool in the summer and warm in the winter. Adobe is still used throughout the southwestern United States.

Image **B** shows a mission in San Antonio, Texas. How is it different from the mission in image **A**?

Mission San José, San Antonio, Texas.

THINK
ABOUT ART

Why are building styles different in different locations?

157

DID YOU KNOW?

Use the facts below to talk about the San Antonio Missions National Historical Park.

- This national historical park was established to preserve the Spanish missions that were built along the San Antonio River.

- The park includes tours of the four Spanish frontier missions, hiking trails, and educational programs for families and schools. The park covers about 819 acres.

- The largest of the missions, Mission San José, founded in 1720, continues to be an active Roman Catholic parish today.

THINK
ABOUT ART

Why are building styles different in different locations? (Possible response: Builders have to work with local materials.) **CRITICAL THINKING**

ARTIST'S EYE ACTIVITY

Architecture Tour Poster Tell students that many visitors come every year to see the architecture of these missions. Have students make a poster advertising a tour of one of the missions. They should invent ways to produce the poster, using a variety of art media and art materials. Be sure the poster includes a vivid description of the buildings and the reasons why visitors should see them. TEKS 4.2B, TEKS 4.2C

Social Studies Connection

A Day at the Mission Tell students that life in a mission was highly structured. Bells woke the residents at sunrise. To keep the mission self-sufficient, residents worked until sunset.

For additional cross-curricular suggestions, see Art Transparency 14.

TEKS 4.4B
Student Art Show

Poster Exhibit Display the posters that the students created in the Artist's Eye Activity. Ask students to respond to peers' artworks, interpreting the ideas and interpreting the ideas and describing the intent of the posters and forming conclusions about their effectiveness.

Lesson 23

Garden Design

PDAS Domains I, II

OBJECTIVES
- Identify movement and unity in artworks
- Create a design for a park
- Summarize and paraphrase ideas in artworks

RESOURCES
- Art Print 17
- Reading Skill Card 5
- Discussion Cards 1, 4, pp. R34, R35
- Electronic Art Gallery CD-ROM, Intermediate

GO ONLINE
Multimedia Art Glossary and Biographies
Visit *The Learning Site*
www.harcourtschool.com

5 Minutes

Warm-Up

Build Background Access prior knowledge about gardens by having students communicate ideas about gardens their families have or gardens in their communities using sensory knowledge and life experiences. Tell students that in this lesson they will examine the work of garden designers.
TEKS 4.1A

Lesson 23

Garden Design

Vocabulary
movement
unity

Look at image **A**. The designer arranged the lines in the garden to show **movement**, or to guide the viewer's eyes from place to place. As you look at image **A**, think about the way your eyes move along the diagonal lines.

Now look at the different parts of the garden. This garden design shows unity. **Unity** is a sense of completeness in an artwork. An artwork has unity when its parts fit together well.

 **A** Garden at Villandry, France.

158

Background Information

Art History
For almost 5,000 years, people have created gardens as places of retreat from everyday life. The oldest known plan for a garden came from ancient Egypt. It shows a very formal, symmetrical design, with plants and trees laid out along straight lines. In the Middle Ages, garden designers in what is now Turkey created a sense of fantasy by using artificial trees of gold or silver whose branches sprayed perfume. In eighteenth-century England, gardens were actually planned to look unplanned and wild.

For related artworks, see **Electronic Art Gallery CD-ROM, Intermediate.**

TEKS 4.1A communicate ideas; TEKS 4.1B discuss elements and principles; PDAS Domain I active participation; PDAS Domain II learner-centered instruction; TAKS Reading Objective 1 demonstrate understanding of texts; *(continued)*

Flower Conservatory, Golden Gate Park, San Francisco, California.

Landscape designers choose color schemes for their gardens. How would you describe the color scheme shown in image **B**? Does the garden have symmetrical balance or asymmetrical balance? How did the designer give this garden a sense of unity?

159

TAKS Reading Objectives 1, 3, 4

Science Connection

Cactus Types Scientists have classified about 2,000 species of cactus. Cacti grow mainly in the arid regions of the Southwestern United States, Mexico, Central America, and southern South America. Have students use an encyclopedia or online resources to find interesting facts, such as the largest, smallest, and oldest varieties of cactus known. Ask volunteers to present their findings to the class.

Saguaro Cactus

10-15 Minutes

Teach

Preview the Art Ask students to look at images A through C on pages 158–160. Have them describe what they see. Use Discussion Card 1 and the questions below to guide the discussion. Then have students read pages 158–160.

A *Garden at Villandry, France* **Does this garden look like a place you would want to visit? Why or why not?**

B *Flower Conservatory, Golden Gate Park* **What kinds of lines and colors do you see in this garden?** TEKS 4.1B

C *Desert Pavilion at the Brooklyn Botanical Garden* **What do you think the climate would be like in this garden?** TEKS 4.1A

Discuss Art Concepts After you discuss with students the principle of movement, have them use their fingers to trace the movement their eyes take through the garden in image A.

In image B, students should note the use of warm colors and symmetrical balance. Discuss with students the way the parts of the garden fit together to give it a sense of unity.

In the garden in image C, have students note that the sense of unity was created by including many kinds of desert plants called cactus. Have students note their different shapes but similar bristly textures. TEKS 4.1B

Teach (continued)

LOCATE IT Have students turn to pages 206–207 to locate Brooklyn, New York. Tell students that the Desert Pavilion at the Brooklyn Botanic Garden houses plants from desert regions throughout the world.

Summarize and Paraphrase Ask students to look at the gardens in images A and B. Ask them to summarize

- the color schemes used in the gardens.

- the shapes used in the garden designs.

Then have students describe in their own words what they see in the images, including the way the designers showed movement and unity.
TEKS 4.1B, TEKS 4.3A, TEKS 4.3B, TEKS 4.4B

Think Critically

Use the questions below to check students' understanding of lesson concepts.

1. **(Focus Skill) READING SKILL Summarize what you have learned about unity in one or two sentences.** (Possible response: Unity is a sense of completeness in an artwork when all the parts fit together.) SUMMARIZE AND PARAPHRASE
TEKS 4.1B

2. **What kind of balance is shown in image C? How do you know?** (Possible response: asymmetrical balance; the plants on each side of the garden are different shapes and sizes, but the tall, thin cacti on the left side seem to have the same visual weight as the short, wide cacti on the right) PERCEPTION/AESTHETICS TEKS 4.1B

3. **WRITE Which one of the gardens shown in this lesson would you most like to visit? Write a paragraph describing what you might see, smell, and feel if you visited that garden.** DESCRIPTIVE TEKS 4.1A; TAKS Writing Objective 1

LOCATE IT
The garden in image C is located in Brooklyn, New York.

See Maps of Museums and Art Sites, pages 206–209.

C Desert Pavilion at the Brooklyn Botanic Garden, Brooklyn, New York.

Now look at image **C**. What kinds of plants do you see in this garden? What textures do these plants have? The designer of this garden used plants with similar textures and colors to create a sense of unity.

Think Critically

1. **(Focus Skill) READING SKILL** Summarize what you learned about unity in one or two sentences. SUMMARIZE AND PARAPHRASE

2. What kind of balance is shown in image **C**? How do you know?

3. **WRITE** Which one of the gardens shown in this lesson would you most like to visit? Write a paragraph describing what you might see, smell, and feel if you visited that garden.

160

TEKS 4.1B
Art Print 17

Display **Art Print 17** and distribute to students Discussion Card 4: *Principles of Design*. Have students discuss the use of movement and unity in this abstract artwork.

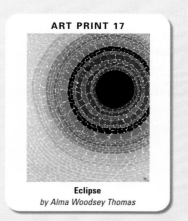

ART PRINT 17

Eclipse
by Alma Woodsey Thomas

★ TEKS 4.1A communicate ideas; TEKS 4.1B discuss elements and principles; TEKS 4.2A integrate ideas in artworks; TEKS 4.2B design original artworks; TEKS 4.2C produce artworks; TEKS 4.3A identify main ideas; TEKS 4.3B compare and contrast artworks; *(continued)*

Artist's Workshop

Design a Park

PLAN

Imagine a park where you would enjoy spending time. Think about the kinds of trees, plants, rocks, and other objects you would like in your park. Sketch your ideas.

CREATE

1. Use your sketches as a guide to draw your park design on white paper. Arrange the parts of your design in a way that shows movement.

2. Choose a color scheme for the plants and other objects in your park.

3. Find magazine pictures with colors and textures you like. Cut them out, and glue them onto your drawing.

REFLECT

How does your drawing show unity? What would you name your park?

MATERIALS

- pencil
- sketchbook
- colored pencils or markers
- magazines
- scissors
- glue

Quick Tip
You may want to include such things as ponds, benches, statues, or fountains to make your park more interesting.

161

30-40 Minutes

Artist's Workshop

Design a Park

PLAN Have students read the activity steps on page 161. Provide students with magazines or flower catalogs from which to cut pictures.

CREATE Have students integrate a variety of ideas about self, life events, family, and community in their park designs. They should invent ways to explore the photographic imagery they chose, using a variety of art media and art materials. Before students glue pictures to their drawing, have them experiment with the arrangement to achieve a sense of unity. TEKS 4.2A, TEKS 4.2B, TEKS 4.2C

REFLECT Ask students to share their park names.
SELF-EVALUATION

5-10 Minutes

Wrap-Up

Informal Assessment PDAS Domain III

- **What art elements did you use to create unity in your design?** (Responses will vary.)
  PERCEPTION/AESTHETICS TEKS 4.1B

- **Summarize the ideas in a peer's park design.** (Responses will vary.) **SUMMARIZE AND PARAPHRASE** TEKS 4.4B

Extend Through Writing TAKS Writing Objectives 1, 3

DIARY ENTRY Have students write a diary entry recounting a day spent in their park. Ask them to include as many sensory details as they can.

Recommended Reading

The Legend of the Indian Paintbrush by Tomie dePaola.
G. P. Putnam's Sons, 1988.
EASY

PDAS Domain IV

Activity Options

Quick Activity Have students sketch a park design that shows unity.

Early Finishers Have students draw a map for visitors to their park.

Challenge See *Teacher Resource Book*, p. 73.

PDAS Domain IV

ESL Encourage students to share cultures by having them describe plants and flowers native to their home country.

Challenge Encourage interested students to conduct a survey of friends and family members asking them about their favorite park in the community and their reasons for their choice.

TEKS 4.4B interpret artworks by peers and others; PDAS Domain III evaluation and feedback; PDAS Domain IV classroom management; TAKS Writing Objective 1 composition; TAKS Writing Objective 3 organization

LESSON 23 *Garden Design* **161**

Architectural Balance

PDAS Domains I, II

OBJECTIVES

- Choose appropriate vocabulary to discuss the use of balance in architecture
- Design an original building
- Summarize and paraphrase ideas in artworks

RESOURCES

- Art Prints 14, 15
- Reading Skill Card 5
- Discussion Cards 1, 10, pp. R34, R38
- Electronic Art Gallery CD-ROM, Intermediate

Multimedia Art Glossary and Biographies
Visit *The Learning Site*
www.harcourtschool.com

5 Minutes

Warm-Up

Build Background Display **Art Print 14,** an image of the glass pyramid at the entrance to the Louvre Museum in Paris, France. Ask volunteers to describe what they see and to give their opinions of the structure. Ask students whether they think the pyramid has symmetrical or asymmetrical balance and why they think so. Tell students that in this lesson they will learn how architects use balance in their building designs. TEKS 4.1B

Lesson 24

Architectural Balance

Vocabulary

architect

An **architect** is a person who designs buildings. Architects design houses, churches, and schools. They design skyscrapers for large cities. Skyscrapers were developed in the late nineteenth century in the United States because of the growing population of the cities. Land was expensive, so tall buildings were built on small pieces of land. Today we see skyscrapers in almost every major city in the world.

Look at the skyscraper in image **A**. Does this building have symmetrical balance or asymmetrical balance? How do you know?

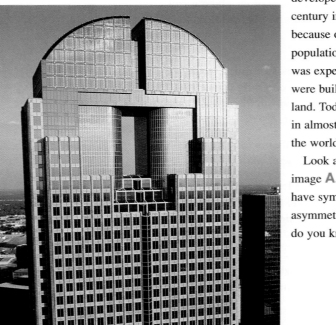

A Chase Building, Dallas, Texas.

162

Background Information

About the Architect

B English architect Norman Foster (1935–) is known for his imaginative use of glass, steel, and other materials to create buildings that have an unusual, abstract design. In 1999, Foster won the Pritzker Architecture Prize, considered by many to be the Nobel Prize of architecture.

For additional information about Norman Foster, see pp. R44–R65.

For related artworks, see **Electronic Art Gallery CD-ROM, Intermediate.**

★ TEKS 4.1B discuss elements and principles; TEKS 4.2B design original artworks; TEKS 4.4B interpret artworks by peers and others; **PDAS Domain I** active participation; **PDAS Domain II** learner-centered instruction; **TAKS Reading Objective 1** demonstrate understanding of texts

**Norman Foster,
City Hall,
London, England.**

Have you ever seen a building like the one in image **B**? How would you describe it? Move your finger down the vertical axis of the building. Notice that the bottom left side of the building has the same visual weight as the top right side. This gives the building asymmetrical balance.

163

TEKS 4.2B; TAKS Reading Objective 1

Social Studies Connection

Architecture Throughout History Discuss with students how different societies around the world and throughout history have developed their own styles of architecture, especially for important buildings. Have students use an encyclopedia to find an example of one kind of architecture designed during one of the following historical periods: the Mayan Empire; the Middle Ages in Europe, pre-Columbian America, or colonial America. Then ask students to create a drawing showing an example of the architecture.

Teach

10-15 Minutes

Preview the Art Have students preview images A through C on pages 162–164. Ask them to discuss details that they find interesting in the buildings. Use Discussion Card 1 and the questions below to guide the discussion. Then have students read pages 162–164.

A *Chase Building* **What is the first thing you notice about this building?**

B *City Hall* **Do you like the design of this building? Why or why not?**

C *Hotel Nice* **If you did not know the purpose of this building, what would you think it was?**

Discuss Art Concepts Have students trace their fingers along the vertical axis in image A to note the building's symmetrical balance. Tell students that this building in Dallas, Texas, is also known as the Keyhole Building because of the ornamental seven-story space, or "keyhole," near the top of the building.

Invite students to describe the building in image B. Tell them that when this building opened in 2002, at least one critic compared it to a large, sliced, hard-boiled egg in glass.

In image C, students should note that without the pendulum, the building would have symmetrical balance. Encourage students to discuss the idea the architect may have wanted to express by adding the colorful pendulum to the front of the building. TEKS 4.1B, TEKS 4.4B

Social Studies Link Have students turn to pages 208–209 to locate Taipei, Taiwan. Tell them that the design of Taipei 101 includes double-deck elevators that travel twice as fast as any other elevators in the world.

Summarize and Paraphrase Ask students to look back at the buildings in this lesson and summarize

- the kinds of lines and shapes used by the architect in each design.

- the features that give each design balance.

Then ask students to select the building they found most interesting and describe in their own words its most interesting features. TEKS 4.1B, TEKS 4.4B

Think Critically

Use the questions below to check students' understanding of lesson concepts.

1. **Focus Skill READING SKILL** **Paraphrase the information about image B on page 163.** (Possible response: The building has asymmetrical balance. The bottom left side of the building has the same visual weight as the top right side.) SUMMARIZE AND PARAPHRASE TEKS 4.1B

2. **How did the architect of the building in image A show unity?** (Possible response: It is balanced, and all of its parts fit together well.) PERCEPTION/AESTHETICS TEKS 4.1B

3. **WRITE** **Choose one of the buildings in this lesson. Imagine you are inside the building, on the top floor looking out. Write a description of what you might see.** DESCRIPTIVE
TAKS Writing Objective 1

Social Studies Link
As of 2004, the tallest building in the world is Taipei 101, located in Taipei, Taiwan. It has 106 stories and is 1,667 feet high.

C Hotel Nice, Nice, France.

Look at the building in image **C**. Imagine the building without the decorative pendulum. Does the building have symmetrical balance or asymmetrical balance? Does the pendulum make the building more interesting or less interesting? Why do you think so?

Think Critically

1. **Focus Skill READING SKILL** Summarize what you learned about image **B**. Paraphrase the information about it on page 163. SUMMARIZE AND PARAPHRASE

2. How did the architect of the building in image **A** show unity?

3. **WRITE** Choose one of the buildings in this lesson. Imagine you are inside the building, on the top floor looking out. Write a description of what you might see.

164

TEKS 4.1A, TEKS 4.3B
Art Print 15

Display **Art Print 15** and distribute to students Discussion Card 10: *Community Art.* Have students communicate ideas about community and school using sensory knowledge and life experiences to compare the architectural design in the building in **Art Print 15** to buildings they know well.

ART PRINT 15

The Alamo
by Unknown Architect

★ TEKS 4.1A communicate ideas; TEKS 4.1B discuss elements and principles; TEKS 4.2B design original artworks; TEKS 4.2C produce artworks; TEKS 4.3B compare and contrast artworks; *(continued)*

Artist's Workshop

Design a Building

PLAN

Look at some photographs of buildings in books or magazines. Decide what kind of building you would like to design. Choose symmetrical balance or asymmetrical balance for your design. Make some sketches of your building.

MATERIALS

- books or magazines
- pencil
- sketchbook
- white paper
- colored pencils or markers

CREATE

1. Choose your best sketch, and copy it onto white paper.

2. Use color and shape to balance the visual weight in your drawing. Use line and value to show visual texture.

3. Finish your design by drawing a setting for your building.

REFLECT

What kind of building did you design? What kind of setting did you place it in? What kind of balance did you show?

Quick Tip
Use a ruler and a round plastic lid to help you draw the geometric shapes in your design.

165

Artist's Workshop
30-40 Minutes

Design a Building

PLAN Have students read the activity steps on page 165 and brainstorm a list of the kinds of buildings they might design. Provide students with books and art magazines containing architectural photographs to help them decide.

CREATE Have students invent ways to explore photographic imagery of architecture, using a variety of art media and art materials as they design their original artworks. TEKS 4.2B, TEKS 4.2C

REFLECT Have students describe the buildings and settings they drew and point out how they created symmetrical or asymmetrical balance in their designs. SELF-EVALUATION TEKS 4.4A

5-10 Minutes

Wrap-Up

Informal Assessment PDAS Domain III

- **Describe the balance shown in a peer's building design.** (Responses will vary.) EVALUATION/CRITICISM TEKS 4.4B

- **Summarize the design of your building.** (Responses will vary.) SUMMARIZE AND PARAPHRASE TEKS 4.4A

Extend Through Writing TAKS Writing Objective 1

TRAVEL GUIDE Have each student write a page of a travel guide that describes the intent of his or her building, its setting, and its purpose.

Recommended Reading

Going to the Getty by J. Otto Seibold and Vivian Walsh. The J. Paul Getty Museum, 1997. AVERAGE

PDAS Domain IV

Activity Options

Quick Activity Have students sketch a building that has symmetrical balance.

Early Finishers Have students draw a sketch of a similar building, but with a different kind of balance from their original design.

Challenge See *Teacher Resource Book*, p. 74.

PDAS Domain IV

ESL Use **visuals** to support **comprehensible input** for names of kinds of buildings. Display *Picture Cards Collection* cards 17, 103, and 115.

See also *Picture Card Bank* CD-ROM, Category: Places I Go.

building

TEKS 4.4A form conclusions about personal artworks; **TEKS 4.4B** interpret artworks by peers and others; **PDAS Domain III** evaluation and feedback; **PDAS Domain IV** classroom management; **TAKS Writing Objective 1** composition

LESSON 24 *Architectural Balance* **165**

PDAS Domains I, II

I.M.Pei

ARTIST BIOGRAPHY

DISCUSS THE IMAGES

Have students read pages 166 and 167.

- Explain to students that image B shows the Rock and Roll Museum and Hall of Fame, a 162-foot tower designed by I. M. Pei that sits next to Lake Erie in Cleveland, Ohio. Have students identify the geometric shapes and forms in the building.

- Display **Art Print 14,** and explain that this glass pyramid was designed by Pei as an underground extension of gallery space for the Louvre Museum in Paris, France. Invite students to compare the pyramid-shaped entrance to the Louvre to the building in image B.

- Tell students that image C shows the Meyerson Symphony Center in Dallas, Texas. This building, home to the Dallas Symphony Orchestra, opened its doors in the fall of 1989. Ask students to describe what they see and discuss the asymmetrical balance in the design of the building.

- Ask students to identify the roles of art in American society by discussing the impact architects such as I. M. Pei have had in communities such as Cleveland and Dallas, and how the construction of buildings like the ones in this lesson might affect a community.
TEKS 4.3C

I.M.Pei

How do architects use art concepts in their designs?

The architect I. M. Pei (PAY) has been designing buildings in the United States and around the world for more than fifty years. Born in China in 1917, Pei moved to the United States when he was seventeen to study architecture. He became well known for his use of geometric shapes and forms in large buildings made of concrete and glass. His style includes open, airy spaces for both work and entertainment.

  I. M. Pei, architect.

  I. M. Pei, The Rock and Roll Museum and Hall of Fame, Cleveland, Ohio.

FYI

Background Information

About the Artist

In the late 1960s, architect **I. M. Pei** (PAY) (1917–) began to use bold geometric shapes, especially the triangle and the prism, to create some of the world's most famous buildings. Pei's modernist designs fit beautifully with more traditional buildings.

For additional information about I. M. Pei, see pp. R44–R65.

For related artworks, see **Electronic Art Gallery CD-ROM, Intermediate.**

★ TEKS 4.1A communicate ideas; TEKS 4.2B design original artworks; TEKS 4.3C identify roles of art; TEKS 4.4B interpret artworks by peers and others; PDAS Domain I active participation; PDAS Domain II learner-centered instruction

Throughout his career, Pei has had a deep interest in the arts and education. Many of Pei's buildings are connected with art and music. These buildings include world-famous libraries, museums, and concert halls.

Look at images **B** and **C**. What geometric shapes and forms do you see? What types of balance can you see in Pei's designs?

 I. M. Pei, Morton H. Meyerson Symphony Center, Dallas, Texas.

Think About Art

Imagine that you could walk through one of the buildings in image **B** or **C**. What do you think the building would look like from the inside?

 Multimedia Biographies
Visit *The Learning Site*
www.harcourtschool.com

167

DID YOU KNOW?

Use the facts below to talk about how technology has changed the field of architecture.

- Architects routinely use computer design software and 3-D modeling software. These tools allow architects to show their clients not only where objects, furniture, and walls are placed, but also their colors and textures and even the way that light shines on them. With the use of a computer, architects can take clients on a "virtual reality" tour of their future building.

- Computers are used for tracking resources, accounting for space, and creating technical specifications for builders to follow. Most drafting work, previously done by hand, is also done on a computer.

Think About Art

Imagine that you could walk though one of the buildings in image B or C. What do you think the building would look like from the inside?

(Possible response: The rooms would be filled with light shining through all the windows.)

PERCEPTION/AESTHETICS TEKS 4.1A

ARTIST'S EYE ACTIVITY

Designing a School Architects design practical spaces in which people live and work, but they also treat their buildings as art. Have students communicate ideas about school using sensory knowledge and life experiences. Then have them integrate these ideas into a design for a new school. Have students share their designs with classmates. TEKS 4.1A, TEKS 4.2B

 Multimedia Biographies
Visit *The Learning Site*
www.harcourtschool.com

 ### Music Connection

The Perfect Sound Tell students that concert halls are designed to make music sound as perfect as possible. Architects must consider noises like air conditioning and outside traffic.

For additional cross-curricular suggestions, see Art Transparency 15.

 TEKS 4.4B
Student Art Show

School Designs Display the school designs created by students in the Artist's Eye Activity. Have students view each of the designs and take note of interesting details and features. Then have them interpret and discuss the ideas expressed by their peers in the artworks.

Lesson 25

Outdoor Murals

OBJECTIVES
- Identify the characteristics of murals
- Design and create a class mural
- Summarize and paraphrase ideas in artworks

RESOURCES
- Art Print 15
- Reading Skill Card 5
- Discussion Cards 1, 10, pp. R34, R38
- Electronic Art Gallery CD-ROM, Intermediate

Multimedia Art Glossary and Biographies
Visit *The Learning Site*
www.harcourtschool.com

5 Minutes

Warm-Up

Build Background   Have students communicate ideas about community using life experiences to describe public artworks they have seen. Then have them discuss the ways outdoor artwork is different from artwork found in museums and galleries. Tell students that in this lesson they will learn about artists who create artwork in public places for the community to enjoy.   TEKS 4.1A, TEKS 4.3B

Lesson 25

Vocabulary

mural

trompe l'oeil

Outdoor Murals

A **mural** is a painting created on a wall or ceiling. Murals can be painted on surfaces that are indoors or outdoors. Many murals are painted on the outside of buildings. Outdoor murals may give a message or tell something about a community.

Look at the mural in image **A**. It is made up of several smaller paintings by different artists. Each artist created his or her own version of a sunflower. How does this mural have unity?

 Unknown artist, *Sunflower Mural on Fence,* Cape Town, South Africa.

168

 Background Information

About the Artists

B Meg Saligman's public murals can be seen in Philadelphia, Pennsylvania, and other U.S. cities.

C John Pugh enjoys painting life-size illusions that visually trick the viewer.

For additional information about the artists, see pp. R44–R65.

 For related artworks, see **Electronic Art Gallery CD-ROM, Intermediate.**

★ **TEKS 4.1A** communicate ideas; **TEKS 4.3B** compare and contrast artworks; **PDAS Domain I** active participation; **PDAS Domain II** learner-centered instruction; **TAKS Reading Objective 1** demonstrate understanding of texts

Movement

Describe what you see in image **B**. What do you think this mural represents? The artist arranged parts of this mural to create movement. Your eyes are guided along the triangular shape formed by the figures. Then your eyes are guided around the circle at the bottom of the mural.

 Meg Fish Saligman, *Common Threads,* 1998, mural paint over sealant and primer, 8 stories tall. Philadelphia, Pennsylvania.

169

TAKS Reading Objective 1

Social Studies Connection

Mural Search The mural in image B was painted as part of the Philadelphia Mural Arts Program. Many communities have similar programs that offer artists the opportunity to create artwork on public walls, buildings, and other spaces. Have students locate a mural in their own community and write a description of it and its location. If public murals do not exist in the community, help students use reference sources to locate a mural in another part of the state. Ask students to report their findings and to display pictures or give descriptions of the murals they have located.

Teach

Preview the Art Have students preview images A through C on pages 168–170. Ask them to describe what they see and discuss the setting in each one. Use Discussion Card 1 and the questions below to guide the discussion. Then have students read pages 168–170.

A *Sunflower Mural on Fence* **What kind of feeling does this artwork express?**

B *Common Threads* **How do you think the artist painted this artwork?**

C *Seven Point One (Siete Punto Uno)* **Describe what might be happening in this artwork.**

Discuss Art Concepts Discuss with students how the pattern of sunflowers in image A gives the mural a sense of unity and completeness. Students may suggest that the sunflowers represent cheerful feelings.

Tell students that the mural in image B is 100 feet tall and covers an area of 7,500 square feet. Discuss the subject matter in the mural—historical figures paired with contemporary young people. Point out that the main idea in this mural may be the common thread of history that runs though all the citizens of Philadelphia—past, present, and future. Then have students trace the path their eyes take around the mural.

In image C, have students point out the details that trick the eye and create a sense of depth in the mural, such as the "damaged" wall that seems to allow viewers to look inside the building, and the woman in the red jacket staring into the room.

Teach (continued)

LOCATE IT Have students turn to the map on pages 206–207 to find Los Gatos, California. The mural was painted on the only building on the block left standing after the 1989 Loma Prieta earthquake. The mural's title may refer to the earthquake's measurement on the Richter scale.

Summarize and Paraphrase Ask students to think about the murals in this lesson and to summarize

- the subjects in each mural.

- the ways the artists created unity in each mural.

Then ask students to describe one of the murals in their own words. TEKS 4.4B

Think Critically

Use the questions below to check students' understanding of lesson concepts.

1. (Focus Skill) *READING SKILL* **Paraphrase the definition of *trompe l'oeil*.** (Possible response: a painting that tricks viewers into thinking they are looking at a real-life object or scene) **SUMMARIZE AND PARAPHRASE**

2. **How are the murals in this lesson alike? How are they different from each other?** (Possible responses: They are all in public places; they are all colorful. They have different subjects; they are different sizes; they are in different locations.) **PERSONAL RESPONSE** TEKS 4.3B

3. **WRITE** **Write a paragraph describing a mural you could create to tell something about your community.** **DESCRIPTIVE**
TEKS 4.1A; TAKS Writing Objective 1

LOCATE IT
The mural in image **C** is located in Los Gatos, California.

CALIFORNIA

Los Gatos

See Maps of Museums and Art Sites, pages 206–209.

Trompe L'oeil

Look at the mural in image **C**. It makes you think you could walk right into the building. This mural is an example of **trompe l'oeil** (TRAWMP LOY), which means "trick the eye" in French. Trompe l'oeil is a style of painting that creates the illusion, or false idea, of a realistic three-dimensional object or scene.

Notice that the artist of image **C** used value to create movement. The darkest values draw your eye to the left side of the scene and create the illusion of depth.

 John Pugh,
*Seven Point One,
(Siete Punto Uno)*
1990, acrylic on panel
mounted on wall,
16 ft. × 24 ft. Los Gatos,
California.

Think Critically

1. (Focus Skill) *READING SKILL* Paraphrase the definition of *trompe l'oeil*. **SUMMARIZE AND PARAPHRASE**

2. How are the murals in this lesson alike? How are they different from each other?

3. **WRITE** Write a paragraph describing a mural you could create to tell something about your community.

170

TEKS 4.1A

Art Print 15

Display **Art Print 15** and distribute to students Discussion Card 10: *Community Art.* Have them discuss how art and architecture relate to a community.

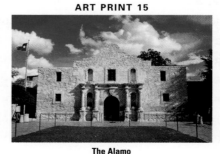

ART PRINT 15

The Alamo
by Unknown Architect

★ TEKS 4.1A communicate ideas; TEKS 4.2A integrate ideas in artworks; TEKS 4.2B design original artworks; TEKS 4.3A identify main ideas;
TEKS 4.3B compare and contrast artworks; TEKS 4.4A form conclusions about personal artworks; *(continued)*

Artist's Workshop

Create a Class Mural

PLAN

With your classmates, brainstorm ideas for a mural. Try to express ideas or feelings about your school or community. As a group, decide which part of the mural each of you will create.

CREATE

1. Sketch your section of the mural on a large sheet of butcher paper.

2. Work with your classmates to decide on the colors to paint your mural. Use large brushes to paint the background and large areas. Use small brushes to paint details and small areas.

REFLECT

What ideas or feelings did you and your classmates express in your mural?

MATERIALS

- pencil
- sketchbook
- butcher paper
- tempera paint
- large and small paintbrushes
- water bowl

Quick Tip
Work with your classmates as you paint to be sure that all the parts of the mural fit together well.

171

Artist's Workshop
30-40 Minutes

Create a Class Mural

PLAN Have students read the activity steps on page 171. Help students list possible mural subjects such as school events, community heroes, local landmarks, or cultural celebrations.

CREATE Students should work together to integrate a variety of ideas about school and community into their mural. Students may sketch the mural on a grid before enlarging it proportionally onto the butcher paper. See *Teacher Resource Book* page 41. TEKS 4.2A, TEKS 4.2B

REFLECT Have students discuss the ideas or feelings they expressed in their mural and talk about how they worked together. SELF-EVALUATION TEKS 4.4A

Wrap-Up
5-10 Minutes

Informal Assessment   PDAS Domain III

- **How does your mural show unity?**
  (Responses will vary.) PERCEPTION/AESTHETICS TEKS 4.4A
- **Summarize the ideas expressed in your mural.** (Responses will vary.) SUMMARIZE AND PARAPHRASE TEKS 4.3A

Extend Through Writing   TAKS Writing Objective 1

NEWS STORY Have students write a news story for the local paper describing their class mural, its location, and the ideas expressed in it.

Recommended Reading

Diego
by Jonah Winter.
Alfred A. Knopf, 1991.
EASY

PDAS Domain IV

Activity Options

Quick Activity Have students sketch a scene for a mural independently.

Early Finishers Have students think of text to add to the mural.

Challenge See *Teacher Resource Book*, p. 75.

PDAS Domain IV

ESL Invite students to **share cultures** as they brainstorm ideas for the class mural.

Challenge Have interested students add an interactive component by making an audio recording about the mural's subject.

TEKS 4.4B interpret artworks by peers and others; PDAS Domain III evaluation and feedback; PDAS Domain IV classroom management; TAKS Writing Objective 1 composition

Unit 5

Review and Reflect

 Have students reflect on what they have learned about the ways artists use space and movement to create new environments. Display **Art Prints 13, 14, 15, 17,** and **4.** Encourage small groups of students to use Discussion Cards 3, 4, and 10 and their completed Word Knowledge Charts to discuss what they learned about the vocabulary and concepts in this unit.

Vocabulary and Concepts

Have students read each sentence and choose the letter of the word or phrase that best completes it.
(1. D; 2. F; 3. C; 4. F; 5. C)

 READING SKILL

Summarize and Paraphrase

Remind students that when you summarize, you tell only the main ideas. When you paraphrase, you use your own words to restate information. Have students reread the information on page 148 and summarize it in two sentences. Then have them retell the information in their own words. Have students use the chart to organize their ideas.

TAKS Reading Objective 4

Summary: Main Ideas Only
Artists show space by creating a sense of depth. One way to do this is to divide an artwork into a foreground, middle ground, and background.

Paraphrase: Main Ideas and Details in Your Own Words
Artists can make a flat artwork seem to show distance. They divide the artwork into three sections. The foreground seems closest to the viewer. The middle ground is farther back, and the background is farthest in the distance.

Unit 5 Review and Reflect

Vocabulary and Concepts

Choose the letter of the word or phrase that best completes each sentence.

1 The area around, between, and within objects is called ___.

   A horizon line   **C** depth

   B foreground   **D** space

2 The ___ is the place where the sky seems to meet the land.

   F horizon line   **H** space

   G foreground   **J** mural

3 An artwork has ___ when its parts fit together well.

   A depth   **C** unity

   B middle ground   **D** space

4 ___ means "trick the eye."

   F Trompe l'oeil   **H** Mural

   G Architecture   **J** Space

5 An artwork painted on a wall or ceiling is called a ___.

   A horizon line   **C** mural

   B vanishing point   **D** space

 **READING SKILL**

Summarize and Paraphrase

Reread page 148 and summarize the information in two sentences. Then paraphrase the text by retelling it in your own words. Use this chart to organize your ideas.

Summary: Main Ideas Only

Paraphrase: Main Ideas and Details in Your Own Words

172

TEKS 4.2A, TEKS 4.2B, TEKS 4.4B

Home and Community Connection

School-Home Connection
Copy and distribute *Teacher Resource Book* pages 93–94. After completing the unit, students can work at home to draw a sketch of a mural that expresses an idea about their family. Encourage students to show movement in their sketches.

Community Connection
You may want to contact local businesses, your town or city hall, or your public library to arrange an exhibition of students' art portfolios. Have students photograph the class mural to include in the exhibition. During the exhibition, provide time for students to analyze the portfolios of their peers to identify the ideas expressed in the artworks.

⭐ TEKS 4.2A integrate ideas in artworks; TEKS 4.2B design original artworks; TEKS 4.3B compare and contrast artworks; TEKS 4.4B interpret artworks by peers and others; PDAS Domain I active participation; PDAS Domain III evaluation and feedback; *(continued)*

Write About Art

Write a summary and a paraphrase of the information on page 156. Use the chart to plan your writing.

REMEMBER — YOU SHOULD

- tell only the most important ideas in your summary.
- write your paraphrase as though the reader has not seen your artwork.

Critic's Corner

Look at *Night Scene in the Saruwaka Street in Edo* by Ando Hiroshige (hee•roh•shee•gay) to answer the questions below.

DESCRIBE What is the subject of the artwork? How would you describe it?

ANALYZE How did the artist create a sense of distance in the artwork? What kind of perspective techniques did he use?

INTERPRET What feeling do you think the artist was trying to express in the artwork?

EVALUATE What is your opinion of this artwork compared to other artworks that show perspective techniques?

Ando Hiroshige, *Night Scene in the Saruwaka Street in Edo*, 1856, wood block print, colored pigments on paper, 13¼ in. × 8⅝ in. Burstein Collection.

PDAS Domain III

Assessment

Portfolio Assessment

Have students choose for their portfolios a piece of artwork that best fulfilled an assignment or that they liked best for another reason.
You may want to provide specific feedback that targets students' use of the elements, principles, and techniques. See also Portfolio Recording Form, page R32.

Formal Assessment

- Progress Recording Form, p. R33
- Artist's Workshop Rubrics (Self/Teacher and Peer), pp. R30–R31
- Unit 5 Test, *Teacher Resource Book* p. 103

Write About Art

Summarize and Paraphrase Read aloud the writing prompt with students. Remind them that their summaries should not be more than one or two sentences and should only include the main ideas. Suggest that they save additional details for their paraphrases. TAKS Writing Objective 1

Critic's Corner

RESPONSE/EVALUATION Use the steps below to guide students in analyzing *Night Scene in the Saruwaka Street in Edo* by Ando Hiroshige (hee•roh•shee•gay). See also Discussion Card 2, p. R34.

DESCRIBE Discuss with students the busy city street at nightfall. Note that the full moon causes the figures to cast shadows on the crowded street.

ANALYZE Students should point out the use of linear perspective shown by the converging lines of the street and buildings. They should also note the artist's use of diminishing size and detail in the objects in the background.

INTERPRET Students may say that despite the crowds, the moonlit night gives the scene a calm, peaceful feeling. TEKS 4.4B

EVALUATE Have students compare and contrast this painting with the others in this unit in terms of the various perspective techniques they have learned about. TEKS 4.3B

 TAKS Test Preparation: Reading and Writing Through Art, pp. 53–57

Unit 6 Variety

Stretch Your Imagination

Artists continue to search for new ways to capture viewers' imaginations. In this unit students will learn about artists, art movements, and art techniques that have changed the way people view and appreciate art.

Resources

- Unit 6 Art Prints (16–18)
- Additional Art Prints (8, 12)
- Art Transparencies 16–18
- Test Preparation: Reading and Writing Through Art, pp. 58–78
- Artist's Workshop Activities: English and Spanish, pp. 51–60
- Encyclopedia of Artists and Art History, pp. R44–R65
- Picture Cards Collection, cards 10, 27, 34, 60, 68, 72, 90, 119

Using the Art Prints

- Discussion Cards, pp. R34–R38
- Teaching suggestions, backs of Art Prints
- Art Print Teaching Suggestions: Spanish

Teacher Resource Book

- Vocabulary Cards in English and Spanish, pp. 27–30
- Reading Skill Card 6, p. 36
- Copying Master, p. 39
- Challenge Activities, pp. 76–80
- School-Home Connection: English/Spanish, pp. 95–96
- Unit 6 Test, p. 104

Technology Resources

 Electronic Art Gallery CD-ROM, Intermediate
Picture Card Bank CD-ROM

 GO **ONLINE** Visit *The Learning Site* www.harcourtschool.com

- Multimedia Art Glossary
- Multimedia Biographies
- Reading Skills and Activities

ART PRINT 16

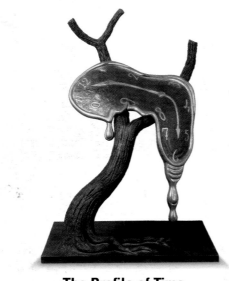

The Profile of Time
by Salvador Dalí

ART PRINT 17

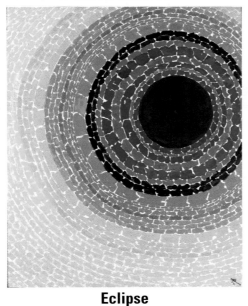

Eclipse
by Alma Woodsey Thomas

ART PRINT 18

California Crosswalk
by John Outterbridge

Art Prints for This Unit

ART PRINT 8

The Family
by Marisol

ART PRINT 12

Three Flags
by Jasper Johns

Lesson	Objectives and Vocabulary	Art Images	Production/Materials

Focus Skill **Author's Purpose, pp. 176–177**

26 **ABSTRACT EXPRESSION-ISM** pp. 178–181 ⏰ 30–60 minutes	• Identify the characteristics of Abstract Expressionism in artworks • Design and create an action painting • Identify the characteristics of action painting **Focus Skill** Determine artist's purpose **Vocabulary: Abstract Expressionism, action painting**	• **Convergence** by Jackson Pollock • **The Bay** by Helen Frankenthaler • **Bird Talk** by Lee Krasner • **Untitled** by Eric, age 9	**Create an Action Painting** ❑ newsprint ❑ white paper ❑ tempera paint ❑ paintbrushes ❑ water bowl
27 **SURREALISM** pp. 182–185 ⏰ 30–60 minutes	• Identify the characteristics of Surrealism in artworks • Choose appropriate vocabulary to discuss variety in artworks • Design and create an original Surrealist painting **Focus Skill** Determine artist's purpose **Vocabulary: Surrealism, variety**	• **The Listening Room (La Chambre d'Ecoute)** by René Magritte • **Memory of the Voyage** by Victor Brauner • **Telephone-Homard** by Salvador Dalí	**Create a Surrealist Painting** ❑ pencil ❑ sketchbook ❑ white paper ❑ tempera paint ❑ paintbrushes ❑ water bowl

Art ↔ Social Studies Connection: Maya Lin, pp. 186–187

28 **CONSTRUCTIONS** pp. 188–191 ⏰ 30–60 minutes	• Identify constructions as sculptures • Identify the use of found objects in an assemblage • Design and create an original construction using found objects **Focus Skill** Determine artist's purpose **Vocabulary: construction, found objects**	• **Luminous Zag: Night** by Louise Nevelson • **Piano Piece** by Nam June Paik • **Celestial Navigation** by Joseph Cornell	**Create a Construction with Found Objects** ❑ yarn, paper clips, rubber bands ❑ shoe box lid ❑ glue ❑ tempera paint ❑ paintbrushes ❑ water bowl
29 **POP ART** pp. 192–195 ⏰ 30–60 minutes	• Identify characteristics of Pop Art • Design and create an original Pop Art collage **Focus Skill** Determine artist's purpose **Vocabulary: Pop Art, silkscreen**	• **Six Self-Portraits** by Andy Warhol • **Cubist Still-Life with Apple** by Roy Lichtenstein • **Bakery Counter** by Wayne Thiebaud	**Create a Pop Art Collage** ❑ magazines ❑ scissors ❑ glue ❑ construction paper

Art ↔ Science Connection: Vehicle Design, pp. 196–197

30 **COMPUTER ART** pp. 198–201 ⏰ 30–60 minutes	• Identify the characteristics of computer-generated art • Design and create an original computer-generated artwork **Focus Skill** Determine artist's purpose **Vocabulary: computer-generated art**	• **No. 49D** by Angelo di Cicco • **Plaid Construct Swirl** by Joan Myerson Shrager • **Annnciation II** by John Clive	**Create a Computer-Generated Artwork** ❑ pencil ❑ sketchbook ❑ computer

Review and Reflect, pp. 202–203

Author's Purpose, pp. 176–177

Focus Skill

Opportunities for application of the skill are provided on pp. 180, 184, 190, 194, 200, 202, and 203.

Resources and Technology	Suggested Literature	Across the Curriculum
• Art Print 17 • Reading Skill Card 6 • Discussion Cards 1, 8, pp. R34, R37 • Electronic Art Gallery CD-ROM, Intermediate	*Action Jackson* by Jan Greenberg	**Social Studies** The United States in the 1950s, p. 179 **Reading** Author's Purpose, 180 **Writing** Poem, p. 181
• Art Print 16 • Reading Skill Card 6 • Discussion Cards 1, 9, pp. R34, R38 • Electronic Art Gallery CD-ROM, Intermediate	*Start with Art: Landscapes* by Sue Lacey	**Math** Proportions in Surrealism, p. 183 **Reading** Author's Purpose, p. 184 **Writing** Surrealistic Story, p. 185
• Art Prints 17, 18 • Reading Skill Card 6 • Discussion Cards 1, 4, pp. R34, R35 • Electronic Art Gallery CD-ROM, Intermediate	*The Jumbo Book of Art* by Irene Luxbacher 	**Science** Recycling, p. 189 **Reading** Author's Purpose, p. 190 **Writing** Interview, p. 191
• Art Prints 8, 12 • Reading Skill Card 6 • Discussion Cards 1, 9, pp. R34, R38 • Electronic Art Gallery CD-ROM, Intermediate	*Visiting the Art Museum* by Laurene Krasny Brown and Marc Brown	**Language Arts** Comic Strip Dialogue, p. 193 **Reading** Author's Purpose, p. 194 **Writing** Personal Narrative, p. 195
• Art Print 16 • Reading Skill Card 6 • Discussion Cards 1, 3, pp. R34, R35 • Electronic Art Gallery CD-ROM, Intermediate	*3-D Planet: The World as Seen Through Stereograms* by Hiroshi Kunoh and Eiji Takaoki	**Social Studies** Computers and Animation, p. 199 **Reading** Author's Purpose, p. 200 **Writing** E-Mail, p. 201

Art Puzzlers

Present these art puzzlers to students at the beginning or end of a class or when students finish an assignment early.

• Cut narrow strips of construction paper in a variety of colors. Arrange them on white paper to create a work of **Abstract Expressionism.** TEKS 4.2B

• Choose a simple object. List three different ways you could show that object in a scene that shows **Surrealism.**

• How could you arrange some of your school supplies in a **construction?**

• Find a product advertisement in a magazine or newspaper. Tell how you would show the product in a **Pop Art** painting.

• **Draw** a pattern that you could use in a piece of **computer-generated art.** TEKS 4.2B

 School-Home Connection
The activities above are included in the School-Home Connection for this unit. See *Teacher Resource Book,* pp. 95–96.

Assessment Options

• Rubrics and Recording Forms, pp. R30–R33
• Unit 6 Test, *Teacher Resource Book,* p. 104

 Visit *The Learning Site* **www.harcourtschool.com**

Artist's Workshops PREVIEW

Use these pages to help you gather and organize materials for the production activity in each lesson.

LESSON	MATERIALS

26 Create an Action Painting p. 181

- newsprint
- white paper
- tempera paint
- paintbrushes
- water bowl

Objective: To design and create an original action painting in the Abstract Expressionist style

🕐 30–40 minutes

Challenge Activity: See *Teacher Resource Book*, page 76.

LESSON

27 Create a Surrealist Painting p. 185

- pencil
- sketchbook
- white paper
- tempera paint
- paintbrushes
- water bowl

Objective: To design and create an original painting in the Surrealist style

🕐 30–40 minutes

Challenge Activity: See *Teacher Resource Book*, page 77.

 For safety information, see Art Safety, p. R4, or Art Safety Poster.

 For information on media and techniques, see pp. R15–R23.

LESSON	MATERIALS

28 Create a Construction with Found Objects

p. 191

Objective: To design and create an original construction using found objects

🕐 **30–40 minutes**

Challenge Activity: See *Teacher Resource Book*, page 78.

- found objects, such as yarn, paper clips, and rubber bands
- shoe box lid
- glue
- tempera paint
- paintbrushes
- water bowl

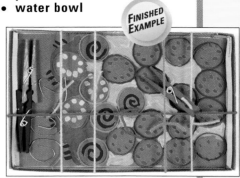

---

29 Create a Pop Art Collage p. 195

Objective: To design and create an original collage in the Pop Art style

🕐 **30–40 minutes**

Challenge Activity: See *Teacher Resource Book*, page 79.

- magazines
- scissors
- glue
- construction paper

---

30 Create a Computer-Generated Artwork

p. 201

Objective: To design and create an original computer-generated artwork

🕐 **30–40 minutes**

Challenge Activity: See *Teacher Resource Book*, page 80.

- pencil
- sketchbook
- computer

Unit 6

Stretch Your Imagination

PREVIEW THE UNIT

Tell students that in this unit they will view artworks that stretch the imagination and change the way people see and appreciate art. Invite students to preview this unit by reading the lesson titles and examining the art images.

STEP INTO THE ART

Have students examine the sculpture on pages 174 and 175 and describe what they see. Then read page 175 with students, and discuss the sculpture:

- **What part of it would you look at first?** Discuss with students what they might see first from different points of view.

- **What do you think its textures would feel like?** Ask students to use sensory language to communicate their ideas. Students should recognize the smooth texture around the eyes and the bumpiness of the ball in front of and on top of the animal. TEKS 4.1A

- **If you could display this sculpture anywhere, where would you place it?** Students may suggest a museum, a nearby park, or a local zoo.

SHARE BACKGROUND INFORMATION

Tell students that Salvador Dalí often incorporated rhinoceroses into his artwork. For example, many of his well-known oil paintings use intricate color images of rhino horns. This sculpture weighs 3 1/2 tons and is 6 1/2 feet tall.

 See **Using the Maps of Museums and Art Sites,** p. R2.

Salvador Dalí, *Rhinoceros Dressed in Lace*, 1955, bronze sculpture, 78$\frac{7}{10}$ in. high.

LOCATE IT

More than 1,400 works by the artist can be found in the Salvador Dalí Museum in St. Petersburg, Florida.

See Maps of Museums and Art Sites, pages 206–209.

FLORIDA

St. Petersburg

174

FYI Background Information

About the Artist

One of the most imaginative artists of the twentieth century, Salvador Dalí (DAH•lee) (1904–1989) was also known for his eccentricity. In 1936, Dalí opened the London Surrealist Exhibition dressed in a diving suit.

For additional information about Salvador Dalí, see the Encyclopedia of Artists and Art History, pp. R44–R65, and the Gallery of Artists, *Student Edition* page 243.

 For related artworks, see **Electronic Art Gallery CD-ROM, Intermediate.**

Unit 6

Variety

Stretch Your Imagination

Step into the Art

Imagine that you could stand next to this sculpture. What part of it would you look at first? What do you think its textures would feel like? If you could display this sculpture anywhere, where would you place it?

ABOUT THE ARTIST

See Gallery of Artists, pages 240–253.

Unit Vocabulary

Abstract Expressionism	found objects
action painting	Pop Art
Surrealism	silkscreen
variety	computer-generated art
construction	

Multimedia Art Glossary
Visit *The Learning Site*
www.harcourtschool.com

175

Language Arts Connection

Students may create a chart like the one below to identify familiar and unfamiliar vocabulary terms. Encourage them to add information to their charts as they work through this unit.

WORD KNOWLEDGE CHART		
I know this term.	I have seen this term before.	I have never seen this term.

Unit Vocabulary

Read aloud the terms with students, and use the Word Knowledge Chart below to assess and discuss their prior knowledge.

Abstract Expressionism a twentieth-century art movement in which artists believed in the freedom to express feelings and emotions through their artwork

action painting a technique of dripping, pouring, and splattering paint onto large canvases

Surrealism an art style that focuses on impossible, dreamlike images

variety a design principle used to add interest in an artwork by including different objects and art elements

construction a type of sculpture that is made by joining pieces together. It can be made from a variety of materials or from one kind of material.

found object a common object that has a specific purpose. Found objects are often used in assemblages.

Pop Art a twentieth-century art movement that was inspired by popular media, such as comic books and advertisements

silkscreen a printing process in which ink is forced through silk onto paper, cloth, or another surface

computer-generated art artwork that is created with software on a computer

Vocabulary Resources

- Vocabulary Cards in English and Spanish: *Teacher Resource Book,* pp. 27–30
- Student Edition Glossary, pp. 254–261

Multimedia Art Glossary
Visit *The Learning Site*
www.harcourtschool.com

Focus Skill **READING SKILL**

PDAS Domains I, II

Author's Purpose

SKILL TRACE	
AUTHOR'S PURPOSE	
Introduce	pp. 176–177
Review	pp. 180, 184, 190, 194, 200, 202

DISCUSS THE SKILL

Access Prior Knowledge   Discuss with students different kinds of books, such as novels, biographies, textbooks, dictionaries, instruction manuals, and joke books. Explain to students that authors have specific purposes for writing and that artists have specific purposes for creating art. Tell students that determining the author's or artist's purpose can help them better understand the texts they read and the artworks they view.

APPLY TO ART

Determine Artist's Purpose   Have students read page 176 and discuss what they see in the painting. Ask students to point out the parts of the artwork that seem realistic and the parts that do not. Explain to students that the artist placed realistic objects—the fish in the aquarium and the man's reflection—in an impossible setting: the ocean floor. Point out that the artist's purpose might have been to surprise and entertain the viewer. Ask students to comment on whether or not they think the artist was successful and why.   TEKS 4.4B

Focus Skill **READING SKILL**

Author's Purpose

Authors have *purposes*, or reasons, for writing. An author's purpose may be one of the following:

- to express, or to share ideas
- to entertain, or to amuse
- to inform, or to give information
- to influence, or to make someone want to do something

When creating an artwork, an artist has a purpose as well.

Look at the image below, and read its title. In this image the artist has shown a person's reflection in an aquarium that seems to be under water. The artist's purpose may have been to **entertain** and to surprise the viewer by showing an object and a place that do not go together in real life.

Ricardo Maffei,
Aquarium (Acuario),
1997, pastel on paper.
Private collection.

176

Background Information

About the Artist

Ricardo Maffei (1953–) was born in Santiago, Chile, where he currently lives and works. He often places realistic images in a highly imaginative setting to achieve an element of surprise. Often considered one of Latin America's most creative contemporary artists, Maffei has exhibited in South America, Europe, and the United States.

For additional information about the artist, see pp. R44–R65.

 For related artworks, see **Electronic Art Gallery CD-ROM, Intermediate.**

⭐ **TEKS 4.4B** interpret artworks by peers and others; **PDAS Domain I** active participation; **PDAS Domain II** learner-centered instruction; **PDAS Domain IV** classroom management; **TAKS Reading Objective 1** demonstrate understanding of texts;   *(continued)*

Now read the passage below. Think about the author's purpose for writing it. Was it to express, to entertain, to inform, or to influence?

In the early part of the twentieth century, painters like Salvador Dalí and René Magritte began creating artworks using images from their imaginations. Their artworks often showed people and objects in realistic detail surrounded by dreamlike landscapes or backgrounds. The images were so strange and realistic at the same time that many people found the art surprising and even shocking. This was exactly what the artists had intended.

List the details that helped you figure out the author's purpose. Use a chart like this to help you.

Author's Purpose		
Detail	Detail	Detail
Dalí and Magritte painted images from their imaginations.		

On Your Own

As you look at the artworks in this unit, use charts like the one above to help you figure out the purposes of the text and the artworks. Look back at your charts when you see questions with READING SKILL .

177

APPLY TO READING

Determine Author's Purpose Tell students that as they read, they should look for details that can help them determine the author's purpose.

Have students read the passage on page 177. Work with them to complete the chart, and have them state the author's purpose.
TAKS Reading Objectives 1, 3, 4

Author's Purpose		
to inform		
Detail	Detail	Detail
Dalí and Magritte painted images from their imaginations.	Their work showed realistic people and objects surrounded by dreamlike backgrounds.	The images were so strange and realistic that many people found the art surprising and shocking.

ON YOUR OWN

As students read about and view the artworks in this unit, have them use a chart such as the one on page 177 to help them determine the author's purpose in writing the text and the artist's purpose in creating the artwork.

TAKS Reading Objective 4

Reading Skill Card

Distribute Reading Skill Card 6, *Teacher Resource Book* page 36. Have students determine the artists' purposes in this unit.

Extend the Skill
For additional teaching suggestions, see *Art Transparency 16.*

PDAS Domain IV

ESL Pair students with English-fluent peers and have them read the passage together. To support **language acquisition,** help students paraphrase the passage.

Challenge Have interested students use the chart on page 177 to analyze the sculpture on pages 174–175.

Reading Skills and Activities
Visit *The Learning Site*
www.harcourtschool.com

Lesson 26

Lesson 26

PDAS Domains I, II
Abstract Expressionism

OBJECTIVES
- Identify the characteristics of Abstract Expressionism in artworks
- Identify the characteristics of action painting
- Design and create an original action painting
- Determine artist's purpose

RESOURCES
- Art Print 17
- Reading Skill Card 6
- Discussion Cards 1, 8, pp. R34, R37
- Electronic Art Gallery CD-ROM, Intermediate

GO ONLINE
Multimedia Art Glossary and Biographies
Visit *The Learning Site*
www.harcourtschool.com

5 Minutes

Warm-Up

Build Background   Have students look through their textbooks for artworks that seem to express various moods. Discuss with students the characteristics of artworks that might express calm, excited, lively, or melancholy moods. Then tell students that in this lesson they will learn about an art movement in which artists used new techniques to express their feelings directly in their work. TEKS 4.4B

Lesson 26

Vocabulary

Abstract Expressionism

action painting

Abstract Expressionism

Abstract Expressionism was an art movement that was popular in the United States in the 1950s. Abstract Expressionists wanted to express their feelings and emotions. They did not feel the need to show real objects in their artworks.

Action Painting

Jackson Pollock, the artist of the painting in image **A**, was the best-known Abstract Expressionist. He was known for his technique of dripping, pouring, and splattering paint onto large canvases. This method of painting is called **action painting**. How would you describe this painting? What kinds of emotion does it express?

Jackson Pollock, *Convergence,* 1952, oil on canvas, 93½ in. × 155 in. Albright-Knox Art Gallery, Buffalo, New York.

Background Information

About the Artists

A American painter **Jackson Pollock** (PAHL•uhk) (1912–1956) placed large canvases on the floor and used heavily loaded brushes, sticks, and even turkey basters to apply paint.

C **Lee Krasner** (1908–1984) sometimes tore apart her paintings and those of her husband, Jackson Pollock, to create her collages.

For more information about the artists, see pp. R44–R65.

For related artworks, see the **Electronic Art Gallery CD-ROM, Intermediate.**

★ TEKS 4.1B discuss elements and principles; TEKS 4.4B interpret artworks by peers and others; PDAS Domain I active participation; PDAS Domain II learner-centered instruction; TAKS Reading Objective 1 demonstrate understanding of texts

 Helen Frankenthaler, *The Bay*,
1963, acrylic on canvas, 6 ft. 8¾ in. × 6 ft. 8¾ in.
Detroit Institute of Arts, Detroit, Michigan.

The painting in image **B** is another example of Abstract Expressionism. The artist used thinned oil paints to stain, or soak, the canvas. This style was very different from the thick buildup of paint in action paintings.

LOCATE IT

The painting in image A is located in Buffalo, New York.

179

Preview the Art Have students preview images A through D on pages 178–180. Ask them to describe each artwork and talk about the mood they think it expresses. Use Discussion Card 1 and the questions below to guide the discussion. Then have students read pages 178–180.

A *Convergence* **What kind of feeling do you get from this painting? Why?**

B *The Bay* **What do the title and the colors tell you about the subject of this painting?** TEKS 4.4B

C *Bird Talk* **Describe the color scheme the artist used in this collage.** TEKS 4.1B

D *Untitled* **What title would you give this artwork, and why?**

Discuss Art Concepts Discuss with students the energetic, busy, even angry mood created by the obvious splattering of paint on the canvas in image A. Students should understand that the artist's technique of flinging the paint over a large canvas, was not a calm, gentle process.

Have students compare and contrast image A and image B. Students should note that though both images show works of Abstract Expressionism, the organic shapes and cool colors in image B create a calm, gentle mood. TEKS 4.1B, TEKS 4.4B

Discuss with students the placement of the shapes in image C. Point out that removing any of the shapes would make the artwork seem unfinished. Similarly, in image D, losing one area of color would disrupt the unity of the artwork.

LOCATE IT Tell students that the painting in image A is about 8 feet tall and 13 feet wide. Compare these dimensions to a classroom.

TAKS Reading Objective 1

Social Studies Connection

The United States in the 1950s Remind students that Abstract Expressionism flourished in the early 1950s. Have students work in small groups to research that decade to find information about historical events, inventions, or popular products of the period. Encourage them to share their findings.

Teach (continued)

Author's/Artist's Purpose   Discuss with students the artist's purpose in creating the painting in image B. Ask students to think about these questions:

- What is the subject of this painting?

- How did the artist show her subject?

Help students conclude that the artist's purpose was probably to express her ideas about her subject, a bay. Point out that a realistic painting of a bay might indicate that the artist's purpose was to inform.   TEKS 4.4B

Think Critically

Use the questions below to check students' understanding of lesson concepts.

1. **READING SKILL** **What do you think the artist's purpose was for creating the collage in image C?** (to show what the sound of birds chirping might look like) **AUTHOR'S/ARTIST'S PURPOSE**   TEKS 4.4B

2. **How are the paintings in images A and D alike? How are they different?** (Possible response: Both are colorful; image A has primary colors, white, and black, but image D also has secondary colors; image A is an action painting, but image D is not.) **PERCEPTION/AESTHETICS**
   TEKS 4.1B, TEKS 4.3B

3. **WRITE**   **Choose an artwork from this lesson, and write a paragraph to explain your opinion of it. Be sure to support your opinion with reasons and details.** **EXPOSITORY**
   TAKS Writing Objective 1

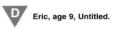
Lee Krasner, *Bird Talk*, 1955, oil, paper, and canvas on cotton duck cloth, 58 in. × 56 in.

The Abstract Expressionist artwork in image **C** is a collage. How has the artist created unity? Now look at image **D**. What gives it unity?

Eric, age 9, Untitled.

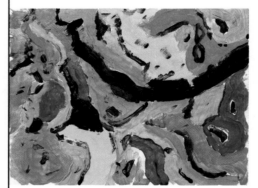

180

Think Critically

1. **READING SKILL**   What do you think the artist's purpose was for creating the collage in image **C**? **AUTHOR'S/ARTIST'S PURPOSE**

2. How are the paintings in images **A** and **D** alike? How are they different?

3. **WRITE**   Choose an artwork from this lesson, and write a paragraph to explain your opinion of it. Be sure to support your opinion with reasons and details.

TEKS 4.3B, TEKS 4.4B

Art Print 17

Display **Art Print 17** and distribute to students Discussion Card 8: *Abstract Art* and Reading Skill Card 6. Have students compare this artwork with the artworks in this lesson and then determine the artist's purpose.

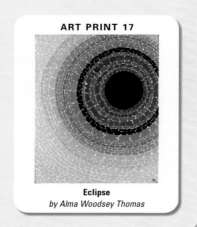
ART PRINT 17

Eclipse
by Alma Woodsey Thomas

★ TEKS 4.1B discuss elements and principles; TEKS 4.2B design original artworks; TEKS 4.2C produce artworks; TEKS 4.3B compare and contrast artworks; TEKS 4.4A form conclusions about personal artworks; *(continued)*

Artist's Workshop

Create an Action Painting

PLAN

Think of the colors you would like to use in an action painting.

CREATE

1. Cover your work area with newsprint, and center your paper on it.

2. Using one color of paint at a time, hold your paintbrush over your paper, and drip or splatter paint onto it.

3. Drip one color over another. Try to drip paint to the edges of your paper.

4. Stand back from your painting now and then to see where you would like to add paint or change colors. Try to give your painting a sense of unity.

REFLECT

How did you create unity in your painting? What kind of feeling do you think it expresses?

MATERIALS

- newsprint
- white paper
- tempera paint
- paintbrushes
- water bowl

 Quick Tip

Drizzle the paint in layers, making it thick in some places to add texture.

181

 30-40 Minutes

Artist's Workshop

Create an Action Painting

PLAN Have students read page 181. Then have them think about the feeling or mood they want to express before choosing their colors.

CREATE Ask students to invent ways to produce their artworks using a variety of art media such as different types of paint to create different effects in their painting. TEKS 4.2B, TEKS 4.2C

REFLECT Have students describe the feelings they expressed in their action paintings. **SELF-EVALUATION** TEKS 4.4A

5-10 Minutes

Wrap-Up

Informal Assessment PDAS Domain III

- **Interpret the ideas or feelings expressed in one of your peers' action paintings.**
  (Responses will vary.) **PERSONAL RESPONSE** TEKS 4.4B

- **Give your painting a title that includes your purpose.** (Responses will vary.) **FACT AND OPINION** TEKS 4.4A

Extend Through Writing TAKS Writing Objective 1

POEM Ask students to brainstorm adjectives describing the mood in their painting and use them to write a short rhymed or unrhymed poem. TEKS 4.4A

Recommended Reading

Action Jackson
by Jan Greenberg
and Sandra Jordan.
Roaring Brook Press, 2002.
AVERAGE

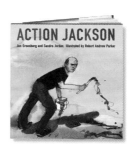

 PDAS Domain IV

Activity Options

Quick Activity Have students experiment with action painting on a smaller sheet of paper using only one color.

Early Finishers Have students use watercolors to create a painting in Frankenthaler's style.

Challenge See *Teacher Resource Book*, p. 76.

 PDAS Domain IV

ESL Work with students to create a list of action verbs related to action painting, such as *splatter, drip, fling, drizzle,* and *pour*. **Model** each action as students **pantomime** each movement while saying the corresponding word aloud.

TEKS 4.4B interpret artworks by peers and others; **PDAS Domain III** evaluation and feedback; **PDAS Domain IV** classroom management; **TAKS Writing Objective 1** composition

LESSON 26 *Abstract Expressionism* **181**

Lesson 27

PDAS Domains I, II
Surrealism

OBJECTIVES
- Identify the characteristics of Surrealism in artworks
- Choose appropriate vocabulary to discuss variety in artworks
- Design and create an original Surrealist painting
- Determine artist's purpose

RESOURCES
- Art Print 16
- Reading Skill Card 6
- Discussion Cards 1, 9, pp. R34, R38
- Electronic Art Gallery CD-ROM, Intermediate

 GO ONLINE Multimedia Art Glossary and Biographies
Visit *The Learning Site*
www.harcourtschool.com

 5 Minutes

Warm-Up

Build Background Display **Art Print 16,** a sculpture by Salvador Dalí, and ask volunteers to describe what they see. Ask students to tell what is "normal" about the sculpture and what is not. (The tree looks normal, but the melted clock does not.) Tell students that in this lesson they will learn about an art style that focuses on strange, dreamlike images, like this sculpture.

Lesson 27

Surrealism

Vocabulary

Surrealism

variety

Surrealism is an art style that focuses on impossible, dreamlike images. Often, realistic objects are shown in settings where they do not belong.

What object and setting do you see in image **A**? The artist painted the object and setting in a realistic style. Notice how the light from the window shines on the left side of the apple while a shadow forms on the right side. How did the artist use values to show this? Where did the artist use linear perspective in this painting?

 A René Magritte, *The Listening Room (La Chambre d'Ecoute),* 1953, oil on canvas, 31 in. × 39⅜ in. William M. Copley Collection.

182

 Background Information

About the Artists

A The paintings of Surrealist artist René Magritte (ruh•NAY ma•GREET) (1898–1967) regularly show symbols such as a castle, a rock, a window, and a man in a hat.

C Salvador Dalí (DAH•lee) (1904–1989) once described his paintings as "hand-painted dream photographs."

For more information about the artists, see pp. R44–R65.

 For related artworks, see **Electronic Art Gallery CD-ROM, Intermediate.**

★ TEKS 4.1B discuss elements and principles; TEKS 4.4B interpret artworks by peers and others; PDAS Domain I active participation; PDAS Domain II learner-centered instruction

Victor Brauner,
*Memory of
the Voyage,*
1957, oil on canvas,
65 cm × 50 cm.
Private collection.

Now look at the painting in image **B**. Which part of this painting shows an object you recognize, and which part does not? Point out the different lines, shapes, colors, and values you see. The artist used many different art elements to create **variety**. Variety can make an artwork more interesting.

183

Math Connection

Proportions in Surrealism Have students look back at image A and note the artist's use of proportion to achieve a surrealistic effect. Ask students to imagine that the apple in the painting is 8 feet tall, and remind them that a real apple is about 3 or 4 inches tall. Have students calculate how many times taller the apple in the painting is than a real apple. (32 or 24 times taller)

10-15 Minutes

Teach

Preview the Art Have students preview images A through C on pages 182–184. Ask them to think about what is unusual about each image. Use Discussion Card 1 and the questions below to guide the discussion. Then have students read pages 182–184.

A *The Listening Room (La Chambre d'Ecoute)* **What do you think was the artist's purpose in creating this image? Why do you think that?** TEKS 4.4B

B *Memory of the Voyage* **What patterns do you see in this painting?** TEKS 4.1B

C *Telephone-Homard* **How would you describe this sculpture to someone who had not seen it?** TEKS 4.4B

Discuss Art Concepts Have students identify the realistic details in image A. They should point out the artist's use of value to show light, shadow, and texture in the apple and the floor. Students should also note the use of linear perspective shown in the lines of the floor and ceiling. Students should recognize that though the apple and the room are each painted realistically, combining them in one scene creates a surrealistic effect.

Have students identify the ship at the top of the painting in image B. Discuss with students that what appears to be under the water is not what the viewer would expect. Students should choose appropriate vocabulary to note that the colorful squares that form the figure create variety. TEKS 4.1B

Students should point out the artist's use of emphasis in image C in the form, color, and object he used for the telephone receiver. Discuss rotary telephones with students who are unfamiliar with them. TEKS 4.1B

Science Link Newborn babies spend about half of their total sleep time in REM sleep. By about age ten, that proportion drops to about one-quarter.

Author's/Artist's Purpose Ask students to look at image B and talk about the artist's purpose in creating the artwork. Encourage students to think about these questions:

- What is happening in the painting?

- What does the artist want you to think about?

Then help students conclude that the artist's purpose was probably to express ideas about his memories of a sea voyage. TEKS 4.4B

Think Critically

Use the questions below to check students' understanding of lesson concepts.

1. (Focus Skill) **READING SKILL** **What do you think the artist's purpose was for creating the artwork in image C?** (Possible response: to surprise and entertain viewers)
AUTHOR'S/ARTIST'S PURPOSE TEKS 4.4B

2. **How could you change image A from a surrealistic scene to a realistic scene?** (Possible response: by painting the apple in realistic proportion to the setting)
PERCEPTION/AESTHETICS

3. **WRITE** **Write a short story about the memory that is shown in image B.** NARRATIVE
TAKS Writing Objective 1

▷ **C** Salvador Dalí,
Telephone-Homard,
1936, assemblage: telephone
with synthetic lobster,
$11\frac{3}{4}$ in. × $5\frac{7}{8}$ in. × $6\frac{5}{8}$ in.
Private collection.

Science Link

During some of your dreams when you are asleep, your eyes make rapid eye movements (REMs), and you breathe faster. This type of sleep, called REM sleep, occurs in all humans and in many other mammals.

Image **C** shows a Surrealistic sculpture. The artist combined two ordinary objects—a telephone and a lobster—in an unusual way. How did the artist use emphasis? What kind of feeling do you get from image **C**?

Think Critically

1. (Focus Skill) **READING SKILL** What do you think the artist's purpose was for creating the artwork in image **C**? AUTHOR'S/ARTIST'S PURPOSE

2. How could you change image **A** from a Surrealistic scene to a realistic scene?

3. **WRITE** Write a short story about the memory that is shown in image **B**.

184

 Art Print 16

Display **Art Print 16** and distribute to students Discussion Card 9: *Art Criticism.* Have students discuss the features of the artwork that distinguish it as Surrealist art.

ART PRINT 16

The Profile of Time
by Salvador Dalí

★ **TEKS 4.1A** communicate ideas; **TEKS 4.2B** design original artworks; **TEKS 4.4A** form conclusions about personal artworks; **TEKS 4.4B** interpret artworks by peers and others; **PDAS Domain III** evaluation and feedback; **PDAS Domain IV** classroom management; *(continued)*

Artist's Workshop

Create a Surrealist Painting

MATERIALS
- pencil
- sketchbook
- white paper
- tempera paint
- paintbrushes
- water bowl

PLAN

Think of a familiar setting. Then think of an object that does not belong in that setting. Make some sketches of the object in the setting.

CREATE

1. Copy your best sketch onto white paper.

2. Experiment with changing the sizes and shapes of the objects in your scene. Think of ways to add variety.

3. Paint your scene. Use tints and shades to show areas of light and shadow in the object or setting.

REFLECT

How does your painting show a Surrealistic scene? How did you add variety?

Quick Tip Look through magazines to get ideas for settings and objects to use to create your scene.

185

Artist's Workshop
30-40 Minutes

Create a Surrealist Painting

PLAN Have students read the activity steps on page 185. Provide students with magazine photographs of familiar settings and objects.

CREATE As students design their artworks, have them think about how they can use value, proportion, and variety to show a Surrealist style. Have students mix and match the objects with the settings to create a Surrealist scene. TEKS 4.2B

REFLECT Ask students to describe the intent of their artworks. SELF-EVALUATION TEKS 4.4A

Wrap-Up
5-10 Minutes

Informal Assessment PDAS Domain III

- **Exchange artworks with a peer. How does your peer's artwork show Surrealism?** (Responses will vary.) PERSONAL RESPONSE TEKS 4.4B

- **What purpose did you have in mind as you created your painting?** (Responses will vary.) AUTHOR'S/ARTIST'S PURPOSE

Extend Through Writing
TAKS Writing Objective 1

SURREALISTIC STORY Have students use sensory knowledge to communicate ideas in a surrealistic story about school. TEKS 4.1A

Recommended Reading

Start with Art: Landscapes by Sue Lacey. Copper Beech Books, 2000. AVERAGE

Activity Options
PDAS Domain IV

Quick Activity Have students combine a few magazine photos in a Surrealistic collage.

Early Finishers Have students add symbols to their painting.

Challenge See *Teacher Resource Book*, p. 77.

ESL
PDAS Domain IV

Use **visuals** to provide **comprehensible input** for familiar settings and common objects. Display *Picture Cards Collection,* cards 10, 27, 68, 72, and 119 for students to discuss and reference.

beach

See also *Picture Card Bank* CD-ROM, Category: Places People Go.

PDAS Domains I, II

Maya Lin

ARTIST BIOGRAPHY

DISCUSS THE IMAGES

Have students read pages 186–187.

- Encourage students to describe the artworks in image A. Tell students that the pyramid is nineteen feet high and is composed of eleven tons of blue-green glass particles. Discuss with students the way the sculptures and the setting work together—the pyramid seems to pour out from the corner and onto the floor.

- Tell students that Maya Lin created the environmental artwork in image B on approximately 10,000 square feet of land at the University of Michigan in Ann Arbor. Point out the pattern of waves in the sculpture, and have students compare it to the pattern of waves in image A. Discuss with students the soft, grassy texture of the surface of image B, and tell them that university students enjoy sitting in the spaces between the waves. Ask students what they think the artist's purpose was for creating the artworks on pages 186–187. Have them interpret the moods and ideas in this small exhibition of Maya Lin's work. TEKS 4.4B

In what ways can an artist use unusual materials to create new art experiences?

Architect Maya Lin is best known for her designs of memorials, public parks, homes, and libraries. However, she is also a sculptor. Lin's sculptures are usually large artworks made of unusual materials. Image A shows a sculpture made entirely from tiny pieces of recycled glass that seems to flow out of the corner and onto the floor. A slight tremble can cause an unexpected shower of glass to flow down.

Maya Lin, *Avalanche*, 1998, crushed recycled glass, approximately 10 ft. x 19 ft. x 21 ft., Private collection, and in foreground, *Untitled (Topographic Landscape)*, 1997, vertical slices of trimmed particle board, 16 ft. x 18 ft. x 2 ft. Columbus Museum of Art, Columbus, Ohio.

Background Information

About the Artist

The American sculptor and architect Maya Lin (1959–) was born in Athens, Ohio, to parents who had moved in the 1940s to the U.S. from China. As a child, Lin spent a great deal of time reading, hiking, and making pottery.

For additional information about Maya Lin, see pp. R44–R65.

For related artworks, see **Electronic Art Gallery CD-ROM, Intermediate.**

★ **TEKS 4.2B** design original artworks; **TEKS 4.3C** identify roles of art; **TEKS 4.4B** interpret artworks by peers and others; **PDAS Domain I** active participation; **PDAS Domain II** learner-centered instruction

Image **B** shows one of Lin's larger sculptures. Fifty grass waves are arranged in eight rows. Each of the waves was sculpted out of soil and sand and then covered with grass. The result is a large open space for people to sit on or walk through. How would you describe the texture shown in image **B**?

Think About Art

Why do you think the glass sculpture in image **A** is titled *Avalanche*?

Multimedia Biographies
Visit *The Learning Site*
www.harcourtschool.com

B **Maya Lin, *The Wave Field,*** 1995, earth and grass, 90 ft. x 90 ft. with waves about 5–6 ft. high. University of Michigan, Ann Arbor, Michigan.

187

DID YOU KNOW?

Use the facts below to talk about the Vietnam Veterans Memorial.

- Explain to students that the names of more than 58,000 men and women killed or missing in the Vietnam War are etched on the black granite panels of the Memorial. The names are listed chronologically, by year, from first casualty to last.

- The Memorial is nearly 494 feet long. It has seventy etched panels and four blank panels at each end. The panels are arranged in two arms extending from a central point to form a wide angle.

- To locate a particular name, visitors can use one of the alphabetical directories located on either end of the Memorial.

Think About Art

Why do you think the glass sculpture in image A is titled *Avalanche*? (because a tremble in the floor can cause some of the glass particles to slide down the side of the sculpture, as snow or rocks would in a real avalanche) **EVALUATION/CRITICISM**
TEKS 4.4B

ARTIST'S EYE ACTIVITY

Unusual Materials   Suggest that students draw a sketch of a sculpture they would like to create out of unusual material, such as the recycled glass in image A or the soil, sand, and grass in image B. Encourage students to share their design with classmates and to explain their choice of materials.
TEKS 4.2B

Multimedia Biographies
Visit *The Learning Site*
www.harcourtschool.com

Science Connection

Ocean Waves   The idea for the artwork in image B came from oceanography. Explain that ocean waves are generated by wind. The wind may be local or from a distant storm.

For additional cross-curricular suggestions, see *Art Transparency 17.*

TEKS 4.3C, TEKS 4.4B
Viewing Public Artworks

Memorials and Monuments Arrange for students to visit public art sites in your community. Have students identify the roles of public artworks in American society and interpret the ideas and moods expressed in them.

PDAS Domains I, II

Constructions

OBJECTIVES
- Identify constructions as a type of sculpture
- Identify the use of found objects in an assemblage
- Design and create an original construction using found objects
- Determine artist's purpose

RESOURCES
- Art Prints 17, 18
- Reading Skill Card 6
- Discussion Cards 1, 4, pp. R34–R35
- Electronic Art Gallery CD-ROM, Intermediate

Multimedia Art Glossary and Biographies
Visit *The Learning Site*
www.harcourtschool.com

Warm-Up

5 Minutes

Build Background Display **Art Print 18,** a sculpture by John Outterbridge. Discuss with students the subject of the artwork and the materials the artist used—metal, wire, cloth, and other materials. Tell students that in this lesson they will learn how some artists create sculptures by combining different materials.

Lesson 28

Constructions

Vocabulary
construction
found objects

The artwork in image **A** is an example of a construction. A **construction** is a type of sculpture that is made by joining different pieces. It can be made from a variety of materials or from one kind of material. The construction in image **A** was made from one kind of material—wood. The artist stacked wooden boxes together to form a wall. She arranged other wooden objects, such as chair legs and railings, inside the boxes. Where do you see variety in image **A**? How did this artist create unity?

 Louise Nevelson, *Luminous Zag: Night,* 1971, painted boxes, 120 in. × 193 in. × 10¾ in. Solomon R. Guggenheim Museum, New York, New York.

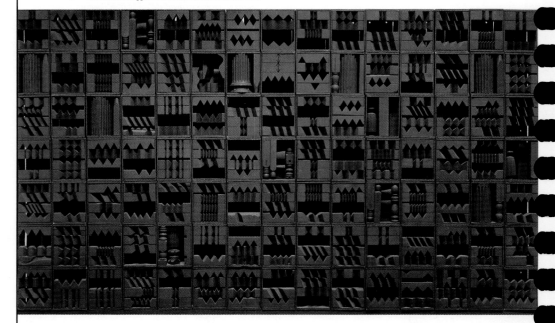

188

 Background Information

About the Artists

A Louise Nevelson (1899–1988) created large, abstract sculptures in wood and other materials.
B Korean-born Nam June Paik (1932–) is considered a pioneer in the use of video technology to create art.
C American artist Joseph Cornell (1903–1972) was one of the originators of the form of sculpture called assemblage.

For additional information about the artists, see pp. R44–R65.

For related artworks, see **Electronic Art Gallery CD-ROM, Intermediate.**

LOCATE IT

The artwork in image A is located at the Guggenheim Museum in New York City.

NEW YORK

New York City

See Maps of Museums and Art Sites, pages 206–209.

B Nam June Paik, *Piano Piece*, 1993, closed-circuit video sculpture, 120 in. × 84 in. × 48 in. Albright-Knox Art Gallery, Buffalo, New York.

Assemblages and Found Objects

An assemblage is a type of construction that is made up of a variety of materials. Sometimes assemblage artists use found objects in their artworks. **Found objects** are things that an artist has found, rather than created. They include common items that have specific purposes. It is usually easy to identify found objects in an assemblage because the artist has not changed them.

Look at image **B**. What found objects did the artist use in this artwork? He created unity by using materials associated with entertainment. How did he add variety?

189

Science Connection

Recycling Tell students that using found objects to create an artwork is one example of recycling. Explain that recycling conserves natural resources, reduces the amount of trash sent to landfills, and saves energy needed to make new products. Have students find out about the recycling efforts in their school or local community, or work in pairs to take a poll to find out how their classmates and family members help the recycling effort in their daily lives.

10-15 Minutes

Teach

Preview the Art Ask students to look at images A through C on pages 188–190. Have them compare each artwork to other three-dimensional artworks they have seen. Use Discussion Card 1 and the questions below to guide the discussion. Then have students read pages 188–190.

A *Luminous Zag: Night* **What do you think the title of this artwork means?**

B *Piano Piece* **What do you think is the main idea of this artwork?**

C *Celestial Navigation* **What does the title tell you about this artwork?**

Discuss Art Concepts Have students point out that the different lines and shapes in the boxes in image A create variety. Ask students whether the construction would look complete if one of the boxes were removed or were painted a different color. (no) Students should conclude that image A shows unity. TEKS 4.1B

Explain to students that found objects include small, everyday items, as well as much larger, heaver objects like those shown in image B. Have students name the found objects in the construction—televisions, a piano, a camera, a light, and a stool—in image B. Discuss with students the way the artist created variety by showing a different view of the piano on each television screen.

In image C, discuss the way the artist showed unity by placing the clear glass goblets in a neat row. The small blue objects on the right and one large blue ball on the left create variety.

LOCATE IT Have students turn to pages 206–207 to locate New York City. Tell students that the Guggenheim Museum is home to many famous pieces of modern art.

Author's/Artist's Purpose Discuss with students the artist's purpose for creating the assemblage in image B. Encourage students to think about these questions:

- How are the objects related?

- How did the artist arrange these objects in the construction?

Then ask students what ideas the artist may have wanted to express or how he may have wanted to influence his viewers. TEKS 4.4B

Think Critically

Use the questions below to check students' understanding of lesson concepts.

1. (Focus Skill) **READING SKILL** **What do you think the artist's purpose was for creating the artwork in image A?** (Possible response: to express ideas or to entertain) AUTHOR'S/ARTIST'S PURPOSE TEKS 4.4B

2. **How do the artworks in images A and B show rhythm?** (Possible response: In image A, the lines and shapes in the repeated squares show rhythm. In image B, the pattern of repeated television monitors shows rhythm.)
PERCEPTION/AESTHETICS TEKS 4.1B

3. **WRITE** Write two paragraphs telling how the artworks in images A and C are alike and how they are different. DESCRIPTIVE
TEKS 4.3B, TAKS Writing Objective 1

 **Joseph Cornell,** *Celestial Navigation,* about 1950–1959, mixed media shadowbox, 9⅝ in. × 16¼ in. × 4 in. Whitney Museum of American Art, New York, New York.

Look at image **C**. What found objects do you see in this assemblage? How did the artist add variety? How did he use color and shape to give this artwork unity?

Think Critically

1. (Focus Skill) **READING SKILL** What do you think the artist's purpose was for creating the artwork in image **A**? AUTHOR'S/ARTIST'S PURPOSE

2. How do the artworks in images **A** and **B** show rhythm?

3. **WRITE** Write two paragraphs telling how the artworks in images **A** and **C** are alike and how they are different.

190

ART PRINT

TEKS 4.1B

Art Print 17

Display **Art Print 17** and distribute to students Discussion Card 4: *Principles of Design.* Have students discuss unity and variety in the artwork.

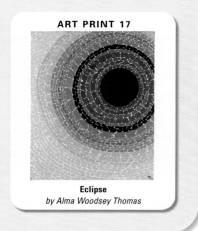

ART PRINT 17

Eclipse *by Alma Woodsey Thomas*

★ TEKS 4.1B discuss elements and principles; TEKS 4.2B design original artworks; TEKS 4.2C produce artworks; TEKS 4.3B compare and contrast artworks; TEKS 4.4A form conclusions about personal artworks; *(continued)*

Artist's Workshop

Create a Construction with Found Objects

PLAN

Gather some found objects to put together in a construction. Think of ways to add variety to your artwork.

CREATE

1. Use the shoe box lid as the base for your construction.

2. Experiment with different arrangements of your found objects on your base.

3. Glue the objects to the base in the arrangement you like best.

4. Paint some or all of the objects in your construction. You may also paint the base.

REFLECT

How would you describe your construction? How did you add variety?

MATERIALS
- found objects, such as yarn, paper clips, and rubber bands
- shoe box lid
- glue
- tempera paint
- paintbrushes
- water bowl

Quick Tip
You may want to add variety by painting part of your construction a different color from the rest of it.

191

30-40 Minutes Artist's Workshop

Create a Construction with Found Objects

PLAN Ask students to read the activity steps on page 191. Students should paint the base of their construction before designing their artwork.

CREATE Have students invent ways to produce their constructions using a variety of materials. Students should think of ways to add variety to their constructions by using found objects of different sizes, shapes, and textures.
TEKS 4.2B, TEKS 4.2C

REFLECT Ask students to describe the intent of their artwork and discuss how they added variety to it. **SELF-EVALUATION** TEKS 4.1B, TEKS 4.4A

5-10 Minutes Wrap-Up

Informal Assessment PDAS Domain III

- **What ideas from this lesson helped you plan your construction?** (Responses will vary.)
  PERCEPTION/AESTHETICS

- **Exchange artworks with a classmate. Interpret the ideas in your peer's construction.** (Responses will vary.)
  AUTHOR'S/ARTIST'S PURPOSE TEKS 4.4B

Extend Through Writing
TAKS Writing Objective 1, 3

INTERVIEW Have partners interview each other about their constructions. Have them each write a list of questions and take turns conducting an interview.

Recommended Reading

The Jumbo Book of Art by Irene Luxbacher. Kids Can Press, 2003. AVERAGE

PDAS Domain IV

Activity Options

Quick Activity Have students sketch an idea for a construction made of found objects.

Early Finishers Suggest that students design a setting for their construction.

Challenge See *Teacher Resource Book,* p. 78.

PDAS Domain IV
MEETING INDIVIDUAL NEEDS

ESL Use **visuals** to support **comprehensible input** for typical classroom objects. Display *Picture Cards Collection* cards 34, 60, and 90 for students to discuss and reference.

crayons

See also **Picture Card Bank CD-ROM,** Category: At School.

TEKS 4.4B interpret artworks by peers and others; **PDAS Domain III** evaluation and feedback; **PDAS Domain IV** classroom management; **TAKS Writing Objective 1** composition; **TAKS Writing Objective 3** organization

LESSON 28 *Constructions* **191**

Lesson 29

Pop Art

OBJECTIVES
- Identify characteristics of Pop Art
- Design and create an original Pop Art collage
- Determine artist's purpose

RESOURCES
- Art Prints 8, 12
- Reading Skill Card 6
- Discussion Cards 1, 9, pp. R34, R38
- Electronic Art Gallery CD-ROM, Intermediate

GO ONLINE Multimedia Art Glossary and Biographies
Visit *The Learning Site*
www.harcourtschool.com

5 Minutes

Warm-Up

Build Background Display **Art Print 12,** a Jasper Johns collage composed of painted images of American flags. Have students compare the artwork with a real American flag. Then discuss with them the way the artist depicted this familiar object in his artwork. Tell students that in this lesson they will learn how artists show ordinary objects in new and unusual ways.

Lesson 29

Pop Art

Vocabulary

Pop Art
silkscreen

Pop Art was an art movement that was inspired by popular media such as comic books and advertisements. Ordinary objects are the subjects of Pop Art.

Silkscreen Prints

Andy Warhol was the best-known Pop Artist. Warhol created silkscreen prints that showed everyday items and famous people. **Silkscreen** is a process of printing. A design is created on a piece of silk and ink is forced through the silk onto paper, cloth, or another surface. For the print in image **A**, Warhol repeated the silkscreen process, using different colors. How does the print show both unity and variety?

Andy Warhol, *Six Self-Portraits,* 1967, screen print: acrylic paint and silkscreen ink on canvas, six canvases each 22 in. × 22 in. Private collection.

192

Background Information

About the Artists

A Andy Warhol (1928–1987) often used images of common objects like soup cans in his artworks.

B Roy Lichtenstein's (LIHK•tuhn•styn) (1923–1997) artwork drew on the styles of popular comic strips.

C Wayne Thiebaud (TEE•boh) (1920–) worked as a commercial artist before becoming a well-known painter.

For additional information about the artists, see pp. R44–R65.

For related artworks, see **Electronic Art Gallery CD-ROM, Intermediate.**

★ TEKS 4.1A communicate ideas; TEKS 4.1B discuss elements and principles; PDAS Domain I active participation; PDAS Domain II learner-centered instruction; TAKS Reading Objective 1 demonstrate understanding of texts; *(continued)*

 Roy Lichtenstein,
Cubist Still-Life with Apple,
about 1974, oil and magna on canvas,
20 in. × 24 in. Private collection.

Roy Lichtenstein was another famous Pop Artist. His painting style imitated what he saw in newspapers and comic books. He enlarged the tiny dots that made up the comic-strip images. He also used bold, black lines and primary colors. Look at image **B**. How did the artist add variety to the artwork? What kinds of patterns do you see?

Social Studies Link

Action-adventure comic strips and comic books first appeared in the United States in the 1930s. They introduced characters such as Tarzan, Dick Tracy, and Superman to young readers.

193

 TAKS Reading Objectives 1, 3, 4

Language Arts Connection

Comic Strip Dialogue Tell students that comic books first appeared at the beginning of the twentieth century. By 1963, there were more than 300 different comic strips in the United States.

Ask pairs of students to each select a comic strip from the local newspaper and cut out or obscure the text in the speech balloons. Then have partners exchange their comic strips and write dialogue for each speech balloon.

 10-15 Minutes

Teach

Preview the Art Have students preview images A through C on pages 192–194. Ask them to point out the ordinary objects they see. Use Discussion Card 1 and the questions below to guide the discussion. Then have students read pages 192–194.

A *Six Self-Portraits* **What is the first thing you notice about this artwork? Why?**

B *Cubist Still-Life with Apple* **Describe the lines the artist used.** TEKS 4.1B

C *Bakery Counter* **Use sensory knowledge and life experience to describe this painting.** TEKS 4.1A

Discuss Art Concepts Before discussing image A, remind students that a self-portrait is an artwork in which the artist is the subject. Students should note that the pattern of the artist's face creates unity in the artwork, while the different color schemes give the artwork variety.

Ask a volunteer to read the title of the painting in image B aloud. Remind students that Cubism was an art style in which artists rearranged pieces of the subject and showed more than one view at the same time. Have students point out the objects in image B that might appear in a still life. Have students point out the way the patterns of dots, lines, and color create variety.

Help students recognize that the painting in image C fits the definition of Pop Art because of the use of ordinary objects as its subject. Students should note that the artist used different shapes, colors, and patterns to add variety. TEKS 4.1B

Social Studies Link Have students ask adult family members which comic strips they enjoyed as children and what they liked about them, and have them share this information with classmates.

Author's/Artist's Purpose Discuss with students the artist's purpose in creating the artwork in image A. Encourage students to think about these questions:

- What are some reasons why artists might create self-portraits?

- Why do you think the artist shows six different versions of the same portrait?

Then discuss with students the artist's possible purposes, such as to express ideas or to entertain the viewer. TEKS 4.4B

Think Critically

Use the questions below to check students' understanding of lesson concepts.

1. (Focus Skill) *READING SKILL* **What do you think the artist's purpose was for creating the painting in image C?** (Possible response: to persuade viewers that ordinary objects can be the subject of artworks) **AUTHOR'S/ARTIST'S PURPOSE** TEKS 4.4B

2. **How does image B show a Cubist art style?** (Possible response: The artist showed more than one view of the subject at the same time.) **PERCEPTION/AESTHETICS**

3. **WRITE** **Write a paragraph describing Pop Art in your own words.** **DESCRIPTIVE** TAKS Writing Objective 1

Now describe the artwork in image **C**. How does this artwork fit the definition of Pop Art? Point out repeated lines, shapes, and colors. How did this artist add variety to the painting? How are the artworks in images **A** and **C** alike, and how are they different?

C Wayne Thiebaud, *Bakery Counter,* 1962, oil on canvas, $54\frac{7}{8}$ in. × $71\frac{7}{8}$ in. Private collection.

Think Critically

1. (Focus Skill) *READING SKILL* What do you think the artist's purpose was for creating the painting in image **C**? AUTHOR'S/ARTIST'S PURPOSE

2. How does image **B** show a Cubist art style?

3. WRITE Write a paragraph describing Pop Art in your own words.

194

TEKS 4.4B

Art Print 8

Display **Art Print 8** and distribute to students Discussion Card 9: *Art Criticism.* Have students discuss how the artwork fits the definition of Pop Art. Then ask students what they think the artist's purpose was for creating the sculpture.

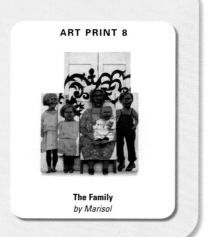

ART PRINT 8

The Family by Marisol

⭐ TEKS 4.1A communicate ideas; TEKS 4.2A integrate ideas in artworks; TEKS 4.4A form conclusions about personal artworks; TEKS 4.4B interpret artworks by peers and others; PDAS Domain III evaluation and feedback; PDAS Domain IV classroom management; *(continued)*

Artist's Workshop

Create a Pop Art Collage

PLAN

Find magazine photographs that represent a topic that interests you, such as sports, music, or fashion. Think about how you will arrange the photographs in a collage.

MATERIALS

- magazines
- scissors
- glue
- construction paper

CREATE

1. Cut your photographs into various sizes and shapes.

2. Try several arrangements of your photographs. You might overlap them or place them side by side. Think of a way to add variety to your collage.

3. After you have chosen an arrangement, glue your photographs to a sheet of construction paper.

REFLECT

How does your collage show your interests? How did you add variety to your collage?

 Quick Tip
You may want to include your own photographs or drawings in your collage.

195

Activity Options

PDAS Domain IV

Quick Activity Have students use colored pencils to draw a common object in the Pop Art style.

Early Finishers Have students mount and frame their collages and complete a museum card. See *Teacher Resource Book,* p. 39.

Challenge See *Teacher Resource Book,* p. 79.

PDAS Domain IV

ESL As students brainstorm topics for their collages, encourage them to **share cultures** by talking about the sports, music, and products that are popular in their home cultures.

Challenge Have students add a found object, such as a food can or an empty CD case, to their collages.

 Artist's Workshop 30-40 Minutes

Create a Pop Art Collage

PLAN Have students read the activity steps on page 195. As students look through the magazines, have them use life experiences to communicate ideas about self and school to use in their collages. **TEKS 4.1A**

CREATE Have students integrate a variety of ideas about life events into their collages. **TEKS 4.2A**

REFLECT Have students describe the intent of their collages and form conclusions about variety in them. **SELF-EVALUATION** TEKS 4.1B, TEKS 4.4A

5-10 Minutes
Wrap-Up

Informal Assessment PDAS Domain III

- **Look at a classmate's collage. What does it tell you about your classmate?** (Responses will vary. Students should interpret moods in their peers' artwork.) **EVALUATION/CRITICISM** TEKS 4.4A

- **What was your purpose for including the pictures you used in your collage?** (Responses will vary.) **AUTHOR'S/ARTIST'S PURPOSE** TEKS 4.4A

Extend Through Writing TAKS Writing Objective 1

PERSONAL NARRATIVE Have students write a paragraph about the significance of the objects and colors they included in their collage.

Recommended Reading

Visiting the Art Museum by Laurene Krasny Brown and Marc Brown. Dutton, 1986. EASY

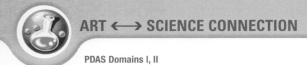

Vehicle Design

CAREERS IN ART

DISCUSS THE IMAGES

Have students read pages 196 and 197.

- Ask students to talk about the kinds of cars they like and what they like about them. Discuss with students the different kinds of designers who take part in producing a concept car. TEKS 4.1A

- Have students describe the concept car in image C and discuss their opinions of it. Have them summarize the steps in the process, from market tests to final concept car. Then encourage students to share any interests they may have in one of the careers associated with vehicle design.

ART ↔ SCIENCE CONNECTION

A Concept car design

B Computer-generated drawing

How do designers use computers to create the cars of the future?

Automobile companies conduct tests to find out car buyers' likes and dislikes. Vehicle designers use this information to create their designs.

Vehicle designers begin their work four to five years before the company expects to sell the car. Image **A** shows a sketch of a concept car, a design that shows many new ideas. Some designers design the outside of the car. Other designers, called color engineers, plan the car's color schemes.

Designers' sketches are scanned into a computer. Then the designers can add colors, values, textures, and even background to complete their designs. Look at image **B**. Where do you see different values? What kinds of texture do you see?

196

Background Information

Art History

The art of automobile design began in 1927, when General Motors created what eventually became its style department. For thirty years, Harley J. Earl led this department. In the 1940s, Earl came up with the idea of putting tail fins on cars after seeing them on World War II fighter planes.

Cadillac tail fins

★ TEKS 4.1A communicate ideas; TEKS 4.1B discuss elements and principles; TEKS 4.2B design original artworks; TEKS 4.4B interpret artworks by peers and others; PDAS Domain I active participation; PDAS Domain II learner-centered instruction

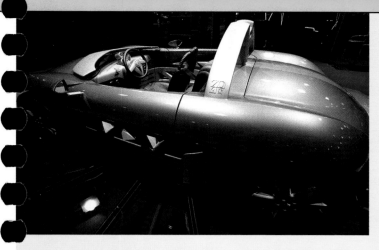

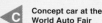
Concept car at the World Auto Fair

Finally, designers called clay modelers use the computer image to create three-dimensional models of the concept car. These designers sculpt a small model and then a full-size model like the model in image **C**. Both models are covered with colored plastic to make them look realistic.

Think About Art

Name five elements of art and principles of design that you think would be important when designing a car. Tell why.

197

DID YOU KNOW?

Use the facts below to talk about sources of energy used to power cars.

- Automobile manufacturers have to think about more than just style when designing cars to sell to the public. Designers like Ed Welburn have to design cars that are also practical, fuel-efficient, and friendly to the environment. Hybrid cars, which run on both electricity and gasoline and produce less air pollution, are just one example of designers' efforts to create a car that is both environmentally conscious and practical to car buyers.

- Battery-powered vehicles do not pollute the environment. However, the distance these cars can travel is limited by the amount of power their batteries provide. Current batteries take hours to recharge.

- Solar-powered vehicles use solar energy to run an electric motor directly or to charge a battery. However, solar cells produce energy only when the sun is shining, and they convert just a small amount of solar rays to usable energy.

Think About Art

Name five elements of art and principles of design you think would be important when designing a car. Tell why. (Accept reasonable responses.) PERCEPTION/AESTHETICS TEKS 4.1B

ARTIST'S EYE ACTIVITY

Designing a Car   Car designers create cars that are functional—they need to move people from one place to another. But car designers also think of cars as artworks. Have students think about the things they would include in a design of a new car. Have students sketch a design and share their sketches with classmates. TEKS 4.2B

Social Studies Connection

Jobs in the Auto Industry
Explain to students that car companies employ chemists, physicists, metallurgists, and engineers to test new car designs for safety.

For additional cross-curricular suggestions, see *Art Transparency 18.*

TEKS 4.4B

Student Art Show

Design Exhibit   Display the students' concept car designs from the Artist's Eye Activity. Ask students to interpret ideas and moods in their peers' designs by forming conclusions about their functionality and design appeal.

Lesson 30

Computer Art

PDAS Domains I, II

OBJECTIVES
- Identify the characteristics of computer-generated art
- Design and create an original computer-generated artwork
- Determine artist's purpose

RESOURCES
- Art Print 16
- Reading Skill Card 6
- Discussion Cards 1, 3, pp. R34, R35
- Electronic Art Gallery CD-ROM, Intermediate

Multimedia Art Glossary and Biographies
Visit *The Learning Site*
www.harcourtschool.com

Warm-Up
5 Minutes

Build Background Ask students to brainstorm a list of uses for a computer—including playing games, word processing, finding information, editing photographs, reading and writing e-mail, and watching movies. Explain to students that computers can also be used to create art, and that computer software today can do many of the things that artists have traditionally done with pencils and paints. Tell students that in this lesson they will learn how artists apply the elements of art and principles of design to create artwork on computers.

Lesson 30

Computer Art

Vocabulary
computer-generated art

Computer software can do many of the things that pencils, paints, and markers can do. Art that is created on a computer is called **computer-generated art**.

Look at the computer-generated art shown in image **A**. What kinds of lines and shapes do you see? Point out the colors and textures. How did this artist add variety to the artwork?

 A Angelo di Cicco, *No. 49D*, 2001, digital art, 2126 × 2690 pixels. Museum of Computer Art.

198

 Background Information

About the Artists

B Joan Myerson Shrager, a professional artist for over twenty-five years, taught herself to create art on the computer as a way to "combine technology with artistry."

C British artist, writer, and film director John Clive (1953–) is considered a pioneer in the field of digital arts.

For additional information about the artists, see pp. R44–R65.

 For related artworks, see **Electronic Art Gallery CD-ROM, Intermediate.**

Math Link

The world's first general-use computer was built by two American engineers in 1946. It was 18 feet tall and 80 feet long and weighed more than 30 tons.

 B Joan Myerson Shrager, *Plaid Construct Swirl*, 2003, digital art. Museum of Computer Art.

Suppose you didn't know that the artwork in image **B** was created using a computer. What kind of materials would you think the artwork was made from?

Computer-generated art can look like a painting or even a sculpture. What kinds of shapes and colors do you see in image **B**? Where do you see shades and tints?

199

Social Studies Connection

Computers and Animation In the early 1900s, simple animated films were made by a technique called stop-motion photography. Objects or drawn figures were photographed, and then repositioned and photographed again. In the 1970s, computers began to play an important role as an efficient alternative to hand-painting individual animation frames. Today, artists can use computers to insert lifelike animated images into a film; viewers cannot distinguish these images from real actors! Have students discuss animated films they enjoy.

 10-15 Minutes

Teach

Preview the Art Have students preview images A through C on pages 198–200. Ask them to describe what they see and to look for familiar details in the artworks. Use Discussion Card 1 and the questions below to guide the discussion. Then have students read pages 198–200.

 A *No. 49D* **What does this artwork look as if it is made of?**

 B *Plaid Construct Swirl* **Describe the track your eyes follow as you look at this artwork.**

 C *Annnciation II* **What does this artwork remind you of?**

Discuss Art Concepts As students view image A, they should point out the straight and curved lines, organic and geometric shapes, and complementary colors. Students should conclude that the artist's use of these different elements adds variety to the artwork.

As students look at image B, they might suggest that it was made with ribbons, tissue paper, and construction paper. Have them point out the artist's use of overlapping, value, and linear perspective in the geometric forms to create a sense of depth in the artwork.

Discuss with students the silky visual texture in image C. Have students point out areas where the artist used tints and shades to create shiny ripples in the "cloth." TEKS 4.1B

Math Link Tell students that in 1953 there were only about 100 computers in the world. Today there are hundreds of millions. Today's personal computers can perform up to one billion operations per second.

Author's/Artist's Purpose   Discuss with students the artist's purpose in creating the artwork in image B. Encourage students to think about these questions:

• What kinds of objects did the artist show?

• Why might the artist want to make her artwork look three-dimensional?

Discuss with students that the artist may have wanted to surprise or entertain the viewer by using an unexpected art material—the computer—to show ordinary objects like paper or ribbons.
TEKS 4.4B

Think Critically

Use the questions below to check students' understanding of lesson concepts.

1. *READING SKILL* **What do you think the artist's purpose was for creating the artwork in image A?** (Possible response: to entertain the viewer) **AUTHOR'S/ARTIST'S PURPOSE**
TEKS 4.4B

2. **Compare and contrast images A and B.** (Possible responses: Both show overlapping; image A has actual lines, while image B has both actual lines and implied lines.)
EVALUATION/CRITICISM TEKS 4.3B

3. **WRITE   Describe how you could re-create image B as a collage. Write what you would do first, next, and last. EXPOSITORY**
TAKS Writing Objective 1

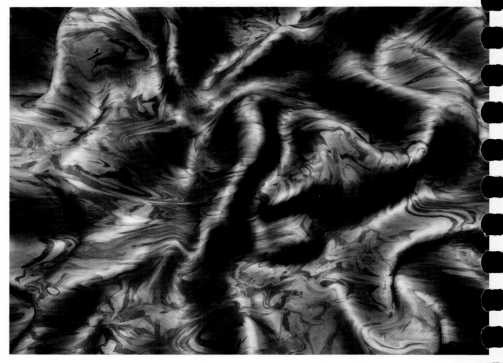

C John Clive, *Annnciation II*, 2001, digital abstraction, giclée print on paper, $14\frac{7}{10}$ in. × 11 in. Museum of Computer Art.

Now look at image **C**. Notice that this artist used value to create visual texture. What does this artwork remind you of? How are images **B** and **C** alike, and how are they different?

Think Critically

1. *READING SKILL*   What do you think the artist's purpose was for creating the artwork in image **A**? **AUTHOR'S/ARTIST'S PURPOSE**

2. Compare and contrast images **A** and **B**.

3. **WRITE**   Describe how you could re-create image **B** as a collage. Write what you would do first, next, and last.

200

TEKS 4.1B

Art Print 16

Display **Art Print 16** and distribute to students Discussion Card 3: *Elements of Art.* Have students describe the textures they see in the artwork.

ART PRINT 16

The Profile of Time
by Salvador Dalí

★ **TEKS 4.1B** discuss elements and principles; **TEKS 4.3B** compare and contrast artworks; **TEKS 4.4A** form conclusions about personal artworks; **TEKS 4.4B** interpret artworks by peers and others; **PDAS Domain III** evaluation and feedback; **PDAS Domain IV** classroom management; *(continued)*

Artist's Workshop

Create a Computer-Generated Artwork

PLAN

Brainstorm some ideas for a design you can create on a computer. Sketch your ideas. Use simple lines and shapes.

MATERIALS

- pencil
- sketchbook
- computer

CREATE

1. Choose one sketch to use as a guide.

2. Use the computer menu and drawing tools to make the simple lines and shapes from your sketch. Arrange the lines and shapes on the screen to match your sketch.

3. Add color to complete your design.

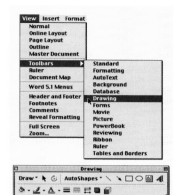

REFLECT

How is your computer-generated artwork similar to and different from your sketch?

Quick Tip You can use the drawing tools to create geometric and organic shapes.

201

PDAS Domain IV

Activity Options

Quick Activity If computers are unavailable, have students create their artworks with traditional media, such as colored pencils.

Early Finishers Have students experiment with the computer drawing tools.

Challenge See *Teacher Resource Book*, p. 80.

PDAS Domain IV

ESL Read the steps aloud and model each one for students. To support **vocabulary development,** ask them to name the different menus and tools used in the activity and describe in their own words how to access and use them to create an artwork.

Artist's Workshop

30-40 Minutes

Create a Computer-Generated Artwork

PLAN After students have read the activity steps on page 201, tell them to keep their sketches simple so they can re-create them successfully on the computer.

CREATE Encourage students to practice playing with the drawing tool and adding and erasing colors until they feel comfortable with the procedure.

REFLECT After students talk about the similarities and differences between their artworks and their sketches, set up an exhibition of their artwork around the classroom. Have classmates interpret the moods and ideas in this exhibition of peers' artworks. **SELF-EVALUATION** TEKS 4.4B

Wrap-Up

5-10 Minutes

Informal Assessment PDAS Domain III

- **Describe how you added variety to your artwork.** (Responses will vary.) **PERSONAL RESPONSE** TEKS 4.4A

- **What purpose did you have for your computer-generated artwork?** (Responses will vary.) **AUTHOR'S/ARTIST'S PURPOSE** TEKS 4.4A

Extend Through Writing

 TAKS Writing Objective 1

E-MAIL Have students write an e-mail message to a friend or relative explaining how they created their artwork. Students should attach a file of their artwork before sending their e-mails. TEKS 4.4A

Recommended Reading

3-D Planet: The World as Seen Through Stereograms by Hiroshi Kunoh and Eiji Takaoki. Cadence Books, 1994. AVERAGE

Unit 6

Review and Reflect

Have students reflect on what they have learned about the ways artists create variety in artworks that stretch the viewers' imagination. Display **Art Prints 8, 12, 16, 17,** and **18.** Encourage small groups of students to use Discussion Cards 4 and 8 and their completed Word Knowledge Charts to discuss what they learned about the vocabulary and concepts in this unit.

Vocabulary and Concepts

Have students read each sentence and choose the letter of the word or phrase that best completes it.
(1. B; 2. H; 3. A; 4. H; 5. C)

READING SKILL

Author's Purpose

Remind students that an author's or artist's purpose may be to express, to entertain, to inform, or to influence. After students have selected an artwork and text passage, have them use Reading Skill Card 6 to list details that give them clues to the artist's purpose.

Author's/Artist's Purpose		
Responses will vary.		
Detail	Detail	Detail

Unit 6 Review and Reflect

Vocabulary and Concepts

Choose the letter of the word or phrase that best completes each sentence.

1 The main characteristic of ___ was the belief in freedom to express feelings and emotions.

  A Cubism   **C** Surrealism

  B Abstract Expressionism   **D** Pop Art

2 ___ focuses on dreamlike images.

  F Variety   **H** Surrealism

  G Action painting   **J** Pop Art

3 ___ may be made up of found objects.

  A Assemblages   **C** Paintings

  B Silkscreens   **D** Variety

4 ___ is a printing process.

  F Action painting   **H** Silkscreen

  G Construction   **J** Surrealism

5 Using different elements in an artwork creates ___.

  A assemblage   **C** variety

  B construction   **D** Surrealism

READING SKILL

Author's Purpose

Select an artwork from an earlier unit, and read the text about it. Think about why the artist created the piece. Use a chart to list details that help you identify the purpose.

Author's/Artist's Purpose		
Detail	Detail	Detail

202

TEKS 4.1A, TEKS 4.2A, TEKS 4.2B, TEKS 4.2C, TEKS 4.4B

Home and Community Connection

School-Home Connection

Copy and distribute *Teacher Resource Book* pages 95–96. After completing the unit, students can work at home to create a collage that integrates a variety of ideas, thoughts, and feelings about their families.

Community Connection

You may want to contact the editor of a local newspaper and explore the possibility of having photographs of students' artwork published, such as on a community news page. In class, provide time for students to analyze the portfolios of their peers to interpret the ideas and moods expressed in the artworks and to choose artworks to be published. Students can take photographs of the artworks to be submitted.

★ TEKS 4.1A communicate ideas; TEKS 4.1B discuss elements and principles; TEKS 4.2A integrate ideas in artworks; TEKS 4.2B design original artworks; TEKS 4.2C produce artworks; TEKS 4.4A form conclusions about personal artworks; TEKS 4.4B interpret artworks by peers and others; *(continued)*

Write About Art

Choose a piece of your own artwork from this unit. Write a paragraph describing your purpose for creating it. Use a chart to list the details in your artwork.

REMEMBER — YOU SHOULD

- include details to help viewers understand your purpose.
- use correct grammar, spelling, and punctuation.

Critic's Corner

Look at *Accent in Pink* by Wassily Kandinsky to answer the questions below.

DESCRIBE How would you describe this artwork?

ANALYZE How did the artist show unity? How did he add variety?

INTERPRET What do you think the title of this artwork means?

EVALUATE What is your opinion of the way the artist used elements of art in this artwork?

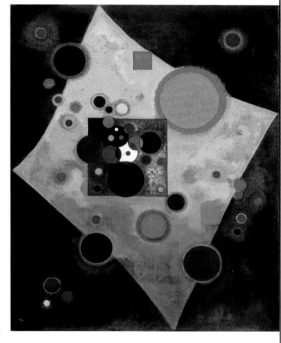

Wassily Kandinsky, *Accent in Pink*,
1926, oil on canvas, 101 cm × 81 cm.
National Museum of Modern Art, Paris, France.

203

PDAS Domain III

Assessment

Portfolio Assessment

Work with students to choose a piece of their artwork to include in their portfolios. Suggest that they decide which piece best fulfilled the assignment or which piece they liked best for another reason. You may want to provide specific feedback that targets students' use of the elements of art, principles of design, and techniques. See also Portfolio Recording Form, page R32.

Additional Assessment Options

- Progress Reading Form, p. R33
- Artist's Workshop Rubrics (Self/Teacher and Peer), pp. R30–R31
- Unit 6 Test, *Teacher Resource Book* p. 104

Write About Art

Author's/Artist's Purpose Paragraph Read aloud the prompt with students. Suggest that students choose a piece of their artwork that has a relatively obvious purpose. Remind students to use the chart on page 202 to help them plan their writing. Encourage them to use appropriate unit vocabulary words in their writing.
TEKS 4.4A; TAKS Writing Objective 1

Critic's Corner

RESPONSE/EVALUATION Use the steps below to guide students in analyzing *Accent in Pink* by Wassily Kandinsky. See also Discussion Card 2, p. R34.

DESCRIBE Discuss with students the shapes and colors in this abstract artwork. TEKS 4.1B

ANALYZE Student responses should note that the artist created unity by including a pattern of circles all over the artwork. The artist used color and shapes of varying sizes to add variety. TEKS 4.1B

INTERPRET Help students conclude that the title may refer to the artist's emphasis on the large, pink circle in the artwork. TEKS 4.4B

EVALUATE Remind students to support their opinions with reasons. TEKS 4.4B

TAKS Test Preparation: Reading and Writing Through Art, pp. 58–78

Student Art Exhibitions

When students display their work in art exhibitions, they gain confidence in their abilities to create and evaluate artworks.

PREPARATION

- Decide whether to hold the exhibition at the end of the school year as a culminating activity or at intervals throughout the year.
- Decide whether to include the work of several grade levels or groups or just one at a time.
- Ask students to create and distribute invitations to family members, friends, and classmates.
- Have students use the ideas on *Student Edition* pages 226–227 to mount, frame, and label their artworks to prepare them for display. See *Teacher Resource Book*, page 39, for an example of a museum card.

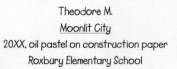

Theodore M.
Moonlit City
20XX, oil pastel on construction paper
Roxbury Elementary School

▲ **museum card**

DISPLAYS

Two-Dimensional Artworks

- Tack to bulletin boards in the classroom or hallway.
- Clip with clothespins to drying racks or a clothesline.
- Line up along chalk trays.
- Prop up on makeshift easels.

Three-Dimensional Artworks

- Place on a large table, bookcase, or a group of desks.
- Cover surfaces with cloth or colored paper.
- Place boxes of varying heights under the cloth.
- Arrange larger artworks behind smaller ones.

RECORDING THE EVENT

- Videotape the art show in progress.
- Take digital photographs before and during the art show. You can use these images to create a slide show or a digital portfolio.

Resources and Correlations

Using the Student Handbook R2

Media and Techniques R15

Meeting Individual Needs R24

Assessment Options R28

Discussion Cards R34

Materials List R39

Free and Inexpensive Materials R41

Alternative Planners R42

Encyclopedia of Artists and Art History R44

Scope and Sequence R66

Index R70

Correlations R76

Using the Student Handbook

Introduce the Student Handbook by having students turn to page 205. Do a walk-through with students, explaining how they can use the sections throughout the year.

USING THE MAPS OF MUSEUMS AND ART SITES

Guide students in looking at the maps on pages 206–209 of their Student Handbook.

- Explain that art comes from all over the United States and the world and that these maps show only a small number of the world's art museums and art sites.
- Model how to select one site on the map and locate the corresponding page in the *Student Edition*.
- Have volunteers follow the same process to locate several art sites.

Use the following optional map activities to extend the learning.

TREASURE HUNT

MATERIALS: paper, pencil, box or bag

DIRECTIONS:

- Using either the United States map or the world map, write the name of each art site from the map on slips of paper, and place them in a box or bag.
- Divide the class into two teams.
- Draw from the bag one slip at a time and read it aloud. Teams should find the site on the map, match its number to the LOCATE IT key, and find the corresponding *Student Edition* page.
- The first team to correctly identify the title of an artwork gets a point. The team with the most points at the end of the game wins.

TRUTH OR CONSEQUENCES

MATERIALS: paper, pencil, two boxes

DIRECTIONS:

- Label one box *Truth* and the other *Consequences*. Give each student two slips of paper.
- Have students write one question based on either of the maps on one slip of paper. Then have them write a simple command on the other slip of paper. Place the slips of paper in the appropriate boxes.
- Students will draw from the *Truth* box and answer the question. Students who answer incorrectly must draw from the *Consequences* box and perform the command.

ELEMENTS AND PRINCIPLES

MATERIALS: slips of paper numbered 1–5, paper bag

DIRECTIONS:

- Have pairs of students open one of their *Student Editions* to pages 20–23, which show the elements of art and principles of design.
- Have partners draw a number from the bag.
- Each student should find the number in the LOCATE IT key and then find the artwork on the corresponding *Student Edition* page.
- Have students use the terms on pages 20–23 to describe the artwork on that page.

 Use the **Electronic Art Gallery CD-ROM, Intermediate,** for additional images in the United States.

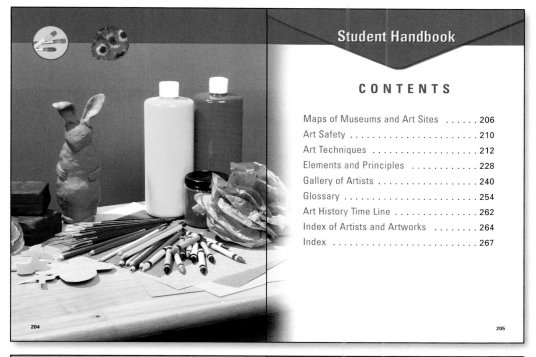

Student Handbook

C O N T E N T S

Maps of Museums and Art Sites 206
Art Safety 210
Art Techniques 212
Elements and Principles 228
Gallery of Artists 240
Glossary 254
Art History Time Line 262
Index of Artists and Artworks 264
Index 267

204

205

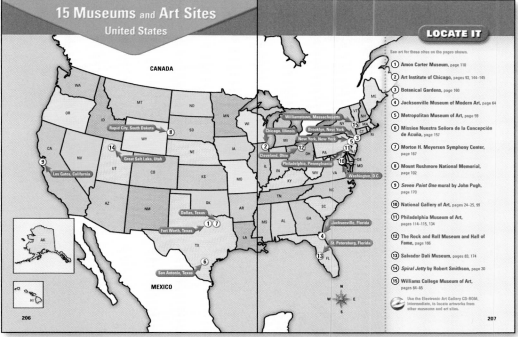

15 Museums and Art Sites
United States

CANADA

MEXICO

LOCATE IT

See art for these sites on the pages shown.

1 Amon Carter Museum, page 110
2 Art Institute of Chicago, pages 93, 144–145
3 Botanical Gardens, page 160
4 Jacksonville Museum of Modern Art, page 64
5 Metropolitan Museum of Art, page 59
6 Mission Nuestra Señora de la Concepción de Acuña, page 157
7 Morton H. Meyerson Symphony Center, page 167
8 Mount Rushmore National Memorial, page 102
9 *Seven Point One* mural by John Pugh, page 170
10 National Gallery of Art, pages 24–25, 99
11 Philadelphia Museum of Art, pages 114–115, 134
12 The Rock and Roll Museum and Hall of Fame, page 106
13 Salvador Dali Museum, pages 83, 174
14 *Spiral Jetty* by Robert Smithson, page 30
15 Williams College Museum of Art, pages 84–85

Use the Electronic Art Gallery CD-ROM, Intermediate, to locate artworks from other museums and art sites.

206

207

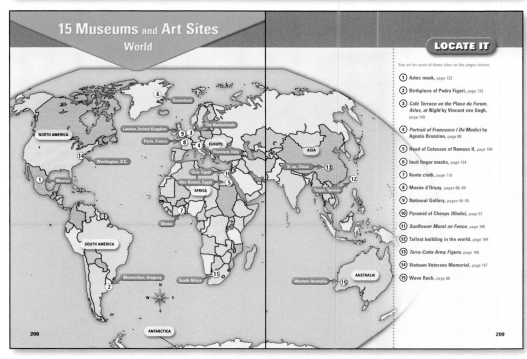

15 Museums and Art Sites
World

NORTH AMERICA

EUROPE

ASIA

AFRICA

SOUTH AMERICA

AUSTRALIA

ANTARCTICA

LOCATE IT

See art for each of these sites on the pages shown.

1 Aztec mask, page 122
2 Birthplace of Pedro Figari, page 133
3 *Café Terrace on the Place du Forum, Arles, at Night* by Vincent van Gogh, page 149
4 *Portrait of Francesco I De'Medici* by Agnolo Bronzino, page 89
5 Head of Colossus of Ramses II, page 104
6 Inuit finger masks, page 124
7 Kente cloth, page 118
8 Musée d'Orsay, pages 68–69
9 National Gallery, pages 54–55
10 Pyramid of Cheops (Khufu), page 67
11 *Sunflower Mural on Fence*, page 168
12 Tallest building in the world, page 164
13 Terra-Cotta Army Figure, page 109
14 Vietnam Veterans Memorial, page 187
15 Wave Rock, page 66

208

209

Art Safety

Listen carefully when your teacher explains how to use art materials.

Wear a smock or apron to keep your clothes clean.

Read the labels on materials before you use them.

Use tools carefully. Hold sharp objects so that they cannot hurt you or others. Wear safety glasses to protect your eyes.

Tell your teacher if you have allergies.

210

Use the kind of markers and inks that will not stain your clothes.

Show respect for other students. Walk carefully around their work. Never touch classmates' work without asking first.

Clean up spills right away so no one will slip and fall.

Always wash your hands after using art materials.

Cover your skin if you have a cut or scratch.

211

Art Techniques

Trying Ways to Draw

There are lots of ways to draw. You can sketch quickly to show a rough idea of your subject, or you can draw carefully to show just how it looks to you. Try to draw every day. Keep your drawings in your sketchbook so you can see how your drawing skills improve.

Here are some ideas for drawing. To start, get out some pencils and either your sketchbook or a sheet of paper.

GESTURE DRAWING

Gesture drawings are quick sketches that are made with loose arm movements. The gesture drawing on the left shows a rough idea of what a baseball player looks like. The more careful drawing on the right shows details of the player's uniform and face. ▶

◀ Find some photographs of people or animals. Make gesture drawings of them. Draw quickly. Don't try to show details.

◀ Ask a friend to pose for a gesture drawing. Take no more than two or three minutes to finish your sketch.

212

CONTOUR DRAWING

Contour drawings show only the outlines of the shapes that make up objects. They do not show the objects' color or shading. The lines that go around shapes are called **contour lines.** Use your finger to trace around the contour lines of the truck in this picture. Trace the lines around each of the shapes that make up the truck.

◀ A blind contour drawing is made without looking at your paper as you draw. Choose a simple object to draw, like a leaf. Pick a point on the object where you will begin drawing. Move your eyes slowly around the edge of the object. Without looking at your paper, move your pencil in the same way that your eyes move. Your first drawings may not look like the object you are looking at. Practice with different objects to improve your skill.

Continuous contour drawings are made without ▶ lifting your pencil off the paper. Draw something simple, like a chair. Look back and forth between the object and your paper. You will have to go over some lines more than once to keep from lifting your pencil off the paper.

◀ Now try making a contour drawing of another object, such as a shoe. Look at your paper and lift your pencil whenever you want to. Then add details.

213

Art Techniques

TONAL DRAWING

Tonal drawings show the dark and light areas of objects using tones, or shades, of one color. They do not include contour lines. Look at the photograph at the right. Notice which areas are dark and which are light. Now look at the tonal drawing. Even without contour lines, you can tell what the drawing shows. ▶

◀ Experiment with your pencils. You can use **cross-hatching,** or a pattern of crossed lines, to show dark areas in a tonal drawing. Try smudging some of the lines together with your fingers. To darken large areas, use the flat edge of a dull pencil point. Use an eraser to lighten some of your marks.

Try a tonal drawing of a simple object ▶ like a spoon. Look at the object closely. Do not draw contour lines. Notice the shapes of the dark and light areas on the object. Use the edge of your pencil point to copy the dark shapes. Use cross-hatching in some areas. Use an eraser to lighten marks where needed.

214

CONTOURS AND TONES

Try combining tonal drawing with contour drawing. Start by making a tonal drawing of something with an interesting shape, like a backpack. Look at it carefully to see the tones of dark and light. ▶

Then look at the object again to see its contours. Draw contour lines around the shapes that make up the object. ▶

You might prefer to start with a contour drawing. Be sure you draw the outline of each shape in the object. Then add tones with shading or cross-hatching. ▼

Did you prefer to start with shading or with contours?

215

Art Techniques

Experimenting with Paint

Working with colors is always fun. Experimenting with paint will help you learn about color and how you can use it in your artwork.

These are some things you should have when you paint: old newspapers to cover your work area, an old shirt to cover your clothes, tempera paints or watercolors, plastic plates or plastic egg cartons for mixing paint, paper, paintbrushes, a jar or bowl of water, and paper towels.

TEMPERA PAINTS

Tempera paints are water-based, so they are easy to clean up. The colors are bright and easy to mix.

GETTING STARTED

Start experimenting with different kinds of brushstrokes. Try painting with lots of paint on the brush and then with the brush almost dry. (You can dry the paintbrush by wiping it across a paper towel.) Make a brushstroke by twisting the paintbrush on your paper. See how many different brushstrokes you can make by rolling, pressing, or dabbing the brush on the paper.

Now load your brush with as much paint as it will ▶ hold, and make a heavy brushstroke. Use a craft stick or another tool to draw a pattern in it.

Use what you've learned to paint a picture. Use as many different brushstrokes as you can. ▶

216

MIXING COLORS

Even if you have only a few colors of tempera paint, you can mix them to make almost any color you want. Use the **primary colors** red, yellow, and blue to create the **secondary colors** orange, green, and violet.

◀ Mix dark and light colors. To make darker colors (**shades**), add black. To make lighter colors (**tints**), add white. See how many shades and tints of a single color you can make.

TECHNIQUES TO TRY

Pointillism is a technique that makes the viewer's eyes mix the colors. Use colors, such as blue and yellow, that make a third color when mixed. Make small dots of color close together without letting the dots touch. In some areas, place the two different colors very close together. Stand back from your paper. What happens to the colors as your eyes "mix" them? ▶

◀ Impasto is a technique that creates a thick or bumpy surface on a painting. You can create an impasto painting by building up layers of paint, or by thickening your paint with a material such as wheat paste. Mix some paint and wheat paste in a small bowl. Spread some of the mixture on a piece of cardboard. Experiment with tools such as a toothpick, a plastic fork, or a comb to make textures in the impasto. Mix more colors and use them to make an impasto picture or design.

217

Art Techniques

WATERCOLORS

Watercolors usually come in little dry cakes. You have to add the water! So keep a jar of clean water and some paper towels nearby as you paint. Use paper that is made for watercolors.

GETTING STARTED

Dip your paintbrush in water and then dab it on one of the watercolors. Try a brushstroke. Watercolors are transparent. Since you can see through them, the color on your paper will never be as dark as the color of the cake. Use different amounts of water. What happens to the color when you use a lot of water?

Now rinse your brush in water and use another color. Try different kinds of brushstrokes—thick and thin, squiggles and waves, dots and blobs. Change colors often.

Try using one color on top of a different color that is already dry. Work quickly. If your brushstrokes are too slow, the dry color underneath can become dull. If you want part of your painting to be white, don't paint that part. The white comes from the color of the paper.

218

MIXING COLORS

Experiment with mixing watercolors right on your paper! Try painting with a very wet brush. Add a wet color on top of, or just touching, another wet color. Try three colors together. ▶

You can also mix colors on your paintbrush. Dip your brush into one color and then another before you paint. Try it with green and yellow. Clean your paintbrush and try some other combinations. To clean any paint cakes that you have used for mixing, just wipe them with a paper towel. ▶

TECHNIQUES TO TRY

◀ Try making a watercolor wash. Start with a patch of dark green. Then clean your paintbrush and get it very wet. Use it to "wash" the color down the page. (You can also do this with a foam brush or a sponge.)

You can wet all of one side of the paper, brush a stroke of color across it, and let the color spread. Try two or three color washes together. For a special effect, sprinkle salt onto the wet paper.

Try using tempera paints and watercolors together. ▶ Start with a two-color watercolor wash. Let it dry. Then use several kinds of brushstrokes to paint a design on top of the wash with tempera paint.

Remember these techniques when you paint designs or pictures. Be sure to clean your paintbrushes and work area when you have finished.

219

Art Techniques

Working with Clay

Clay is a special kind of mud or earth that holds together and is easy to shape when it is mixed with water. Clay objects can be fired, or heated at a high temperature, to make them harden. They can also be left in the air to dry until hard.

To make an object with clay, work on a clean, dry surface. (A brown paper bag makes a good work surface.) Have some water handy. If the clay starts to dry out, add a few drops of water at a time. When you are not working with the clay, store it in a plastic bag to keep it moist.

You can use an assortment of tools. Use a rolling pin to make flat slabs of clay. Use a plastic knife or fork, keys, a comb, or a pencil to add texture or designs to the objects you make out of clay.

Start working with a piece of clay by making sure it has no air bubbles in it. Press it down, fold it over, and press it down again. This process is called **kneading**.

220

MODELING

Try making different forms with your ▶ clay. If one of your forms reminds you of an animal or a person, continue to mold the form by pinching and pulling the clay.

◀ You can join two pieces of clay together. Carve small lines on the edges that will be joined. This is called **scoring**. Then use **slip**, or clay dissolved in water, to wet the surfaces. Press the pieces together and smooth the seams.

To make a bigger form, wrap a slab of clay around a tube or crumpled newspaper.

Try adding patterns, textures, or details to your form. Experiment with your tools. Press textured objects into the clay and lift them off. Brush a key across the clay. Press textured material like burlap into your clay, lift it off, and add designs. If you change your mind, smooth the clay with your fingers and try something else.

221

Art Techniques

USING SLABS

Roll your clay out flat, to between $\frac{1}{4}$ inch and $\frac{1}{2}$ inch thick. Shape the clay by molding it over something like a bowl or crumpled paper. ▶

◀ To make a slab box, roll your clay out flat. Use a plastic knife to cut six equal-sized squares or rectangles for the bottom, top, and sides of your box. Score the edges, and then let the pieces dry until they feel like leather.

Join the pieces together with slip. ▶
Then smooth the seams with your fingers.

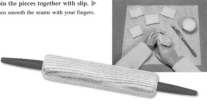

USING COILS

To make a coil pot, roll pieces of clay against a hard surface. Use your whole hand to make long clay ropes. ▶

◀ Make the bottom of your pot by coiling a clay rope into a circle. Smooth the seams with your fingers. To build the sides, attach coils of clay on top of one another. Score and wet the pieces with slip as you attach them. Smooth the inside as you work. You may smooth the outside or let the coils show.

MAKING A CLAY RELIEF ▶

A relief is a sculpture raised from a surface. To make a relief, draw a simple design on a slab of clay. Roll some very thin ropes and attach them to the lines of the design. This is called the **additive method** because you are adding clay to the slab.

◀ You can also make a relief sculpture by carving a design out of your clay slab. This is called the **subtractive method** because you are taking away, or subtracting, clay from the slab.

222 223

Art Techniques

Exploring Printmaking

When you make a print, you transfer color from one object to another. If you have ever left a muddy footprint on a clean floor, you know what a print is. Here are some printmaking ideas to try.

COLLOGRAPH PRINTS

A **collograph** is a combination of a **collage** and a **print**. To make a collograph, you will need cardboard, glue, paper, newspapers, a brayer (a roller for printing), printing ink or paint, a flat tray such as a foam food tray, and some paper towels or sponges. You will also need some flat objects to include in the collage. Try things like old keys, string, lace, paper clips, buttons, small shells, or burlap.

Arrange objects on the cardboard ▶
in a pleasing design. Glue the objects to the surface, and let the glue dry.

Prepare your ink while the collage ▶
is drying. Place a small amount of ink or paint on your foam tray. Roll the brayer through the ink until it is evenly coated. Gently run the brayer over the collage. Most of the ink should be on the objects.

Now press a piece of paper onto ▶
the inked collage. Gently rub the paper. Peel off the paper and let the ink dry. You've made a collograph!

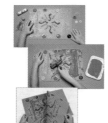

MULTICOLOR PRINTS

You can use different colors of tempera paint to make a multicolor print with repeated shapes. You will need poster board or a foam tray (such as a food tray), cardboard, scissors, glue, paper, water, tempera paint, and a paintbrush.

First cut out some interesting shapes from the poster board or foam tray. Carve or poke holes and lines into the shapes. ▶

Arrange the shapes on the cardboard to make an interesting design. Glue down the pieces. When the glue is dry, paint the shapes with different colors of tempera paint. Try not to get paint on the cardboard. ▶

◀ While the paint is wet, place a sheet of paper on top of your design. Gently rub the paper, and peel it off carefully. Let the paint dry.
After the shapes dry, paint them again with different colors. Print the same paper again, but turn it so that the designs and colors overlap.

Try using different colors, paper, and objects to make prints.

224 225

Art Techniques

Displaying Your Artwork

Displaying your artwork is a good way to share it. Here are some ways to make your artwork look its best.

DISPLAYING ART PRINTS

Select several pictures that go together well. Line them up along a wall or on the floor. Try grouping the pictures in different ways. Choose an arrangement that you like. Attach a strong string across a wall. Use clothespins or paper clips to hang your pictures on the string.

Make a frame. Use a piece of cardboard that is longer and wider than the art. In the center of the cardboard, draw a rectangle that is slightly smaller than your picture. Have an adult help you cut out the rectangle. Then decorate your frame. Choose colors and textures that look good with your picture. You can paint the frame or use a stamp to print a design on it. You can add texture by gluing strips of cardboard or rows of buttons onto your frame.

Mount your picture. Tape the corners of your artwork to the back of the frame. Cut a solid piece of cardboard the same size as the frame. Then glue the framed artwork to the cardboard. Tape a loop of thread on the back. Hang up your framed work.

DISPLAYING SCULPTURES

To display your clay objects or sculptures, find a location where your work will be safe from harm. Look for a display area where people won't bump into your exhibit or damage your work.

Select several clay objects or sculptures that go together well. Try grouping them in different ways. Place some of the smaller objects on boxes. When you find an arrangement that you like, remove your artworks, tape the boxes to the table, and drape a piece of cloth over the boxes. Pick a plain cloth that will look good under your artworks, try adding a few interesting folds in the cloth, and place your artworks back on the table.

Now invite your friends and family over to see your work!

226 227

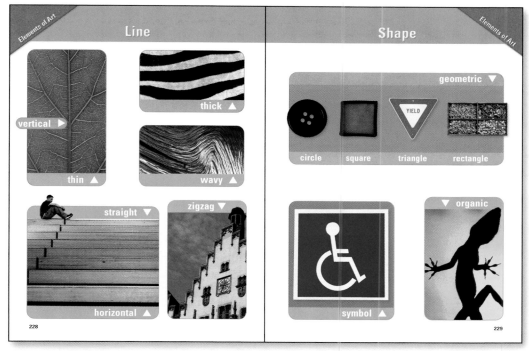

Line

Elements of Art

- vertical ▶
- thin ▲
- thick ▲
- wavy ▲
- straight ▼
- zigzag ▼
- horizontal ▲

228

Shape

Elements of Art

geometric ▼

- circle
- square
- triangle
- rectangle

YIELD

- symbol ▲
- ▼ organic

229

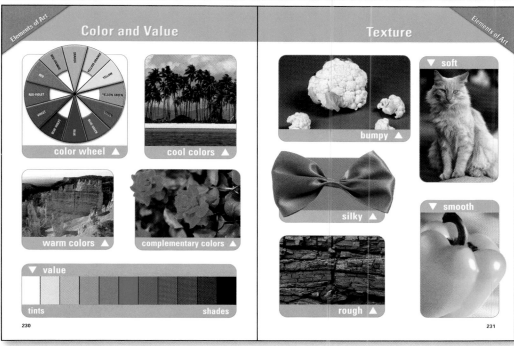

Color and Value

Elements of Art

- color wheel ▲
- cool colors ▲
- warm colors ▲
- complementary colors ▲
- ▼ value
- tints
- shades

230

Texture

Elements of Art

- ▼ soft
- bumpy ▲
- silky ▲
- ▼ smooth
- rough ▲

231

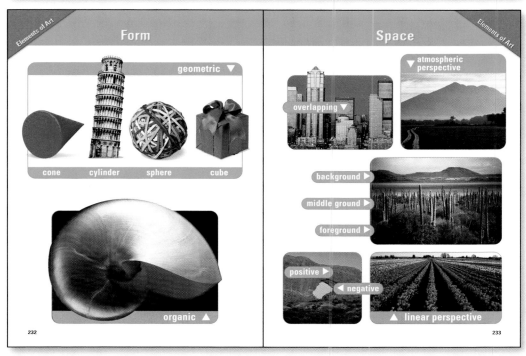

Form

Elements of Art

geometric ▼

- cone
- cylinder
- sphere
- cube
- organic ▲

232

Space

Elements of Art

- atmospheric perspective
- overlapping ▼
- background ▶
- middle ground ▶
- foreground ▶
- positive ▶
- ◀ negative
- ▲ linear perspective

233

STUDENT HANDBOOK R7

Pattern

Rhythm and Movement

Proportion

Emphasis

Balance

▼ radial

asymmetrical ▲

symmetrical ▲

Unity and Variety

Gallery of Artists

Meredith Brooks Abbott
(1938–) United States, painter. Abbott grew up in rural California with a great appreciation for the land. She paints Impressionistic landscapes. **page 58**

Josef Albers
(1888–1976) Germany, painter. Albers studied art while teaching elementary school. He is best known for his abstract paintings of overlapping monochromatic squares. **page 60**

Giacomo Balla
(1871–1958) Italy, painter. Balla was particularly interested in how light and movement were represented in his work. His paintings are considered very inventive. **page 100**

Bruce Barnbaum
(1943–) United States, photographer. Barnbaum is recognized as one of the finest photographers today. His work is featured in many art galleries in the United States. **page 72**

Thomas Hart Benton
(1889–1975) United States, painter. Benton began his career as a cartoonist. He later became known for his pictures of rural America. **page 26**

Albert Bierstadt
(1830–1902) United States, painter. Born in Germany, Bierstadt [BEER•stat] spent his childhood in Massachusetts. He is best known for his landscapes of the American West. **page 152**

240

John Biggers
(1924–2001) United States, painter. Biggers was a former teacher who believed that art can help African Americans better understand their culture. His paintings, drawings, and murals have won many awards. **page 143**

Gutzon Borglum
(1867–1941) United States, sculptor. Borglum was a successful painter before he became well known as a sculptor. His best-known sculptures are of the four U.S. Presidents shown on the face of Mount Rushmore. **page 102**

Victor Brauner
(1903–1966) Romania, painter/sculptor. Brauner is known for his artworks of the human figure. He was heavily influenced by the Surrealists. **page 183**

Agnolo Bronzino
(1503–1572) Italy, painter. Bronzino was a court artist to the Medici family. **page 89**

Gustave Caillebotte
(1848–1894) France, painter. Caillebotte's [ky•yuh•bawt] paintings show bold perspectives and delicate light. **page 144**

Bobbi A. Chukran
(1956–) United States, folk artist. Chukran's inspiration comes mostly from nature. **page 50**

Angelo di Cicco
(1953–) Italy, digital artist/painter. Di Cicco is a physician who enjoys painting in his spare time. **page 198**

241

Gallery of Artists

John Clive
England, digital artist. Clive directs film, theatre, and commercials. **page 200**

Joseph Cornell
(1903–1972) United States, sculptor. Cornell was an assemblage artist best known for his glass-fronted shadow boxes. **pages 80, 190**

Jean Baptiste Camille Corot
(1796–1875) France, painter/printmaker. Corot believed that a sketch captured a nature scene better than a painting. **page 148**

Salvador Dalí
(1904–1989) Spain, painter. Dalí [DAH•lee] was the most famous Surrealist artist. He also designed jewelry, advertisements, costumes, and stage sets. **pages 83, 174, 184**

Edgar Degas
(1834–1917) France, painter. Degas [duh•GAH] was fascinated by photographic techniques. He painted many pictures of dancers, often in rehearsal or backstage. **page 98**

Raymond Depardon
(1942–) France, photographer. Depardon is self-taught. His more recent work has been in film and advertising. **page 78**

Robert S. Duncanson
(about 1821–1872) United States, painter. Duncanson is best known for his landscapes. He is thought to be the first African American artist not only to make a living from selling his paintings but also to become famous for them. **page 24**

242

W. Herbert Dunton
(1878–1936) United States, painter/illustrator. Dunton is considered one of America's most popular artists of cowhand and frontier life. **page 136**

M. C. Escher
(1898–1972) Holland, graphic artist. Escher [ESH•er] studied architecture but became a graphic artist instead. He is famous for his drawings that surprise viewers with optical illusions. **page 73**

Marisol Escobar
(1930–) France, sculptor. Escobar creates life-size figure arrangements. Her work is heavily influenced by Mexican and American folk art. **pages 106–107**

Lyonel Feininger
(1871–1956) United States, painter/printmaker/illustrator. Feininger's work combines qualities of both Cubism and Expressionism. **page 99**

Pedro Figari
(1861–1938) Uruguay, painter. Figari had a degree in law but was gifted in art. His paintings celebrate Uruguayan culture. **page 133**

Norman Foster
(1935–) England, architect. Foster is considered one of the leading modernist architects. **page 163**

Helen Frankenthaler
(1928–) United States, painter/printmaker. Frankenthaler was one of the leading artists of the Abstract Expressionist movement. **page 179**

243

Gallery of Artists

Paul Gauguin
(1848–1903) France, painter. Gauguin [goh•GAN] was a sailor in the French navy and a stockbroker before he became a painter. He moved to the tropical island of Tahiti in 1895 where he lived and painted for the rest of his life. **page 48**

William James Glackens
(1870–1938) United States, painter/illustrator. Glackens began his art career as an illustrator. He went on to study painting and later produced artworks in a very realistic style. **page 146**

Glenna Goodacre
(1939–) United States, sculptor. **page 102**

Sante Graziani
(1920–) United States, muralist. Graziani drew medical illustrations while he served in the United States Army. He was influenced by Surrealism and by famous paintings of the past. **page 140**

Juan Gris
(1887–1927) France, painter. Gris [GREES] was considered one of the leading Cubist painters in France, where he spent most of his life as an artist. He was a friend of the Cubist painter Pablo Picasso. **page 93**

Jack Gunter
United States, painter. Gunter has also worked with photography and ceramics. **page 150**

244

Richard Haas
(1936–) United States, muralist/printmaker/architect. Haas has created more than 120 murals and is renowned for his trompe l'oeil paintings. **page 137**

Ole Juul Hansen
page 44

Frederick Childe Hassam
(1859–1935) United States, painter/printmaker. Hassam painted landscapes of New England and rural New York. **page 138**

Ando Hiroshige
(1797–1858) Japan, painter/printmaker. Hiroshige [hee•roh•shee•gay] became famous for his many landscape paintings and views of the city of Edo, now called Tokyo. **page 173**

David Hockney
(1937–) United States, mixed media. Born in England, Hockney now lives in southern California. He was eleven years old when he decided he wanted to be an artist. Hockney has said, "The smallest event can become a story if you tell it in the right way." **page 79**

Winslow Homer
(1836–1910) United States, painter/illustrator. Fascinated by the ocean, Winslow Homer painted many works that show the coast of Maine, where he lived. Many of his works show people struggling against powerful seas. **page 84**

Don Jacot
(1949–) United States, painter. Don Jacot [jahk•OH] paints in the photorealistic style. **page 154**

245

Alexej von Jawlensky
(1864–1941) Russia, painter. Von Jawlensky [yah•VLEN•skee] spent much of his early artistic career traveling, which introduced him to a variety of artists, techniques, and theories. **pages 29, 92**

Bernadine Jendrzejczak
United States, folk artist. Jendrzejczak (yin•JAY•chek) is known for her traditional Polish paper cuttings. **page 129**

Frida Kahlo
(1907–1954) Mexico, painter. Kahlo is best known for her self-portraits. Many of her paintings show her Mexican heritage. **page 90**

Wassily Kandinsky
(1866–1944) Russia, painter. Kandinsky is often considered one of the founders of abstract art. **page 203**

Warren Kimble
United States, folk artist. Kimble's paintings focus on nature scenes near his Vermont home. **page 139**

Paul Klee
(1879–1940) Switzerland, painter. Klee's [KLAY] paintings, drawings, and etchings have been described as childlike. Klee was a professional violinist before becoming an artist. **pages 46–47**

Lee Krasner
(1908–1984) United States, painter. Krasner was married to artist Jackson Pollock. She created expressive paintings, abstract still-lifes, and collages. **page 180**

Roy Lichtenstein
(1923–1997) United States, painter. Lichtenstein [LIK•tuhn•styn] was one of the best-known American painters in the Pop Art movement. His most famous paintings imitate comic strips. **page 193**

Maya Lin
(1959–) United States, sculptor. Maya Lin is best known for her Vietnam Veterans Memorial in Washington, D.C. Lin has also created small sculptures and stage sets. **pages 186–187**

Carmen Lomas Garza
(1948–) United States, illustrator. Lomas Garza is best known for her artworks that show Chicano family life. **page 130**

Ricardo Maffei
(1953–) Chile, painter. **page 176**

René Magritte
(1898–1967) Belgium, painter. Magritte [ma•GREET] once worked as a wallpaper designer. Many of his paintings include patterns like those used on wallpaper. Magritte often painted dreamlike scenes. **pages 113, 182**

Franz Marc
(1880–1916) Germany, painter. Marc used bright color to show emotion in his paintings. He co-founded the Blue Rider group, which included other artists who also used color in an expressive way. **page 32**

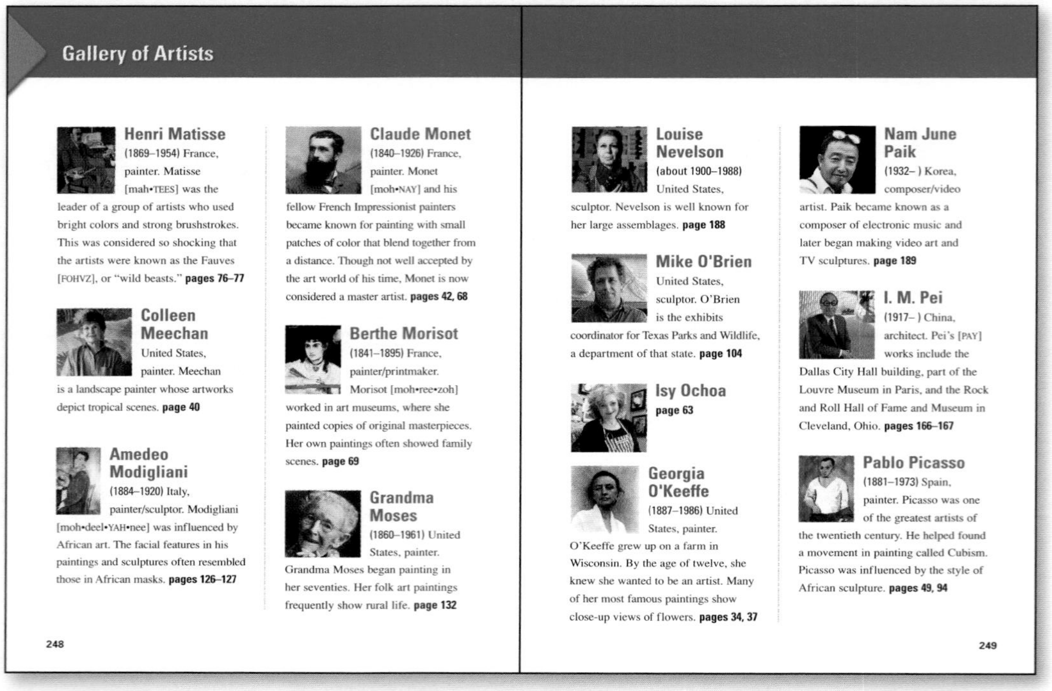

Henri Matisse
(1869–1954) France, painter. Matisse [mah•TEES] was the leader of a group of artists who used bright colors and strong brushstrokes. This was considered so shocking that the artists were known as the Fauves [FOHVZ], or "wild beasts." **pages 76–77**

Colleen Meechan
United States, painter. Meechan is a landscape painter whose artworks depict tropical scenes. **page 40**

Amedeo Modigliani
(1884–1920) Italy, painter/sculptor. Modigliani [moh•deel•YAH•nee] was influenced by African art. The facial features in his paintings and sculptures often resembled those in African masks. **pages 126–127**

Claude Monet
(1840–1926) France, painter. Monet [moh•NAY] and his fellow French Impressionist painters became known for painting with small patches of color that blend together from a distance. Though not well accepted by the art world of his time, Monet is now considered a master artist. **pages 42, 68**

Berthe Morisot
(1841–1895) France, painter/printmaker. Morisot [moh•ree•zoh] worked in art museums, where she painted copies of original masterpieces. Her own paintings often showed family scenes. **page 69**

Grandma Moses
(1860–1961) United States, painter. Grandma Moses began painting in her seventies. Her folk art paintings frequently show rural life. **page 132**

Louise Nevelson
(about 1900–1988) United States, sculptor. Nevelson is well known for her large assemblages. **page 188**

Mike O'Brien
United States, sculptor. O'Brien is the exhibits coordinator for Texas Parks and Wildlife, a department of that state. **page 104**

Isy Ochoa
page 63

Georgia O'Keeffe
(1887–1986) United States, painter. O'Keeffe grew up on a farm in Wisconsin. By the age of twelve, she knew she wanted to be an artist. Many of her most famous paintings show close-up views of flowers. **pages 34, 37**

Nam June Paik
(1932–) Korea, composer/video artist. Paik became known as a composer of electronic music and later began making video art and TV sculptures. **page 189**

I. M. Pei
(1917–) China, architect. Pei's [PAY] works include the Dallas City Hall building, part of the Louvre Museum in Paris, and the Rock and Roll Hall of Fame and Museum in Cleveland, Ohio. **pages 166–167**

Pablo Picasso
(1881–1973) Spain, painter. Picasso was one of the greatest artists of the twentieth century. He helped found a movement in painting called Cubism. Picasso was influenced by the style of African sculpture. **pages 49, 94**

Horace Pippin
(1888–1946) United States, painter. Pippin began painting seriously after his right arm was partially paralyzed as the result of an injury. Many of his works show scenes from the Bible or from the daily life of African American families. **page 53**

Jackson Pollock
(1912–1956) United States, painter. Pollock's [PAHL•uhk] paintings express powerful moods without showing objects. He was known for a style of Abstract Expressionism called Action Painting. **page 178**

Anna Pugh
England, folk artist. Anna Pugh's work has been influenced by middle-eastern painting styles. **page 86**

John Pugh
United States, painter. Pugh is best known for his detailed trompe l'oeil murals, which trick the eye. **page 170**

Man Ray
(1890–1976) United States, photographer/painter/sculptor. Man Ray was best known for the unusual subjects in his artworks. He was part of the Surrealist movement. **page 110**

Frederic S. Remington
(1861–1909) United States, sculptor/painter. Although born in New York, Remington spent a good deal of time in the frontier of the American West, documenting the lives of soldiers and cowhands. **pages 56, 110**

Faith Ringgold
(about 1930–) United States, painter/sculptor. Ringgold's paintings and quilts reflect the issues facing African Americans and women. **page 114**

Thomas Rogers
United States, sculptor. Rogers is best known for his image of an eagle, which appears on the tail side of the Sacagawea American coin. **page 102**

Henri Rousseau
(1844–1910) France, painter. Rousseau [roo•SOH] taught himself to paint and began painting full time at age forty-nine. The ideas for his paintings came from gardens and illustrated books. **page 59**

Meg Fish Saligman
United States, muralist. **page 169**

Matiros Sarian
(1880–1972) Armenia, painter/museum director. Sarian painted many fantasy scenes, often based on folktales. His style is very colorful and bright, with rhythmic patterns. **page 43**

Georges Seurat
(1859–1891) France, painter. Seurat [suh•RAH] painted huge compositions that seem to shimmer. His technique of showing light by using tiny dots of contrasting colors is called Pointillism. **pages 54, 153**

Joan Myerson Shrager
United States, painter/sculptor/ digital artist. Shrager experiments with a variety of media and techniques in her art. **page 199**

Paul Sierra
(1944–) Cuba, painter. Sierra's use of bright color and vast spaces often gives his paintings a dreamlike quality. **page 38**

Robert Smithson
(1938–1973) United States, sculptor. *Spiral Jetty*, one of Smithson's most famous works, is an example of environmental art. Also called land art or earthworks art, this kind of art involves large-scale changes to the surface of the Earth. **page 30**

Joaquín Sorolla y Bastida
(1863–1923) Spain, painter. Sorolla y Bastida [soh•ROH•yah ee bahs•TEE•dah] used the Mediterranean seashore as his inspiration for beach scene paintings. **page 70**

Alice Kent Stoddard
(1885–1976) United States, painter. Stoddard is known for her portraits and landscapes. **page 88**

Wayne Thiebaud
(1920–) United States, painter. Thiebaud [TEE•boh] was born in Mesa, Arizona, and held various art-related jobs in New York and California. He is best known for his texture paintings of ice cream, cakes, and hot dogs. **page 194**

Vincent van Gogh
(1853–1890) Holland, painter. Van Gogh [van GOH] sold only one painting when he was alive, but today he is recognized as one of the most famous painters in history. He used bright colors, thick oil paint, and visible brushstrokes. **pages 33, 149**

José María Velasco
(1840–1912) Mexico, painter. Velasco [vay•LAHS•koh] was known as a landscape painter. He is considered a "scientific" artist because he created many sketches of nature and the human body. **page 29**

Diego Velázquez
(1599–1660) Spain, painter. Velázquez [vay•LAHS•kes] was the court painter for King Philip IV of Spain. One of the artist's favorite techniques was to focus intense light on his subjects and set them against dark backgrounds. **page 96**

Robert Wagstaff
United States, painter. Wagstaff was born and raised in Hawaii. Native Hawaiian plants and animals are often the subjects of his artworks. **page 39**

Andy Warhol
(about 1928–1987) United States, painter. Warhol was one of the most important artists in the Pop Art movement. He used familiar commercial images but played with their colors and sizes, often repeating the images. **page 192**

Memphis Wood
United States, folk artist. Wood has been a member of the Jacksonville, Florida, art community for years. She has taught all over the state. **page 64**

252

253

Glossary

abstract art   assemblage

The Glossary contains important art terms and their definitions. Each word is respelled as it would be in a dictionary. When you see this mark ′ after a syllable, pronounce that syllable with more force than the other syllables.

a add	e end	o odd	ōō pool	oi oil	th this		a in above
ā ace	ē equal	ō open	u up	ou pout	zh vision	ə =	e in sicken
â care	i it	ô order	û burn	ng ring			i in possible
ä palm	ī ice	ŏŏ took	yōō fuse	th thin			o in melon
							u in circus

A

abstract art [ab′strakt ärt] Art that does not look realistic. Artists may show either real objects in unusual ways or no real objects at all. (page 92)

Abstract Expressionism [ab′strakt ik•spresh′ən•iz•əm] A twentieth-century art movement in which artists believed in the freedom to express feelings and emotions. (page 178)

action painting [ak′shən pān′ting] A technique of dripping, pouring, and splattering paint onto large canvases. (page 178)

actual line [ak′shōō•əl līn] A line that clearly outlines an object. (page 29)

actual lines

architect [är′kə•tekt] A person who designs buildings. (page 162)

artwork [ärt′wûrk] A piece of art, such as a drawing, a painting, or a sculpture. (page 28)

assemblage [ə•sem′blij] A sculpture made from various objects and materials. (page 80)

254

asymmetrical balance   construction

asymmetrical balance [ā•sə•me′tri•kəl ba′ləns] A type of balance achieved when two sides of an artwork are different but visually equal in weight. (page 130)

atmospheric perspective [at•məs•fēr′ik pər•spek′tiv] A technique used to create a sense of depth in a two-dimensional artwork by using dull colors and fuzzy edges in the background. (page 152)

B

background [bak′ground] The part of an artwork that seems farthest from the viewer. (page 148)

background

blending [blen′ding] Mixing or smudging areas in an artwork to create gradual value changes. (page 74)

C

close-up view [klōs•up vyōō] A detailed view of an object or part of an object. (page 34)

collage [kə•läzh′] An artwork made by gluing materials, such as paper or cloth, onto a flat surface. (page 50)

color scheme [kul′ər skēm] An artist's plan for choosing colors for an artwork. (page 40)

complementary colors [kom•plə•men′tər•ē kul′ərz] Colors that are opposite each other on the color wheel. (page 39)

complementary colors

computer-generated art [kəm•pyōō′tər•jen′ər•ā•təd ärt] Artwork that is created with software on a computer. (page 198)

construction [kən•struk′shən] A type of sculpture that is made of parts joined together. It can be made from a variety of materials or from one kind of material. (page 188)

255

---

contrast   fiber

contrast [kon′trast] A sharp difference between two things, making one or both stand out. (page 39)

cool colors [kōōl kul′ərz] The colors blue, green, and violet. These colors create a calm, peaceful mood. (page 42)

cool colors

Cubism [kyōō′biz•əm] A style of abstract art in which the artist may show more than one view of a subject at the same time. (page 93)

D

depth [depth] The appearance of space or distance in a two-dimensional artwork. (page 148)

distortion [dis•tôr′shən] A technique used to change the way a subject looks, by bending, stretching, or twisting its shape. (page 93)

distortion

dominant color [dom′ə•nənt kul′ər] The color a viewer sees most in an artwork. (page 58)

E

emphasis [em′fə•sis] The special importance given to one part of an artwork. (page 78)

F

facial proportions [fā′shəl prə•pôr′shənz] The way the features of the human face, such as eyes, nose, and mouth, are related to each other in size and placement. (page 89)

fiber [fī′bər] A material such as cloth, yarn, or thread. (page 64)

fiber

256

folk art   landscape

folk art [fōk ärt] A style of art made by people who have had little formal training in art. (page 133)

foreground [fôr′ground] The part of an artwork that seems closest to the viewer. (page 148)

form [fôrm] An object that has height, width, and depth. (page 108)

forms

found object [found ob′jikt] A common object that has a specific purpose. Found objects are often used in assemblages. (page 189)

G

geometric shape [jē•ə•met′rik shāp] A shape, such as a triangle or a circle, that has regular outlines. (page 32)

gesture drawing [jes′chər drō′ing] A sketch created with loose arm movements. (page 98)

gray scale [grā skāl] The range of values from pure black to pure white. (page 72)

gray scale

H

horizon line [hə•rī′zən līn] A line that shows where the sky meets the land or the water. (page 153)

I

impasto [im•pas′tō] A technique of painting that creates a bumpy surface by using thick brushstrokes. (page 70)

implied line [im•plīd′ līn] A line that is suggested rather than drawn. (page 29)

implied lines

Impressionism [im•pre′shə•ni•zəm] An art movement of the late nineteenth century in which artists painted the way light and color looked at a certain moment in time. (page 68)

L

landscape [land′skāp] A painting of an outdoor scene. (page 28)

257

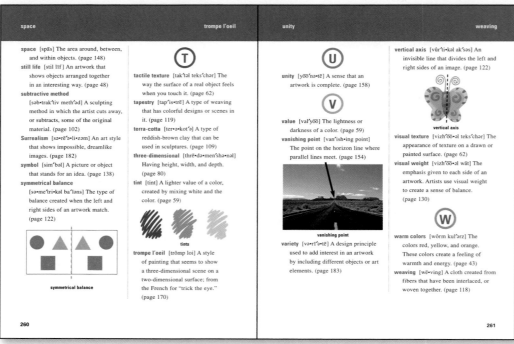

linear perspective   **plein air**

linear perspective [li′nē•ər pər•spek′tiv] A technique used to create a sense of depth in a two-dimensional artwork by making parallel lines meet at a vanishing point. (page 154)

linear perspective

middle ground [mi′dəl ground] The part of an artwork that is between the foreground and the background. (page 148)

monochromatic color [mo•nə•krō•ma′tik kul′ər] A group of values of one color. (page 60)

movement [mōōv′mənt] The way a viewer's eyes travel from one element to another in an artwork. (page 158)

mural [myŏŏr′əl] A painting that is created on a wall or ceiling. A mural can be painted on an indoor or an outdoor surface. (page 168)

negative space [ne′gə•tiv spās] The area in a three-dimensional artwork where material has been removed. (page 103)

organic shape [ôr•gan′ik shāp] A shape that is made up of curved, irregular lines. (page 32)

organic shapes

overlapping [ō•vər•lap′ing] Relating to objects that are partly in front of or behind other objects. (page 48)

pattern [pa′tərn] A design made up of repeated lines, shapes, or colors. (page 118)

plein air [plān âr] The practice of painting outdoors; from the French for "open air." (page 69)

Pop Art   **silkscreen**

Pop Art [pop ärt] A twentieth-century art movement that was inspired by popular media, such as comic books and advertisements. (page 192)

portrait [pôr′trət] An artwork that shows what a person, a group of people, or an animal looks like. (page 88)

portrait

positive space [pä′zə•tiv spās] The raised part of a three-dimensional artwork. (page 103)

primary colors [prī′mâr•ē kul′ərz] The colors red, yellow, and blue. They are mixed together to create the other colors on the color wheel. (page 38)

radial balance [rā′dē•əl ba′ləns] A type of balance in which a pattern extends from the center of the artwork, like the spokes of a wheel. (page 129)

radial balance

relief sculpture [ri•lēf′ skulp′chər] A three-dimensional artwork in which part of the image stands out from the background surface. (page 102)

rhythm [ri′th̸əm] The visual beat created by repeated lines, shapes, colors, or patterns. (page 99)

seascape [sē′skāp] An outdoor scene that shows the sea and sky. (page 42)

secondary colors [se′kən•dâr•ē kul′ərz] The colors orange, green, and violet. Each one is created by combining two primary colors. (page 39)

self-portrait [self•pôr′trət] An artwork of a person, made by that person. (page 90)

shade [shād] A darker value of a color, created by mixing black and the color. (page 59)

shades

silkscreen [silk′skrēn] A printing process in which ink is forced through silk onto paper, cloth, or another surface. (page 192)

258   259

---

space   **trompe l'oeil**

space [spās] The area around, between, and within objects. (page 148)

still life [stil līf] An artwork that shows objects arranged together in an interesting way. (page 48)

subtractive method [səb•trak′tiv meth′əd] A sculpting method in which the artist cuts away, or subtracts, some of the original material. (page 102)

Surrealism [sə•rē′ə•li•rzəm] An art style that shows impossible, dreamlike images. (page 182)

symbol [sim′bəl] A picture or object that stands for an idea. (page 138)

symmetrical balance [sə•me′tri•kəl ba′ləns] The type of balance created when the left and right sides of an artwork match. (page 122)

symmetrical balance

tactile texture [tak′əl teks′chər] The way the surface of a real object feels when you touch it. (page 62)

tapestry [tap′is•trē] A type of weaving that has colorful designs or scenes in it. (page 119)

terra-cotta [ter•ə•kot′ə] A type of reddish-brown clay that can be used in sculptures. (page 109)

three-dimensional [thrē•də•men′shə•nəl] Having height, width, and depth. (page 80)

tint [tint] A lighter value of a color, created by mixing white and the color. (page 59)

tints

trompe l'oeil [trŏmp loi] A style of painting that seems to show a three-dimensional scene on a two-dimensional surface; from the French for "trick the eye." (page 170)

unity   **weaving**

unity [yōō′nə•tē] A sense that an artwork is complete. (page 158)

value [val′yōō] The lightness or darkness of a color. (page 59)

vanishing point [van′ish•ing point] The point on the horizon line where parallel lines meet. (page 154)

vanishing point

variety [və•rī′ə•tē] A design principle used to add interest in an artwork by including different objects or art elements. (page 183)

vertical axis [vûr′ti•kəl ak′səs] An invisible line that divides the left and right sides of an image. (page 122)

vertical axis

visual texture [vizh′ōō•əl teks′chər] The appearance of texture on a drawn or painted surface. (page 62)

visual weight [vizh′ōō•əl wāt] The emphasis given to each side of an artwork. Artists use visual weight to create a sense of balance. (page 130)

warm colors [wôrm kul′ərz] The colors red, yellow, and orange. These colors create a feeling of warmth and energy. (page 43)

weaving [wē′ving] A cloth created from fibers that have been interlaced, or woven together. (page 118)

260   261

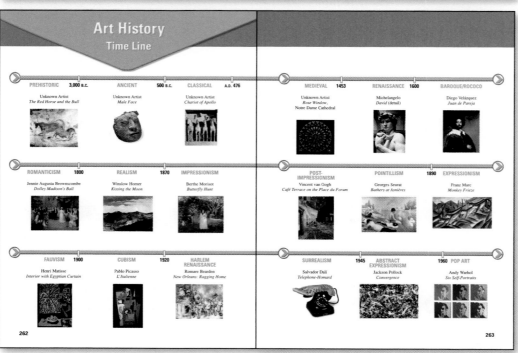

Art History
Time Line

| PREHISTORIC | 3,000 B.C. | ANCIENT | 500 B.C. | CLASSICAL | A.D. 476 |

Unknown Artist
The Red Horse and the Bull

Unknown Artist
Male Face

Unknown Artist
Chariot of Apollo

| MEDIEVAL | 1453 | RENAISSANCE | 1600 | BAROQUE/ROCOCO |

Unknown Artist
Rose Window,
Notre Dame Cathedral

Michelangelo
David (detail)

Diego Velázquez
Juan de Pareja

| ROMANTICISM | 1800 | REALISM | 1870 | IMPRESSIONISM |

Jennie Augusta Brownscombe
Dolley Madison's Ball

Winslow Homer
Kissing the Moon

Berthe Morisot
Butterfly Hunt

| POST-IMPRESSIONISM | | POINTILLISM | 1890 | EXPRESSIONISM |

Vincent van Gogh
Café Terrace on the Place du Forum

Georges Seurat
Bathers at Asnières

Franz Marc
Monkey Frieze

| FAUVISM | 1900 | CUBISM | 1920 | HARLEM RENAISSANCE |

Henri Matisse
Interior with Egyptian Curtain

Pablo Picasso
L'Italienne

Romare Bearden
New Orleans: Ragging Home

| SURREALISM | 1945 | ABSTRACT EXPRESSIONISM | 1960 | POP ART |

Salvador Dalí
Telephone-Homard

Jackson Pollock
Convergence

Andy Warhol
Six Self-Portraits

262   263

Abbott, Meredith Brooks *Kathy's Bowl* 58
Albers, Josef *Homage to the Square/Red Series, Untitled III* 60
Anna, grade 4, *Untitled* 94
Balla, Giacomo *Child Who Runs on the Balcony* 100
Barnbaum, Bruce *Dance of the Corn Lilies* 72
Benton, Thomas Hart *June Morning* 26
Bierstadt, Albert *Among the Sierra Nevada Mountains, California* 152
Biggers, John *Four Seasons* 143
Borglum, Gutzon *Mount Rushmore National Memorial* 102
Brauner, Victor *Memory of the Voyage* 183
Bronzino, Agnolo *Portrait of Francesco I De' Medici* 89
Caillebotte, Gustave *Paris Street, Rainy Day* 144
Caleb, age 4, *Paper sculpture mask* 124
Chukran, Bobbi A. *Bluebonnet Collage* 50
Cicco, Angelo *de No. 49D* 198
Clive, John *Annnciation II* 200
Cornell, Joseph *Toward the Blue Peninsula* 80, *Celestial Navigation* 190
Corot, Jean Baptiste Camille *Cows Grazing* 148
Dali, Salvador *Basket of Bread* 83, *Rhinoceros Dressed in Lace* 174, *Telephone-Homard* 184
Degas, Edgar *Two Blue Dancers* 98, *Study of a Dancer* 98
Depardon, Raymond *Palm Tree in Mauritania* 78
Duncanson, Robert S. *Loch Long* 24
Dunton, W. Herbert *Old Texas* 136
Eric, age 4, *Untitled* 180
Escher, M. C. *Dewdrop* 73
Escobar, Marisol *President Charles DeGaulle* 106, *The Generals* 107
Feininger, Lyonel *The Bicycle Race* 99
Figari, Pedro *Creole Dance* 133
Fiore, Johanna *Portrait of Gordon Parks* 78
Foster, Norman *City Hall, London, England* 163
Frankenthaler, Helen *The Bay* 179
Gauguin, Paul *Still Life with Teapot and Fruit* 48
Glackens, William James *Outdoor Swimming Pool* 146
Golding, A. Maureen *Windy Day in England* 28
Goodacre, Glenna *Sacagawea coin* 102
Graziani, Sante *George Washington* 140
Gris, Juan *Portrait of Picasso* 93
Gunter, Jack *The Discovery* 150

264

Haas, Richard *Cowgirl Mural. National Cowgirl Museum and Hall of Fame, Fort Worth, Texas* 137
Hansen, Ole Juul *Possibilities* 44
Hassam, Frederick Childe *The Fourth of July* 138
Hiroshige, Ando *Night Scene in the Saruwaka Street in Edo* 173
Hockney, David *A Bigger Splash* 79
Homer, Winslow *Children on a Fence* 84
Jacot, Don *Commuter Trains, Union Station* 154
Jawlensky, Alexej von *Landscape of Murnau* 29, *Mystical Head: Crow Wings (Mystischer Kopf: Rabenflügel)* 92
Jendrzejczak, Bernadine *Paper cutting in Polish traditional style* 129
Kahlo, Frida *Self-Portrait with Loose Hair* 90
Kandinsky, Wassily *Accent in Pink* 203
Kenny, Chris *Flowering Tree* 62
Kimble, Warren *The American Farm* 139
Kirstie, grade 4, *Prairie Flower* 34
Klee, Paul *Moving Landscape* 46, *The Goldfish* 47
Krasner, Lee *Bird Talk* 180
Lichtenstein, Roy *Cubist Still-Life with Apple* 193
Lin, Maya *Avalanche and Untitled (Topographic Landscape)* 186, *The Wave Field* 187, *Vietnam Veterans Memorial, Washington, D.C.* 187
Lomas Garza, Carmen *Flowery Words: Stories, Poems, Song, History & Wisdom* 130
Maffei, Ricardo *Aquarium* 176
Magritte, René *Golconda* 113, *The Listening Room* 182
Marc, Franz *Monkey Frieze* 32
Matthew, grade 4, *Untitled* 74
Matisse, Henri *Self-Portrait, 1918* 76, *Interior with Egyptian Curtain* 77, *The Trapeze Performers (Les Codomas)* 77
Meechan, Colleen *Blue Fronds* 40
Modigliani, Amedeo *Self-Portrait* 126, *Head of a Caryatid (Tête de Cariatide)* 126, *Head (Tête)* 126, *Jeanne Hebuterne* 127
Monet, Claude *The Beach at Sainte-Adresse* 42, *Rouen Cathedral, Impression of Morning* 68, *Rouen Cathedral, Bright Sun* 68
Morisot, Berthe *The Butterfly Hunt* 69
Moses, Grandma *The Old Checkered House* 132
Nevelson, Louise *Luminous Zag: Night* 188
O'Brien, Mike *Moon Landing* 104
Ochoa, Isy *Velvet Cat I* 63
O'Keeffe, Georgia *Poppies* 34, *Summer Days* 37
Paik, Nam June *Piano Piece* 189
Pei, I. M. *Rock and Roll Museum and Hall of Fame, Cleveland, Ohio* 166, *Morton H. Meyerson Symphony Center, Dallas, Texas* 167

265

Picasso, Pablo *L'Italienne* 49, *Woman Seated in an Armchair* 94
Pippin, Horace *Man on a Bench* 53
Pollock, Jackson *Convergence* 178
Pugh, Anna *A Day in the Country* 86
Pugh, John *Seven Point One (Siete Punto Uno)* 170
Ray, Man *Man Ray* 110
Remington, Frederic S. *The Fall of the Cowboy* 56, *The Rattlesnake* 110
Ringgold, Faith *The Sunflower Quilting Bee at Arles* 114
Rogers, Thomas *Sacagawea coin* 102
Rousseau, Henri *The Banks of the Bièvre near Bicêtre* 59
Saligman, Meg *Fish Common Threads* 169
Sorian, Matiros *Gazelles* 43
Seurat, Georges *Bathers at Asnières* 54, *Alfalfa Fields, Saint-Denis* 153
Shroger, Joan Myerson *Plaid Construct Swirl* 199
Sierra, Paul *Elegy for Summer* 38
Smithson, Robert *Spiral Jetty* 30
Sorolla y Bastida, Joaquin *Children at the Beach* 70
Stoddard, Alice Kent *Young Man in Blue Suit* 88
Thiebaud, Wayne *Bakery Counter* 194
Unknown artists
  African kente cloth detail 118
  African Kwele mask 123
  Aztec mask 122
  Bird Tree 134
  British herald's tunic 116
  Chinese Emperor's Twelve Symbol Robe 119
  Embarkation on Ship of Roman Troops (Detail from Trajan's Column) 103
  Head of Colossus of Ramses II 104
  Indian warrior's shirt 116
  Inuit finger masks 124
  Navajo traditional shawl 118
  Neron Child 108
  Sunflower Mural on Fence 168
  Terra-Cotta Army Figure 109
  Window Flowers for New Year 128
van Gogh, Vincent *Irises* 33, *Café Terrace on the Place du Forum, Arles, at Night* 149
Velasco, José Maria *A Small Volcano in Mexican Countryside* 29
Velázquez, Diego *Las Meninas* 96
Vicky, age 4, *Reverse weaving* 120
Wagstaff, Robert *Visitors to the Rainforest* 39
Warhol, Andy *Six Self-Portraits* 192
Wood, Memphis *Elysian Fields* 64

266

A

Abstract Expressionism, 178–181
Abstract portrait, 92–95
Action painting, 178, 181
Activities
  See Artist's Workshop.
Architect, 162, 166–167
Artist Biographies
  Escobar, Marisol, 106–107
  Klee, Paul, 46–47
  Lin, Maya, 186–187
  Matisse, Henri, 76–77
  Modigliani, Amedeo, 126–127
  Pei, I. M., 166–167
Artists
  See Gallery of Artists, 240–253; Index of Artists and Artworks, 264–266.
Artist's Workshop
  abstract portrait drawing, 95
  action painting, 181
  building design, 165
  charcoal still-life drawing, 75
  class mural, 171
  close-up view painting, 35
  collage, 51
  collage with texture, 65
  complementary colors painting, 41
  computer-generated artwork, 201
  drawing with depth, 151
  drawing with linear perspective, 155
  folk art painting, 135
  found object construction, 191
  landscape drawing, 31
  monochromatic painting, 61
  outdoor scene painting, 71
  panel drawing, 101
  paper cutting, 131

paper mask, 125
park design, 161
pastel drawing, 81
Pop Art collage, 195
portrait drawing, 91
print, 141
relief sculpture, 105
reverse weaving, 121
seascape or desert landscape painting, 45
soap sculpture, 111
Surrealist painting, 185
Artworks
  See Index of Artists and Artworks, 264–266.
Assemblage, 80, 189–190
Asymmetrical balance, 130
Atmospheric perspective, 152

B

Background, 148
Balance, 23, 122, 125, 128–135, 140, 158–160, 162–165, 238
  asymmetrical, 130
  radial, 129
  symmetrical, 122
Blending, 74–75

C

Careers in Art
  architect, 166–167
  vehicle designer, 196–197
Close-up view, 34–35
Collage, 50, 51, 65, 195
Color, 20, 38–41, 42–45, 58–61, 68–71, 230
  complementary, 39

267

cool, 42
  dominant, 58
  monochromatic, 60
  primary, 38
  secondary, 39
  warm, 43
Color scheme, 40, 58–61
Computer-generated art, 198–201
Construction, 188–191
Cross-Curricular Connections
  math, 154, 199
  reading skills, 26–27, 52, 56–57, 82, 86–87, 112, 116–117, 142, 146–147, 172, 176–177, 202
  science, 36–37, 44, 64, 66–67, 184, 196–197
  social studies, 34, 40, 46–47, 50, 73, 76–77, 79, 96–97, 106–107, 119, 124, 126–127, 130, 136–137, 140, 156–157, 164, 166–167, 186–187, 193
Cubism, 93

D

Depth, 148–151
Distortion, 93
Dominant color, 58
Drawing, 31, 75, 81, 91, 95, 101, 151, 155, 161, 165

E

Elements and Principles, 20–23, 228–239
  See also Elements of art; Principles of design.

Elements of art
  color, 20, 38–41, 42–45, 58–61, 68–71, 230
  form, 21, 108, 232
  line, 20, 28–31, 33, 153, 228
  shape, 20, 32, 34–35, 48–51, 79, 92, 229
  space, 21, 103–105, 148, 233
  texture, 21, 62–65, 66–67, 72–73, 231
  value, 21, 59–61, 63, 69–70, 72–75, 78, 230
Emphasis, 78–81
Environmental art, 30

F

Facial proportion, 89, 91
Fiber art, 64, 118–121
Folk art, 132–135
Foreground, 148
Form, 21, 108, 232
Found objects, 189

G

Geometric shape, 32, 79
Gesture drawing, 98
Glossary, 254–261
Gray scale, 72

H

Horizon line, 153

I

Impasto, 70
Implied line, 29, 33
Impressionism, 68–71

268

K

Keeping a Sketchbook, 12–13

L

Landscape, 28, 31
Line, 20, 28–31, 33, 153, 228
  actual, 29, 33
  horizon, 153
  implied, 29, 33
Linear perspective, 154–155

M

Maps of Museums and Art Sites, 206–209
Mask, 122–125
Middle ground, 148
Monochromatic, 60–61
Movement, 158, 235
Mural, 168–171

N

Negative space, 103

O

Organic shape, 32, 79
Overlapping, 48–51

P

Painting, 35, 41, 45, 61, 71, 135, 171, 181, 185
Paper cutting, 128–131
Pattern, 23, 118–121, 128–129, 234

Perspective
  atmospheric, 152
  linear, 154–155
  Plein air, 69
Pop Art, 192–195
Portrait
  abstract, 92–95
  self-portrait, 90
Positive space, 103
Primary colors, 38
Principles of design
  balance, 23, 122, 125, 128–135, 140, 158–165, 238
  emphasis, 78–81
  movement, 158, 235
  pattern, 23, 118–121, 128–129, 234
  proportion, 23, 89, 91, 236
  rhythm, 23, 99–100, 235
  unity, 22, 158–161, 239
  variety, 22, 183, 188–195, 239
Print, 141
Production Activities
  See Artist's Workshop.
Proportion, 23, 236

R

Radial balance, 129
Reading Skills
  author's purpose, 176–177, 202
  compare and contrast, 116–117, 142
  fact and opinion, 56–57, 82
  main idea and details, 26–27, 52
  narrative elements, 86–87, 112
  summarize and paraphrase, 146–147, 172
Reading Your Textbook, 16–19

269

Relief sculpture, 102–105
Review and Reflect, 52–53, 82–83, 112–113, 142–143, 172–173, 202–203
Rhythm, 23, 99–100, 235

S

Safety, 210–211
Sculpture, 108–111
Seascape, 42
Secondary colors, 39
Self-portrait, 90
Shades, 59
Shape, 20, 32, 34–35, 48–51, 79, 92, 229
geometric, 32, 79
organic, 32, 72, 79
Silkscreen, 192
Space, 21, 103–105, 148, 233
negative, 103
positive, 103
Surrealism, 182–185
Symbol, 138–141
Symmetrical balance, 122

T

Tapestry, 119
Techniques, 212–227
Terra-cotta, 109
Texture, 21, 62–65, 66–67, 72–73, 231
tactile, 62
visual, 62
Three-dimensional, 80
Tints, 59
Trompe l'oeil, 170

U

Unity, 22, 158–161, 239

V

Value, 21, 59–61, 63, 69–70, 72–75, 78, 230
Vanishing point, 154
Variety, 22, 183, 188–195, 239
Vertical axis, 122
Visiting a Museum, 14–15
Visual texture, 62
Visual weight, 130

W

Warm colors, 43
Watercolors, 71
Weaving, 118–121
Writing Activities
author's purpose paragraph, 203
compare-and-contrast composition, 143
fact-and-opinion paragraph, 83
main idea and details paragraph, 53
story, 113
summary and paraphrase, 173

Acknowledgments

Photo Credits:

Page Placement Keys: (t)-top (c)-center (l)-left (fg)-foreground (bg)-background.

All photos property of Harcourt except for the following:

Frontmatter:

5 (tl) Roy King/Superstock; (tr) Kirstie Silverthorn; 6 (tr) Artist Rights Society (ARS), New York, NY/Art Institute of Chicago, Illinois/Lauro-Giraudon, Paris/Superstock; (tc) Licensed by VAGA, New York, NY/Christopher Felver/Corbis; 7 (tl) Victoria Lantz; (tr) Caleb Cloud; 8 (tl) Charles O'Rear /Corbis; 9 (tl) Eric; 12 (tl) Francisco Matarazzo Sobrinho Collection, Sao Paulo/Superstock; (br) Christie's Images/Superstock 14 (tr) Mark E. Gibson/Corbis; (bl) Angelo Hornak/Corbis; 15 (bl) David Woo Photo; 16 (b) The Metropolitan Museum of Art; 17 (c) Artist Rights Society (ARS), New York, NY/Cameraphoto Arte, Venice/Art Resource, NY; 18 (c) Original collage artwork by Bobbi A. Chukran, bobbichukran.com.

Unit 1:

25 (b) Notman Photographic Archives/McCord Museum of Canadian History, Montreal; 26 (b) (copyright) T.H. Benton and R.P. Benton Testamentray Trusts/ Licensed by VAGA, New York, NY/The Cummer Museum of Art and Gardens, Jacksonville/Superstock; 28 (b) The Grand Design, Leeds, England/Superstock; 29 (t) Artist Rights Society (ARS), New York, NY/Superstock; (b) Nardoni Galerie, Prague, Czech Republic/INDEX/Bridgeman Art Library; 30 Art (copyright) Estate of Robert Smithson/Licensed by VAGA, New York, NY/Estate of Robert Smithson, Courtesy James Cohan Gallery, New York; Collection: DIA Center for the Arts, New York; Photo by Gianfranco Gorgoni; Copyright Estate of Robert Smithson; 32 (b) Superstock; 33 (t) The J. Paul Getty Museum; 34 (tr) Artist Rights Society (ARS), New York, NY/Milwaukee Art Museum, Gift of Mrs. Harry Lynde Bradley; (bl) Kirstie Silverthorn; 36 (tr, bl) Illinois State Museum; 37 (b) Caron (NPP) Philippe/Corbis Sygma; (tl) Artist Rights Society (ARS), New York, NY/The Whitney Museum of American Art; 38 (b) Paul Sierra; 39 (tr) Robert Wagstaff; 40 (c) Colleen Meechan; 42 (b) The Art Institute of Chicago; 43 (t) Tretyakov gallery, Moscow/Superstock; 44 (t) Ole Juul Hansen/Superstock; 46 (b) Artist Rights Society (ARS), New York, NY/Private Collection/Peter Willi/Superstock; (tr) Hulton/Archive; 47 (t) Artist Rights Society (ARS), New York, NY/Hamburg Kunsthalle, Hamburg, Germany/The Bridgeman Art Library; 48 (b) The Metropolitan Museum of Art, the Walter H. and Leonore Annenberg Collection, Gift of Walter H. and Leonore Annenberg, 1997, Bequest of Walter H. Annenberg, 2002. (1997.391.2) Photograph (c) 1994 the Metropolitan Museum of Art; 49 (t) Artist Rights Society (ARS), New York, NY/Cameraphoto Arte, Venice/Art Resource, NY; 50 (t) Original collage artwork by Bobbi A. Chukran, bobbichukran.com; 53 (c) Geoffrey Clements/Corbis.

Unit 2:

54 (t) National Gallery, London/Superstock; 55 (bl) Reunion des Musees Nationaux/Art Resource, NY; 56 (b) Artist Rights Society (ARS), New York, NY/Amon Carter Museum; 58 (b) Meredith Brooks Abbott; 59 (t) 2006 Artist Rights Society (ARS), New York/ADAGP, Paris/The Metropolitan Museum of Art, Gift of Marshall Field, 1939. (39.15) Photograph (c) 1981 The Metropolitan Museum of Art; 60 (c) Artist Rights Society (ARS), New York, NY/Norton Simon Museum, Pasadena, CA; 62 (b) The Grand Design, Leeds, England/Superstock; 63 (c) Isy Ochoa/Superstock; 64 (c) Jacksonville Museum of Modern Art, Florida/Superstock; 66 (b) Steve Vidler/Superstock; 67 (b) Harcourt Index; (tl) Mark Keller/Superstock; 68 (br, bl) Musee d'Orsay, Paris/Superstock; 69 (t) Musee d'Orsay, Paris/E.T. Archive, London/Superstock; 70 (t) Archivo Iconografico, S.A./Corbis; 72 (b) Bruce Barnbaum Photography; 73 (t) 2003 Cordon Art B.V. -Baarn-Holland; 74 (b) Matthew Alvarado; 76 (b) Artist Rights Society (ARS), New York, NY/Bridgeman Art Library, London/Superstock; 77 (br) Artist Rights Society (ARS), New York, NY/CNAC/MNAM/Dist. Reunion des Musees Nationaux/Art Resource, NY; (tl) Artist Rights Society (ARS), New York, NY/Phillips Collection, Washington, D.C./Lauros-Giraudon, Paris/Superstock; 78 (tr) Raymond Depardon/Magnum Photos; (bl) Johanna Fiore; 79 (t) Art Resource, NY/Tate Gallery, London, England; 80 (bl) (copyright) The Joseph and Robert Cornell Memorial Foundation/Licensed by VAGA, New York, NY/Art Resource; 83 (br) Artist Rights Society (ARS), New York,NY/Salvador Dali Museum, Inc.

Unit 3:

84 (t) Williams College Museum of Art, Museum purchase, with funds provided by the Assyrian Relief Exchange; 85 (bl) Bettmann/Corbis; 86 (bl) Feldman & Associates/ Lucy B. Campbell Gallery, London; 88 (b) David David Gallery, Philadelphia/Superstock; 89 (t) Superstock; 90(b) Christie's Images/Superstock; 92 (b) Artist Rights Society (ARS), New York, NY/Christie's Images/Superstock; 93 (tl) Artist Rights Society (ARS), New York, NY/Art Institute of Chicago, Illinois/Lauro-Giraudon, Paris/Superstock; 94 (tl) Artist Rights Society (ARS), New York, NY/Christie's Images/Superstock; (br) Anna Handelsman; 96 (tr) Bettmann/Corbis; 97 (bl) Corbis; (br) Michael Freeman/Corbis; (cr) National Portrait Gallery, Smithsonian Institution/Art Resource, NY; 98 (bl) Christie's Images/Superstock; (t) Von Der Heydt Museum, Wuppertal, Germany/Giraudon, Paris/Superstock; 99 (b) Artist Rights Society (ARS), New York, NY/National Gallery of Art, Washington D.C.; 100 (b) Artist Rights Society (ARS), New York, NY/Civica Galleria d'Arte Moderna, Milan/Fratelli Alinari/Superstock; 102 (tr) Harcourt; 103 (c) Superstock; 104 (bl) Royalty-Free/Corbis; (c) Don Couch Photography;106 (t) Christopher Felver/Corbis; (b) (copyright) Marisol/Licensed by VAGA, New York, NY/Smithsonian American Art Museum, Washington, DC/Art Resource; 107 (b) (copyright) Marisol/Licensed by VAGA, New York, NY/Albright-Knox

Art Gallery/Corbis; 108 (t) Musee du Louvre, Paris/Superstock; 109(cr) Tomb of Qin shi Huang Di, Xianyang, China/33Bridgeman Art Library; 110 (bl) Artist Rights Society (ARS), New York, NY/Christie's Images/Superstock; (tr) Buffalo Bill Historical Center, Cody, WY, Gift of The Coe Foundation;113 (c) Artist Rights Society (ARS), New York, NY/Menil Foundation, Houston, Texas/Lauros-Giraudon, Paris/Superstock.

Unit 4:

114 (t) Philadelphia Museum of Art; 115 (bl) Grace Matthews/FaithRinggold.com; 116 (cl) Philadelphia Museum of Art/Corbis; (br) Christie's Images/Corbis; 118 (bl) Lowe Art Museum/Superstock; (br) The British Museum; 119 (t) Lowe Art Museum/Superstock; 120 Hailey Marosi; 122 (b) Peabody Museum, Harvard University N36551; 123 (tr) Christie's Images/Superstock; 124 (tr) The Detroit Institute of Arts; (bl) Caleb Cloud; 126 (bl) Francisco Matarazzo Sobrinho Collection, Sao Paulo/Superstock; (b) Christie's Images/Superstock; (br) Superstock; 127 (tl) Artist Rights Society (ARS), New York, NY/Christie's Images/Superstock; 128 (c) Museum of Internaitonal Folk Art/Museum of New Mexico Girard Foundation Collection, Photo: Michel Monteaux; 129 (t) Bernie Jendrzejczak; 130 (tr) Rudy Gomez Photo Arts/Collection of Carmen Lomas Garza; 132 (b) Chisholm Gallery, West Palm Beach, Florida/Superstock; 133 (t) Christie's Images/Superstock; 134 (cr) Philadelphia Museum of Art/Corbis; 136 (c) San Antonio Art League Museum; 137 (br) (copyright) Richard Haas/Licensed by VAGA, New York, NY/National Cowgirl Museum & Hall of Fame/Fort Worth, Texas; (t) Rhonda Hole/National Cowgirl Museum & Hall of Fame, Fort Worth, Texas; 138 (br) Christie's Images/Superstock; 139 (t) Warren Kimble/Kimble House; 140 (c) Burstein Collection/Corbis; 143 (br) Earlie Hudnall, Jr./Hazel Biggers.

Unit 5:

144 (t) Gustave Caillebotte, French, 1848-1894, Paris Street; Rainy Day, 1877, oil on canvas, 212.2 x 276.2 cm, Charles H. and Mary F.S. Worcester Collection/The Art Institute of Chicago; 145 (bl) Erich Lessing/Art Resource, NY; 146 (bl) Christie's Images/Superstock; 148 (b) Christie's Images/Corbis; 149 (l) Superstock; 150 (c) Jack Gunter; Corbis; 152 (l) The Art Archive; 153 (t) National Gallery of Scotland, Edinburgh; 154 (c) Louis K. Meisel Gallery/Corbis; 156 (b) Ben Mangor/Superstock; 157 (tl) George H. H. Huey/Corbis; (cr) San Antonio Missions National Historical Park; 158 (b) Superstock; 159 (t) Roy King/Superstock; 160 (t) Lisa Quinones/Black Star; 162 (bl) Nathan Benn/Corbis; 163 (t) Steve Vidler/Superstock; 164 (t) Superstock; 166 (b) Bill Ross/Corbis; (cl) Phil Huber/Stock Photo; 167 (c) Art on File/Corbis; 168 (b) Charles O'Rear Corbis; 169 (t) Meg Saligman; 170 (c) RJD Enterprises; 173 (br) Burstein Collection/Corbis.

Unit 6:

174 (t) Artist Rights Society (ARS), New York, NY/AFP/Corbis; (bg) Royalty-Free/Corbis; 175 AP/Wide World Photos; 176 (br) Kactus Foto, Santiago, Chile/Superstock; 178 (b) Artist Rights Society (ARS), New York, NY/Albright-Knox Art Gallery/Corbis; 179 (t) Geoffrey Clements/Corbis; 180 (tr) Artist Rights Society (ARS), New York, NY/Burstein Collection/Corbis; (bl) Eric; 182 (b) Artist Rights Society (ARS), New York, NY/Christie's Images/Superstock; 183 (tr) Artist Rights Society (ARS), New York, NY/Superstock; 184 (t) Artist Rights Society (ARS), New York,NY/Christie's Images/Superstock; 186 (bl) Courtesy of the Southeastern Center for Contemporary Art (SECCA), Winston-Salem, NC, Photo by Jackson Smith/Maya Lin Studio; (tl) Layne Kennedy/Corbis; 187 (b) Balthazar Korab/Maya Lin Studio; (cr) James P. Blair/Corbis; 188 (b) Artist Rights Society (ARS), New York, NY/Solomon R. Guggenheim Museum, New York, gift, Mr. & Mrs. Sidney Singer, 1977, photo by Robert E. Mates; 189 (tl) Albright-Knox Art Gallery/Corbis; 190 (t) (copyright) The Joseph and Robert Cornell Memorial Foundation/Licensed by VAGA, New York, NY/Geoffrey Clements/Corbis; 192 (b) Artist Rights Society (ARS), New York, NY/Burstein Collection/Corbis; 193 (t) Geoffrey Clements/Corbis; 194 (c) (copyright) Wayne Thiebaud/Licensed by VAGA, New York, NY/Christie's Images/Corbis; 196 (tl) Eranian PH/Corbis Sygma; (br) Lowell Georgia/Corbis;197 (br) General Motors Corporation; (t) Durand Patrick/Corbis Sygma; 198 (b) Angelo Di Cicco/Museum of Computer Art; 199 (tr) Joan Myerson Shrager/Museum of Computer Art; 200 (t) Museum of Computer Art; 203 (cl) Artist Rights Society (ARS), New York, NY/National Museum of Modern Art, Paris, France/Lauros-Giraudon, Paris/Superstock.

Backmatter:

Gallery of Artists:

240 (tl) Duncan H. Abbott/Meredith Abbott; (cl) Norton Simon Museum, Pasadena, CA; (bl) Artists Rights Society (ARS), NY/Roger-Viollet, Paris/Bridgeman Art Library; (tr) Bruce Barnbaum; (cr) Bettmann/Corbis; (br) PictureHistory; 241 (tl) Earlie Hudnall Jr.; (cl) Corbis; (tr) H.O. Havemeyer Collection, Bequest of Mrs. H.O. Havemeyer, 1929/Metropolitan Museum of Art; (cr) Erich Lessing/Art Resource, NY; (cr) Original collage artwork by Bobbi A. Chukran, bobbichukran.com; (br) Angelo Di Cicco; 242 (tl) John Clive; (cl) Smithsonian American Art Museum, Washington, DC/Art Resource, NY; (cl) Gianni Dagli Orti/Corbis; (bl) AP/Wide World Photos; (tr) Giraudon/Art Resource, NY; (cr) Robert S. Duncanson, artist, Montreal, QC, 1864. I-11978; Notman Photographic Archives, McCord Museum of Canadian History, Montreal; (cr) Raymond Depardon/Magnum Photos; 243 (cl) M.C. Escher's "Selfportrait" © 2003 Cordon Art B.V. - Baarn - Holland. All rights reserved; (bl) Christopher Felver/Corbis; (tr) Sarah Campbell Blaffer Foundation, Houston, TX/Artists Rights Society (ARS), NY/AKG Images; (cr) Boterell Roy/Corbis Sygma; (br) Christopher Felver/Corbis; 244 (cl) AKG Images; (bl) The Barnes Foundation, Merion Station, Pennsylvania/Corbis; (tr) The Barnes Foundation, Merion Station, Pennsylvania/Corbis; (cr) Images of Yale individuals (RU684). Papers, Manuscripts and Archives, Yale University Library; (cr) Getty Images; (br) Karla Matzke/Jack Gunter; 245 (tl) Superstock; (cl) Corbis; (bl) Peter Harholdt/Corbis; (tr) Rufus F. Folkks/Corbis; (cr) Bettmann/Corbis; (br) Nina Hauser Swanson/Don Jacot; 246 (tl) Artists Rights Society (ARS), NY/AKG Images; (cl) Bettmann/Corbis; (bl) National Museum of Modern Art, Paris, France/Lauros-Giraudon, Paris/Superstock; (tr) Edward Loedding/Kimble House, Inc.; (cr) Edward Loedding/Kimble House, Inc.; (br) Hulton Archive/Getty Images; 247 (tl) Christopher Felver/Corbis; (bl) Layne Kennedy/Corbis; (tr) Dale Higgins/Harcourt; (cr) Superstock; (cr) Hulton Archive/Getty Images; (br) AKG Images; 248 (tl) Succession, H. Matisse, Paris/Artists Rights Society (ARS), NY/AKG Images; (cl) Colleen Meechan; (bl) Giraudon/Art Resource, NY; (tr) Reunion des Musees Nationaux/Art Resource, NY; (cr) Archivo Iconografico, S.A./Corbis; (br) Bettmann/Corbis; 249 (bl) Charles Moore/Stockphoto.com/Stock Photo; (cl) Mike O'Brien; (cl) Florence Levillain/Isy Ochoa; (bl) National Portrait Gallery, Smithsonian Institution/Art Resource, NY; (tr) Albright-Knox Art Gallery/Corbis; (cr) Phil Huber/Stock Photo; (br) Philadelphia Museum of Art/Corbis; 250 (bl) Hulton Archive/Getty Images; (tr) Courtesy of Anna Pugh/Lucy B. Campbell Gallery, London; (cr) John Pugh; (cr) Bruno Barbey/Magnum Photos; (br) AP/Wide World Photos; 251 (tl) Grace Matthews/FaithRinggold.com; (cl) Courtesy of the American Numismatic Association; (bl) Erich Lessing/Art Resource, NY; (tr) Meg Saligman; (cr) Bettmann/Corbis ; (br) Reunion des Musees Nationaux/Art Resource, NY; 252 (tl) Joan Myerson Shrager; (cl) Paul Sierra; (bl) Angelika Platen/AKG Images; (tr) Photos12.com; (br) Christopher Felver/Corbis; 253 (tl) Reunion des Musees Nationaux/Art Resource, NY; (bl) Galleria degli Uffizi Florence/Dagli Orti/Art Archive ; (tr) N. Robert Wagstaff/Wagstaff Fine Art; (cr) Corbis; 254 (tl) Don Ray/The Florida Times Union

Media & Techniques

Creating art is an exhilarating process of self-expression.

Children who are experienced in basic art techniques have the confidence to take risks and try new approaches, with surprisingly original pieces of artwork often resulting. Here are some brief descriptions of media and techniques suitable for students in elementary school.

• TYPES OF PAPER

BUTCHER PAPER
Available in wide rolls and several colors, this hard-surfaced paper is useful for murals and other large art projects.

CONSTRUCTION PAPER
Available in different colors, this paper is useful for crayon and tempera projects. It is easy to cut or tear, and can be used in collages and paper sculptures.

DRAWING AND PAINTING PAPER
This slightly rough paper is useful for drawing and watercolor painting projects, especially at the elementary level.

NEWSPRINT
This thin, inexpensive paper is good for sketching, printmaking, and making papier-mâché.

TISSUE PAPER
Available in bright colors, tissue paper is especially useful for making collages and for projects that require transparent color.

OTHER KINDS OF PAPER
Wallpaper and gift-wrapping paper can be cut into shapes and used in collages. Photographs in old magazines can be cut out and arranged into photomontages.

• ART BOARDS

POSTER BOARD
This lightweight, flexible art board comes in a variety of colors. It has a smooth, hard surface and is easily cut with dull scissors. It can be used for tempera painting projects, collages, and for mounting paper artworks.

CARDBOARD
Used boxes are a good source of cardboard. Pieces of cardboard can be used to back a framed artwork or to build three-dimensional forms. They can also be used as bases for sculptures. Teachers should use sharp scissors to cut boxes ahead of time.

FOAMCORE BOARD
This lightweight board is made by laminating a layer of foam between two pieces of poster board. Foam boards come in various thicknesses and are easy to cut. They are useful for mounting artwork and building three-dimensional forms.

MATBOARD
Matboard is a stiff, heavy, professional-quality board used for framing photographs and paper artworks. Matboards are cut with a razor-edge mat knife.

Closely supervise students when they are using hard or pointed instruments.

• GLUE, STARCH, AND PASTE

WHITE GLUE

This nontoxic, creamy liquid comes in plastic squeeze bottles and in larger containers. It is recommended for use with cardboard, wood, cloth, plastic foam, and pottery. White glue causes wrinkling when used with paper, especially when too much is used.

POWDERED ART PASTE OR STARCH

Mixed to a thin, watery consistency, this material is recommended for use in making tissue-paper collages.

SCHOOL PASTE (LIBRARY PASTE)

Although this substance is nontoxic, young children like its smell and may be tempted to eat it. It should be used by the teacher for pasting pieces of paper onto other pieces of paper or onto cardboard. School paste and glue sticks are not recommended for more elaborate projects because they may not hold the materials together.

USING GLUE OR PASTE

1. Spread out sheets of newspaper.
2. Place the artwork to be glued facedown. Spread the glue or paste evenly from the center, using a finger or a piece of cardboard. Be sure the edges and corners of the paper are covered.
3. Lift the paper and carefully lay it in the desired position on the surface to which it will be affixed. Place a sheet of clean paper over the artwork and smooth it with the palm of the hand.

Starch and powdered art paste should be mixed by the teacher without students present.

• DRAWING TOOLS AND TECHNIQUES

PENCILS

Many different effects can be created with an art pencil, depending on how it is held and how much pressure is applied. Art pencil leads vary from 6B, which makes the darkest, softest mark, to 9H, which makes the lightest, hardest mark.

Students can also achieve a variety of effects with regular number 2 or $2\frac{1}{2}$ pencils. Shading or making light and dark values can be made by using the flat side of the lead.

Colored pencils are most effectively used by first making light strokes and then building up the color to develop darker areas.

CRAYONS

When applied with heavy pressure, crayons produce rich, vivid colors. Always save crayon stubs. Allow students to unwrap them so they can experiment with using the side of the crayon rather than the tip.

Crayon etching is a technique in which layers of light-colored crayon are built up on shiny, nonabsorbent paper. The colors are covered with black crayon or black tempera paint that has been mixed with a small amount of liquid soap. Students must press hard with all the crayons to apply enough wax to the paper. With a toothpick, fingernail, or other pointed tool, students etch, or scratch away, the black layer to expose the colors or the white paper underneath (**Figure 1**).

Figure 1. Crayon etching

OIL PASTELS

Softer than wax crayons, oil pastels produce bright, glowing color effects. Pressing an oil pastel hard on the paper creates rich, vibrant color; less pressure produces a softer color. Oil pastels smudge more easily than crayons. As with crayons, drawing can be done with the points or with the unwrapped sides, and students may wish to break their oil pastels in half.

Colors can be mixed by adding one over another or by placing dots of different colors side by side and blending them by rubbing.

COLORED MARKERS

Nonpermanent felt- or plastic-tipped markers are safe and easy to use, and they are available in a wide range of colors and sizes. They are useful for outdoor sketching, for making contour drawings, and for other art assignments. Dried-out markers can be renewed by running warm water on the tip.

PAINTING TOOLS AND TECHNIQUES

TEMPERA

Tempera paint works best when it has the consistency of thick cream. It is available in powder or, more commonly, liquid form. Tempera is opaque—the paper beneath cannot be seen through paint of normal consistency.

Tempera powder is available in cans or boxes, and it should be mixed in small amounts. Mix water and powder to the desired consistency. Tempera may be mixed with wheat paste to make a very thick paint for impasto painting. Dried-out tempera paint should not be used again.

Safety Tips

Powdered tempera can irritate eyes and nasal passages during mixing. If you use powdered tempera, wear a mask and mix it ahead of time.

Liquid tempera is available in jars or plastic containers and is ready to use. Shake the container well before using. Keep a lid on the paint when it is not being used, and keep paint cleaned out of the cap to prevent sticking.

Some manufacturers supply helpful pouring spouts. If you use them, put a galvanized nail in the spout openings when not in use to keep them from stopping up.

WATERCOLORS

Watercolors should be softened ahead of time by placing a drop of water on each color cake. Paintings can be done with a dry or wet brush for different effects. Students may use the top of the open box to mix colors. Small, soft-bristle brushes are used with watercolors to achieve the transparent, fluid quality of the medium.

Interesting effects with watercolors include
- making a watercolor wash by painting a line and then smudging the line with a wet brush.
- blotting watercolors with crumpled paper.
- sprinkling salt on a wet watercolor picture.
- painting on wet paper.

BRUSHES

Choose well-made brushes with metal ferrules (the ring around the paintbrush shaft near the bristles). Ferrules should be tightly bonded to the handles so the bristles will not come off onto students' paintings.

Dozens of sizes and varieties of brushes are available, from nylon-bristle brushes to fairly expensive sable brushes. Students should have access to a wide variety of brushes—round and flat, thick and thin, square-ended and oval-tipped. After each art session, brushes should be cleaned in a warm solution of mild detergent and water. Students can experiment with other painting tools, such as toothbrushes, eye-makeup brushes, sponges, and cotton swabs.

PAINT CONTAINERS

Mixing trays or paint palettes can be made from many free or inexpensive materials, such as pie pans, muffin tins, plastic food trays, and paper plates. Egg cartons make good mixing trays because they can be closed, labeled with the student's name, and stored for later use.

When storing tempera paint in a mixing tray for later use, add a little water to keep the paint from drying out overnight. You can use a spray bottle to wet the paints before storing.

Always provide students with containers of water for cleaning their brushes while painting. Use plastic margarine containers or other small plastic tubs. Demonstrate for students how to rinse the brush in water before dipping it into a new color. Students can dry the brush as needed by stroking it across a folded paper towel.

Quick Tip

Make your own portable paint holder by cutting holes in the lid of a shoe box. Place babyfood jars filled with paint into the openings.

COLOR-MIXING TECHNIQUES

When mixing **tints**, start with white and gradually add small amounts of a color to make the desired tint. When mixing **shades**, gradually add small amounts of black to a color.

Mix the **primary colors** (red, yellow, and blue) to create the **secondary colors** (green, orange, and violet).

- To make green, add small amounts of blue to yellow.
- To make orange, add small amounts of red to yellow.
- To make violet, add small amounts of blue to red.

To make **neutral colors**, such as brown, combine **complementary color pairs** (red plus green, yellow plus violet, blue plus orange).

PRINTMAKING TOOLS AND TECHNIQUES

Prints can be made from a wide variety of materials, including plastic foam meat trays with indented designs, dried glue lines on cardboard, and flat shapes or objects glued to cardboard.

The following technique may be used for printmaking:

1. Pour water-based printing ink on a plastic tray or a cookie sheet.
2. Roll a brayer or roller over the ink.
3. Roll the coated brayer over the printing surface until it is evenly covered. Roll first in one direction and then at right angles.
4. Place a piece of paper on top of the inked surface. Rub the back of the paper with the fingertips or the back of a spoon, being careful not to move it.
5. Pull the paper away from the surface. This is called "pulling the print." The print is ready to dry.

Safety Tips

Even water-based ink stains clothing. Have students wear smocks or old shirts when they are making prints.

PRINTMAKING PAPER

Recommended paper for printing includes newsprint, construction paper, and tissue paper. Avoid using paper with a hard, slick finish because it absorbs ink and paint poorly.

To use paint instead of ink for a relief print, mix several drops of glycerine (available in drugstores) with one tablespoon of thick tempera paint. If brayers are not available, have students apply the ink or the paint with a foam brush.

CLEANUP

Drop a folded piece of newspaper into the pan filled with printmaking ink. Roll the brayer on the newspaper. This removes most of the ink from both the pan and the brayer. Lift the newspaper, refold it with the ink inside, and throw it away. Repeat until most of the ink is out of the pan, and then rinse the pan and the brayer at the sink.

ASSEMBLAGE

An assemblage is an artwork made by joining three-dimensional objects. It can be either free-standing or mounted on a panel, and it is usually made from "found" materials—scraps, junk, and objects from nature. Students can help you collect and sort objects such as

- carpet, fabric, foil, leather, paper, and wallpaper scraps.
- boxes in all sizes, film cans, spools, corks, jar lids.
- packing materials such as foam peanuts and cardboard.
- wire, rope, twine, string, yarn, ribbon.

SCULPTING TOOLS AND TECHNIQUES

Sculpture is three-dimensional art. It is usually made by carving, modeling, casting, or assembling. Sculptures can be created by adding to a block of material (**additive**) or taking away from a block of material (**subtractive**).

Materials recommended for additive sculpture include clay, papier-mâché, wood, and other materials that can be joined together.

Materials appropriate for subtractive sculpture in school include child-safe clay, wax, soft salt blocks, and artificial sandstone. Synthetic modeling materials are also available.

In the primary grades, salt dough may be substituted for clay in some art activities. Combine 2 cups of flour with 1 cup of salt. Add 1 cup of water and mix thoroughly. Press the mixture into a ball and then knead for several minutes on a board.

Foil offers interesting possibilities for sculpture and embossing. Heavy aluminum foil works best. In addition to making three-dimensional forms with foil, students can smooth it over textured objects to make relief sculptures or jewelry.

Wire, including pipe cleaners, telephone wire, and floral wire, is easily shaped and reshaped. Teachers should cut wire into pieces ahead of time. When using long wires, tape the ends to prevent injury. Students should wear safety goggles and sit a safe distance from each other.

PAPER SCULPTURE

Stiff paper or poster board, cut in a variety of shapes and sizes, yields colorful and inventive three-dimensional forms. For best results, students should always use glue, not paste, when assembling a paper sculpture. They can use a paper clip or tape to hold parts together while the glue is drying.

CLAY

Clay comes from the ground and usually has a gray or reddish hue. It is mixed with other materials so that it is flexible, yet able to hold a shape.

Oil-based clay is mixed with oil, usually linseed, and cannot be fired or glazed. It softens when it is molded with warm hands. When the clay becomes old and loses oil, it becomes difficult to mold and will eventually break apart. Oil-based clay is available in a variety of colors.

Water-based or wet clay comes in a variety of textures and can be fired to become permanent. It should be stored in a plastic sack to keep it moist until it is used. If the clay begins to dry out, dampen it with a fine spray of water. If it has not been fired, dried water-based clay can be recycled by soaking it in water.

Before firing, or baking clay in a kiln, there are two important considerations:

- Read and carefully follow the instructions for operating the kiln.
- Be certain that the clay has been kneaded before being molded to prevent air pockets that can explode during firing.

PREPARING CLAY

If clay is reused or made from a powder mix, knead thoroughly to remove air pockets.

- Take a chunk of soft clay and form it into a ball. Then use a wire cutting tool to cut the ball in half. From a standing position, throw the clay onto a tabletop to flatten it.
- Press down on the clay with the palms of both hands against a hard surface. Fold the clay, and press hard again. Keep folding and pressing in this manner until the air pockets have been removed.

Figure 2. Pinch method

METHODS FOR MOLDING CLAY

Clay can be molded and formed using the pinch, slab, and coil methods.

- To make a pot using the **pinch method (Figure 2)**, mold a chunk of clay into a ball. Holding the ball in one hand, press the thumb in and carefully squeeze the clay between thumb and forefinger. Begin at the bottom, and gradually work upward and out. Continually turn the ball of clay while pinching it.
- To make a **slab**, use a rolling pin to flatten a chunk of clay between a quarter of an inch and half an inch thick. Shapes cut from the slab (**Figure 3**) can be draped over bowls or crumpled newspapers and left to dry. Clay shapes can also be joined together to form containers or sculptures.

Figure 3. Slab method

Textures can be added by pressing found objects, such as combs, coins, buttons, bottle caps, and other interesting objects, into the clay. Designs can also be etched with tools such as pencil points, paper clips, and toothpicks.

To create a **coil**, use the whole hand to roll a chunk of clay against a hard surface until it forms a rope of even thickness (**Figure 4**). Ropes can be attached to each other and coiled into a shape, or they can be added to a slab base and smoothed out.

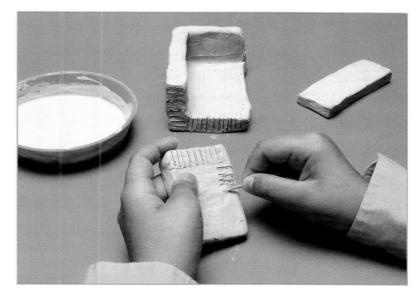

Figure 5. Joining clay pieces

JOINING CLAY TOGETHER

Oil-based clay pieces can be pressed together and blended with the fingertips.

Water-based clay pieces should be joined by **scoring**, or scratching the surface, of the adjoining pieces with the tip of a toothpick. Adding **slip**, or water-thinned clay, will make the two pieces adhere (**Figure 5**).

Figure 4. Coil method

Plastic spray bottles provide an easy way to keep clay pieces moist.

Clean up dry clay with a wet cloth or a wet mop to keep silica dust from dispersing into the air.

• PAPIER-MÂCHÉ

This art material is made by mixing paper pulp or strips with art paste or glue. It can be molded into three-dimensional forms or applied to a foundation form, or **armature**, then painted when dry.

Good forms that can be used as foundations for papier-mâché include inflated balloons, plastic bottles, paper sacks stuffed with newspapers, and wire armatures shaped into skeletal forms.

PREPARING PULP

Shred pieces of soft paper, such as newsprint, paper towels, or facial tissue, into small bits or thin strips. Soak them for several hours in water, then drain them, squeeze out the extra water, and mix the pulp with prepared paste until it reaches the consistency of soft clay. Let the mixture stand for an hour before beginning to work with it.

PREPARING STRIPS

Tear newsprint into long strips about one-half inch wide. Dip the strips into art paste or a white-glue mixture, and put down a layer of wet strips over the foundation form. Allow the piece to dry after every two layers of application. Continue putting strips on the form until there are five or six layers. This thickness is strong enough to support most papier-mâché projects.

Do not use pages from a printed newspaper to make papier-mâché. The printing inks may contain toxic pigments.

• MAKING PAPER

Help children rip up scrap paper and put in a blender with water to make pulp. Pour it into a basin. Children can add things from nature like seeds, flower petals, or leaves. Dip a section of screen into the pulp and raise it up, covering

it with a thin, even layer. Place a towel over the pulp, push on it to drain out the water, and flip it over carefully so that the layer of pulp is lying on the towel. Place another towel over the pulp and iron until it is dry. Spray on starch to make the paper easier to write on.

• FABRIC ARTS

BATIK

The traditional batik method of dyeing fabric is a **wax-resist** technique. First, patterns are drawn on the fabric with wax. When the fabric is dyed, waxed areas resist the dye. When the wax is removed, the pattern emerges. To make an acrylic batik, draw patterns on the fabric with acrylic white paint, rather than wax. Then dye the fabric or brush it with a water-based paint. After it has dried, scratch the white paint off to reveal the pattern **(Figure 6)**.

Figure 6. Simple batik

• WEAVING

A weaving is an artwork created on a **loom** by lacing together or interlocking strands of thread, yarn, or other materials. Simple square looms can be made by stretching thick rubber bands across stiff cardboard. Circular weavings can be made on looms formed from wire hangers bent into a circle. Students can weave a variety of materials through the loom, including ribbon, yarn, strands of beads, twine, and fabric strips **(Figure 7)**.

Figure 7. Weaving

• DISPLAYING ARTWORK

Frames usually improve the appearance of artwork, and they make attractive displays.

MOUNTING

The simplest kind of frame is a **mount**, or a solid sheet of paper or cardboard attached to the back of an artwork. It should be at least an inch larger than the work on all sides.

MATTING

A **mat** is a piece of paper or cardboard with a cut-out center. A picture is taped in place behind it, with the mat forming a border. Professional-style mats made from matboard should be cut only by the teacher.

To make a mat, use a piece of cardboard that extends two or three inches beyond the picture on all sides. On the back of the board, mark the position where the art is to be placed. Then measure one-fourth inch in from the outer edge of the artwork. This will make the picture overlap the cutout window on all sides.

FRAMING

Students can turn cardboard mats into finished frames. Have them paint and decorate a mat, attach their artwork to the back of it, and then attach a solid piece of cardboard to the back of the mat.

Teachers should work carefully when using a mat knife. Keep the blade pointed away from you, and retract the blade or return the knife to its container when not in use.

Art instruction can be particularly useful in helping to meet a wide spectrum of individual needs in the classroom. Knowing some of the characteristics of the developmental stages in art can help teachers make better decisions concerning individual needs.

STAGES OF ARTISTIC DEVELOPMENT

Students' interests and skills in art develop at different rates, just as they do in other disciplines. The following information describes five basic stages of artistic development. Of course, at any age, individual students may show characteristics of various stages.

Scribbling (2–4 YEARS)

- Children begin drawing disorganized scribbles, progress to controlled scribbling, and then advance to named scribbling.
- Children work with art materials for the joy of manipulating them.

Preschematic (4–6 YEARS)

- Drawings are often direct, simple, and spontaneous, showing what children believe is most important about the subject.
- There is usually little concern about technical skill or physical appearance, and color is selected for emotional reasons.
- There is little understanding of space, and objects may be placed haphazardly throughout pictures. The self often appears in the center.

Schematic (7–9 YEARS)

- An understanding of space is demonstrated in most drawings, and objects have a relationship to what is up and down.
- In drawings, a horizon becomes apparent, and items are spatially related.
- Exaggeration between figures, such as humans taller than a house, is used to express strong feelings about subjects.

Beginning of Realism (9–11 YEARS)

- Children begin using perspective.
- Overlapping objects and three-dimensional effects are achieved, along with shading and use of subtle color combinations.
- Drawings may appear less spontaneous than in previous stages because of the students' attempts at achieving realism.

Increasing Realism (11–13 YEARS)

- Students may value the finished product over the process.
- Students strive to show things realistically and in three dimensions.
- Perspective and proportion are used.

▲ **Preschematic Stage**

▲ **Late Schematic Stage**

ESL

Art instruction provides an exceptional opportunity for English-language learners to build both language ability and self-esteem because of the abundance of visual images, hands-on experiences, and peer interaction involved.

Strategies for Success

To help English-language learners:

Use physical movement and gestures, realia, and visuals to make language comprehensible and to encourage oral language development. You may want to use Harcourt's *Picture Card Collection* and *Picture Card Bank CD-ROM* to reinforce concepts visually.

Introduce concepts and words using rhymes and poetry. At Grades 1–3, you will find rhymes and poems in the unit openers.

Explain concepts, using the Grades 1–2 *Big Books* and Grades 1–5 *Art Prints*.

Encourage students to speak, but never force them to do so. All responses should be voluntary.

Display the *Posters of Elements, Principles, and Safety* in both English and Spanish. *Artist's Workshop Activities: English and Spanish* are also available.

EXTRA SUPPORT

Students may need extra support due to insufficient background experiences or home support or because of learning disabilities that affect the way they receive and process information. Some of the problems these students may have include difficulty in organizing work, expressing ideas through speech and language, following directions, or maintaining attention.

Strategies for Success

To help students who need extra support:

Involve students in setting goals and in determining rubrics.

Modify art instruction to meet students' learning styles.

Maintain a consistent art-program schedule.

Simplify complex directions or use fewer words to explain them.

Give students a desk copy of board work or directions.

Model directions for art activities.

Provide concrete examples of concepts and vocabulary to aid retention.

Review regularly what students have previously done or learned.

Allow student choice, and build on student interests.

Look for

CHALLENGE NOTES

Gifted children may

- become bored with routine tasks.

- be overly critical of others or perfectionistic.

- dominate or withdraw in cooperative learning situations.

- resist changing from activities they find interesting.

GIFTED AND TALENTED

Gifted and talented students are those who consistently perform at a high level in art.

Characteristics

When gifted and talented students produce art, they typically:

- show willingness to experiment and try new materials and techniques.
- appear keenly interested in the art of other artists.
- produce art frequently.
- show originality.
- display ease in using materials and tools.

Strategies for Success

Use these strategies with gifted and talented students:

Provide more challenging art assignments and projects. See the Challenge Activities in the *Teacher Resource Book*.

Enable students to participate in long-term projects in which they explore techniques or styles in depth.

Encourage and provide opportunities for individual exploration.

Challenge students with cross-disciplinary experiences in which they combine aspects of two disciplines, such as making a "sound collage."

Plan for additional outlets and audiences for students' work—in the community as well as at school.

Arrange for additional art opportunities, such as noon "drop-in" classes or after-school classes.

SPECIAL NEEDS

Special-needs students may have mobility, visual, or hearing impairments; be multiply disabled; or have behavioral or developmental disabilities. Art experiences can provide these students with unique opportunities to express their ideas and feelings and to improve their self-esteem and independence.

Strategies for Success

Here are a few of the many strategies you can use to help these students achieve success. Not all strategies work with all students or situations. Check individualized educational plans for each student's personal goals as well as the objectives of your curriculum.

Mobility Impairments

Consider whether a different medium might be easier to use, such as oil pastels instead of tempera paints.

Use assistive technology, or use or make adaptive devices. For example, for a student who has trouble gripping a crayon, place the crayon inside a foam curler.

Tape paper to the table to hold it in place while students draw.

Visual Impairments

Demonstrate for the child, allowing the student to touch your hands as you model.

Provide tactile materials in lieu of primarily visual ones, such as yarn for forming lines, clay for sculpting, and finger paints for painting.

Tape a shallow box lid or frame in the student's workspace, where the student's tools can be kept and easily located.

Hearing Impairments

Provide additional visual models.

Repeat demonstrations of skills, such as mixing colors.

Use signing, if known.

Behavioral Disabilities

Praise students for all tasks well done.

Provide opportunities for working with three-dimensional materials.

Make these students your helpers.

Developmental Disabilities

Explain each task separately, allowing it to be done before starting another.

Allow frequent opportunities for free drawing.

Repeat each direction, demonstrating it several times.

Look for
SPECIAL NEEDS NOTES

KEEP IN MIND

You may want to share the work of some artists with disabilities:

■ **Chuck Close (mobility)**

■ **Dale Chihuly (vision)**

■ **Francisco Goya (hearing)**

■ **Auguste Renoir (mobility)**

■ **Frida Kahlo (mobility)**

For more information and resources:

- http://www.vsarts.org
- http://finearts.esc20.net/fa_forall.htm
- http://www.vsatx.org

Assessment Options

Assessment involves the selection, collection, and interpretation of information about student performance. The goal of assessment is to help students show what they know and what they can do. Effective assessment in an art program should include both creating and responding experiences that engage a variety of knowledge and skills in studio production, art criticism, art history, and aesthetics. Student learning may be demonstrated in products, paper-pencil format, and discussions or conferences.

Art Everywhere includes a variety of tools that teachers may use to construct a complete picture of a student's accomplishments.

TOOLS AND STRATEGIES

Student Edition Review and Reflect Pages

Use to determine whether the student

- Responds to questions of art and design using appropriate vocabulary through discussion, writing, and visual analysis

- Applies knowledge in art criticism, art history, and aesthetics

Two pages at the end of each instructional unit in the *Student Edition* provide exercises and activities for students to review and reflect upon the unit content. These activities encourage students to demonstrate their knowledge of visual art vocabulary, to apply reading and thinking skills to art, to write in response to art, and to describe, analyze, interpret, compare, and evaluate works of art.

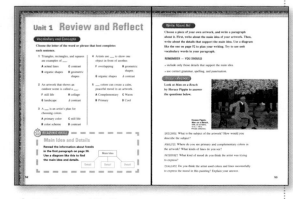

▲ Review and Reflect

Studio Production Activities

Use to determine whether the student

- Demonstrates and applies technical skills and control of media and tools in studio production

- Constructs and communicates meaning by using different media, techniques, and processes to communicate ideas and experiences and solve problems

The Artist's Workshop, a production activity in each lesson in the *Student Edition*, provides an opportunity for students to demonstrate technical skills and control of media and tools and to apply elements and principles taught in the lesson. The Artist's Workshop Rubrics on pages R30–R31 may be used to help students assess their own work and to discuss personal artworks with peers and the teacher. The completed form may serve to guide a student-teacher conference or a student-student discussion.

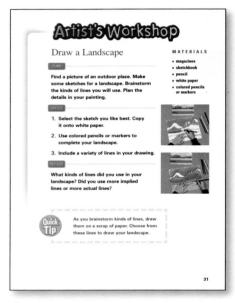

▲ Artist's Workshop

Unit Tests

Use to determine whether the student

- Uses appropriate vocabulary to respond to questions of art and design through discussion, writing, and visual analysis

The *Teacher Resource Book* includes a set of multiple-choice and short-answer questions, in blackline master format, which may be duplicated and used to assess students' knowledge of visual art vocabulary and concepts orally or in writing.

Portfolio

Use to determine whether the student

- Recognizes personal strengths and weaknesses and discusses own work

- Constructs and communicates meaning by using different media, techniques, and processes

A portfolio, a purposeful collection of a student's work, provides a continuous record of a student's growth and learning. It is an effective strategy to be used to compare a student's current work to earlier work.

Organized chronologically, a portfolio benefits both the student and the teacher. Students reflect on their own growth and development as they self-assess and select materials to include in their portfolio. For the teacher, a portfolio provides a forum for a student-teacher discussion or conference. See page R32 for the Portfolio Recording Form.

Art Prints and Discussion Cards

Use to determine whether the student

- Responds to works of art and design, using appropriate vocabulary, through discussion and visual analysis

- Identifies specific works of art as belonging to particular cultures, times, and places

- Recognizes connecting patterns, shared concepts, and connections between and among works of art

The Discussion Cards, found on pages R34–R38, may be used to help students focus their thoughts as they view the program *Art Prints*. Each card provides a framework for students to respond to works of art and design using technical vocabulary appropriately and to demonstrate an understanding of the nature and meaning of artworks.

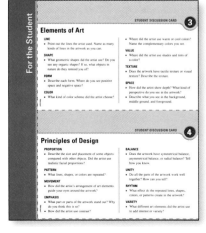

▲ Student Discussion Card

Observations

Use to determine whether the student

- Demonstrates and applies technical skills and control of media, tools, and processes

- Applies art knowledge in art criticism, art history, and aesthetics

A checklist or inventory is one of the easiest tools for recording students' progress. Observe students at various times and in various circumstances, and record observations. The Progress Recording Form, found on page R33, is a checklist based on instructional objectives that may be used for monitoring students' acquisition of art skills and knowledge.

Self- and Peer Assessment

Use to determine whether the student

- Describes, analyzes, interprets, and judges or evaluates design or artwork done by self, peers, or other artists

- Recognizes personal strengths and weaknesses and discusses own work

- Responds to works of art and design, using technical vocabulary that describes visual experiences and supports assertions

Self-assessment helps students learn to reflect on their own artwork and on their strengths and weaknesses as artists. The Artist's Workshop Rubric for Self/Teacher Assessment, on page R30, provides a format for both the student and the teacher to assess student artwork and habits.

▲ Peer Assessment Rubric

Peer assessment provides students with a forum to share their ideas as artists and as viewers of art in a positive and constructive setting. In evaluating each other's work, students can use art-specific vocabulary and knowledge, exercise their art-response skills, and reflect on their own learning and development. Use the Artist's Workshop Rubric for Peer Assessment on page R31 to guide students' responses.

Artist's Workshop Rubric
Self/Teacher Assessment

Artist _____ Artwork _____

Teacher _____ Date _____

Knowledge and Skills	Rate your own work.	Teacher Rating
Creativity Work shows creativity. Work is imaginative and original.	☆ ☆ ☆ ☆	☆ ☆ ☆ ☆
Design Work shows application of art principles and elements.	☆ ☆ ☆ ☆	☆ ☆ ☆ ☆
Technique Shows skillful use of tools, techniques, and media.	☆ ☆ ☆ ☆	☆ ☆ ☆ ☆
Following Directions Stays on task. Completes activity as directed.	☆ ☆ ☆ ☆	☆ ☆ ☆ ☆
Work Habits Applies self to activity. Shows safe and proper use of tools.	☆ ☆ ☆ ☆	☆ ☆ ☆ ☆

Excellent	Above Average	Satisfactory	Unsatisfactory
☆ ☆ ☆ ☆	☆ ☆ ☆	☆ ☆	☆

Comments

Harcourt

Artist's Workshop Rubric
Peer Assessment

Artist _____ Artwork _____

Reviewer _____ Date _____

Make a checkmark in the boxes that tell about this artwork.

Creativity	
Uses imagination.	
Takes risks or experiments.	

Communication	
Shows original ideas.	
Expresses ideas clearly.	
Shows attention to detail.	

Focus	
Meets objective.	
Uses good technique and skills.	
Shows good effort.	

Elements and Principles	
Uses elements of art such as	
color	
texture	
form	
line	
space	
value	
Uses principles of design such as	
emphasis	
pattern	
rhythm	
balance	
proportion	
unity	

Something that makes this artwork special is _____

_____.

Harcourt

Portfolio Recording Form

Name _____

Artwork/Date Done	Notes
_____	_____
_____	_____
_____	_____
_____	_____
_____	_____
_____	_____
_____	_____
_____	_____
_____	_____

My portfolio includes

_____ plans or sketches.

_____ finished work.

_____ photos of finished work.

_____ writing about finished work.

_____ only my best work.

_____ some of my early artwork.

_____ artworks that show how I have improved.

My favorite artwork in my portfolio is _____

because _____.

My least favorite artwork in my portfolio is _____

because _____.

Harcourt

Progress Recording Form

Name _____ Teacher _____

Knowledge and Skills

Date

Perception						
Communicates ideas about self, family, school, and community, using sensory knowledge and life experiences.						
Chooses appropriate vocabulary to discuss the use of art elements such as color, texture, form, line, space, and value and art principles such as emphasis, pattern, rhythm, balance, proportion, and unity.						
Creative Expression/Performance						
Integrates a variety of ideas about self, life events, family, and community in original artworks.						
Designs original artworks.						
Invents ways to produce artworks and to explore photographic imagery, using a variety of art media and materials.						
Historical/Cultural Heritage						
Identifies simple main ideas expressed in art.						
Compares and contrasts selected artworks from a variety of cultural settings.						
Identifies the roles of art in American society.						
Response/Evaluation						
Describes intent and forms conclusions about personal artworks.						
Interprets ideas and moods in original artworks, portfolios, and exhibitions by peers and others.						

Key: R = Rarely or never exhibits behavior
        S = Sometimes exhibits behavior
        C = Consistently exhibits behavior

Comments

Harcourt

Looking at Art

1. **Have students describe the subject and details in the artwork.**
   - What do you see? What is happening here?

2. **Use prompts such as these to encourage students to talk about the artwork's elements, principles, materials, and meaning.**

   ELEMENTS
   - What kinds of shapes do you see? **SHAPE**
   - Where do you see tints and shades? **VALUE**

   PRINCIPLES
   - What part of the artwork do you notice first? **EMPHASIS**
   - Does the artwork look complete? **UNITY**

   MATERIALS
   - What is the artwork made of? **MEDIA**
   - How was this artwork created? **TECHNIQUE**

   MEANING
   - What feeling does the artwork express? **IDEAS AND FEELINGS**
   - Why do you think the artist created the artwork? **PURPOSE**

3. **Present historical information about the artwork and artist, as appropriate.**

Harcourt

Art Criticism

DESCRIBE

1. **Have students describe the subject of the art-work and share facts about what they see. Ask:**
   - What is the subject of the artwork? Does the artwork show people, a place, or something else?
   - What details do you see in the artwork?

ANALYZE

2. **Students should describe how the artist uses the elements of art and the principles of design. Ask questions such as these:**
   - What kinds of lines, shapes, and colors do you see?
   - How did the artist create movement?

INTERPRET

3. **Have students discuss the artist's message or the mood of the artwork. Ask:**
   - Does the artwork tell a story? Does it show a mood? How?
   - What do you think the artist wanted viewers to know about the subject of the artwork?

EVALUATE

4. **Have students give reasons for their opinions about the artwork. Ask:**
   - Do you think the artist clearly expressed a mood or message? Explain your answer.
   - What will you remember most about this art-work? Why?

Harcourt

Elements of Art

LINE

- Point out the lines the artist used. Name as many kinds of lines in the artwork as you can.

SHAPE

- What geometric shapes did the artist use? Do you see any organic shapes? If so, what objects in nature do they remind you of?

FORM

- Describe each form. Where do you see positive space and negative space?

COLOR

- What kind of color scheme did the artist choose?

- Where did the artist use warm or cool colors? Name the complementary colors you see.

VALUE

- Where did the artist use shades and tints of a color?

TEXTURE

- Does the artwork have tactile texture or visual texture? Describe the texture.

SPACE

- How did the artist show depth? What kind of perspective do you see in the artwork?
- Describe what you see in the background, middle ground, and foreground.

Harcourt

Principles of Design

PROPORTION

- Describe the size and placement of some objects compared with other objects. Did the artist use realistic facial proportions?

PATTERN

- What lines, shapes, or colors are repeated?

MOVEMENT

- How did the artist's arrangement of art elements guide your eyes around the artwork?

EMPHASIS

- What part or parts of the artwork stand out? Why do you think this is so?
- How did the artist use contrast?

BALANCE

- Does the artwork have symmetrical balance, asymmetrical balance, or radial balance? Tell how you know.

UNITY

- Do all the parts of the artwork work well together? How can you tell?

RHYTHM

- What effect do the repeated lines, shapes, colors, or patterns create in the artwork?

VARIETY

- What different art elements did the artist use to add interest or variety?

Harcourt

For the Student

STUDENT DISCUSSION CARD 5

Portraits

1. DESCRIBE
- Who is the subject of the portrait? Is it one person or more than one? Is this a self-portrait?
- What is the subject wearing? What details did the artist include to show the setting?

2. ANALYZE
- What kind of balance do you see in the portrait?
- Is the portrait realistic or abstract? How do you know?
- Describe how the artist used proportion.

3. INTERPRET
- What was the artist trying to tell you about the subject's personality?
- What do you think the subject of this portrait was thinking or feeling?
- How do lines, shapes, or colors express ideas in this portrait?

4. EVALUATE
- What do you think of the way the artist showed the subject of this portrait? Explain your answer.

Harcourt

STUDENT DISCUSSION CARD 6

Landscapes

1. DESCRIBE
- What kinds of lines do you see in the landscape?
- Does the landscape look realistic? Why or why not?

2. ANALYZE
- Where do you see overlapping?
- What part of the landscape seems closest to you? What part seems farthest away?
- How did the artist show depth?

3. INTERPRET
- What mood or feeling does this landscape express?

4. EVALUATE
- Would you like to visit the place shown in this artwork? Why or why not?
- If you could give this artwork a new title, what would you name it?

Harcourt

R36 *ART EVERYWHERE*

Stories

1. DESCRIBE
- Describe the characters you see in this artwork.
- What are the characters doing? Where are they?
- What story do you think the artist is telling?

2. ANALYZE
- What kinds of materials did the artist use? What effect does this create?
- What part of the artwork seems most important?

3. INTERPRET
- What is the main idea in this artwork? What details support the main idea?
- Does the scene in this artwork show the beginning, middle, or end of a story? Explain.

4. EVALUATE
- Would you like to meet any of the characters in the artwork? Explain.
- What do you think of the way the artist told this story?

Harcourt

Abstract Art

1. DESCRIBE
- Describe what you see in this artwork. Does it have a recognizable subject?
- Is the artwork two-dimensional or three-dimensional? What materials is it made of?

2. ANALYZE
- What kinds of shapes and colors do you see in this artwork?
- What kind of balance did the artist show?
- Can you see more than one view of the subject?
- Did the artist use distortion? How do you know?

3. INTERPRET
- What idea do you think the artist was trying to express in this artwork?
- What kind of mood do the lines or colors in the artwork express?

4. EVALUATE
- What do you think of the way the artist expressed a feeling? Explain your answer.
- What part of this artwork do you think is most interesting?

Harcourt

Art Criticism

1. DESCRIBE
- What is happening in this artwork? Describe what you see.
- What materials is the artwork made of?

2. ANALYZE
- What kinds of lines, shapes, forms, or colors did the artist use? How did the artist organize them in the artwork?
- How did the artist show emphasis?

3. INTERPRET
- Did the artist use lines or colors to express a feeling? If so, what feeling does the artwork express?
- Do you think the artwork has a message? Tell what you think it is.

4. EVALUATE
- Would you tell a friend to go to a museum to see this artwork? Why or why not?

Harcourt

Community Art

1. DESCRIBE
- What kind of artwork is this? What is its subject?
- Is the artwork realistic or abstract?

2. ANALYZE
- How did the artist use shapes, form, or space? What kind of balance do you see?
- How did the artist add variety to this artwork?
- How do your eyes move around the artwork?

3. INTERPRET
- What do you think is the main idea of the artwork? Explain.
- What is the mood or message of the artwork?

4. EVALUATE
- Compare this artwork with others you have seen in your community.
- Would you want this artwork displayed in your community? Why or why not?

Harcourt

For the Student

Materials

PAPER	UNIT 1	2	3	4	5	6
butcher paper					●	
colored paper	●			●		
construction paper						●
newsprint			●			●
poster board	●	●		●		
sketchbook	●	●	●	●	●	●
white paper	●	●	●	●	●	●

PAINTING, DRAWING, PRINTMAKING	1	2	3	4	5	6
charcoal pencil		●				
colored pencils					●	
colored pencils or markers	●		●	●	●	
crayons		●	●			
eraser		●				
large and small paintbrushes					●	
markers	●					
markers or paint				●		
oil pastels		●	●		●	
paintbrushes	●	●		●		●
pencil	●	●	●	●	●	●
tempera paint	●	●		●	●	●

CLAY	1	2	3	4	5	6
clay			●			
craft stick			●			
plastic knife			●			
sharpened pencil or paper clip			●			

continued

OTHER MATERIALS

	UNIT 1	2	3	4	5	6
6 in. x 6 in. burlap pieces				●		
bar of soap			●			
books or magazines					●	
classroom objects		●				
colored yarn				●		
computer						●
decorative materials				●		
eraser		●				
foam brush				●		
foam tray				●		
found objects, such as yarn, paper clips, and rubber bands						●
glue		●		●	●	●
glue stick	●					
magazines	●	●			●	●
magazines or newspapers			●			
natural object such as plants or fruit	●					
objects with different textures		●				
paper plates		●				
ruler				●	●	
scissors		●		●	●	●
scrubber sponge			●			
shoe box lid						●
tissue		●				
tissue paper		●				
toothpick or paper clip			●			
water bowl	●	●		●	●	●
yarn or string		●				

FREE AND INEXPENSIVE MATERIALS

GENERAL CLASSROOM MATERIALS	WHERE TO FIND THEM
artificial flowers, leaves	fabric stores, department stores, craft stores
building materials (dowels, scrap lumber, wood shavings, bricks, screws, nuts, bolts)	contractors, builders, lumberyards
carpet scraps, foam	carpet manufacturers and retailers
fabric scraps, ribbon, yarn	fabric stores, craft stores
hangers	discount department stores, consignment shops, thrift stores
leaves, woodchips	local lawn services
magazines, catalogs, and newspapers	libraries, bookstores
packing supplies (Styrofoam™ noodles, cardboard scraps, bubble wrap, etc.)	storage and moving suppliers
shoe boxes	shoe stores, discount department stores
straws, napkins	fast food or restaurant chains
Styrofoam™	packing supply stores, hardware stores, retail stores
tile (damaged, samples, seconds)	hardware/paint stores, plumbers, tile manufacturers
wallpaper samples	home improvement stores, discount stores
watercolor paints, regular paints	art supply stores, school resources
wire	television repair shops, florists, hardware stores, plumbers, telephone/power companies
wood scraps	home improvement stores, lumberyards

TECHNOLOGY RESOURCES

Visit *The Learning Site*
www.harcourtschool.com

Link Bank for Teachers
- Links to museum sites
- Links to sites that offer free and inexpensive materials
- Links to key educational organizations

Alternative Planners

TEACHING BY MEDIA

The following chart shows the pages you can use if you wish to teach with the same media across different grades.*

MEDIA	PAGES GRADE 1	GRADE 2	GRADE 3	GRADE 4	GRADE 5
Clay	73, 89	87, 93	39, 127	105	71, 135
Colored Pencils/ Crayons/Markers	27, 35, 39, 75, 93, 109, 129	27, 29, 39, 59, 79, 109, 113, 135, 139	27, 29, 49, 59, 67, 89, 95, 99, 107, 139	31, 91, 125, 131, 155, 161, 165	31, 35, 65, 91, 105, 121, 141, 171, 195
Computers	– –	57	– –	201	201
Drawing Pencils/ Charcoal	93	39, 115, 133	29, 67, 89, 95, 99, 107, 139	75	– –
Fiber/Textiles	87, 129	75, 135	55, 73, 75, 119	121	185
Found Objects	79, 87, 95, 127	67, 75, 79, 95, 109, 119	135	191	111
Oil Pastels	49	55, 73, 109, 113, 115, 139	69, 109	81, 95, 151	151, 155
Paper/Foil/Tissue Paper	33, 59, 69, 93, 109, 127, 129, 135, 139	27, 29, 33, 35, 47, 67, 69, 75, 79, 107, 113, 127	33, 119, 133	51, 65, 125, 131, 195	121
Photographic Imagery	133	113	133	51, 161, 195	45
Tempera Paints	29, 47, 53, 55, 67, 107, 113, 115, 127	39, 47, 49, 53, 69, 99, 107, 119, 129, 133	35, 47, 53, 79, 93, 113, 115, 129, 135	35, 41, 45, 61, 71, 125, 135, 141, 171, 181, 185, 191	41, 131
Watercolor Paints	99, 119, 135	59, 99, 107, 139	59, 87	71	51, 61, 81, 95, 101, 125, 161, 165

* See also **Challenge Activities**, *Teacher Resource Book*.

TEACHING BY ELEMENTS AND PRINCIPLES

The following chart shows the pages you can use if you wish to teach the same elements and principles across different grades.

ELEMENTS & PRINCIPLES	PAGES GRADE 1	GRADE 2	GRADE 3	GRADE 4	GRADE 5
Balance	106–107, 108–109, 110–111, 120	112–113, 114–115, 116–117, 118–119	106–107, 108–109, 112–113, 120–121	122–125, 128–131, 132–135, 138–141, 159, 162–165	148–151, 152–155, 158–161, 162–165
Color	42–43, 46–47, 48–49, 52–53, 54–55, 58–59, 60	46–47, 48–49, 50–51, 52–53, 54–55, 58–59	30–31, 46–47, 48–49, 50–51, 52–53, 60–61, 72–73, 94–95, 98–99, 106–107, 114–115	38–41, 42–45, 48–51, 58–61, 68–71, 152–155, 159, 183, 193–194, 198–199	38–41, 42–45, 48–51, 98–101, 148–151, 158–161, 162–165, 168–171, 178–181, 183–185, 188–191, 193, 200
Emphasis	102–103, 112–113, 114–115, 118–119, 120	106–107, 108–109, 110–111	94–95, 98–99, 100–101	78–81, 182–185	88–91, 158–161, 163–164, 169, 194
Form	82–83, 86–87, 88–89, 92–93, 94–95, 96–97, 100	86–87, 88–89, 90–91, 92–93, 94–95, 96–97	38–39, 40–41, 98–99, 134–135	102–105, 108–111	72–75, 78–81, 132–135
Line	26–27, 28–29, 30–31, 32–33, 36–37, 40	26–27, 28–29, 58–59	26–27, 28–29, 30–31, 40–41, 72–73, 92–93, 94–95, 106–107	28–31, 62, 149, 153–154, 183, 193–194, 198	28–31, 32–35, 58–59, 102–105, 130, 162
Movement	28–29, 68–69	28–29, 72–73	68–69, 78–79, 80–81	158–161, 168–171	93–94, 163, 192–195
Pattern	58–59, 62–63, 66–67, 68–69, 70–71, 76–77, 80	66–67, 68–69, 70–71, 72–73, 74–75, 78–79	72–73, 74–75, 77, 79, 80–81	118–121, 128–131	58–61, 68–71
Proportion	– –	98–99, 108–109	66–67, 80–81	88–91, 92–95	92–95, 103, 119, 124, 125
Rhythm	62–63, 66–67, 68–69, 76–77, 80	72–73	128–129, 132–133, 140–141	98–101	178–185, 189–191, 192–195
Shape	32–33, 34–35, 36–37, 38–39, 40, 86–87	32–33, 34–35, 36–37, 38–39, 86–87	30–31, 32–33, 34–35, 36–37, 40–41, 72–73, 74–75, 92–93, 94–95, 112–113, 126–127	32–35, 48–51, 79, 92–95, 99, 183, 198–199	28–31, 32–34, 58, 62–65, 148–151, 152–155
Space	94–95, 96–97, 98–99, 100	88–89, 92–93, 94–95, 96–97, 98–99	86–87, 88–89, 91, 92–93, 97, 100–101	102–105, 148–151, 152, 155	68–71, 89–91, 92–95, 98–101, 103, 164
Texture	62–63, 72–73, 74–75, 78–79, 80	74–75, 78–79	54–55, 58–59, 60–61, 94–95, 118–119	62–65, 72–75, 160, 198, 200	129–131, 135, 198
Unity	122–123, 132–133, 136–137, 138–139, 140	126–127, 128–129, 130–131, 132–133, 134–135, 138–139	114–115, 118–119, 120–121	158–161, 162–165, 168–171, 178–181, 188–190, 192	152–155
Value	42–43, 52–53, 54–55, 60	52–53, 58–59	52–53, 60–61, 115	58–61, 62–65, 68–71, 72–75, 78, 183, 200	38–41, 48–49, 129, 159, 168–171, 199
Variety	122–123, 126–127, 128–129, 130–131, 136–137, 140	132–133, 134–135, 138–139	126–127, 129, 132–133, 134–135, 138–139, 140–141	178–181, 182–185, 188–191, 192–195, 198–201	178–181, 182–185, 189–191

These pages provide additional information about the artists and art history terms in this grade level.

Abbott, Meredith Brooks (1938–)

American landscape painter whose works combine Impressionism and Realism to produce scenes that are somewhat more true to life than those of the traditional Impressionists. Abbott was born in rural California and raised in a family of artists. She trained in California and New York and now works from a studio on a California avocado and lemon ranch. Although she also paints portraits and studio still lifes, Abbott does much of her work *en plein air,* or outdoors. Her still-life paintings are characterized by rich, vibrant colors and an array of textures, while her landscapes depict truth and spontaneity. Abbott belongs to a group of artists who paint pictures of scenic areas that are being taken over by development, in hopes of raising awareness about the importance of nature preservation. *Images by this artist: Student Edition p. 58.*

Abstract Expressionism
Mid-twentieth-century extension of abstract art characterized by an emotional approach to artistic concepts. Abstract art consists of colors and forms for their own sake, rather than to depict reality. Abstract Expressionism flourished in New York City from the mid-1940s to the mid-1950s and influenced the development of art in Europe. Painters practice Abstract Expressionism to express personal emotions and to implement unstructured techniques rather than conventional structured composition. They use different techniques to emphasize color and the physical quality of paint to express emotion in an abstract composition. Painting techniques include making sweeping, slashing brushstrokes, dripping or spilling paint directly onto the canvas, and spreading large areas of flat, thin paint over the canvas, which is typically large. The most prominent Abstract Expressionists include Jackson Pollock and Willem de Kooning.

Albers, Josef (1888–1976)
German-born painter, art teacher, and color theorist. As a young man in Germany, Albers studied art while working as an elementary school teacher. In 1920, he enrolled in the then-new Bauhaus School. He was soon teaching at the Bauhaus, which became Germany's most important school of design. When the school closed in 1933, Albers and his wife immigrated to the United States, where he continued to teach and experiment with painting styles. He is best known for his series of paintings titled *Homage to the Square,* begun in 1950 and continued until his death. The works are completely abstract color-field studies of overlapping solid-colored squares. Albers was the first living artist to receive a solo exhibition at the Metropolitan Museum of Art in New York City. *Images by this artist: Student Edition p. 60.*

DID YOU KNOW?

Josef Albers was the longest-serving member of the Bauhaus, as well as one of its most popular instructors. When the Bauhaus closed, he taught at Black Mountain College in North Carolina and also at Yale. He maintained his popularity as a teacher in the United States, just as he did in Europe.

Ashcan School
Term loosely applied to early twentieth-century American artists who portrayed ordinary aspects of city life in their paintings. Ashcan School painters rebelled against the influence of French Impressionism and the sentimental subjects painted by nineteenth-century American painters. They chose to paint city scenes of ordinary people in commonplace settings. Painters used a dark, somber palette. The Ashcan School style can be found in the works of William James Glackens and Maurice Prendergast.

Balla, Giacomo [BAHL•lah, JAH•koh•moh]
(1871–1958) Italian painter, sculptor, and designer who was one of the pioneers of Futurism, an artistic style concerned with the representation of light and movement. Born in Turin, Italy, Balla taught himself to paint and sculpt. He became interested in the effects of light and movement in his paintings. Balla's first Futuristic painting, *Dynamism of a Dog on a Leash,* depicts the effects of a dog running, illustrating the movement of the leash, tail, and legs simultaneously. *Images by this artist: Student Edition p. 100. See also* **Futurism.**

Bannister, Edward Mitchell

(1828–1901) Canadian-born American artist who became one of the first African American painters to be recognized as an important landscape artist. Bannister was born in St. Andrews, New Brunswick. He was one of the first African Americans to take art classes at the Lowell Institute of Art in Lowell, Massachusetts. There, he painted portraits, landscapes, and religious pictures. He also took an interest in photography as an art form. Bannister moved to Rhode Island, where he continued to paint landscapes that reflected the Barbizon style, a school of art that focused on nature and its changing moods. Bannister founded the Providence Art Club, which later became the Rhode Island School of Design. He was the first African American to win a national art award—a bronze medal at the 1876 World Centennial Exhibition in Philadelphia for his painting *Under the Oaks. Images by this artist: Art Print 1.*

DID YOU KNOW?

Edward Mitchell Bannister's interest in art developed as a child. His mother encouraged him to pursue his art and, at the young age of ten, he created his first watercolor paintings. Before gaining recognition as an artist, he worked as a cook, a sailor, and a barber.

Barnbaum, Bruce (1943–) American

environmental and architectural photographer. Barnbaum was a mathematical physicist and hobby photographer until 1970, when he decided to pursue photography full time. He became known for his unusual landscapes, shot close-in or from angles that render the subject almost abstract, and he used darkroom techniques to further dramatize the swirling lines and contours of his images. Barnbaum is an ardent environmentalist who, in 1974, won the Sierra Club's Ansel Adams Award for Photography and Conservation. He also teaches and has published several books, including one that pairs architectural photographs with piano music. He lives and works in Granite Falls, Washington. *Images by this artist: Student Edition p. 72.*

Baroque Term used to describe a style that developed

mainly in Italy around 1580 and influenced many forms of art in Europe for more than a century. The Baroque movement spread to western Europe and Latin America, undergoing modifications as it migrated. Artists rebelled against the restrained, orderly, and symmetrically balanced art of the Renaissance period. Painters and sculptors used dramatic details and ornate forms to convey grandeur, realism, illusion, movement, and emotion. Architects designed buildings to create an illusion of great space. The Baroque style can be found in the works of Giovanni Lorenzo Bernini, Caravaggio, and Diego Velázquez.

Benton, Thomas Hart (1889–1975)

Painter and muralist who was part of the American Regionalist movement of the 1930s. Benton, who was born on a farm in Neosho, Missouri, studied for a year at the Art Institute of Chicago and then in Paris and New York. His early works were abstracts, but by 1920, he had rejected modernism and begun painting straightforward, recognizable scenes based on American history, daily life, folktales, and song lyrics. He used strong colors and dark, dramatic outlines, depicting people and objects with distorted, almost cartoon-like features. Benton received commissions to paint numerous murals for public buildings, including the New School for Social Research in New York City, the Missouri State Capitol in Jefferson City, and the Truman Presidential Museum & Library in Independence, Missouri. He settled in Kansas City, Missouri, in the mid-1930s and directed the Kansas City Art Institute from 1935 to 1941. Benton, who also produced lithographs and wrote books and essays, painted from his Kansas City studio until his death and is said to have died with a paintbrush in his hand. *Images by this artist: Student Edition p. 26.*

Bierstadt, Albert [BEER•stat] (1830–1902)

German-born American painter known for his landscapes of the American West. Bierstadt was born near Düsseldorf and moved with his parents to New Bedford, Massachusetts, as a child. Little is known of his early life or artistic training. In the mid-1850s, Bierstadt went back to Düsseldorf for three years of art training. He returned to the United States and joined an expedition surveying the western frontier, where he drew sketches and painted small studies of the spectacular scenery. When Bierstadt returned to his New York studio, the dramatic, oversized landscapes he created made him one of the most popular and highly paid painters in America. His luminous scenes shaped the way many people viewed the American West. Bierstadt's work became less popular late in his career, and he eventually declared bankruptcy. The 1960s saw a renewed interest in his sketches and more realistic paintings. *Images by this artist: Student Edition p. 152.*

Biggers, John (1924–2001) American painter, sculptor, illustrator, and educator known for his murals depicting African and African American historical and cultural themes. Biggers was born in Gastonia, North Carolina. His influences include American Regionalist painters, Mexican muralists, writers and artists of the Harlem Renaissance, and painter and art professor Viktor Lowenfeld. Lowenfeld, who taught Biggers at Hampton Institute in Virginia and at Pennsylvania State University, encouraged his students to explore their heritage as it was reflected in African art. In 1949, Biggers went to Houston, Texas, to launch an art program at what is now Texas Southern University. Many of his murals are on walls at the university and in other public buildings in Texas. In 1983, he retired from teaching and began to devote all of his energy to his art. *Images by this artist: Student Edition p. 143.*

Blue Rider group (Blaue Reiter) Organization
whose goal was to promote freedom of expression through an array of colors and distorted forms. The Blue Rider group, founded by Wassily Kandinsky and Franz Marc, was based in Munich, Germany, from 1911 to 1914. The name of the group evolved from the founders' favorite color, combined with the masculine characteristics of knights and horses, the latter of which were featured in Kandinsky's and Marc's artworks. These artists were influenced by Futurism, Fauvism, and Cubism, and much of their work was abstract. The Blue Rider group paved the way for German Expressionism and abstract art.

Borglum, Gutzon [BAWR•gluhm, GUHT•suhn] (1867–1941) American painter and sculptor best known for his huge-scale public carvings, particularly the Mount Rushmore National Memorial in South Dakota. The child of Danish immigrants, Borglum was born in Idaho and raised in Nebraska. After studying art in San Francisco and Paris, he established himself as a painter and sculptor in England. By 1902, he was living and working in New York City. He made a name for himself with large public works, including the six-ton head of Abraham Lincoln in the Capitol Rotunda in Washington, D.C. In 1916, Borglum began work on a Confederate memorial carving on Stone Mountain, near Atlanta, Georgia. He completed the head of Robert E. Lee in 1924 but quit the project over disputes with its patrons. The memorial was redesigned and completed by others. Three years later, Borglum was commissioned to carve Mount Rushmore into another giant memorial. He invented new

methods using dynamite and pneumatic jackhammers to sculpt 60-foot-high heads of George Washington, Thomas Jefferson, Abraham Lincoln, and Theodore Roosevelt. The project took fourteen years to complete, and Borglum died during its final months. His son Lincoln Borglum, who had also worked at Mount Rushmore since 1933, completed the memorial's last details. *Images by this artist: Student Edition p. 102.*

Brauner, Victor (1903–1966) Romanian-born painter,
sculptor, and ceramicist. Brauner attended the School of Fine Arts in Bucharest and became interested in Surrealist painting. In 1930, he moved to Paris and became part of the Surrealist movement. During World War II, when painting materials were scarce, Brauner began making his candle drawings. He painted with coffee or walnut stain on relief drawings made with wax. His best-known work is a sculpture titled *Wolftable*. It depicts a wolf's head and tail mounted on a table that forms the animal's body and legs. *Images by this artist: Student Edition p. 183. See also* **Surrealism.**

Bronzino, Agnolo [brawn•DZEE•noh, AHN•yoh•loh] (1503–1572) Italian painter best known for his portraits of Italian nobility. Bronzino spent nearly half his life as court painter to the Medici family in Florence. His Mannerist-style portraits are described as sophisticated, refined, and unemotional, and they expressed a chilly austerity that his sitters admired. Bronzino's portraits were extremely popular and influenced European portraiture for hundreds of years. *Images by this artist: Student Edition p. 89.*

Caillebotte, Gustave [ky•yuh•BAWT, goos•TAHV] (1848–1894) French painter best known for the financial help that he gave the Impressionist painters. Born in Paris into a wealthy family, Caillebotte trained to be an engineer. However, he changed his mind and decided to study art in Paris. In 1874, Caillebotte joined the Impressionist group and participated in their exhibitions. Later, he organized these exhibitions. In his own Impressionist paintings, Caillebotte painted scenes of everyday life in Paris. His painting titled *Paris Street, Rainy Day* became very popular. Caillebotte left instructions that sixty-seven of his paintings were to be given to the French government when he died. They now hang in the Musée d'Orsay in Paris. *Images by this artist: Student Edition p. 144. See also* **Impressionism.**

Chukran, Bobbi A. (1956–) American printmaker, writer, and mixed-media folk artist. Chukran was born in Fort Worth, Texas, and is largely self-taught. She specializes in semi-abstract collages, aiming to bring an array of patterns, textures, and color to her art. Chukran is inspired by the wildlife and nature that surround her ranch. One of her hobbies is caring for her antique rose and herb gardens. *Images by this artist: Student Edition p. 50.*

Cicco, Angelo di (1953–) Italian anesthesiologist and intensive care doctor who enjoys painting in his free time. Di Cicco's art is characterized by thick lines, rich forms, and vibrant colors, giving it an almost childlike, yet mysterious, quality. He uses various computer programs to enhance his artwork. Di Cicco pursues his art because he feels it allows him to express his love and appreciation of life. *Images by this artist: Student Edition p. 198.*

Clive, John London-based digital artist who trained at Ealing College of Art in London. Clive uses computers to manipulate imagery and to simulate interactions of color, form, light, and texture. His artworks are recognized for their unique surfaces. Clive has worked as a consultant and special-effects designer for prominent filmmakers, including Mel Gibson. He has won international awards as a commercial, film, and theater director, including the Canon Award in the Canon Digital Creators Competition in 2002. *Images by this artist: Student Edition p. 200.*

Cornell, Joseph (1903–1972) American collage artist and sculptor, best known for his assemblages of found objects in glass-fronted boxes. Cornell was born in Nyack, New York. He began his working life as a textile salesman and taught himself about art by studying reviews and going to exhibitions. Cornell lost a sales job in 1931, the same year he began frequenting a gallery that showcased Surrealist art. A year later, he exhibited collages in a Surrealist show at the same gallery. Cornell soon began assembling his shadow boxes, which contained arrangements of small objects with pieces of engravings and photographs. He also designed textiles, made films, and produced magazine layouts and illustrations. *Images by this artist: Student Edition pp. 80, 190.*

DID YOU KNOW?

Joseph Cornell designed layouts and created illustrations for famous magazines, including *Harper's Bazaar, Vogue,* and *House and Garden.* He also wrote articles for the publications *View* and *Dance Index.* However, he worked as a freelancer, so that he was able to focus primarily on his art.

Corot, Jean Baptiste Camille [kaw•ROH, ZHAHN baht•TEEST ka•MEE•yuh] (1796–1875) French painter whose interpretation of certain characteristics of nature—including light, atmosphere, temperature, and mood—created a bridge between classical landscape painting and what became Impressionism. Corot was born in Paris into a well-to-do family. He painted in relative obscurity until 1846, when a government award led to commercial success. His most successful paintings, sometimes called "landscape poems," are dreamy, nostalgic, and highly decorative scenes with feathery trees and hazy, indefinite features. Late in his career, he also produced portraits and figure studies for his own amusement. After his death, the rediscovery of those works plus oil studies he had painted directly from nature enhanced his reputation. *Images by this artist: Student Edition p. 148.*

Cubism Movement in twentieth-century painting and sculpture developed jointly by Pablo Picasso and Georges Braque from around 1907 to 1914. Cubists reacted against the Impressionists' use of color and their style of painting from a single viewpoint. Cubists paint a subject as it appears to them rather than paint an imitation. The Cubist style is divided into two categories—analytical and synthetic. In analytical Cubism, painters use monochromatic colors and fragmented geometric shapes to place subjects in different presentations in a composition. Synthetic Cubists use color and the technique of collage to give texture and illusion to the painting. Other artists who have worked in the Cubist style include Robert Delaunay and Juan Gris.

Dada Twentieth-century artistic and literary movement originating in Switzerland in 1916 that protested traditional values and pretension in the art world and focused on the absurd. It flourished from 1916 to 1922 in Switzerland, New York, and Berlin. Dadaists were not united by a common style. They organized to protest World War I, traditional art, and the established values of society. Artists practiced Dada to shock and provoke the public with absurd and illogical works of art. Dadaists abandoned traditional forms of painting and sculpture and replaced them with collage, photomontage, objects, and ready-mades, or items chosen by the artist and put into an artistic context. They believed that art should be a group activity and involve accident and chance, rather than fine materials and craftsmanship. The Dada style can be found in the works of Kurt Schwitters, Man Ray, and Marcel Duchamp.

Dalí, Salvador [DAH•lee] (1904–1989) Spanish painter, illustrator, sculptor, writer, and filmmaker renowned for his Surrealist style that mixed reality with fantasy. Dalí was born in Figueras, Spain. He studied art at the San Fernando Royal Academy of Fine Arts in Madrid. Dalí reportedly told his professors that he knew more about art than they did. His flamboyant behavior and unconventional lifestyle became his trademark. Dalí developed his own artistic style after reading Freud's writings about the subconscious. He also became part of the French Surrealist movement, whose members painted images of dreams and nightmares into realistic scenes. Later in life, Dalí adopted a style of the Renaissance masters, painting historical and religious themes. *Images by this artist: Student Edition pp. 83, 174, 184; Art Print 16. See also* **Surrealism.**

DID YOU KNOW?

Dalí had trouble with some everyday situations. For example, he did not know how to count money, he was afraid of germs, and he feared all types of transportation except taxis.

Degas, Edgar [duh•GAH] (1834–1917) French painter, sculptor, and draftsman known as the painter of dancers. Degas came from a wealthy Parisian family. He originally studied law, but at the age of twenty, he convinced his father to support his interest in art. In 1861, he met Edouard Manet, who introduced him to the Impressionists. Like the Impressionists, Degas painted scenes that seemed spontaneous and unplanned. Unlike these artists, however, he painted only indoors and did not work directly from nature; his work also reflected his intense training and his mastery of drawing the human form. He may be best known for his scenes of female ballet dancers. When Degas's eyesight began to fail in the 1880s, he turned to creating bold, simple pastels, primarily of women, and wax sculptures of dancers and horses. *The Little 14-Year-Old Dancer,* perhaps Degas's most recognized sculpture, was the only one exhibited during his lifetime. For the last twenty years of his life, Degas was almost completely blind and lived in seclusion in Paris. *Images by this artist: Student Edition p. 98.*

Depardon, Raymond (1942–) French-born photographer who specializes in advertising and filmmaking. Depardon, who is largely self-taught, has enjoyed much success. He has directed numerous films since 1969, won a Pulitzer Prize in 1977, and has been nominated for an Academy Award. Depardon has a deep love for the Middle East and the desert, which serve as recurrent themes in some of his later work. People all over the world enjoy Depardon's color photographs of the farm where he grew up and the black-and-white photographic diary of his journeys in Africa. *Images by this artist: Student Edition p. 78.*

Duncanson, Robert S. (1821?–1872) African American painter best known for his landscapes. Duncanson is thought to be the first African American artist to make a living by painting as well as the first to become internationally known. Duncanson was born in New York, but was educated in Canada. As an adult, Duncanson returned to the United States and taught himself to paint by producing portraits and copying works by the Hudson River School of landscape artists. Duncanson traveled widely and became known in Europe and Canada as well as in England and Scotland, where he spent the Civil War years. *Images by this artist: Student Edition p. 24.*

Dunton, W. Herbert (1878–1936) American illustrator and painter of Old West genre scenes. Dunton was born in Augusta, Maine. By age eighteen, he was a successful illustrator, drawing for a variety of popular books and magazines. He studied briefly in Boston and New York City and traveled west in the summers to sketch, hunt, and work as a ranch hand. By his early forties, "Buck" Dunton was able to retire permanently to what had been his summer studio in Taos, New Mexico, and devote himself to painting. The untamed West was his favorite theme, and he painted western landscapes, animals, and scenes of the rapidly-disappearing cowboy life. *Images by this artist: Student Edition p. 136.*

Escher, M. C. [ESH•er] (1898–1972) Dutch printmaker and graphic artist known for his reality-altering illustrations. Escher was born in Leeuwarden, the Netherlands. His early works include bold but mostly naturalistic landscape and townscape scenes. Escher's signature style began to develop after a visit to Spain, where he was fascinated by patterns in mosaic-covered buildings. Soon Escher was producing patterns of stylized, interlocking images of animals that move from two-dimensional to three-dimensional areas within the same space. He also produced illustrations of imaginary buildings with impossible physical characteristics, such as never-ending staircases that carry people both up and down at the same time and in the same direction, and curved walls that are simultaneously concave and convex. Escher's work fascinated mathematicians and psychologists who studied the effects of visual perception, but he remained mostly unknown until the 1960s, when a book and a series of exhibitions brought his work to the attention of the general public. *Images by this artist: Student Edition p. 73.*

Escobar, Marisol [es•koh•VAR, mah•ree•SOHL] (1930–) French-born American sculptor known for her satirical, life-sized wooden figures. Born in Paris to Venezuelan parents, Marisol (who uses only her first name) spent much of her childhood in Los Angeles. At age sixteen, she took drawing classes at the Jepson School in Los Angeles. She also studied art in Paris and then moved to New York in 1950, where she studied at the Art Students League and the Hans Hofmann School. After Marisol developed an interest in pre-Columbian art, she abandoned traditional painting and began to produce terra-cotta, wood, and bronze sculptures. During the 1960s, Marisol associated with Roy Lichtenstein and Andy Warhol—members of the Pop Art movement. However, unlike that of other Pop artists, Marisol's work focuses primarily on fictitious and ordinary human subjects, rather than on commercial objects. She also began sculpting portraits of world leaders and other famous people, including President Lyndon Johnson, Queen Elizabeth II, and Bob Hope. The plaster faces, hands, and legs on Marisol's wooden carvings were often cast from her own face and limbs. *Images by this artist: Student Edition pp. 106–107; Art Print 8. See also* **Pop Art.**

Estes, Richard (1932–) American Photorealist painter. Estes was born in Kewanee, Illinois, but spent most of his childhood in Chicago. He studied at the Art Institute of Chicago in the mid-1950s before moving to New York, where he worked as a graphic artist. He is renowned for works that depict anonymous New York City buildings in a super-sharp, photographic style. Estes paints from photographs, and from them he combines details to depict more than the human eye can actually see—the same building from two different directions at once, for example. He pays special attention to reflections in shiny surfaces. For instance, a viewer might see objects behind a window, the surface of the glass itself, and reflections in the glass of objects across the street, all at the same time. Estes continues to paint and make prints from a studio in Maine. *Images by this artist: Art Print 13. See also* **Photorealism.**

DID YOU KNOW?

Upon completing his art studies, Richard Estes worked in the advertising and publishing industries in New York and Spain. He worked in these fields for ten years, before establishing himself as an artist.

Expressionism Late nineteenth- and early twentieth-century artistic movement that is reflected in European art, film, music, literature, and theater of the time. Artists practiced Expressionism to convey emotion, in contrast with Realism. Painters use jarring colors, rapid brushwork, and jagged lines to express emotions such as joy, sadness, fear, or horror. Expressionism can be found in the works of artists such as Vincent van Gogh, Wassily Kandinsky, Franz Marc, and Paul Klee.

Fauvism Early twentieth-century artistic movement originating in France. Fauvism flourished in Paris from 1905 to 1907. It is considered the first avant-garde European art movement. Like the Impressionists, Fauvists painted scenes directly from nature, but they rejected the way Impressionists used color. Fauvist painters use pure, brilliant, luminous colors straight from the tube and then aggressively apply them to the canvas in broad, flat areas. They also use rough brushstrokes, thick outlines, and contrasting hues, and they often leave areas of the canvas exposed. Painters practice Fauvism to create a feeling of space and light and to express personal feelings through the vigorous application of color. The Fauvist style can be found in the work of Henri Matisse.

Feininger, Lyonel (1871–1956) American painter who combined the artistic styles of Cubism and Expressionism. Feininger was born in New York City but moved to Germany when he was a teenager. He took an art class in Hamburg and studied Cubism in Paris, developing a style of painting that used spatial exaggeration and bold colors. In 1912, Feininger became affiliated with the Blue Rider group, an association of German Expressionist artists. Feininger painted landscapes, scenes of urban life, and the architecture of Manhattan. *Images by this artist: Student Edition p. 99. See also* **Blue Rider group.**

Figari, Pedro [fee•GAH•ree] (1861–1938) Uruguayan painter who was born in Montevideo. Figari is best known for documenting the geography, gaucho lifestyle, celebrations, and rituals of the black community in Uruguay. He received his law degree in 1886 and then went on to study art in Europe, where he was interested in the works of Post-Impressionist painters. On his return to Uruguay, he established an art school and became a member of Parliament. Beginning in 1921, Figari devoted himself to painting full time. He painted with oil on cardboard and created figurative compositions as arrangements of color. *Images by this artist: Student Edition p. 133.*

Folk art Natural art style that aims to convey simplicity in art while expressing the beliefs and interests that a group of people have in common. Folk art has been created in numerous countries for hundreds of years, but American folk art gained popularity from 1780 to 1860. It represents everyday life and includes pottery, carving, needlework, weaving, quilting, and other decorative art forms. Folk artists are often self-taught. This art style can be found in the works of Grandma Moses and Horace Pippin.

Foster, Norman (1935–) British architect known for his high-tech modern office buildings, public spaces, and transportation centers in locations around the world. Foster's buildings are characterized by soaring interior spaces, glass walls, and visible metal skeletons. Foster was born in Manchester, England, and trained at the Manchester University School of Architecture and at Yale University. His works and projects include the Millennium Bridge in London, Stansted Airport, and the Great Court of the British Museum. Foster was knighted in 1990 and received the Pritzker Prize—the architectural equivalent of the Nobel Prize—in 1999. *Images by this artist: Student Edition p. 163.*

Frankenthaler, Helen (1928–) American painter who was born and raised in New York City. Frankenthaler studied under respected artists in high school, at Bennington College in Vermont, and privately afterward. Influenced by the work of the Abstract Impressionists, especially Jackson Pollock, Frankenthaler became part of a "second generation" of Abstract Expressionists. In a signature technique called staining or color-stain painting, she pours thinned-down paint directly onto an unprimed canvas. The technique creates overlapping, semitransparent fields of color, eliminating paint texture as an element of the composition while emphasizing the texture of the canvas. Her works are abstract, but they often suggest landscape scenes. Frankenthaler had her first one-woman show in 1951, and her work has been highly praised for more than fifty years. *Images by this artist: Student Edition p. 179. See also* **Abstract Expressionism.**

Futurism Early twentieth-century artistic movement originating in Italian art, architecture, literature, and photography in 1909. It started when Italian writer Filippo Tommaso Marinetti published a statement declaring that the art of the past no longer had meaning. He called for innovation in art and promoted speed, power, and movement. Painters use the Futurist style to show motion by depicting multiple images of moving objects in different positions. Their paintings contain vibrant colors, fragmented forms, and vigorous diagonals that often convey a sense of action. The Futurist style can be found in the work of Giacomo Balla.

Gauguin, Paul [goh•GAN] (1848–1903) French painter whose innovative style had a profound influence on the development of modern art. Gauguin was born in Paris. By young adulthood, he had lived in Lima, Peru; spent six years sailing the world in a merchant marine service; and lost both his parents. Between 1871 and 1883, Gauguin lived a typical middle-class life in Paris. He worked as a stockbroker, married, had five children, and developed an interest in collecting art and painting. Gauguin bought works by the major Impressionists, including Edouard Manet, Claude Monet, Camille Pissarro, and Pierre-Auguste Renoir, and he worked with Pissarro on his painting and drawing skills. In 1883, Gauguin made painting his full-time work. He spent much of the next five years with a group of experimental artists in the Brittany region of northwestern France. In 1891, Gauguin left France on a government grant to paint the people and customs of Tahiti. Except for a two-year period when health problems forced him back to France, Gauguin spent the rest of his time living and working in Tahiti and the nearby Marquesas Islands. Three years after his death, a Paris exhibition of nearly 300 of his paintings brought his work to the attention of a new generation of artists, including Edvard Munch, Henri Matisse, and Pablo Picasso. Gauguin's bold use of color and rejection of Realism inspired both the Fauvist and Expressionist movements. *Images by this artist: Student Edition p. 48.*

DID YOU KNOW?

In 1888, Paul Gauguin spent two months in Arles, France, where he worked with Vincent van Gogh. The two appreciated each other's art but quarreled bitterly about almost everything else.

Glackens, William James (1870–1938) American painter and illustrator. Glackens was born in Philadelphia and studied at the Pennsylvania Academy of the Fine Arts. Early in his career, he worked as a newspaper illustrator. Glackens was one of the original members of a group of urban Realist painters who became known as the Ashcan School. Glackens, however, was also drawn to the bright, festive colors of the Impressionists, and instead of the gritty Realism of the Ashcan artists, enjoyed depicting colorful, upbeat scenes of middle-class urbanites enjoying themselves in cafés and parks. Glackens also became a leader in the American arts community. He helped organize the celebrated 1913 Armory Show in New York City, for example, and was elected the first president of the Society of Independent Artists. *Images by this artist: Student Edition p. 146.*

Gogh, Vincent van *See* Van Gogh, Vincent.

Goodacre, Glenna (1939–) American sculptor renowned for her creation of the *Vietnam Women's Memorial,* honoring the women who served in the Vietnam War. Goodacre was born in Texas. Early in her career, she was known for her bronze sculptures and portraits of children in action. Goodacre created the obverse, or head-side, design of the

Sacagawea gold dollar that debuted in 2000. *Images by this artist: Student Edition p. 102. See also* **Rogers, Thomas.**

Graziani, Sante [grahtz•ee•AHN•ee] (1920–) American painter and muralist. Graziani is best known for his murals, painted on the walls of public buildings in the northeastern and midwestern United States, of images connected to local history or culture. He was born in Cleveland, Ohio, and studied at the Cleveland Institute of Art and the Yale University School of Art and Architecture. He has been an influential teacher throughout his career, especially at the School of the Worcester Art Museum in Worcester, Massachusetts. *Images by this artist: Student Edition p. 140.*

Gris, Juan [GREES] (1887–1927) Spanish painter, sculptor, stage designer, graphic artist, and major figure in Cubism. Gris was born in Madrid, the thirteenth of fourteen children. When he was about eighteen, he moved to Paris, where one of his neighbors was the young Pablo Picasso. For four years, Gris supported himself by producing illustrations for newspapers and magazines. He did not begin painting seriously until 1910, but by 1912, he was recognized as a leading painter of the Cubist movement. Between 1913 and 1914, Gris developed his own style of Cubism, called Synthetic Cubism. Whereas Picasso and other Cubists started with objects and broke them down into shapes, Gris started with shapes and transformed them into recognizable objects. Gris was plagued by a variety of health problems. He died in France at the age of forty. *Images by this artist: Student Edition p. 93. See also* **Cubism.**

Gunter, Jack American egg tempera painter from Washington State. Gunter has also worked in photography, ceramics, and pottery and exhibits his art in a museum-like setting at the Pilchuck School near his home. In 1995, he co-created a panoramic mural that portrayed turn-of-the-century Stanwood in a fun, humorous way. This commemorative masterpiece measures 240 feet long by 24 feet high. *Images by this artist: Student Edition p. 150.*

Haas, Richard

Haas, Richard [HAHS] (1936–) American muralist, printmaker, and architect who was born in Spring Green, Wisconsin. Haas has created more than 120 murals and is renowned for his *trompe l'oeil* paintings that deceive the eye. His large-scale murals consist of architectural details, including the illusion of windows. At a young age, Haas moved to Chicago, where he was inspired by its modern architecture. Among his works is a series of perspective boxes that are three-dimensional replicas of interiors previously illustrated by famous artists, such as Jan Vermeer's *The Artist's Studio.* Haas currently lives and works in New York. *Images by this artist: Student Edition p. 137.*

Hassam, Frederick Childe

(1859–1935) American painter and printmaker known for Impressionistic scenes of life in New York City and the New England coast and countryside. Hassam was born in Dorchester, Massachusetts. Trained as a wood-block engraver, he supported himself by illustrating books while he developed his painting skills. He studied in Boston and in Paris, where he incorporated the short brushstrokes and bright colors of the French Impressionists into his work. Hassam achieved success by the late 1880s and was able to support himself solely on the sale of his popular paintings and later, his prints. *Images by this artist: Student Edition p. 138.*

Hiroshige, Ando (other first names also

include Ichiryusai or Ichiryusu or Utagawa) [hee•roh•shee•gay] (1797–1858) Japanese painter and printmaker, renowned for his full-color landscape prints. Hiroshige was born in Edo, Japan (present-day Tokyo). As a child, Hiroshige liked to sketch. The prints of the great artist Katsushika Hokusai inspired him to become an artist. From 1830 to 1844, he traveled throughout Japan, creating a series of landscape prints. His most successful print series, titled *Fifty-three Stages on the Tokaido,* was made from sketches about life along the Tokaido highway connecting the ancient Japanese cities of Edo and Kyoto. Hiroshige's technique of using sweeping brushstrokes to suggest vast landscapes influenced the Impressionist movement. His prints, seen by many Europeans along with the prints of other mid-nineteenth-century Japanese landscape printmakers, profoundly affected Westerners' views of Japanese life. *Images by this artist: Student Edition p. 173.*

Hockney, David

Hockney, David (1937–) British painter, printmaker, photographer, and stage designer, considered one of the most popular and versatile artists of the twentieth century. He studied at the Bradford College of Art from 1953 to 1957 and became an international success as a painter while still a postgraduate student at the Royal College of Art in London. He was associated with the Pop Art movement early in his career because of the lighthearted mood of his early works and their references to consumer goods and popular culture. Hockney's mature style is spare, unfussy, naturalistic, and saturated with intense color. He visited Los Angeles, California, often in the 1960s and 1970s, and he made it his permanent home in 1978. Scenes from his life there—including portraits of himself and his friends and surrounding landscapes with swimming pools and exotic plants—are common subjects of his work. *Images by this artist: Student Edition p. 79.*

DID YOU KNOW?

During the 1960s, much of David Hockney's work was a tribute to artists whom he admired, including Henri Matisse and Pablo Picasso. Hockney was an inspiration to others as well, and in 1988, he received an honorary doctorate from the University of Aberdeen, Scotland.

Homer, Winslow

Homer, Winslow (1836–1910) American painter, illustrator, and lithographer, known as the era's leading representative of Realism. Homer was born in Boston and grew up in Cambridge, Massachusetts. Both parents encouraged his interest in art. In 1855, he became a lithographer's apprentice; he then moved on to work as a freelance magazine illustrator. In 1859, the magazine *Harper's Weekly* hired Homer and eventually made him an artist-correspondent covering the Civil War. He traveled south with the Union army, making illustrations of the daily routine of camp life. After the war, Homer focused on oil painting. His early oils were inspired by his wartime illustrations and were somber in color. His masterpiece from the period, titled *Prisoners from the Front,* was praised as the most powerful painting to come out of the Civil War. During the 1860s and 1870s, Homer began painting in watercolor, choosing rural or idyllic scenes of farm life as his subjects. He spent a year in France and was influenced by French Naturalism and Japanese prints. From 1881 to 1882, Homer spent time painting in an English fishing village. He eventually moved to the Maine coast, and the sea became the leading subject of his paintings. Among his classic seascapes from this period are *Cannon Rock* and *Northeaster.* He also traveled to Canada and the Caribbean to paint seascapes. Homer's paintings are characterized by their directness, realism, objectivity, and splendid color. He said about his art, "When I have selected the thing carefully, I paint it exactly as it appears." *Images by this artist: Student Edition p. 84. See also* **Realism.**

DID YOU KNOW?

Winslow Homer was twenty-four when he received his first important assignment with *Harper's Weekly.* He had to sketch Abraham Lincoln's first inauguration.

Hudson River School Nineteenth-century artistic movement originating in the United States. The Hudson River School flourished primarily in New York City from 1825 to 1870. It was an association of artists who rejected European styles of painting and represented the first native movement of American art. The Hudson River School artists painted landscapes in the Hudson River Valley of New York and in the newly opened lands of the West. They used realistic compositions, accurate details, and sketches to paint romantic views of wilderness areas. The paintings reflect pride in the American landscape and culture. Some Hudson River School artists used contrasts of light and dark in a technique called luminism to convey emotion in their artworks. The style of the Hudson River School can be found in the work of Albert Bierstadt.

Impressionism Late nineteenth-century artistic movement that flourished in France from 1860 to 1900. The Impressionists were a group of artists with different styles who exhibited their work together. They reacted against traditional painting techniques and the Romantics' belief that paintings should portray emotion. Impressionists attempt to capture the visual impression made by a scene, usually a landscape or city scene painted outdoors. Their primary goal is to show the effect of natural light and color on a subject and quickly transmit it to the canvas. Painters use unmixed bright, soft colors applied with swift, loose brushstrokes to intensify luminosity and brilliance. The Impressionist style can be found in the works of Claude Monet, Pierre-Auguste Renoir, Edgar Degas, and Mary Cassatt.

Jacot, Don [jahk•OH] (1949–) American painter of urban landscapes. Jacot first photographs a city scene and then paints from those photos. He combines elements from different views and alters specific components of them to produce an image that is as sharp as a photograph but that no camera could physically produce. Jacot took only basic drawing classes at Wayne State University in his home state of Michigan and considers himself essentially self-taught. His subject matter includes city streets, buildings, and a series of shop window displays. *Images by this artist: Student Edition p. 154.*

Jawlensky, Alexej von [yah•VLEN•skee, ah•LEKS•yee fawn] (1864–1941) Russian-born painter and printmaker who lived and worked mostly in Germany. In 1889, Jawlensky gave up an established career in the prestigious Russian Imperial Guard to study painting. In 1896, tired of the realistic style of his training and early work, he moved to Munich, Germany. There, influenced by Wassily Kandinsky and later by Henri Matisse and the Fauves, Jawlensky's work became more experimental and expressive. His paintings emphasized color and line over the realistic depiction of form. Among his best-known paintings are a series of semi-abstract faces he produced in the 1920s and 1930s. In 1929, Jawlensky developed crippling arthritis that severely limited the use of his hands. He continued to paint, but by 1938, the arthritis forced him to quit entirely. *Images by this artist: Student Edition pp. 29, 92.*

Jendrzejczak, Bernadine [yin•JAY•chek] Polish-American folk artist known for her *wycinanki,* which is the art of Polish paper cuttings. As of 2003, Jendrzejczak was acting president of Polanki—the Polish Women's Cultural Club of Milwaukee, Wisconsin. Polanki's mission is to promote appreciation and understanding of Polish culture in the Milwaukee area. Polanki is a nonprofit organization with more than 150 members. It celebrated its fiftieth anniversary in 2003. Jendrzejczak showed her craft of *wycinanki* in 2001 at a Polanki-sponsored exhibit. *Images by this artist: Student Edition p. 129.*

Johns, Jasper (1930–) American painter, sculptor, and printmaker. Johns was born in Augusta, Georgia, and grew up in South Carolina. In the early 1950s, he worked in a bookstore and as a commercial artist in New York City, designing store window displays with friend and artist Robert Rauschenberg. In 1954, Johns created the first of his now-famous flag paintings. In 1958, his first solo exhibition made him one of the world's best-known—and best-paid—living artists. Along with Rauschenberg, Johns is credited with laying the groundwork for Pop Art. He painted full, flat renderings of common and instantly recognizable objects, including flags, targets, maps, and stenciled numbers and letters. His sculptures included light bulbs and cans of artists' brushes faithfully duplicated in bronze. Johns experimented with styles and media throughout his career. In the 1960s, he made prints, and in the 1970s, he incorporated found objects and repeated diagonal lines he called "crosshatching" into his canvases. The 1980s saw less abstract, more autobiographical work. Johns has also designed costumes and sets for numerous dance works. Since the late 1990s, he has lived and worked in Connecticut. *Images by this artist: Art Print 12. See also* **Pop Art.**

Kahlo, Frida [KAH•loh, FREE•dah] (1907–1954) Mexican painter noted for her self-portraits and primitive artistic style. Kahlo was born in Coyoacan, Mexico. She never planned to become an artist, wanting instead to go to medical school. However, devastating injuries in a traffic accident left her permanently disabled. During her slow recovery, Kahlo taught herself to paint. She painted mostly self-portraits and still lifes. In 1929, Kahlo married Diego Rivera, Mexico's most famous artist. Rivera encouraged Kahlo to focus on her Mexican heritage as the subject of her paintings. In her second self-portrait, Kahlo took Rivera's advice and portrayed herself in traditional Mexican folk dress. Kahlo used bright colors in her paintings to create a mixture of realism and fantasy. Many have described her work as Surrealist fantasy. However, she disliked having her artistic style linked to Surrealism. Kahlo said that she painted her own reality, rather than dreams. Throughout her life, she refused to let her physical problems interfere with her art. *Images by this artist: Student Edition p. 90.*

DID YOU KNOW?

As a result of her accident, Frida Kahlo endured thirty-two operations. She could not paint for more than an hour at a time. At one exhibit of her paintings, Kahlo was too ill to leave her bed, so she had it moved into the gallery in order to become a part of the exhibit.

Kandinsky, Wassily [kan•DIN•skee, vuh•SEEL•yee] (1866–1944) Russian-born painter who is renowned as one of the most important pioneers of abstract art. Kandinsky was born in Moscow, Russia. He learned to play the piano and cello at an early age, and his love of music had a profound impact on his art. Kandinsky admired the work of Paul Gauguin. He was also influenced by an exhibition of Islamic art, which does not permit showing images of human figures. In 1910, he painted his first abstract watercolor. His early paintings were expressive, colorful compositions with figures. In his later work, figures gradually disappeared. Describing how he came to understand the power of nonrepresentational art, or art without figures, Kandinsky said that one night he went into his art studio and failed to recognize one of his paintings because it was upside down. Seeing it that way, he began to appreciate how light transformed the shapes and colors. He decided that the figures in a painting should not be recognizable. In his book *Concerning the Spiritual in Art* he compared painting and music. He believed that painting could elicit the same emotional response as music. *Images by this artist: Student Edition p. 203.*

Kimble, Warren American painter whose highly stylized animals and rural scenes are reminiscent of early American folk art. Kimble grew up in New Jersey and graduated from the Syracuse University Fine Arts program in 1957. He worked in advertising and taught art at both the elementary and college levels. In 1983, Kimble retired from teaching to paint full time, often using salvaged or antique wooden boards as a painting surface. Kimble's images have been widely reproduced on products that include wallpaper, rugs, dishware, and decorative accessories. He lives and works in Brandon, Vermont. *Images by this artist: Student Edition p. 139.*

Klee, Paul [KLAY] (1879–1940) Swiss-born painter, printer, teacher, and writer, best known for creating a modern artistic style combining elements of fantasy and satire. Klee studied art at the Academy of Fine Arts in Munich, Germany and continued his artistic education by visiting Italy and Paris. While in Germany, Klee met Expressionist artists Wassily Kandinsky and Franz Marc. He began to participate in their Blue Rider art group, where he was exposed to the use of bright colors and a childlike way of painting. Klee painted on paper or small canvases using a variety of materials including chalk and crayons. He used bright colors as well as figures, numbers, and letters as symbols. In his abstract pieces, however, he used only colors and shapes. Klee is remembered as one of the most individualistic figures of twentieth-century art. During his life, he produced more than 9,000 works. *Images by this artist: Student Edition pp. 46–47; Art Print 2.*

Krasner, Lee (1908–1984) American painter whose work is credited as being the forerunner of Abstract Expressionism. Krasner was born in Brooklyn, New York, and was admitted in 1921 to Washington Irving High School, the only public high school in New York City that offered girls professional art training. She went on to study at several prestigious art schools, including Hans Hofmann School of Fine Arts. There, she studied Fauvism and Cubism and also created abstract still lifes. In 1945, Krasner married artist Jackson Pollock, and she became part of the largely male-dominated New York art world of the 1940s. In 1946, Krasner created her *Little Images* paintings using dots and drips of paint. In 1956, she produced a series of enormous paintings filled with thick, expressive brushstrokes. Later in her career, she concentrated on collages. *Images by this artist: Student Edition p. 180.*

DID YOU KNOW?

In the early 1940s, Lee Krasner met her future husband, Jackson Pollock, when their works were exhibited at a prestigious show in a New York gallery. Krasner dedicated much of her time and energy to promoting her husband's work, and she contributed greatly to his success.

Lichtenstein, Roy [LIK•tuhn•styn] (1923–1997) American painter, printer, and sculptor who is credited with being a pioneer in the Pop Art movement. Born in New York City, Lichtenstein became interested in art in high school. He painted pictures of jazz musicians and admired the paintings of Pablo Picasso. He studied art at Ohio University, served in World War II, and then resumed his studies when he returned home. Lichtenstein worked as a graphic artist and taught at several universities. In his early work, Lichtenstein painted scenes from the American West in a modern style. Artist Allan Kaprow introduced Lichtenstein to cartoon imagery, and in 1960, Lichtenstein made a painting of Mickey Mouse and Donald Duck for his children. In his comic strip paintings, he used large canvases and words to express sound effects, which he displayed in balloons above the figures. He developed an artistic technique that outlined primary colors with black lines. He also eliminated visible brushstrokes. His paintings looked as though they were mass-produced. Lichtenstein said, "I want my painting to look as if it had been programmed." He also painted Pop Art versions of paintings by modern masters. In 1995, he received the National Medal of the Arts from President Clinton. *Images by this artist: Student Edition p. 193. See also* **Pop Art.**

Lin, Maya (1959–) Asian American sculptor and architect who was born in Athens, Ohio. Lin's parents immigrated to the United States from China. As a child, Lin enjoyed hiking, reading, and making pottery. She studied sculpture and architecture at Yale University. While at Yale, Lin entered a competition to design a Vietnam Veterans' Memorial for Washington, D.C. Her design was chosen from among 1,421 entries. Lin chose a Minimalist design, a departure from more traditional designs typically used for public monuments. The memorial has a low V-shaped black granite wall that descends into the ground—a design used in constructing ancient burial sites. The names of the dead and missing are inscribed on the wall's reflective surface. Lin also designed the Civil Rights Memorial in Montgomery, Alabama, and the Women's Table at Yale. To design memorials, Lin uses computer-enhanced imaging, aerial and satellite photography, and topographic mapping. *Images by this artist: Student Edition pp. 186–187.*

Lomas Garza, Carmen (1948–) Mexican American painter, printmaker, and illustrator. Lomas Garza specializes in simple scenes of Chicano family life, inspired by folk art and usually drawn from memories of her own childhood.

She studied in Austin, Texas, and in Mexico. She wrote and illustrated the children's book *Family Pictures/Cuadros de Familia,* which tells the story of her childhood in the Hispanic community of Kingsville, Texas. The book, published in 1990, includes text in both English and Spanish. Today Lomas Garza, who works in San Francisco, is considered one of America's leading Hispanic American painters and remains active writing and illustrating books and working with several groups that promote Hispanic American art. *Images by this artist: Student Edition p. 130.*

Maffei, Ricardo (1953–) Chilean artist born in Santiago. Maffei has worked hard to achieve his own artistic style. He paints models that represent the cessation of time. Maffei attended two art schools in his native Santiago. *Images by this artist: Student Edition p. 176.*

Magritte, René [ma•GREET, ruh•NAY] (1898–1967) Belgian-born Surrealist whose paintings are known for their elaborate fantasies constructed around everyday situations. Magritte was born in Lessines and began to study art at age ten. After studying at the Brussels Academy of Fine Arts, he designed wallpaper and made sketches for advertisements. His early artistic style showed elements of Cubism and Futurism, but he soon adopted a realistic style, sometimes called Magic Realism. He painted ordinary scenes, but added a combination of elements that normally would not belong in the scene. For example, he painted floating rocks, fish with human legs, and men in hats, floating in the air. His painting *Threatening Weather,* in which a chair, a table, and a torso hover over the sea, is an example of Magic Realism. Magritte also began to produce word-paintings, creating a link between word and image. His artistic style had a profound influence on the Pop Art movement. *Images by this artist: Student Edition pp. 113, 182. See also* **Surrealism.**

Mannerism Movement in European painting, sculpture, and architecture that flourished between 1520 and 1600. In reaction against the idealized Naturalism of the High Renaissance, Mannerist painters valued creativity and the imaginative resolution of composition problems more than the accurate representation of nature. Mannerist portraits frequently use bright, even harsh, colors to depict people with stylized facial features and distorted, especially elongated, heads and limbs against a relatively flat background. Mannerist-style painters include Agnolo Bronzino and Giambologna.

Marc, Franz (1880–1916) German painter who co-founded the Blue Rider group—an association of Expressionists who used brilliant color and strong forms to express emotion in their art. Marc was born in Munich and studied philosophy and theology before deciding to become an artist. After studying at the Munich Academy of Fine Art, he made several trips to Paris. Marc loved to study the habits and characteristics of animals. He began painting animals, especially horses, in a mystical and symbolic style. In 1912, Marc's work became more abstract, taking on a Cubist style. The animals in his paintings became fragmented and merged into the background. *Fighting Forms,* one of his last paintings, is an example of his abstract work. *Images by this artist: Student Edition p. 32; Art Print 3. See also* **Blue Rider group.**

Marisol *See* Escobar, Marisol.

Matisse, Henri [mah•TEES, ahn•REE] (1869–1954) French painter, sculptor, and graphic artist. Matisse is widely considered the greatest French painter of the twentieth century and one of the major figures of contemporary art. Matisse did not become interested in art until he was in his twenties when, against his father's wishes, he left law school to become an artist. He studied in Paris, where the work of Paul Cézanne, Claude Monet, Paul Gauguin, and other revolutionary artists influenced him. Matisse emphasized color and line over the realistic depiction of people and objects. A 1913 New York show that introduced Matisse and other contemporary European artists to the United States only enhanced his reputation, and he was soon one of the world's best-known—and best-paid—living artists. By the 1940s, Matisse's eyesight was failing, and arthritis limited the use of his hands. During this time, he experimented with what he called "drawing with scissors," producing compositions of cut paper that today are among his most recognizable works. *Images by this artist: Student Edition pp. 76–77; Art Print 6. See also* **Fauvism.**

DID YOU KNOW?

Henri Matisse suffered from an attack of appendicitis in 1890. While he was recovering, his mother gave him a set of oil paints to help him pass the time. "Henceforth," he later wrote, "I did not lead my life. It led me."

Meechan, Colleen American landscape painter whose artwork depicts tropical scenery, illustrating her love of nature. Meechan's contemporary paintings are filled with rich yet sensitive color, combined with a mixture of bold and subtle patterns, shapes, and lines. She received her master's degree in fine arts from the University of Hawaii at Manoa. Her artwork can be viewed at her studio in Naples, Florida. *Images by this artist: Student Edition p. 40.*

Minimalism Chiefly American art movement that developed in the late 1960s. As a reaction against the emotional paintings of the Abstract Expressionists, Minimalists reduced their work to its most basic elements, using a minimum of lines, colors, shapes, and textures. The result was a body of highly geometric and intentionally impersonal works not intended to represent any other object or experience. Robert Rauschenberg, Frank Stella, and Robert Smithson are well-known American Minimalists, and Minimalist applications appeared not only in sculpture and painting, but also in architecture, literature, theater, and design. In a more general sense, the term *Minimalism* also describes a style stripped of all but its most necessary elements.

Modigliani, Amedeo [moh•deel•YAH•nee, ah•may•DAY•oh] (1884–1920) Italian painter and sculptor best known for his portraits. Born in Livorno, Modigliani developed a tubercular lung as the result of a childhood illness and suffered ill health throughout his life. In 1906, he moved to Paris, where he made his home for the rest of his life. Paul Gauguin, Paul Cézanne, and Pablo Picasso influenced his early paintings, as did his experience as a sculptor. In his portraits, Modigliani composed his figures with elongated noses and necks and long, slender faces. Many of his friends, including Diego Rivera and Pablo Picasso, posed for his portraits. Modigliani did not have any financial success from his art during his lifetime. However, after a successful exhibition of his work in 1922, his sculptures and paintings became highly prized by collectors. *Images by this artist: Student Edition pp. 126–127; Art Print 11.*

Monet, Claude [moh•NAY] (1840–1926) French painter renowned as the leader of the Impressionist movement. Born in Paris, Monet spent his childhood in Le Havre, France. In 1862, he moved back to Paris to study art. There, he met several other artists, including Pierre-Auguste Renoir. In 1874, Monet and his friends held an independent

exhibition of their paintings, including Monet's landscape titled *Impression: Sunrise.* That apparently inspired one art critic to call the entire exhibition Impressionist, which gave the movement its name. The Impressionists attempted to capture a visual impression of a scene, especially the effect natural light has on the setting. Monet painted the same view many times to capture the light at different times of the day, as can be seen in his *Rouen Cathedral* series. Monet once said, "I want the unobtainable. Other artists paint a bridge, a house, a boat, and that's the end. They are finished. I want to paint the air which surrounds the bridge, the house, the boat, the beauty of the air in which the objects are located, and that is nothing short of impossible." Despite failing eyesight, Monet continued to paint until his death. *Images by this artist: Student Edition pp. 42, 68. See also* **Impressionism.**

Morisot, Berthe [moh•ree•ZOH, BEHRT] (1841–1895) French Impressionist painter and printmaker best known for Edouard Manet's influence on her work. Morisot was born in Bourges, France, into a family that respected art and culture. Morisot studied under landscape painter Jean Baptiste Camille Corot and exhibited her paintings at the Salon in Paris. She met Manet in 1868, and he painted several portraits of her. In 1874, she married Manet's brother Eugene. Morisot's paintings often included women and children in scenes from everyday life. One of her best-known works is *Young Woman at the Dance.* Morisot used a light, delicate style in her pastels, watercolors, lithographs, and drypoints. Her success stood as an inspiration to other women painters. *Images by this artist: Student Edition p. 69. See also* **Impressionism.**

Moses, Grandma (Anna Mary Robertson) (1860–1961) American painter best known for her folk art paintings. Grandma Moses was born Anna Mary Robertson in Greenwich, New York. Robertson had no formal art training. As a child, she drew and painted on unused newsprint. She used berry juice to brighten her pictures. She married Thomas Salmon Moses in 1887, and the couple became farmers. Moses loved to work in needlepoint, and she won prizes for her embroidery. After her husband's death in 1927, she began to paint full time. Her first art exhibition was held in a drugstore in Hoosick Falls, New York, where an art collector discovered her work. In 1940, an exhibition in Manhattan titled *What a Farm Wife Painted* launched her career. Five years later, Hallmark bought the rights to reproduce her paintings on Christmas cards, making her an instant celebrity. Moses published her autobiography, *My Life's History,* in 1952. At the age of one hundred, she illustrated *'Twas the Night Before Christmas* by Clement Moore. *Images by this artist: Student Edition p. 132.*

Nevelson, Louise (1899?–1988) American sculptor, painter, and printmaker known for her large monochromatic abstract sculptures and assemblages. Nevelson was born in Kiev, Ukraine, but her family moved to Rockland, Maine, in 1905. At the age of ten, Nevelson decided to become a sculptor. However, she did not begin studying art seriously until the age of thirty. She studied at the Art Students League under Hans Hofmann, who taught her the artistic techniques of Cubism and collage. In 1933, Nevelson assisted Diego Rivera in painting murals. Surrealism, African art, and pre-Columbian art influenced her work. Her early sculptures were done in wood, terra-cotta, bronze, and plaster. She also began creating assemblages in which she used found objects such as chair backs, furniture legs, moldings, and spindles. In 1976, Nevelson wrote her autobiography, titled *Dawns and Dusks,* in which she said that determination was the key to her success. In 2000, the United States government issued five commemorative stamps in her honor. *Images by this artist: Student Edition p. 188.*

O'Brien, Mike (1954?–) American sculptor and exhibits coordinator for Texas Parks and Wildlife. O'Brien was commissioned by the State Preservation Board to create six relief sculptures for the Bob Bullock Texas State History Museum. The purpose of these panels was to illustrate Texas's history. Each panel measures 11 feet by 16 feet and weighs more than 2 tons. *Images by this artist: Student Edition p. 104.*

O'Keeffe, Georgia (1887–1986) American painter renowned for her abstract paintings and still-life compositions. Born in Sun Prairie, Wisconsin, O'Keeffe became interested in art after she saw a pen-and-ink drawing of a Grecian maiden in one of her mother's books. O'Keeffe studied art at many prestigious schools, including the Art Institute of Chicago and Columbia University. She worked as a teacher and commercial artist but after 1918 began to paint full time. She followed the advice of art teacher Arthur Dow, who told her to express her personal ideas and feelings in her art. O'Keeffe's life changed when she married photographer Alfred Stieglitz in 1924. She learned about photography and began to use certain elements of the photographic process in her work. Her painting *New York With Moon* contained many photographic characteristics. O'Keeffe moved to New Mexico and was inspired by the state's beautiful landscapes. In New Mexico, she painted abstracts and still lifes of flowers, animal bones, mountains, and other natural forms. *Blue Iris* and *Cow's Skull* are two typical works O'Keeffe painted in New Mexico. Near the end of her life, O'Keeffe lost her sight, but she did not give up her art. She pursued pottery instead. *Images by this artist: Student Edition pp. 34, 37.*

DID YOU KNOW?

Georgia O'Keeffe mixed paints on a glass tray on which she also kept a separate brush for each color. In order to keep track of every color, O'Keeffe put a sample of each on a white card. This enabled her to easily reproduce the color to use in another painting.

Outterbridge, John (1933–) African American sculptor known for his found-object assemblages. Outterbridge was born in Greenville, North Carolina. He studied on his own as a soldier in Germany and at the American Academy of Art in Chicago before settling in Los Angeles, where his work shifted from painting to sculpting. Outterbridge's pieces reflect political and social themes, particularly the shared history and culture of African Americans. Outterbridge remains active in the cultural affairs of Los Angeles, where he teaches, exhibits, and serves as a mentor to young people. *Images by this artist: Art Print 18.*

Paik, Nam June (1932–) South Korean-born video artist, performer, musician, sculptor, filmmaker, and writer who pioneered video art in the United States. Born in Seoul, Paik studied music at the University of Tokyo and in Munich, Germany. He trained as a pianist and discovered electronic music while a student in Germany. Paik moved to New York City in 1964. He showed artists how to use the creative medium of television by integrating visual images with music. In an exhibition titled *Fin de Siecle II,* shown at the Whitney Museum, Paik used hundreds of television monitors to display multiple images and sounds. Paik is the first artist to have experimented with the use of television and video as a vehicle for artistic expression. *Images by this artist: Student Edition p. 189.*

Pei, I. M. [PAY] (1917–) Chinese-born American architect best known for his use of simple geometric forms to create contemporary, functional buildings. As a young boy, Pei had been interested in design and building construction. He especially loved the design of the Lion Forest Garden in Suzhou, China, and the new high-rise buildings in Shanghai. In 1935, Pei went to the United States to study architectural engineering at the Massachusetts Institute of Technology. He also earned a graduate degree from Harvard University. He started his own architectural firm in 1955. As he developed his own personal style, Pei's designs often included prism shapes, soaring airy spaces, and skylights in vaulted ceilings. Some of his most famous designs are the John Hancock Tower in Boston, the glass pyramid that was built in the courtyard of the Louvre Museum in Paris, and the JFK Memorial Library in Boston. In 1979, Pei received a Gold Medal from the American Institute of Architects, the organization's highest award, for his design of the JFK Memorial Library. *Images by this artist: Student Edition pp. 166–167; Art Print 14.*

Photorealism Depiction of ordinary life with the sharp detail and impersonality of a photograph; also called Super-Realism or Hyper-Realism. Photorealistic artists often paint from photographs and combine more detail into a scene than the camera would capture, such as exaggerated sharpness of focus, multiple layers of reflection in shiny surfaces, or an impossible point of view—the same building or intersection seen simultaneously from two different points, for example. Photorealism was prominent in the United States and Britain during the late 1960s and 1970s and included the paintings of Richard Estes, Chuck Close, Janet Fish, and Charles Bell.

Picasso, Pablo [pih•KAHS•soh] (1881–1973) Spanish painter, sculptor, printmaker, ceramicist, and illustrator renowned for pioneering the artistic style of Cubism. Picasso was born in Malaga, Spain. His father, an art teacher, recognized Picasso's early talent and gave him art lessons. At fifteen, Picasso qualified to enter the Academy of Fine Arts in Barcelona. After one year, he left school and went to Paris. There, he painted the poor and social outcasts of the city using blue tones to express their sadness. In 1904, Picasso changed his style and began to paint happy circus performers in rose and pink tones. After studying Paul Gauguin's paintings of non-Western cultures and the artistic style of ancient Iberian sculpture, Picasso became inspired to experiment with the element of distortion. In 1907, he collaborated with fellow artist Georges Braque to produce a new artistic style called Cubism. Cubists try to show all sides of an object at once by using geometrical forms. Picasso was also the first artist to create sculptures out of various materials, rather than by carving or modeling. *Images by this artist: Student Edition pp. 49, 94. See also* **Cubism.**

DID YOU KNOW?

Picasso invented an important artistic technique called collage. Collage is an artistic form that attaches flat, ready-made materials to the surface of a canvas or sculpture. Picasso invented collage when he painted *Still Life with Chair Caning.*

Pippin, Horace (1888–1946) African American painter known for his American folk paintings. Pippin's art depicted scenes of African American life and his experiences in World War I. The grandson of slaves, Pippin was born in West Chester, Pennsylvania. He grew up in Goshen, New York, and served in a segregated regiment during World War I. He kept an illustrated diary of his war experiences. His first oil painting was *End of War: Starting Home,* a scene from World War I that protested the war. Pippin painted scenes from African American life, such as his series titled *Cabin in the Cotton.* He also painted historical scenes from the lives of John Brown and Abraham Lincoln. He created simple images painted in bright colors and flat forms, and his work attained considerable recognition. Pippin's style is described as primitive, because his forms and figures lacked specific details. In 1938, the Museum of Modern Art in New York held an exhibition titled *Masters of Popular Painting* that showcased some of his work. *Images by this artist: Student Edition p. 53.*

Pointillism Painting technique developed in France in the 1880s. Pointillism used tiny dots or points of pure color juxtaposed so that from a distance they seemed to blend in the viewer's eye. The painter's intent was to achieve a more vibrant, shimmering, or luminous effect not possible with mixed colors. The term was coined to describe the work of Georges Seurat, but Camille Pissarro was another famous artist who used the technique. An offshoot of Impressionism, Pointillist painting is usually classified as a form of Post-Impressionism.

Pollock, Jackson [PAHL•uhk] (1912–1956) American painter best known as the leading figure in the Abstract Expressionist movement. Pollock was born in Cody, Wyoming, the youngest of five brothers. During the 1940s, he invented a new artistic style called Action Painting. Instead of using traditional brushes and easels, Pollock laid his canvas on the floor and then poured and dripped the paint onto the canvas. He used sticks, trowels, and knives to spread the paint. His paintings had no identifiable parts or composition, and many people criticized them. In 1956, *Time* magazine called him "Jack the Dripper." Pollock said about his Action Painting, "I feel nearer, more a part of the painting, since this way I can walk around it, work from the four sides, and literally be in the painting." One of his most famous paintings, *Lavender Mist,* sold for $1,500 in 1950. In 1976, the National Gallery of Art purchased it for $2 million. *Images by this artist: Student Edition p. 178.*

DID YOU KNOW?

Jackson Pollock studied at the Art Students League in New York, under the direction of Thomas Hart Benton. Although he was initially inspired by Benton, Pollock's paintings of the 1930s were intended to free him from Benton's influence, allowing him to find his own style.

Pop Art Movement in painting, sculpture, and printmaking that began in Britain in the 1950s and shifted to the United States in 1960. Pop Art focused on images from popular culture, including advertising, comic strips, and brand-name packaged goods. Inspired by Dada, which broke new ground in both subject matter and technique, Pop Art is sometimes called Neo-Dada. Major Pop artists include Roy Lichtenstein, Jasper Johns, Claes Oldenburg, and Andy Warhol.

Post-Impressionism General term for trends in modern art that developed as a reaction against Impressionism and Neo-Impressionism. The three major Post-Impressionist artists were Paul Cézanne, Vincent van Gogh, and Paul Gauguin, but Henri Matisse and Pablo Picasso were also involved for part of their careers. All produced early work that was Impressionist in style but later developed styles that used flat areas of bright color and emphasized solid structures and simplified forms. Most Post-Impressionist work was created between 1886 and 1905, but the term was not in general use until 1910.

Pugh, Anna British artist born in Wales during World War II. Pugh is a folk artist whose paintings focus on plants and animals. Her love of Mogul and Persian paintings inspired her creativity. Her early works were small-scale paintings, but she has also painted furniture. Her more recent work utilizes acrylic on wood panels. Today, Pugh lives in Kent, England, with her dog. *Images by this artist: Student Edition p. 86.*

Pugh, John California muralist who mixes architecture, craftsmanship, and wit with fine art. Pugh is a *trompe l'oeil* (meaning "fool the eye") artist. He is gaining international recognition. Many of Pugh's paintings have an incomplete look, which he feels adds to the illusion. He says, "Murals are active art—full of artistic energy and community involvement." Pugh spends his days painting and his nights drawing. *Images by this artist: Student Edition p. 170.*

Ray, Man (1890–1976) American photographer, painter, sculptor, and filmmaker who participated in the Cubist, Dada, and Surrealist art movements. Ray is best known for developing photograms—or what he called rayograms—which were photographs produced without a camera by placing objects directly onto sensitized paper and exposing them to light. Born in Philadelphia with the name Emmanuel Radensky, Ray was the son of an artist and a photographer. He grew up in New York City and briefly studied architecture, engineering, and art before he became a painter. However, his artistic skills were largely self-taught. Ray often visited photographer Alfred Stieglitz, who introduced him to photography. In 1921, Ray moved to Paris and began to experiment with photographic methods. His photographs were published in such magazines as *Harper's Bazaar* and *Vogue*. In 1961, he was awarded the gold medal at the Photograph Biennale in Venice. Although Ray explored many different artistic media, he made his greatest contribution to the art world as a photographer. *Images by this artist: Student Edition p. 110.*

Realism Movement in literature and painting that was based in France in the mid-to-late 1800s. Reacting against the formulas of Neoclassicism and the drama of Romanticism, Realist painters produced scenes from everyday life, often emphasizing the harshness or ugliness of common people's activities and circumstances to make a social or political statement. French painter Jean Baptiste Camille Corot and American artist Winslow Homer were Realists. Realism inspired a number of offshoots and rebirths, including Impressionism, the Ashcan School, American Regionalism, and Social Realism.

Regionalism American art movement of the 1930s, also called American Scene Painting. The best-known Regionalists, Thomas Hart Benton, John Steuart Curry, and Grant Wood, had widely varying styles, but all painted realistic, recognizable scenes of rural, Midwestern life or history. These scenes often took the form of murals in public buildings and were depicted in a clear, simple way that a wide audience could understand.

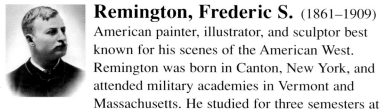

Remington, Frederic S. (1861–1909) American painter, illustrator, and sculptor best known for his scenes of the American West. Remington was born in Canton, New York, and attended military academies in Vermont and Massachusetts. He studied for three semesters at the newly formed Yale School of Fine Arts but quit following his father's death in 1880. Nineteen-year-old Remington took his $9,000 inheritance (about $170,000 in today's dollars) and spent five years traveling through America's western states and territories. He worked as a ranch hand, lumberjack, and prospector while he built a reputation for his drawings, which documented a way of life Remington felt was quickly disappearing. His action-packed and precisely drawn illustrations were published in several popular magazines and by the late 1880s, Frederic Remington was a household name. He began working in bronze in 1885, and his twenty-three sculptures—mostly of cowboys on horseback—have been widely reproduced. *Images by this artist: Student Edition pp. 56, 110.*

Renoir, Pierre-Auguste [REN•wahr, PYAIR•oh•GOOST] (1841–1919) French painter and cofounder of Impressionism. Renoir was born in Limoges, France. He showed an interest in art at an early age and spent time copying Rococo masterpieces in the Louvre. In 1862, Renoir began studying classical painting and met fellow art students Claude Monet, Alfred Sisley, and Jean-Frederic Bazille. Together, these young artists revolted against the rules of the classical art style. They founded a group of painters known as the Impressionists. Outdoor scenes, an emphasis on natural light, quick brushstrokes, and bright colors characterized this new style. Unlike other Impressionist painters, who painted only landscapes, Renoir painted individual human figures and family group portraits. *Luncheon of the Boating Party* is an example of a Renoir group portrait. Renoir traveled to Italy in 1880 to study the Renaissance masters. After that trip, he began to once again paint in a classical style. Near the end of his life, Renoir developed crippling arthritis. However, he continued to paint by using a brush strapped to his hand. *Images by this artist: Art Print 4. See also* **Impressionism.**

Ringgold, Faith (1930?–) African American painter, sculptor, performance artist, and writer known for her soft sculpture figures, painted story quilts, and illustrated children's books. Ringgold was born in Harlem, New York. She earned her master's degree in art from the City College of New York. For many years, Ringgold painted huge murals. For example, her *American People* series is about civil rights and other political issues that affect African Americans and women. However, the murals were too heavy to transport. Exasperated, Ringgold decided to paint art that was lightweight and portable—cloth hangings and soft sculptures. Ringgold uses her portable art during special interactive performances in which she involves the audience. African American themes are also the focus of her portable art pieces. Ringgold has written and illustrated numerous children's books about African Americans. Her book *Tar Beach* has won more than thirty awards, including the Coretta Scott King Award for best-illustrated children's book. *Images by this artist: Student Edition p. 114.*

DID YOU KNOW?

Faith Ringgold is well known for her painted story quilts. Ringgold's book *Tar Beach* is based on the story quilt *Tar Beach* from her story quilt series *The Woman on a Bridge*. Ringgold gets many of her ideas for her books from her story quilts.

Rogers, Thomas Sculptor and engraver for the United States Mint. Rogers designed the reverse, or tail, side of the Sacagawea gold dollar that first appeared in 2000. Rogers also designed the reverse side of the 2001 Vistas of Liberty coin, which is part of the American Eagles series. *Images by this artist: Student Edition p. 102. See also* **Goodacre, Glenna.**

Romanticism Late-eighteenth- to mid-nineteenth-century movement originating in literature but including music, religion, philosophy, and the visual arts—especially painting. Romanticism was not so much a style as a way of thinking and looking at the world. Reacting against the reason, rationality, and restriction of Neoclassicism, Romantics valued emotion, instinct, imagination, and personal, subjective experience. Romantic landscapes were moody, dramatic, and even exotic; portraits reflected the emotions and personality of the sitter. Romantic artists included William Blake and Francisco José de Goya y Lucientes.

Rousseau, Henri [roo•SOH, ahn•REE] (1844–1910) French painter renowned for his modern primitive-style paintings. Born in Laval, France, Rousseau came from a working-class family. His family could not afford art lessons, but he taught himself to paint. In 1884, Rousseau began working as a copyist, making copies of masterpieces in Paris museums. The next year, Rousseau began to exhibit his work. He did not begin painting full time until he retired at the age of forty-nine. At first, critics ridiculed his work, but he believed in himself and continued painting. Rousseau developed an unusual painting technique. He painted from the top to the bottom of the canvas. He also painted the different colors one by one. For example, he would paint first the reds, then the blues, and then the other colors. Rousseau liked to paint jungle landscapes and wild animals. His best-known jungle landscape is entitled *Tiger in a Tropical Storm.* He got his inspiration from walks through Paris gardens and from looking at photographs of wild animals in books. The French Impressionists influenced Rousseau's use of bold colors and decorative patterns. However, Rousseau broke away from the classic Impressionist look and developed his own style. He painted each detail and varnished the surfaces of his paintings to a high gloss. Rousseau's work influenced the Surrealist movement of the 1920s. *Images by this artist: Student Edition p. 59.*

Ruysch, Rachel [ROYS] (1664–1750) Dutch painter known for her floral still lifes. Ruysch came from a wealthy, respected family and received her earliest training from her father, an anatomy and botany professor who was also a talented amateur artist. She achieved widespread fame during her lifetime, and her works were highly prized. A typical Ruysch piece shows a large bouquet of a variety of flowers in a vase on a stone or marble ledge against a plain, dark background. Her paintings are noted for their balanced composition, their use of color, light, and shadow, and their attention to detail, particularly in the depiction of individual flower petals. *Images by this artist: Art Print 5.*

Saligman, Meg Fish American painter who creates collage-like murals. Saligman often depicts contemporary people as allegorical figures in her elaborate paintings. She received a bachelor of fine arts degree from Washington University in St. Louis. Her masterpiece, *Common Threads,* is located in Philadelphia and is one of the largest murals on the East coast. *Images by this artist: Student Edition p. 169.*

Sarian, Matiros (1880–1972) Armenian painter who specialized in landscapes, still lifes, and portraits. Sarian used vibrant colors and rich, rhythmic patterns to depict memorable themes, often based on folktales. He studied at the Moscow School of Painting, Sculpture and Architecture from 1897 to 1903. Sarian was influenced by Impressionists Henri Matisse and Paul Gauguin. *Images by this artist: Student Edition p. 43.*

Seurat, Georges [suh•RAH, zhawrzh] (1859–1891) French painter who invented the painting style called Pointillism that became associated with the artistic movement of Neo-Impressionism. Seurat was born in Paris. When he was a teenager, he began taking informal art lessons from his uncle. He later attended art school in Paris and studied the art of the Impressionist painters. Seurat studied the relationship between lines and images and the effect of light on colors, using this information to develop the artistic technique of Pointillism. Unlike Impressionists, who were interested in recording the natural world, Neo-Impressionists wanted to calculate the emotional effect of colors. One of Seurat's first Pointillist works and his most famous painting is *A Sunday on La Grande Jatte—1884.* Seurat's Pointillist technique and the application of his scientific principles to painting had a lasting impact on the art world into the twentieth century. *Images by this artist: Student Edition pp. 54, 153. See also* **Pointillism.**

Shrager, Joan Myerson

American painter, sculptor, and ceramicist from Pennsylvania. Shrager's work is filled with layers of vivid colors and has been displayed in more than fifty exhibitions. For the past several years, she has been teaching herself how to create digital art on the computer. She finds it challenging to mix technology with artistry. *Images by this artist: Student Edition p. 199.*

Sierra, Paul (1944–) Cuban-born painter

who immigrated to the United States in 1961. Over the years, Sierra's art has exhibited his interest in body language as well as Magic Realism. He paints with bold brushstrokes, filling the canvas with powerful colors. A long-time resident of Chicago, Sierra is inspired by the city's rich artistic culture, as well as by Jackson Pollock's life and art career. *Images by this artist: Student Edition p. 38.*

Smithson, Robert (1938–1973) American

sculptor and painter renowned for his earth sculptures. Smithson was born in Passaic, New Jersey. He studied at the Art Students League in New York and the Brooklyn Museum School. He traveled to Rome and studied Byzantine art, which inspired him to paint in the Abstract Expressionist style. He designed massive earth sculptures—called Earthworks—using natural materials, maps, diagrams, and photographs. Smithson's most famous Earthwork sculpture is called *Spiral Jetty.* He used rocks and debris to build a 15-foot-wide spiral in Utah's Great Salt Lake. *Images by this artist: Student Edition p. 30.*

Sorolla y Bastida, Joaquín [soh•ROH•yah ee bahs•TEE•dah, hwah•KEEN] (1863–1923) Spanish painter known

for painting scenes of the Valencia seacoast in an Impressionist style. Born in Valencia, Sorolla attended art school in Spain and also studied in Rome and Paris. In the Prado, he made copies of Spanish masterpieces. He learned to combine contemporary style with traditional approaches, and he painted historical scenes. However, he received international recognition for his landscapes and paintings of beach scenes. The Hispanic Society of America in New York commissioned Sorolla to paint a series of murals representing scenes of Spain's provinces. He also received a commission to paint President Howard Taft in 1909. In his later years, Sorolla painted beach scenes in Valencia, inspired by the reflection of light off the Mediterranean Sea. *Images by this artist: Student Edition p. 70.*

Stoddard, Alice Kent (1885–1976) American painter

known for her portraits and landscapes. Stoddard was born in Connecticut and trained in Pennsylvania. She spent her adult life between homes in Philadelphia and Monhegan Island, Maine. During summers in Maine, she produced brightly colored landscapes and portraits of children and families. In Philadelphia, her portrait sitters included prominent artists, educators, politicians, federal judges, and justices of the United States Supreme Court. *Images by this artist: Student Edition p. 88.*

Surrealism Movement in visual art and literature that flour-

ished in Europe in the 1920s and 1930s. Surrealist, or "Super Realist," art was seen as a way to give expression to the unconscious part of the mind. Some Surrealists might use spontaneous techniques as a means to unleash their own subconscious. Others might force viewers to expand their sense of what is real by challenging them with a seemingly incomprehensible scene. Surrealist painters, whose specific styles varied widely, included René Magritte, Salvador Dalí, and Joan Miró.

Thiebaud, Wayne [TEE•boh] (1920–)

American painter and commercial artist best known for his still lifes of sweet foods. Thiebaud was born in Mesa, Arizona, and has spent much of his life in California. In the early 1950s, Thiebaud earned a master's degree in art and began working as a college art professor. By the early 1960s, he had begun the paintings for which he is best known—small still lifes of commonplace objects, especially cakes, pies, and other desserts, against an empty, white background. Thiebaud was linked to Pop Art in part because of his everyday subject matter and emphasis on basic shapes, but he has always considered himself a traditional painter, applying paint in what has been described as a thick, juicy style. In the late 1960s, Thiebaud began painting landscapes, especially city scenes viewed at a distance from overhead angles. *Images by this artist: Student Edition p. 194.*

DID YOU KNOW?

As a high school student, Wayne Thiebaud served a summer apprenticeship as an animator at the Walt Disney Studio in California.

Thomas, Alma Woodsey (1891–1978)

African American painter and teacher known for her abstract style of painting that is associated with the Washington Color Field Painters group. Thomas was born in Columbus, Georgia. Her interest in art began on her grandfather's plantation in Alabama, where she molded objects from riverbank clay. Thomas attended Howard University and became the first graduate of its fine arts department in 1924. She also earned a master of fine arts degree from Columbia Teacher's College. She taught art in the Washington Public Schools while painting part time. Thomas used large canvases filled with dense, irregular patterns and bright colors. She had her first major exhibition at the age of eighty and was the first African American woman to have a solo show at the Whitney Museum of American Art. *Images by this artist: Art Print 17.*

Van Gogh, Vincent [van GOH, VIN•sent]

(1853–1890) Dutch painter born in the small village of Groot-Zundert, Holland, renowned as one of the greatest Post-Impressionist artists. In 1869, van Gogh became an apprentice in his uncle's art business and later pursued his interest in religious studies. He became a missionary and went to live in the coal-mining district of southern Belgium. There, he decided to become an artist, and he began to draw pictures chronicling the miners' harsh living conditions. After studying drawing in Brussels and watercolor with Anton Mauve, van Gogh began to paint in oils. He moved to a desolate area of the Netherlands, where he painted the remote landscape and local peasants. In 1885, he produced his first masterpiece based on the daily life of peasants, titled *The Potato Eaters.* The works of Rubens, the Japanese printmakers Hiroshige and Katsushika Hokusai, and the French Impressionists influenced his work. In 1888, he went to paint in southern France; his works created there reflect the sunlight, landscapes, and vivid colors of the countryside. In France, he began to exhibit erratic behavior. Paul Gauguin joined him, they argued, and after cutting off his own earlobe, van Gogh was hospitalized for mental illness. He spent the last nineteen months of his life fighting this illness. *Images by this artist: Student Edition pp. 33, 149. See also* **Post-Impressionism.**

DID YOU KNOW?

Poverty-stricken, van Gogh sold only one painting during his lifetime. In 1987, his painting *Irises,* which he painted while in a mental hospital, sold for $53.9 million. The buyer called it "the most important painting in the world."

Velasco, José María [vay•LAHS•koh] (1840–1912)

Mexican painter known for his realistic, highly detailed landscapes. Velasco learned to paint in private lessons and at Mexico City's San Carlos Academy of Fine Arts, where he later taught Diego Rivera. He also studied scientific subjects, including anatomy, botany, geography, and geology, believing that the knowledge would make him a better painter. Velasco's work includes more than 400 oil paintings, primarily of scenes in and around the Valley of Mexico. *Images by this artist: Student Edition p. 29.*

Velázquez, Diego [vay•LAHS•kes, DYAY•goh]

(1599–1660) Spanish painter who is renowned as the most important painter of the Baroque period. Velázquez was born in Seville, Spain, into a family of minor nobility. While still in his teens, he became a master painter and began to develop his own style. He painted his figures in a lifelike manner, in natural settings, using natural light. Velázquez's style was quite extraordinary in a time when artists typically painted figures in a sterile, idealized setting. His paintings are divided into three categories: kitchen scenes, portraits, and religious scenes. In 1623, he became the official court painter to Spain's King Philip IV. He also made several trips to Italy to study the Italian masters whose work influenced his style. *The Surrender of Breda,* in which Velázquez depicted Spanish troops in battle, has been lauded as one of the world's finest historical paintings. His realistic and emotional depiction was unlike any other battle scene ever painted before that time. Near the end of his life, Velázquez painted *Las Meninas (The Maids of Honor).* He incorporated himself into the painting of various members of the royal family, including the king and queen, who are shown reflected in a mirror. In 1985, a group of art critics voted this the "world's greatest painting." *Images by this artist: Student Edition p. 96.*

Wagstaff, Robert American painter of contemporary botanicals, known as "Maui's Audubon." Wagstaff was born and raised in Hawaii, where he retired to become a painter after a thirty-year career as an advertising art director. Wagstaff works in gouache (opaque watercolor), and his works are realistic, intensely color-saturated depictions of Hawaii's native plants, animals, flowers, and insects. *Images by this artist: Student Edition p. 39.*

Warhol, Andy [WAWR•hawl] (1928?–1987) American painter, printmaker, sculptor, filmmaker, and writer, best known as a leading figure in the Pop Art movement. Warhol was born in Pennsylvania, to parents who were Czechoslovakian immigrants. He studied pictorial design at the Carnegie Institute of Technology and worked as a successful commercial illustrator in New York City before he began to paint in the late 1950s. Warhol is best known for his images of common objects such as soup cans, dollar bills, and soda bottles. His art showed the emptiness of American material culture, and it ridiculed the values of the American middle class. In 1962, he exhibited a group of paintings titled *32 Campbell's Soup Cans.* Warhol explained that one of the reasons he painted soup cans was that he liked to eat soup. He said, "I paint things I always thought beautiful, things that you use every day and don't think about." He worked in a studio called the Factory, where he and his staff mass-produced his paintings, using a mechanical stencil process called silkscreen printing. Later in life, he spent his time making portraits of famous people, including Marilyn Monroe and Mick Jagger. Warhol's successful process of mass-producing his work made him a leading innovator in the Pop Art movement. *Images by this artist: Student Edition p. 192. See also* **Pop Art.**

Wood, Grant (1891–1942) American painter best known for his painting *American Gothic.* Wood was born in Anamosa, Iowa. As a young man, he supported himself as a metalworker and handyman while he studied and practiced painting. He produced Impressionist-inspired landscapes and architectural scenes until the late 1920s, when he began to paint distinctly Midwestern themes in a hard-edged, almost cartoonish American Regionalist style. Wood painted Iowa landscapes and gently satirical portraits of local people, often farmers, in everyday situations and dress. *American Gothic,* which Wood painted in 1930, depicts a gaunt Iowa farmer and his equally stern-looking daughter in front of their farmhouse. The piece made Grant Wood famous and has since become an American icon and one of the most-recognized paintings in the world. Through the 1930s, Wood also worked on numerous New Deal Public Works Art Projects, founded an experimental art colony at Stone City, Iowa, and taught at Iowa State University. *Images by this artist: Art Print 7.*

DID YOU KNOW?

The model for the farmer in *American Gothic* was Dr. Byron W. McKeelby, a Cedar Rapids dentist and friend of Grant Wood. The model for the woman was Wood's sister, Nan. The house, now on the National Register of Historic Places, still stands in Eldon, Iowa.

Wood, Memphis American artist renowned for her vibrant weavings. Wood lived in Florida and taught in the Duval County School System, at Jacksonville University, and at the Jacksonville Museum of Contemporary Art. *Images by this artist: Student Edition p. 64.*

Scope & Sequence

PERCEPTION: DEVELOP AND ORGANIZE IDEAS FROM THE ENVIRONMENT	GRADE 1	2	3	4	5
Use Sensory Knowledge and Life Experiences to Identify Ideas					
About self	•	•	•	•	•
About family, school, community	•	•	•	•	•
About visual symbols, life events		•	•	•	•
Elements of Art					
Line					
Identify and discuss line as an element of art	•	•	•	•	•
Examine and explore line in art	•	•	•	•	•
curved, straight, diagonal	•	•	•	•	•
vertical, horizontal		•	•	•	•
outline; contour; expressive		•	•	•	•
crosshatch; sketched			•	•	•
actual; implied				•	
continuous					•
Shape					
Identify and discuss shape as an element of art	•	•	•	•	•
Recognize shape as two-dimensional	•	•	•	•	•
Examine and explore shape in art	•	•	•	•	•
geometric; organic/free-form; repeated; symbols/pictures	•	•	•	•	•
symbols/letters; positive, negative					•
Color					
Identify and discuss color as an element of art	•	•	•	•	•
Examine and explore color in art	•	•	•	•	•
primary, secondary, neutral	•	•	•	•	•
warm, cool	•	•	•	•	•
intermediate, complementary			•	•	
monochromatic, dominant				•	
analogous; hue; saturation; intensity					•
Space					
Identify and discuss space as an element of art	•	•	•	•	•
Examine and explore space in art	•	•	•	•	•
three-dimensional; horizon line	•	•	•	•	•
foreground, background			•	•	•
overlapping; illusion of depth			•	•	•
placement; proportion		•	•	•	•
atmospheric perspective; linear perspective; vanishing point				•	•
middle ground, positive, negative				•	•
points of view					•
Value					
Identify and discuss value as an element of art	•	•	•	•	•
Examine and explore value in art	•	•	•	•	•
dark, light	•	•	•	•	•
brightness		•	•	•	•
shadows; gray scale; color gradations	•	•	•	•	•
shades, tints	•	•	•	•	•
contrast		•	•	•	•

			GRADE		
	1	2	3	4	5
Texture					
Identify and discuss texture as an element of art	•	•	•	•	•
Recognize texture as simulated (drawn or painted on a surface) and real (tactile); distinguish between visual and tactile textures	•	•	•	•	•
Examine and explore texture in art	•	•	•	•	•
visual, tactile; repeated lines	•	•	•	•	•
values				•	•
Form					
Identify and discuss form as an element of art	•	•	•	•	•
Recognize form as three-dimensional	•	•	•	•	•
Examine and explore form in art	•	•	•	•	•
geometric, organic	•	•	•	•	•

Principles of Design

	1	2	3	4	5
Pattern/Repetition					
Identify and discuss pattern as a principle of design	•	•	•	•	•
Recognize repetition of art elements to create pattern	•	•	•	•	•
Examine and explore pattern in art	•	•	•	•	•
Proportion					
Identify and discuss proportion as a principle of design			•	•	•
Emphasis					
Identify and discuss emphasis as a principle of design	•	•	•	•	•
Identify emphasis by indicating what parts of an artwork are most important	•	•	•	•	•
Examine and explore emphasis in art	•	•	•	•	•
center of interest; color; contrast	•	•	•	•	•
visual weight		•	•	•	•
Balance					
Identify and discuss balance as a principle of design	•	•	•	•	•
Understand balance as a composition that achieves equilibrium in the eyes of the viewer		•	•	•	•
Examine and explore balance in art	•	•	•	•	•
symmetrical	•	•	•	•	•
radial; asymmetrical; midline		•	•	•	•
vertical axis; visual weight				•	•
horizontal axis; exact symmetry, near symmetry					•
Rhythm					
Identify and discuss rhythm as a principle of design	•	•	•	•	•
Understand that rhythm is achieved by repeating elements in artwork	•	•	•	•	•
Examine and explore rhythm in art (repetition; movement)	•	•	•	•	•
Movement					
Identify and discuss movement as a principle of design		•	•	•	•
Examine and explore movement on two-dimensional surfaces		•	•	•	•
Unity					
Identify and discuss unity as a principle of design	•	•	•	•	•
Examine and explore unity in art	•	•	•	•	•
Variety					
Identify and discuss variety as a principle of design	•	•	•	•	•
Examine and explore variety in art (variety in line, color, texture, shape)	•	•	•	•	•

CREATIVE EXPRESSION/PERFORMANCE: EXPRESS IDEAS THROUGH ORIGINAL ARTWORKS

	GRADE				
	1	2	3	4	5

Safety in Art Processes

	1	2	3	4	5
Display an awareness of and respect for art tools and materials	•	•	•	•	•
Demonstrate the proper care for and use of tools, materials, and art area	•	•	•	•	•
Follow art safety rules and procedures	•	•	•	•	•

Develop and Apply Art Knowledge and Skills

	1	2	3	4	5
Apply elements (line, shape, color, form, texture, value, space) in original artworks	•	•	•	•	•
Apply design principles (pattern, rhythm, movement, unity, variety, balance, proportion, emphasis) in original artworks	•	•	•	•	•

Creative Expression

	1	2	3	4	5
Create artworks based on personal observations and experiences	•	•	•	•	•
Integrate a variety of ideas about self, life experiences, family, and community in original artworks	•	•	•	•	•
Combine information from personal observations, experiences, and imagination to express ideas about self, family, and community in original artworks	•	•	•	•	•

Organization and Composition

	1	2	3	4	5
Compare relationships between design and everyday life	•	•	•	•	•
Use design skills to develop effective compositions in original artworks		•	•	•	•

Production

	1	2	3	4	5
Follow directions and solve problems	•	•	•	•	•
Produce artworks using a variety of art media appropriately	•	•	•	•	•
Produce drawings, paintings, prints, constructions, clay/ceramics, textiles/fiberart	•	•	•	•	•
Produce art that reflects knowledge of a variety of cultures		•	•	•	•

HISTORICAL/CULTURAL HERITAGE: UNDERSTAND ART HISTORY AND CULTURE

Understanding the Visual Arts in Relation to History and Cultures

Historical Background

	1	2	3	4	5
Understand that art reflects values, beliefs, traditions, expressions, or experiences in a historical context	•	•	•	•	•
Recognize or describe art as a visual record of humankind	•	•	•	•	•
Recognize that media, tools, materials, and processes available to artists have changed through history	•	•	•	•	•
Relate art to different kinds of jobs in everyday life	•	•	•	•	•
Identify main ideas expressed in art	•	•	•	•	•
Recognize a variety of artworks as being from various historical eras		•	•	•	•
Investigate major themes in historical/contemporary eras			•	•	•
Identify the roles of art in American society				•	•

Cultural Influences

	1	2	3	4	5
Understand that art reflects values, beliefs, traditions, expressions, or experiences in a cultural context	•	•	•	•	•
Compare and contrast art from various cultures	•	•	•	•	•
Recognize a variety of artworks as being from various cultures	•	•	•	•	•
Determine ways in which artworks reflect or express cultural themes	•	•	•	•	•
Acknowledge and appreciate the artistic contributions of various ethnic groups in our culture	•	•	•	•	•
Compare ways individuals and families are depicted in art	•	•	•	•	•
Identify stories and constructions in art		•	•	•	•
Identify the characteristics of art from other cultures, and value the images, symbols, and themes distinguishing a specific culture		•	•	•	•

Artists and Artistic Styles

	1	2	3	4	5
Identify and discuss the artworks of a particular artist	•	•	•	•	•

	GRADE				
	1	2	3	4	5
Value the diverse contributions of artists	•	•	•	•	•
Recognize various artistic styles	•	•	•	•	•
Recognize artists' roles in history and society (to inform, define, interpret, enlighten, entertain; to raise questions and cause reflection; to provide a visual record of humankind; to communicate values, beliefs, feelings; to reveal social and political customs)	•	•	•	•	•
Learn that art is universal, made by people in all cultures throughout history	•	•	•	•	•
Recognize that artists are influenced by artists of the past		•	•	•	•

Understanding the Visual Arts in Relation to the Environment and Everyday Lives

Art in the Environment

	1	2	3	4	5
Develop an awareness of art in natural and human-made environments	•	•	•	•	•
Respond to art elements and design principles (formal structure) found in natural and human-made environments	•	•	•	•	•
Identify art that reflects, celebrates, or communicates sensitivity to natural and human-made environments	•	•	•	•	•

Art in the Community

	1	2	3	4	5
Recognize art as an important part of daily life	•	•	•	•	•
Recognize that art can contribute to the quality of daily life	•	•	•	•	•
Develop awareness of the historical relationship between art and daily life	•	•	•	•	•
Recognize the function of visual arts in the family, the neighborhood, and the community		•	•	•	•
Recognize the importance of art careers		•	•	•	•

RESPONSE/EVALUATION: MAKE INFORMED JUDGMENTS ABOUT ARTWORKS

Apply Simple Criteria to Make Informed Judgments About Art

	1	2	3	4	5
Analyze art elements in art	•	•	•	•	•
Analyze design principles in art	•	•	•	•	•
Analyze media, processes, techniques in art	•	•	•	•	•
Form conclusions about artworks	•	•	•	•	•
Analyze and interpret moods, meanings, symbolism, themes, stories, constructions in art		•	•	•	•

Evaluate Personal Artworks

	1	2	3	4	5
Identify general intent in art	•	•	•	•	•
Identify expressive qualities in art	•	•	•	•	•
Form conclusions about art	•	•	•	•	•
Interpret meaning in art	•	•	•	•	•

Evaluate Artworks by Peers and Others

	1	2	3	4	5
View and respond to original art and reproductions	•	•	•	•	•
Use art vocabulary in discussions about artworks	•	•	•	•	•
Recognize characteristics that make artworks similar and different	•	•	•	•	•
Distinguish characteristics of style in art	•	•	•	•	•
Respond to evidence of skill and craftsmanship found in art	•	•	•	•	•
Respect the differences in others' responses to and perceptions of art	•	•	•	•	•
Identify ideas/moods in original artworks, portfolios, and exhibitions by peers and others	•	•	•	•	•
Recognize that the aim of criticism is to clarify the meaning of and to share discoveries about art		•	•	•	•

CONNECTIONS BETWEEN AND AMONG THE ARTS AND OTHER CONTENT AREAS

	1	2	3	4	5
Discover and identify connections between the visual arts and other disciplines	•	•	•	•	•
Construct meaning and express ideas, feelings, experiences, and responses through connections to the other subjects	•	•	•	•	•
Analyze and interpret similarities and differences between characteristics of the visual arts and other disciplines		•	•	•	•

Index

A

Abbott, Meredith Brooks
About the Artist, 58
Abstract Expressionism, 178–181
Activities
See Artist's Workshops
Adams, Ansel, 73
Albers, Josef
About the Artist, 58
Alternative Planners
Teaching by Elements and Principles, R43
Teaching by Media, R42
Architecture
balance, 162–165
Art and Culture, 96–97, 136–137, 156–157
Art and Nature, 66–67
Art and the Environment, 36–37
Art Criticism
See Criticism
Art History
See also Encyclopedia of Artists and Art History
Abstract Expressionism, 178–181
Aztec art, 122
Ching dynasty, 118
Computer art, 198–201
Folk art, 132–135
Kente cloth, 118
Kwele people, 122
Masks, 122–125
Murals, 168–171
Navajo Indian tribe, 118
Pop Art, 192–195
Spanish missions, 156
Surrealism, 182–185
Art Prints, 24b, 54b, 84b, 114b, 144b, 174b
Art Puzzlers, 24d, 54d, 84d, 114d, 144d, 174d
Artist Biographies, 46–47, 76–77, 106–107, 126–127, 166–167, 186–187

Artists
See also Encyclopedia of Artists and Art History
Abbott, Meredith Brooks, 58
Adams, Ansel, 73
Albers, Josef, 58
Bannister, Edward Mitchell, 24b, 54b
Benton, Thomas Hart, 26
Bierstadt, Albert, 152
Bronzino, Agnolo, 88
Caillebotte, Gustave, 144
Chukran, Bobbi A., 48
Clive, John, 198
Cornell, Joseph, 78, 188
Corot, Jean Baptiste Camille, 148
Dalí, Salvador, 54b, 174, 174b, 182
Degas, Edgar, 98
Duncanson, Robert Scott, 24
Dunton, W. Herbert, 136
Escher, M. C., 72
Escobar, Marisol, 84b, 106–107, 174b
Estes, Richard, 144b
Feininger, Lyonel, 98
Figari, Pedro, 132
Foster, Norman, 162
Garza, Carmen Lomas, 128
Gauguin, Paul, 48
Glackens, William James, 146
Graziani, Sante, 138
Gris, Juan, 92
Hassam, Frederick Childe, 138
Hockney, David, 78
Homer, Winslow, 84
Jawlensky, Alexej von, 28
Johns, Jasper, 114b, 174b
Kahlo, Frida, 88
Klee, Paul, 24b, 46–47, 84b
Krasner, Lee, 178
Lichtenstein, Roy, 192
Lin, Maya, 186–187
Maffei, Ricardo, 176
Magritte, René, 182
Marc, Franz, 24b, 32
Matisse, Henri, 24b, 54b, 76–77

Meechan, Colleen, 38
Modigliani, Amedeo, 84b, 114b, 126–127
Monet, Claude, 42, 68
Morisot, Berthe, 68
Moses, Grandma, 132
Nevelson, Louise, 188
Ochoa, Isy, 62
O'Keeffe, Georgia, 32, 34, 36
Outterbridge, John, 174b
Paik, Nam June, 188
Pei, I. M., 144b, 166–167
Picasso, Pablo, 92
Pollock, Jackson, 178
Pugh, Anna, 86
Pugh, John, 168
Ray, Man, 108
Remington, Frederic S., 56, 57, 108
Renoir, Pierre-Auguste, 54b, 144b
Ringgold, Faith, 114
Ruysch, Rachel, 24b, 54b
Saligman, Meg, 168
Sarian, Matiros, 42
Seurat, Georges, 54, 152
Shrager, Joan Myerson, 198
Smithson, Robert, 28
Thiebaud, Wayne, 192
Thomas, Alma Woodsey, 144b, 174b
Van Gogh, Vincent, 148
Velázquez, Diego, 96
Wagstaff, Bob, 38
Warhol, Andy, 192
Wood, Grant, 84b, 114b
Wood, Memphis, 62
Artist's Eye Activities, 37, 47, 67, 77, 97, 107, 127, 137, 157, 167, 187, 197
See also Production activities
Artist's Workshops
Abstract Portrait, 95
Action Painting, 181
Building Design, 165
Charcoal Still-Life, 75
Class Mural, 171
Close-Up View Painting, 35

Collage, 65
Complementary Colors Painting, 41
Computer-Generated Artwork, 201
Construction with Found Objects, 191
Folk Art Painting, 135
Landscape, 31
Monochromatic Painting, 61
Outdoor Scene Painting, 71
Panel Drawing, 101
Paper Cutting, 131
Paper Mask, 125
Park Design, 161
Pastel Drawing, 81
Pop Art Collage, 195
Portrait, 91
Print, 141
Relief Sculpture, 105
Reverse Weaving, 121
Scene Showing Depth, 151
Scene with Linear Perspective, 155
Soap Sculpture, 111
Still-Life Collage, 51
Surrealist Painting, 185
See also Materials

Assessment
Assessment Options, 24d, 53, 54d, 83, 84d, 113, 114d, 143, 144d, 173, 174d, 203, R28–R33
Informal Assessment, 31, 35, 41, 45, 51, 61, 65, 71, 75, 81, 91, 95, 101, 105, 111, 121, 125, 131, 135, 141, 151, 155, 161, 165, 171, 181, 185, 191, 195, 201
Portfolio Assessment, 53, 83, 113, 143, 173, 203

Aztecs, 122

B

Background Information
See also Encyclopedia of Artists and Art History
About the Artist, 24, 26, 28, 32, 38, 42, 46, 48, 54, 58, 62, 68, 72, 76, 78, 84, 86, 88, 92, 96, 98, 106, 108, 114, 126, 128, 132, 136, 138, 144, 146, 148, 152, 162, 166, 168, 174, 176, 178, 182, 186, 188, 192, 198
Art History, 102, 116, 118, 122, 156, 158, 196

Balance, 122–125, 128, 129, 130, 131, 132, 133, 135, 136, 139, 140, 141, 143, 159, 162–165
Bannister, Edward Mitchell
Untitled (Sunset with Quarter Moon and Farmhouse), 24b, 54b
Benton, Thomas Hart
About the Artist, 26
Bierstadt, Albert
About the Artist, 152
Bronzino, Agnolo
About the Artist, 88

C

Caillebotte, Gustave
About the Artist, 144
Careers in Art, 196–197
Challenge, 31, 121, 141, 161, 171, 177, 195
Ching dynasty, 118
Chukran, Bobbi A.
About the Artist, 48
Classroom Management
Challenge, 31, 35, 41, 45, 51, 61, 65, 71, 75, 81, 91, 95, 101, 105, 111, 121, 125, 131, 135, 141, 151, 155, 161, 165, 171, 181, 185, 191, 195, 201
Early Finishers, 31, 35, 41, 45, 51, 61, 65, 71, 75, 81, 91, 95, 101, 105, 111, 121, 125, 131, 135, 141, 151, 155, 161, 165, 171, 181, 185, 191, 195, 201
Quick Activity, 31, 35, 41, 45, 51, 61, 65, 71, 75, 81, 91, 95, 101, 105, 111, 121, 125, 131, 135, 141, 151, 155, 161, 165, 171, 181, 185, 191, 195, 201
Clive, John
About the Artist, 198
Collage, 51, 65, 195
Color
color schemes, 38–41
complementary, 38–41
light and, 68–71
mood and, 42–45
value and, 58–61
Community Connection, 52, 82, 112, 142, 172, 202
Computer art, 198–201

Constructions, 188–191
Cornell, Joseph
About the Artist, 78, 188
Corot, Jean Baptiste Camille
About the Artist, 148
Creative expression/performance
design original artworks, 31, 35, 41, 45, 51, 52, 61, 65, 67, 71, 75, 81, 82, 91, 101, 105, 111, 121, 125, 127, 151, 155, 157, 161, 165, 167, 171, 172
integrate a variety of ideas about
community in original artworks, 37, 52, 135, 151, 161, 171
family in original artworks, 82, 112, 131, 135, 141, 161, 172
life events in original artworks, 37, 82, 101, 131, 135, 141, 161
self in original artworks, 51, 77, 81, 131, 141, 161
invent ways to explore photographic imagery
using a variety of art materials, 67, 71, 95, 161, 165
using a variety of art media, 67, 71, 81, 95, 161
invent ways to produce artworks
using a variety of art materials, 47, 61, 65, 105, 111, 121, 125, 157
using a variety of art media, 33, 61, 125, 157, 181
Critical thinking
Critic's Corner, 53, 83, 113, 143, 173, 203
Think About Art, 37, 47, 67, 77, 97, 107, 127, 137, 157, 167, 187, 197
Think Critically, 30, 34, 40, 44, 50, 60, 64, 70, 74, 80, 90, 94, 100, 104, 110, 130, 134, 140, 150, 154, 160, 164, 170, 180, 184, 190, 194, 200
Criticism
Critic's Corner, 53, 83, 113, 143, 173, 203
describe intent about personal artworks, 31, 35, 41, 51, 53, 65, 81, 91, 95, 101, 135, 141, 165, 171
evaluation/criticism, 45, 71, 75, 81, 91, 95, 101, 105, 111, 135, 151, 181, 195

form conclusions about personal artworks, 45, 71, 121, 131, 141, 151, 155

Informal Assessment, 31, 35, 41, 45, 51, 61, 65, 71, 75, 81, 91, 95, 101, 105, 111, 121, 125, 131, 135, 141, 151, 155, 161, 165, 171, 181, 185, 191, 195, 201

interpret ideas in exhibitions
  by others, 47, 77, 97, 127, 186
  by peers, 37, 67, 107, 112, 137

interpret ideas in original artworks
  by others, 30, 39, 44, 47, 50, 56, 60, 61, 64, 70, 74, 77, 80, 86, 88, 89, 90, 94, 99, 100, 110, 113, 120, 130, 134, 140, 143, 146, 150, 151, 160, 163, 164, 170, 173
  by peers, 35, 37, 61, 67, 131, 137, 155, 157, 161, 165, 167

interpret ideas in portfolios
  by others, 46, 47, 76, 77, 82, 97, 106, 127, 142
  by peers, 37, 67, 107, 137, 172

interpret moods in exhibitions
  by others, 47, 77, 97, 127, 186
  by peers, 37, 107, 112, 137, 201

interpret moods in original artworks
  by others, 43, 47, 53, 58, 60, 74, 77, 79, 89, 133, 134, 140, 173
  by peers, 37, 127, 137, 195, 197

interpret moods in portfolios
  by others, 46, 47, 76, 97, 106, 127, 142
  by peers, 37, 107, 137, 202

Cross-Curricular Connections
  language arts, 25, 43, 55, 63, 85, 115, 145, 175, 193
  math, 29, 93, 154, 183
  music, 99, 167
  reading, 26–27, 56–57, 86–87, 116–117, 146–147, 176–177
  science, 33, 36–37, 39, 44, 64, 103, 159, 184, 187, 189, 196–197
  social studies, 40, 49, 50, 59, 67, 69, 73, 76–77, 79, 89, 96–97, 106–107, 109, 119, 123, 124, 126–127, 129, 133, 136–137, 139, 140, 149, 153, 156–157, 163, 164, 166–167, 169, 179, 186–187, 193, 197, 199

Culture
  See Historical/cultural heritage

D

Dalí, Salvador
  About the Artist, 174, 182
  The Profile of Time, 54b, 174b

Degas, Edgar
  About the Artist, 98

Design
  See Principles of design

Discussion Cards, R34–R38

Drawing, 31, 75, 81, 91, 101, 155
  See also Production activities

Duncanson, Robert Scott
  About the Artist, 24

Dunton, W. Herbert
  About the Artist, 136

E

Elements of art
  color, 38–41, 42–45, 58–61, 68–71
  form, 109
  line, 28–31
  planning by, R43
  shape, 32–35
  space, 103, 105
  texture, 62–65
  value, 72–75

Emphasis, 78–81

Encyclopedia of Artists and Art History, R44–R65

Escher, M. C.
  About the Artist, 72

Escobar, Marisol
  About the Artist, 106
  Artist Biography, 106–107
  The Family, 84b, 174b

ESL, 27, 31, 35, 41, 45, 51, 57, 61, 65, 71, 75, 81, 87, 91, 95, 101, 105, 111, 117, 121, 125, 131, 135, 141, 147, 151, 155, 161, 165, 171, 177, 181, 185, 191, 195, 201

Estes, Richard
  Bus Interior, 144b

Evaluation/Criticism, 45, 71, 75, 81, 91, 95, 101, 105, 111, 135, 151, 181, 195

F

Feininger, Lyonel
  About the Artist, 98

Fiber art, 118–121

Figari, Pedro
  About the Artist, 132

Figures
  in motion, 98–101

Folk art, 132–135

Form, 109

Foster, Norman
  About the Artist, 162

Free and Inexpensive Materials, R41

G

Garden design, 158–161

Garza, Carmen Lomas
  About the Artist, 128

Gauguin, Paul
  About the Artist, 48

Glackens, William James
  About the Artist, 146

Graziani, Sante
  About the Artist, 138

Gris, Juan
  About the Artist, 92

H

Hassam, Frederick Childe
  About the Artist, 138

Historical/cultural heritage
  See also Art History
  compare selected artworks from a variety of cultural settings, 50, 63, 90, 94, 103, 104, 108, 109, 110, 116, 120, 123, 124, 125, 126, 130, 131, 134, 135, 140, 141, 142, 160, 164, 170, 173
  contrast selected artworks from a variety of cultural settings, 50, 63, 90, 94, 103, 104, 108, 109, 110, 116, 120, 123, 124, 125, 130, 131, 134, 135, 140, 141, 142, 143, 168, 170, 173
  identify simple main ideas expressed in art, 26, 30, 31, 34, 40, 41, 44, 45, 50, 53, 59, 69, 90, 104, 106, 124, 133, 140, 143, 150, 153, 154, 155, 160, 171

identify the roles of art in American
society, 97, 103, 109, 119, 136,
139, 166
Hockney, David
About the Artist, 78
Home and Community Connections,
52, 82, 112, 142, 172, 202
Homer, Winslow
About the Artist, 84

J

Jawlensky, Alexej von
About the Artist, 28
Johns, Jasper
Three Flags, 114b, 174b

K

Kahlo, Frida
About the Artist, 88
Kente cloth, 118
Klee, Paul
About the Artist, 46
Artist Biography, 46–47
Senecio (Head of a Man),
24b, 84b
Krasner, Lee
About the Artist, 178
Kwele people, 122

L

Language Arts
See Reading Skills; Recommended
Reading; Writing Activities
Lichtenstein, Roy
About the Artist, 192
Lin, Maya
About the Artist, 186
Artist Biography, 186–187
Line
in landscapes, 28–31
Literature
See Reading Skills; Recommended
Reading
Locate It, 24, 30, 54, 59, 69, 84, 89,
93, 99, 104, 110, 114, 134, 144,
149, 160, 170, 174, 179, 189

M

Maffei, Ricardo
About the Artist, 176

Magritte, René
About the Artist, 182
Marc, Franz
About the Artist, 32
Sheep, 24b
Masks, 122–125
Materials, R39–R40
free and inexpensive, R41
materials lists for Artist's Workshops,
24e–24f, 54e–54f, 84e–84f,
114e–114f, 144e–144f, 174e–174f
Math, 29, 93, 154, 183, 199
Matisse, Henri
About the Artist, 76
Artist Biography, 76–77
The Large Red Interior, 24b, 54b
Media, planning by, R42
See also Resources
Media and Techniques, R15–R23
Meechan, Colleen
About the Artist, 38
Meeting Individual Needs, R24–R27
See also Challenge; ESL; Special
Needs
Modigliani, Amedeo
About the Artist, 126
Artist Biography, 126–127
Head of a Woman, 84b, 114b
Monet, Claude
About the Artist, 42, 68
Morisot, Berthe
About the Artist, 68
Moses, Grandma
About the Artist, 132
Movement, 159, 160
Murals, 168–171
Music, 99, 167

N

Navajo Indian tribe, 118
Nevelson, Louise
About the Artist, 188

O

Ochoa, Isy
About the Artist, 62
O'Keeffe, Georgia
About the Artist, 32, 34, 36
Outterbridge, John
California Crosswalk, 174b

P

Paik, Nam June
About the Artist, 188
Painting, 35, 41, 45, 61, 71, 135,
181, 185
Paper art, 128–131
Pattern, 119, 120, 121, 134,
139, 140
Pei, I. M.
About the Artist, 166
Artist Biography, 166–167
Pyramid du Louvre, 144b
Perception
choose appropriate vocabulary to
discuss the use of
art elements such as color, texture,
form, line, space, and value,
30, 31, 33, 34, 39, 40, 44,
46, 49, 53, 59, 60, 63, 64,
66, 67, 69, 70, 71, 73, 75,
76, 93, 99, 100, 101, 103,
105, 119, 121, 123, 130,
149, 150, 154, 159, 164
art principles such as emphasis,
pattern, rhythm, balance,
proportion, and unity, 79, 80,
81, 91, 119, 120, 121, 123,
124, 125, 129, 130, 131, 133,
136, 139, 141, 143, 160, 161,
162, 163, 164, 171
communicate ideas about
community using life experiences,
30, 36, 103, 122, 132, 158, 164,
168, 170
community using sensory
knowledge, 30, 103, 133, 134,
158, 164, 170
family using life experiences, 70,
77, 100, 107, 112, 122, 132,
142, 158
family using sensory knowledge,
70, 84, 100, 107, 112, 133, 134,
142, 158
school using life experiences, 28,
32, 72, 96, 101, 122, 164, 167
school using sensory knowledge,
28, 32, 72, 101, 154, 164,
167, 185
self using life experiences, 31,
50, 63, 67, 90, 118, 128, 138,
142, 167

Index

self using sensory knowledge, 24,
  31, 54, 62, 63, 67, 69, 70, 79,
  84, 103, 109, 120, 140, 142,
  144, 149, 159, 160
Perspective
  depth and distance, 148–151
  techniques, 152–155
Picasso, Pablo
  About the Artist, 92
Pollock, Jackson
  About the Artist, 178
Pop Art, 192–195
Portrait
  abstract, 92–95
  proportion in, 88–91
Principles of design
  Balance, 122–125, 128, 129, 130,
    131, 132, 133, 135, 136, 139,
    140, 141, 143, 159, 162–165
  Emphasis, 78–81
  Movement, 159, 160
  Pattern, 119, 120, 121, 134, 139,
    140
  planning by, R43
  Proportion, 88–91
  Rhythm, 99, 101, 190
  Unity, 159, 160, 164, 169, 171, 189
  Variety, 183, 189, 193, 195, 199,
    201
Print, 141
Production activities
  See Artist's Workshops
Proportion, 88–91
Pugh, Anna
  About the Artist, 86
Pugh, John
  About the Artist, 168

R

Ray, Man
  About the Artist, 108
Reading Skills
  See also Recommended Reading
  author's/artist's purpose, 176–177,
    180, 184, 190, 194, 200
  compare and contrast, 50, 116–117,
    120, 124, 130, 134, 140
  fact and opinion, 56–57, 60, 64, 70,
    74, 80
  main idea and details, 26–27, 30, 34,
    40, 44, 50

narrative elements, 86–87, 90, 94,
  100, 104, 110
summarize and paraphrase,
  146–147, 150, 154, 160, 164, 170
Recommended Reading, 31, 35, 41,
  45, 51, 61, 65, 71, 75, 91, 95, 101,
  105, 111, 121, 125, 131, 135, 141,
  151, 155, 161, 165, 171, 181, 185,
  191, 195, 201
Remington, Frederic S.
  About the Artist, 56, 108
Renoir, Pierre-Auguste
  The Bathers, 54b, 144b
Resources
  Alternative Planners, R42–R43
  Assessment Options, R28–R33
  Discussion Cards, R34–R38
  Encyclopedia of Artists and Art
    History, R44–R65
  Free and Inexpensive Materials, R41
  Materials, R39–R40
  materials lists for Artist's Workshops,
    24e–24f, 54e–54f, 84e–84f,
    114e–114f, 144e–144f, 174e–174f
  Media and Techniques, R15–R23
  Meeting Individual Needs, R24–R27
  Scope and Sequence, R66–R69
  Teacher Resource Book, 24a, 54a,
    84a, 114a, 144a, 174a
  Technology Resources, 24a, 54a,
    84a, 114a, 144a, 174a
  Unit Planning Guides, 24c–24d,
    54c–54d, 84c–84d, 114c–114d,
    144c–144d, 174c–174d
  Using Student Handbook, R3–R14
Response/Evaluation
  Critic's Corner, 53, 83, 113, 143,
    173, 203
  describe intent about personal
    artworks, 31, 35, 41, 51, 53, 65,
    81, 91, 95, 101, 135, 141, 165,
    171
  evaluation/criticism, 45, 71, 75, 81,
    91, 95, 101, 105, 111, 135, 151,
    181, 195
  form conclusions about personal
    artworks, 45, 71, 121, 131, 141,
    151, 155
  Informal Assessment, 31, 35, 41,
    45, 51, 61, 65, 71, 75, 81, 91, 95,
    101, 105, 111, 121, 125, 131,
    135, 141, 151, 155, 161, 165,

171, 181, 185, 191, 195, 201
interpret ideas in exhibitions
  by others, 47, 77, 97, 127, 186
  by peers, 37, 67, 107, 112, 137
interpret ideas in original artworks
  by others, 30, 39, 44, 47, 50, 56,
    60, 61, 64, 70, 74, 77, 80, 86,
    88, 89, 90, 94, 99, 100, 110,
    113, 120, 130, 134, 140, 143,
    146, 150, 151, 160, 163, 164,
    170, 173
  by peers, 35, 37, 61, 67, 131, 137,
    155, 157, 161, 165, 167
interpret ideas in portfolios
  by others, 46, 47, 76, 77, 82, 97,
    106, 127, 142
  by peers, 37, 67, 107, 137, 172
interpret moods in exhibitions
  by others, 47, 77, 97, 127, 186
  by peers, 37, 107, 112, 137, 201
interpret moods in original artworks
  by others, 43, 47, 53, 58, 60, 74,
    77, 79, 89, 133, 134, 140, 173
  by peers, 37, 127, 137, 195, 197
interpret moods in portfolios
  by others, 46, 47, 76, 97, 106,
    127, 142
  by peers, 37, 107, 137, 202
Review and Reflect, 52–53, 82–83,
  112–113, 142–143, 172–173,
  202–203
Rhythm, 99, 101, 190
Ringgold, Faith
  About the Artist, 114
Ruysch, Rachel
  Still Life of Summer Flowers, 24b,
    54b

S

Saligman, Meg
  About the Artist, 168
Sarian, Matiros
  About the Artist, 42
School-Home Connection, 52, 82,
  112, 142, 172, 202
Science, 33, 36–37, 39, 44, 64, 103,
  159, 184, 187, 189, 196–197
Scope and Sequence, R66–R69
Sculpture, 105, 111
  in history, 108–111
  relief, 102–105

Seurat, Georges
About the Artist, 54, 152
Shapes
in nature, 32–35
overlapping, 48–51
Shrager, Joan Myerson
About the Artist, 198
Smithson, Robert
About the Artist, 28
Social studies, 40, 49, 50, 59, 67, 69, 72, 73, 76–77, 79, 89, 96–97, 106–107, 109, 119, 123, 124, 126–127, 129, 133, 136–137, 139, 140, 149, 153, 156–157, 163, 164, 166–167, 169, 179, 186–187, 193, 197, 199
Special Needs, 51, R27
Step into the Art, 24, 54, 84, 114, 144, 174
Student Art Exhibition, 137, 157, 167, 197, 204
Student Handbook, R3–R14
Surrealism, 182–185
Symbols, 138–141

T

Technology
Electronic Art Gallery CD-ROM, 24, 26, 28, 32, 38, 42, 48, 54, 56, 58, 62, 72, 76, 78, 84, 86, 88, 92, 96, 98, 102, 106, 108, 114, 116, 118, 122, 126, 128, 132, 136, 138, 144, 146, 148, 152, 162, 166, 168, 174, 176, 178, 182, 186, 188, 198
Multimedia Art Glossary, 25, 28, 32, 38, 42, 48, 55, 58, 62, 68, 72, 78, 85, 88, 92, 98, 102, 108, 115, 118, 122, 128, 132, 138, 145, 148, 152, 158, 162, 168, 175, 178, 182, 188, 192, 198
Multimedia Biographies, 47, 77, 97, 107, 127, 167, 187
Tests
See Assessment
Texture, 62–65
Theme Connections
Art Reflects Culture, 114a–114b, 114–115
The Artist's Environment, 144a–144b, 144–145
Moments in Time, 54a–54b, 54–55
Nature Inspires Art, 24a–24b, 24–25
People in Art, 84a–84b, 84–85
Stretch Your Imagination, 174a–174b, 174–175
Thiebaud, Wayne
About the Artist, 192
Thomas, Alma Woodsey
The Eclipse, 174b
Tunic, 116

U

Unit Planning Guides, 24c–24d, 54c–54d, 84c–84d, 114c–114d, 144c–144d, 174c–174d
Unity, 159, 160, 164, 169, 171, 189

V

Value
of black and white, 72–75
Van Gogh, Vincent
About the Artist, 148
Variety, 183, 189, 193, 195, 199, 201
Vehicle Design, 196–197
Velázquez, Diego
About the Artist, 96

Viewing an Artist's Work, 127
Viewing Public Artworks, 187
Vocabulary
review, 52, 82, 112, 142, 172, 202
Unit Vocabulary, 25, 55, 85, 115, 145, 175

W

Wagstaff, Bob
About the Artist, 38
Warhol, Andy
About the Artist, 192
Weaving, 121
Wood, Grant
American Gothic, 84b, 114b
Wood, Memphis
About the Artist, 62
Writing Activities
author's purpose paragraph, 202
compare-and-contrast composition, 143
descriptive, 30, 40, 60, 64, 70, 74, 90, 94, 104, 120, 124, 160, 164, 170, 190, 194
expository, 34, 50, 80, 130, 140, 180, 200
Extend Through Writing, 31, 35, 41, 45, 51, 61, 65, 71, 75, 81, 91, 95, 101, 105, 111, 121, 125, 131, 135, 141, 151, 155, 161, 165, 171, 181, 185, 191, 195, 201
fact-and-opinion paragraph, 83
main idea and details composition, 53
narrative, 44, 110, 113, 134, 150, 154, 184
summarize and paraphrase, 173

Cross-Curricular
Themes and Topics

READING	Examples of Artworks and Artist's Workshop Activities from *Art Everywhere*, Grade 4	
Biographies	Paul Klee, pp. 46–47 Henri Matisse, pp. 76–77 *Self-Portrait with Loose Hair*, p. 90 Marisol Escobar, pp. 106–107	Amedeo Modigliani, pp. 126–127 I. M. Pei, pp. 166–167 Maya Lin, pp. 186–187
Communities	*June Morning*, p. 26 *Windy Day in England*, p. 28 *The Beach at Sainte-Adresse*, p. 42 *The Old Checkered House*, p. 132 *The American Farm*, p. 139 *Four Seasons*, p. 143	*Outdoor Swimming Pool*, p. 146 San Francisco de Asis Mission, p. 156 *Sunflower Mural on a Fence*, p. 168 *Common Threads*, p. 169 Artist's Workshop: Create a Folk Art Painting, p. 135 Artist's Workshop: Create a Class Mural, p. 171
Cooperation	*A Day in the Country*, p. 86 *The Sunflower Quilting Bee at Arles*, p. 114 *Sunflower Mural on Fence*, p. 168	Artist's Workshop: Create a Class Mural, p. 171 Art Print 10: *Panamanian Cuna Mola with Iguanas and Birds*
Creativity	*Spiral Jetty*, p. 30 *Blue Fronds*, p. 40 *L'Italienne*, p. 49 *Elysian Fields*, p. 64 *Dewdrop*, p. 73 *Toward the Blue Peninsula*, p. 80 *Portrait of Picasso*, p. 93 *Child Who Runs on the Balcony*, p. 100 *The Generals*, p. 107	*Man Ray*, p. 110 *Golconda*, p. 113 *Flowery Words: Stories, Poems, Song, History, and Wisdom*, p. 130 *Sunflower Mural on Fence*, p. 168 *Seven Point One (Siete Punto Uno)*, p. 170 *Rhinoceros Dressed in Lace*, p. 174 *Telephone Homard*, p. 184 Artist's Workshop: Create Texture in a Collage, p. 65
Cultures	*Terra-Cotta Army Figure*, p. 109 British Herald's Tunic, p. 116 Indian Warrior's Shirt, p. 116 Navajo traditional shawl, p. 118 Detail of African kente cloth, p. 118 Chinese Emperor's Twelve Symbol Robe, p. 119 Aztec Mask, p. 122 Inuit Finger Masks, p. 124	*Creole Dance*, p. 133 San Francisco de Asis Mission, p. 156 Mission Nuestra Señora de la Concepción de Acuña, p. 157 *Night Scene in the Saruwaka Street in Edo*, p. 173 Art Print 9: *Limestone Bust of Queen Nefertiti* Art Print 10: *Panamanian Cuna Mola with Iguanas and Birds*
Diversity	*Portrait of Gordon Parks*, p. 78 *The Sunflower Quilting Bee at Arles*, p. 114 Indian Warrior's Shirt, p. 116 *Creole Dance*, p. 133 *Four Seasons*, p. 143	*Common Threads*, p. 169 Art Print 8: *The Family* Art Print 17: *Eclipse* Art Print 18: *California Crosswalk*
Explorations	Sacagawea Coin, p. 102 *Moon Landing*, p. 104	*Old Texas*, p. 136 *Among the Sierra Nevada Mountains, California*, p. 152

Families	Children at the Beach, p. 70 A Day in the Country, p. 86 Las Meninas, p. 96	Artist's Workshop: Create a Folk Art Painting, p. 135 Art Print 7: American Gothic Art Print 8: The Family
Friends	The Butterfly Hunt, p. 69 Children on a Fence, p. 84 Outdoor Swimming Pool, p. 146	Artist's Workshop: Draw a Portrait, p. 91 Artist's Workshop: Carve a Relief Sculpture, p. 105 Art Print 4: The Bathers
Growth and Change	June Morning, p. 26 The Fall of the Cowboy, p. 56 Four Seasons, p. 143	The Rock and Roll Hall of Fame, Cleveland, Ohio, p. 166 Seven Point One, p. 170 Vehicle Design, pp. 196–197
Heroes	Fredrick Douglass, p. 97 Sam Houston, p. 97 Sacagawea Coin, p. 102 Mount Rushmore National Monument, p. 102 Head of Colossus of Ramses II, p. 104 Moon Landing, p. 104	President Charles DeGaulle, p. 106 The Generals, p. 107 Cowgirl Mural, p. 137 George Washington, p. 140 Vietnam Veterans Memorial, p. 187 Art Print 9: Limestone Bust of Queen Nefertiti
Self-Discovery	Self-Portrait, p. 76 Self-Portrait with Loose Hair, p. 90	Self-Portrait, p. 126 Six Self-Portraits, p. 192
Traditions	The Fall of the Cowboy, p. 56 Terra-Cotta Army Figure, p. 109 British Herald's Tunic, p. 116 Detail of African kente cloth, p. 118	Creole Dance, p. 133 The Fourth of July, p. 138 Art Print 10: Panamanian Cuna Mola with Iguanas and Birds

SOCIAL STUDIES	Examples of Artworks and Artist's Workshop Activities from *Art Everywhere*, Grade 4	

GEOGRAPHY
• understanding place
	A Small Volcano in Mexican Countryside, p. 29
	Summer Days, p. 37
	The Fall of the Cowboy, p. 56
	Palm Tree in Mauritania, p. 78
	Mount Rushmore National Monument, p. 102
	Old Texas, p. 136
	The American Farm, p. 139
	Paris Street, Rainy Day, p. 144
		Café Terrace on the Place du Forum, Arles, at Night,
		    p. 149
		San Francisco de Asis Mission, p. 156
		Mission Nuestra Señora de la Concepción de Acuña,
		    p. 157
		Night Scene in the Saruwaka Street in Edo, p. 173
		Artist's Workshop: Draw a Landscape, p. 31
		Art Print 15: The Alamo

• understanding human-environment interactions	Spiral Jetty, p. 30 The Beach at Sainte-Adresse, p. 42	Children at the Beach, p. 70

• understanding regions	Landscape at Murnau, p. 29
	A Small Volcano in Mexican Countryside, p. 29
	Summer Days, p. 37
	Palm Tree in Mauritania, p. 78
	Old Texas, p. 136
		Among the Sierra Nevada Mountains, California,
		    p. 152
		Seven Point One (Siete Punto Uno), p. 170
		Artist's Workshop: Paint a Seascape or Desert
		    Landscape, p. 45

HISTORY • understanding communities in the Western Hemisphere	June Morning, p. 26 A Day in the Country, p. 86 Sam Houston, p. 97 Indian Warrior's Shirt, p. 116	Navajo traditional shawl, p. 118 The American Farm, p. 139 Four Seasons, p. 143 San Francisco de Asis Mission, p. 156

	Mission Nuestra Señora de la Concepcíon de Acuña, p. 157	Common Threads, p. 169 Art Print 15: The Alamo
• understanding explorations and journeys	The Fall of the Cowboy, p. 56 Sacagawea Coin, p. 102 Moon Landing, p. 104 Old Texas, p. 136	Among the Sierra Nevada Mountains, California, p. 152 Mission Nuestra Señora de la Concepcíon de Acuña, p. 157 Art Print 15: The Alamo
• understanding important factors in the formation of Texas	The Fall of the Cowboy, p. 56 Sam Houston, p. 97 The Rattlesnake, p. 110 Old Texas, p. 136	San Francisco de Asis Mission, p. 156 Mission Nuestra Señora de la Concepcíon de Acuña, p. 157 Art Print 15: The Alamo
CULTURE • understanding ideas of shared humanity and unique identity	Terra-Cotta Army Figure, p. 109 The Sunflower Quilting Bee at Arles, p. 114 Indian Warrior's Shirt, p. 116 Navajo traditional shawl, p. 118 Detail of African kente cloth, p. 118 Chinese Emperor's Twelve Symbol Robe, p. 119	Aztec Mask, p. 122 Inuit Finger Masks, p. 124 Creole Dance, p. 133 Common Threads, p. 169 Art Print 10: Panamanian Cuna Mola with Iguanas and Birds
CIVICS AND GOVERNMENT • understanding identity as a resident of Texas	Bluebonnet Collage, p. 50 The Fall of the Cowboy, p. 56 Sam Houston, p. 97 The Rattlesnake, p. 110	Old Texas, p. 136 The Fourth of July, p. 138 Art Print 15: The Alamo
• understanding civic responsibility	Sam Houston, p. 97 Mount Rushmore National Monument, p. 102 The Fourth of July, p. 138 George Washington, p. 140	Vietnam Veterans Memorial, p. 187 Art Print 12: Three Flags Art Print 15: The Alamo
SCIENCE	**Examples of Artworks and Artist's Workshop Activities from Art Everywhere, Grade 4**	
LIFE SCIENCE Animals	June Morning, p. 26 Monkey Frieze, p. 32 Mazon Creek fossil, p. 36 Summer Days, p. 37 Visitors to the Rainforest, p. 39 Gazelles, p. 43 The Fall of the Cowboy, p. 56 Velvet Cat I, p. 63	The Rattlesnake, p. 110 Bird Tree, p. 134 Old Texas, p. 136 Rhinoceros Dressed in Lace, p. 174 Artist's Workshop: Carve a Soap Sculpture, p. 111 Art Print 3: Sheep Art Print 10: Panamanian Cuna Mola with Iguanas and Birds
Plants	June Morning, p. 26 Irises, p. 33 Poppies, p. 34 Mazon Creek fossil, p. 36 Summer Days, p. 37 Elegy for Summer, p. 38 Visitors to the Rainforest, p. 39 Bluebonnet Collage, p. 50 The Banks of the Bièvre near Bicêtre, p. 59	Flowering Tree, p. 62 Dance of the Corn Lilies, p. 72 Dewdrop, p. 73 Palm Tree in Mauritania, p. 78 The Sunflower Quilting Bee at Arles, p. 114 Flower Conservatory, Golden Gate Park, p. 159 Desert Pavillion, Brooklyn Botanical Garden, p. 160 Artist's Workshop: Paint a Close-Up View, p. 35 Art Print 5: Still Life of Summer Flowers

COMPUTER SCIENCE Technology	Vehicle Design, pp. 196–197 No. 49 D, p. 198 Plaid Construct Swirl, p. 199	Annnciation II, p. 200 Artist's Workshop: Create a Computer-Generated Artwork, p. 201
EARTH SCIENCE Weather	Windy Day in England, p. 28 The Fall of the Cowboy, p. 56 Rouen Cathedral, Bright Sun, p. 58 Rouen Cathedral, Impressions of Morning, p. 58	Wave Rock, p. 66 Torrey Pines State Reserve, p. 67 Pyramid of Cheops, p. 67 Paris Street, Rainy Day, p. 144
Land and Water	Loch Long, p. 24 Spiral Jetty, p. 30 Mazon Creek Fossils, p. 36 Wave Rock, p. 66 Torrey Pines State Reserve, p. 67	Artist's Workshop: Draw a Landscape, p. 31 Artist's Workshop: Paint a Seascape or Desert Landscape, p. 45 Artist's Workshop: Design a Park, p. 161 Art Print 4: The Bathers

MATHEMATICS

Examples of Artworks and Artist's Workshop Activities from
Art Everywhere, Grade 4

GEOMETRY Line	Windy Day in England, p. 28 Landscape of Murnau, p. 29 Spiral Jetty, p. 30 Poppies, p. 34 Topographic Landscape, p. 186 Cubist Still-Life with an Apple, p. 193 No. 49D, p. 198	Plaid Construct Swirl, p. 199 Artist's Workshop: Draw a Landscape, p. 31 Artist's Workshop: Paint a Close-Up View, p. 35 Artist's Workshop: Draw a Scene with Linear Perspective, p. 155 Art Print 13: Bus Interior Art Print 14: Pyramid du Louvre
Symmetry and Asymmetry	Flower Conservatory, Golden Gate Park, p. 159 Chase Building, p. 162 City Hall, p. 163	Hotel Nice, p. 164 Art Print 14: Pyramid du Louvre
Shape/Form	Monkey Frieze, p. 32 Homage to the Square/Red Series, Untitled III, p. 60 The Bicycle Race, p. 99 Portrait of Picasso, p. 93 City Hall, p. 163 Avalanche, p. 186	The Wave Field, p. 187 Cubist Still-Life with an Apple, p. 193 No. 49D, p. 198 Plaid Construct Swirl, p. 199 Accent in Pink, p. 203 Art Print 14: Pyramid du Louvre
RELATIONSHIPS Patterns	The Bicycle Race, p. 99 Child Who Runs on the Balcony, p. 100 British Herald's Tunic, p. 116 Indian Warrior's Shirt, p. 116 Navajo traditional shawl, p. 118 Detail of African kente cloth, p. 118 Chinese Emperor's Twelve Symbol Robe, p. 119	Reverse Weaving, p. 120 Garden at Villandry, France, p. 158 Artist's Workshop: Create a Reverse Weaving, p. 121 Art Print 10: Panamanian Cuna Mola with Iguanas and Birds Art Print 17: Eclipse
PROBLEM SOLVING Problem/Solution	Garden at Villandry, France, p. 158 Artist's Workshop: Design a Park, p. 161	Artist's Workshop: Design a Building, p. 165

Texas Essential Knowledge and Skills

This correlation shows where the Texas Essential Knowledge and Skills
are developed in the *Teacher Edition* for grade 4.

ART

(4.1) **Perception.** The student develops and organizes ideas from the environment.

The student is expected to:	Teacher Edition pages
(A) communicate ideas about self, using sensory knowledge;	24, 31, 39, 54, 62, 63, 67, 69, 70, 79, 84, 103, 109, 120, 140, 142, 144, 149, 159, 160
communicate ideas about self, using life experiences;	31, 50, 63, 67, 90, 118, 128, 138, 142, 167
communicate ideas about family, using sensory knowledge;	70, 84, 100, 107, 112, 133, 134, 142, 158
communicate ideas about family, using life experiences;	70, 77, 100, 107, 112, 122, 132, 142, 158
communicate ideas about school, using sensory knowledge;	28, 32, 64, 72, 99, 101, 154, 164, 167, 185
communicate ideas about school, using life experiences;	28, 32, 72, 96, 101, 122, 164, 167
communicate ideas about community, using sensory knowledge;	30, 103, 133, 134, 158, 164, 170
communicate ideas about community, using life experiences.	30, 36, 103, 122, 132, 158, 164, 168, 170
(B) choose appropriate vocabulary to discuss the use of art elements such as color, texture, form, line, space, and value;	30, 31, 33, 34, 39, 44, 46, 49, 53, 59, 60, 63, 64, 65, 66, 67, 69, 70, 71, 73, 75, 76, 93, 99, 100, 101, 103, 105, 119, 121, 123, 130, 149, 150, 154, 159
choose appropriate vocabulary to discuss the use of art principles such as emphasis, pattern, rhythm, balance, proportion, and unity.	79, 80, 81, 91, 119, 120, 121, 123, 124, 125, 129, 130, 131, 133, 136, 139, 141, 143, 160, 161, 162, 163, 164

(4.2) **Creative expression/performance.** The student expresses ideas through original artworks, using a variety of media with appropriate skill.

The student is expected to:	Teacher Edition pages
(A) integrate a variety of ideas about self in original artworks;	51, 77, 81, 131, 141, 161
integrate a variety of ideas about life events in original artworks;	37, 82, 101, 131, 135, 141, 161
integrate a variety of ideas about family in original artworks;	82, 112, 131, 135, 141, 161, 172
integrate a variety of ideas about community in original artworks.	37, 52, 135, 151, 161, 171
(B) design original artworks;	31, 35, 41, 45, 51, 52, 61, 65, 67, 71, 75, 81, 82, 91, 101, 105, 111, 121, 125, 127, 131, 135, 137, 142, 151, 155, 157, 161, 163, 165, 167, 171, 172
(C) invent ways to produce artworks, using a variety of art media;	33, 61, 125, 157, 181

invent ways to produce artworks, using a variety of art materials;	47, 61, 65, 105, 111, 121, 125, 142, 157
invent ways to explore photographic imagery, using a variety of art media;	67, 71, 81, 95, 161
invent ways to explore photographic imagery, using a variety of art materials.	67, 71, 95, 161, 165

(4.3) **Historical/cultural heritage.** The student demonstrates an understanding of art history and culture as records of human achievement.

The student is expected to:	**Teacher Edition pages**
(A) identify simple main ideas expressed in art;	26, 28, 30, 31, 34, 40, 41, 43, 44, 45, 50, 53, 59, 69, 90, 104, 106, 124, 133, 140, 143, 150, 153, 154, 155, 160, 171
(B) compare selected artworks from a variety of cultural settings;	46, 50, 63, 90, 94, 103, 104, 108, 109, 110, 116, 120, 123, 124, 125, 126, 130, 131, 134, 135, 140, 141, 142, 160, 164, 170, 173
contrast selected artworks from a variety of cultural settings.	46, 50, 63, 90, 94, 103, 104, 108, 109, 110, 116, 120, 123, 124, 125, 130, 131, 134, 135, 140, 141, 142, 168, 170, 173
(C) identify the roles of art in American society.	97, 103, 109, 119, 136, 139, 166

(4.4) **Response/evaluation.** The student makes informed judgments about personal artworks and the artworks of others.

The student is expected to:	**Teacher Edition pages**
(A) describe intent about personal artworks;	31, 35, 41, 51, 53, 65, 81, 83, 91, 95, 101, 111, 135, 141, 143, 165, 171
form conclusions about personal artworks.	45, 61, 71, 121, 131, 141, 151, 155
(B) interpret ideas in original artworks by peers;	35, 37, 61, 65, 67, 131, 137, 155, 157, 161, 165, 167
interpret ideas in original artworks by others;	30, 39, 44, 47, 50, 56, 60, 61, 64, 70, 74, 77, 80, 86, 88, 89, 90, 94, 99, 100, 110, 113, 120, 130, 134, 140, 143, 146, 150, 151, 160, 161, 163, 164, 170, 173
interpret ideas in portfolios by peers;	37, 67, 107, 137, 172
interpret ideas in portfolios by others;	46, 47, 76, 77, 82, 97, 106, 127, 142
interpret ideas in exhibitions by peers;	37, 67, 107, 112, 137
interpret ideas in exhibitions by others;	47, 77, 97, 127, 186
interpret moods in original artworks by peers;	37, 127, 137, 194, 197
interpret moods in original artworks by others;	43, 47, 53, 58, 60, 74, 77, 79, 89, 133, 134, 140, 173
interpret moods in portfolios by peers;	37, 107, 137, 202
interpret moods in portfolios by others;	46, 47, 76, 97, 106, 127, 142
interpret moods in exhibitions by peers;	37, 107, 112, 137, 201
interpret moods in exhibitions by others.	47, 77, 97, 127, 186

READING

(4.5) **Listening/speaking/audiences.** The student speaks appropriately to different audiences for different purposes and occasions.

The student is expected to:	Teacher Edition pages
(B) demonstrate effective communication skills that reflect such demands as interviewing, reporting, requesting, and providing information (4–8);	24, 32, 42, 54, 133, 191

(4.6) **Reading/word identification.** The student uses a variety of word recognition strategies.

The student is expected to:	Teacher Edition pages
(C) locate the meanings, pronunciations, and derivations of unfamiliar words using dictionaries, glossaries, and other sources (4–8)	25, 55, 85, 115, 145, 175

(4.7) **Reading/fluency.** The student reads with fluency and understanding in texts at appropriate difficulty levels.

The student is expected to:	Teacher Edition pages
(A) read regularly in independent-level materials (texts in which no more than approximately 1 in 20 words is difficult for the reader) (4);	31, 45, 61, 65, 75, 81, 91, 95, 125, 135, 151, 155, 161, 165, 171, 181, 185, 191, 195
(B) read regularly in instructional-level materials that are challenging but manageable (texts in which no more than approximately 1 in 10 words is difficult for the reader; a "typical" fourth grader reads approximately 90 wpm) (4);	35, 41, 51, 71, 101, 105, 111, 121

(4.8) **Reading/variety of texts.** The student reads widely for different purposes in varied sources.

The student is expected to:	Teacher Edition pages
(C) read for varied purposes such as to be informed, to be entertained, to appreciate the writer's craft, and to discover models for his/her own writing (4–8).	31, 35, 41, 45, 51, 61, 65, 71, 75, 81, 91, 95, 101, 105, 111, 121, 125, 131, 135, 141, 151, 155, 161, 165, 171, 181, 185, 191, 195, 201

(4.9) **Reading/vocabulary development.** The student acquires an extensive vocabulary through reading and systematic word study.

The student is expected to:	Teacher Edition pages
(C) use multiple reference aids such as a thesaurus, synonym finder, dictionary, and software to clarify meanings and usage (4–8/ESL);	25, 55, 85, 115, 145, 175
(E) study word meanings systematically such as across curricular content areas and through current events (4–8)	25, 36, 55, 66, 85, 97, 115, 145, 156, 175, 197

(4.10) **Reading/comprehension.** The student comprehends selections using a variety of strategies.

The student is expected to:	Teacher Edition pages
(F) determine a text's main (or major) ideas and how those ideas are supported with details (4–8);	26–27, 30, 34, 40, 44, 50, 52–53
(G) paraphrase and summarize text to recall, inform, and organize ideas (4–8);	146–147, 150, 154, 160, 164, 170, 172–173

(J)	distinguish fact and opinion in various texts (4–8);	56–57, 60, 64, 70, 74, 80, 82–83
(L)	represent text information in different ways such as in outline, timeline, or graphic organizer (4–8).	27, 57, 87, 117, 147, 177

(4.11) Reading/literary response. The student expresses and supports responses to various types of texts.

The student is expected to:	**Teacher Edition pages**
(D) connect, compare, and contrast ideas, themes, and issues across text (4–8).	116-117, 120, 124, 130, 134, 140, 142-143

(4.12) Reading/text structures/literary concepts. The student analyzes the characteristics of various types of texts (genres).

The student is expected to:	**Teacher Edition pages**
(C) identify the purposes of different types of texts such as to inform, influence, express, or entertain (4–8);	176–177, 180, 184, 190, 194, 200, 202–203

(4.13) Reading/inquiry/research. The student inquires and conducts research using a variety of sources.

The student is expected to:	**Teacher Edition pages**
(C) use multiple sources including electronic texts, experts, and print resources to locate information relevant to research questions (4–8);	29, 33, 39, 49, 59, 69, 73, 79, 89, 103, 109, 119, 123, 129, 149, 153, 159, 169
(D) interpret and use graphic sources of information such as maps, graphs, timelines, tables, and diagrams to address research questions (4-5);	49, 115, 124
(E) summarize and organize information from multiple sources by taking notes, outlining ideas, or making charts (4–8);	27, 52, 53, 57, 82, 83, 87, 112, 113, 117, 140, 141, 147, 172, 173, 177, 202, 203

(4.14) Reading/culture. The student reads to increase knowledge of his/her own culture, the culture of others, and the common elements of cultures.

The student is expected to:	**Teacher Edition pages**
(C) articulate and discuss themes and connections that cross cultures (4–8)	116–117, 123, 127, 130, 132, 134

(4.15) Writing/purposes. The student writes for a variety of audiences and purposes, and in a variety of forms.

The student is expected to:	**Teacher Edition pages**
(A) write to express, discover, record, develop, reflect on ideas, and to problem solve (4–8);	30, 31, 40, 74, 90, 94, 124, 140, 161, 180, 194
(B) write to influence such as to persuade, argue, and request (4–8);	71, 101
(C) write to inform such as to explain, describe, report, and narrate (4–8);	34, 35, 44, 45, 50, 53, 60, 61, 64, 65, 70, 74, 80, 90, 95, 104, 120, 130, 131, 151, 154, 160, 164, 165, 170
(D) write to entertain such as to compose humorous poems or short stories (4–8);	81, 91, 100, 110, 111, 113, 125, 134, 135, 141, 150, 155, 171, 181, 184, 185, 190, 194, 200, 201

(4.19) **Writing/writing processes.** The student selects and uses writing processes for self-initiated and assigned writing.

The student is expected to:	Teacher Edition pages
(A) generate ideas and plans for writing by using such prewriting strategies as brainstorming, graphic organizers, notes, and logs (4–8);	53, 83, 113, 143, 173, 203
(E) edit drafts for specific purposes such as to ensure standard usage, varied sentence structure, and appropriate word choice (4–8);	53, 83, 113, 143, 173, 203
(H) proofread his/her own writing and that of others (4–8);	113, 131

(4.23) **Viewing/representing/interpretation.** The student understands and interprets visual images, messages, and meanings.

The student is expected to:	Teacher Edition pages
(B) interpret important events and ideas gathered from maps, charts, graphics, video segments, or technology presentations (4–8);	24, 30, 34, 36, 37, 40, 54, 59, 144, 149, 170, 179, 189

(4.24) **Viewing/representing/analysis.** The student analyzes and critiques the significance of visual images, messages, and meanings.

The student is expected to:	Teacher Edition pages
(A) interpret and evaluate the various ways visual image makers such as graphic artists, illustrators, and news photographers represent meanings (4–5);	30, 34, 40, 44, 50, 60, 64, 70, 74, 80, 90, 94, 100, 104, 110, 120, 124, 130, 134, 140, 150, 154, 160, 164, 170, 180, 184, 190, 194, 200

MATHEMATICS

(4.4) **Number, operation, and quantitative reasoning.** The student multiplies and divides to solve meaningful problems involving whole numbers.

The student is expected to:	Teacher Edition pages
(B) represent multiplication and division situations in picture, word, and number form;	183

(4.8) **Geometry and spatial reasoning.** The student identifies and describes lines, shapes, and solids using formal geometric language.

The student is expected to:	Teacher Edition pages
(A) identify right, acute, and obtuse angles;	29, 93
(B) identify models of parallel and perpendicular lines; and	29, 76, 93
(C) describe shapes and solids in terms of vertices, edges, and faces.	32, 34

(4.14) **Underlying processes and mathematical tools.** The student applies Grade 4 mathematics to solve problems connected to everyday experiences and activities in and outside of school.

The student is expected to:	Teacher Edition pages
(A) identify the mathematics in everyday situations;	32, 34, 35, 46, 47, 48, 49, 99, 100, 101, 109, 110, 111, 120, 121, 123, 124, 125, 128, 129, 130, 131, 133, 135, 139, 141, 143, 154, 158, 162, 163, 164, 165, 166, 186, 189, 190, 199

| (D) | use tools such as real objects, manipulatives, and technology to solve problems. | 183 |

(4.15) **Underlying processes and mathematical tools.** The student communicates about Grade 4 mathematics using informal language.

The student is expected to:	**Teacher Edition pages**
(A) explain and record observations using objects, words, pictures, numbers, and technology; and	44, 48, 49, 99, 100, 101, 119, 121, 123, 124, 125, 129, 130, 131, 139, 143, 154, 162, 163, 164, 165, 166, 186, 190, 199
(B) relate informal language to mathematical language and symbols.	28, 30, 31, 33, 46, 48, 49, 101, 119, 123, 128

SCIENCE

(4.1) **Scientific processes.** The student conducts field and laboratory investigations following home and school safety procedures and environmentally appropriate and ethical practices.

The student is expected to:	**Teacher Edition pages**
(B) make wise choices in the use and conservation of resources and the disposal or recycling of materials.	189, 197

(4.2) **Scientific processes.** The student uses scientific inquiry methods during field and laboratory investigations.

The student is expected to:	**Teacher Edition pages**
(B) collect information by observing and measuring;	44, 189
(D) communicate valid conclusions; and	44
(E) construct simple graphs, tables, maps, and charts to organize, examine, and evaluate information.	44

(4.3) **Scientific processes.** The student uses critical thinking and scientific problem solving to make informed decisions.

The student is expected to:	**Teacher Edition pages**
(C) represent the natural world using models and identify their limitations;	33
(D) evaluate the impact of research on scientific thought, society, and the environment; and	36, 37, 67, 197
(E) connect Grade 4 science concepts with the history of science and contributions of scientists.	37, 197

(4.6) **Science concepts.** The student knows that change can create recognizable patterns.

The student is expected to:	**Teacher Edition pages**
(A) identify patterns of change such as in weather, metamorphosis, and objects in the sky;	31, 56

(4.7) **Science concepts.** The student knows that matter has physical properties.

The student is expected to:	Teacher Edition pages
(B) conduct tests, compare data, and draw conclusions about physical properties of matter including states of matter, conduction, density, and buoyancy.	103

(4.10) **Science concepts.** The student knows that certain past events affect present and future events.

The student is expected to:	Teacher Edition pages
(A) identify and observe effects of events that require time for changes to be noticeable including growth, erosion, dissolving, weathering, and flow; and	36, 66
(B) draw conclusions about "what happened before" using fossils or charts and tables.	36

(4.11) **Science concepts.** The student knows that the natural world includes earth materials and objects in the sky.

The student is expected to:	Teacher Edition pages
(A) test properties of soils including texture, capacity to retain water, and ability to support life;	66
(B) summarize the effects of the oceans on land;	66

SOCIAL STUDIES

(4.1) **History.** The student understands the similarities and differences of Native-American groups in Texas and the Western Hemisphere before European exploration.

The student is expected to:	Teacher Edition pages
(A) identify Native-American groups in Texas and the Western Hemisphere before European exploration and describe the regions in which they lived;	123, 124

(4.2) **History.** The student understands the causes and effects of European exploration and colonization of Texas and the Western Hemisphere.

The student is expected to:	Teacher Edition pages
(A) summarize reasons for European exploration and settlement of Texas and the Western Hemisphere;	156
(C) explain when, where, and why the Spanish established Catholic missions in Texas;	156, 157
(E) identify leaders important to the founding of Texas as a republic and state, including Sam Houston, Mirabeau Lamar, and Anson Jones.	96, 109

(4.4) **History.** The student understands the political, economic, and social changes in Texas during the last half of the 19th century.

The student is expected to:	Teacher Edition pages
(B) explain the growth and development of the cattle and oil industries;	136

(4.6) **Geography.** The student uses geographic tools to collect, analyze, and interpret data.

The student is expected to:	Teacher Edition pages
(A) apply geographic tools, including grid systems, legends, symbols, scales, and compass roses, to construct and interpret maps;	24, 30, 54, 59, 67, 69, 84, 89, 99, 104, 114, 134, 144, 149, 160, 174, 179

(4.7) **Geography.** The student understands the concept of regions.

The student is expected to:	Teacher Edition pages
(A) describe a variety of regions in Texas and the Western Hemisphere such as political, population, and economic regions that result from patterns of human activity;	136, 156
(B) describe a variety of regions in Texas and the Western Hemisphere such as landform, climate, and vegetation regions that result from physical characteristics;	30, 37, 39, 40, 49

(4.8) **Geography.** The student understands the location and patterns of settlement and the geographic factors that influence where people live.

The student is expected to:	Teacher Edition pages
(B) explain patterns of settlement at different time periods in Texas;	156
(C) describe the location of cities in Texas and explain their distribution, past and present;	156

(4.9) **Geography.** The student understands how people adapt to and modify their environment.

The student is expected to:	Teacher Edition pages
(A) describe ways people have adapted to and modified their environment in Texas, past and present;	136, 156
(B) identify reasons why people have adapted to and modified their environment in Texas, past and present, such as the use of natural resources to meet basic needs; and	136, 156
(C) analyze the consequences of human modification of the environment in Texas, past and present.	136, 156

(4.17) **Citizenship.** The student understands important customs, symbols, and celebrations of Texas.

The student is expected to:	Teacher Edition pages
(A) explain the meaning of selected patriotic symbols and landmarks of Texas, including the six flags over Texas, San José Mission, and the San Jacinto Monument;	109, 156, 157, 166

(4.18) **Citizenship.** The student understands the importance of voluntary individual participation in the democratic process.

The student is expected to:	Teacher Edition pages
(C) identify the importance of historical figures such as Sam Houston, Barbara Jordan, and Lorenzo de Zavala who modeled active participation in the democratic process;	96, 137

(4.19) **Citizenship.** The student understands the importance of effective leadership in a democratic society.

The student is expected to:	Teacher Edition pages
(A) identify leaders in state and local governments, including the governor, selected members of the Texas Legislature, and Texans who have been President of the United States, and their political parties;	137

(4.20) **Culture.** The student understands the contributions of people of various racial, ethnic, and religious groups to Texas.

The student is expected to:	Teacher Edition pages
(B) identify customs, celebrations, and traditions of various culture groups in Texas; and	136, 156
(C) summarize the contributions of people of various racial, ethnic, and religious groups in the development of Texas.	48, 96, 128, 137, 156

(4.22) **Social studies skills.** The student applies critical-thinking skills to organize and use information acquired from a variety of sources including electronic technology.

The student is expected to:	Teacher Edition pages
(A) differentiate between, locate, and use primary and secondary sources such as computer software; interviews; biographies; oral, print, and visual material; and artifacts to acquire information about the United States and Texas;	49, 73, 109, 123, 139, 153, 159, 189
(B) analyze information by sequencing, categorizing, identifying cause-and-effect relationships, comparing, contrasting, finding the main idea, summarizing, making generalizations and predictions, and drawing inferences and conclusions;	26, 29, 31, 33, 34, 35, 39, 40, 41, 45, 46, 47, 50, 52, 53, 63, 64, 75, 76, 84, 88, 90, 93, 95, 103, 104, 109, 110, 111, 116, 117, 120, 121, 124, 125, 126, 130, 131, 134, 140, 141, 142, 143, 146, 147, 150, 151, 152, 154, 155, 156, 157, 160, 161, 164, 165, 170, 171, 173, 179, 180, 184, 196, 200
(C) organize and interpret information in outlines, reports, databases, and visuals including graphs, charts, timelines, and maps;	25, 27, 39, 41, 44, 52, 55, 57, 63, 79, 82, 83, 85, 87, 89, 112, 113, 115, 117, 123, 142, 145, 147, 172, 175, 177, 202
(D) identify different points of view about an issue or topic;	47, 174, 191, 194
(E) identify the elements of frame of reference that influenced the participants in an event;	56, 136

(4.23) **Social studies skills.** The student communicates in written, oral, and visual forms.

The student is expected to:	Teacher Edition pages
(B) incorporate main and supporting ideas in verbal and written communication;	26, 27, 29, 30, 31, 33, 34, 35, 39, 40, 41, 44, 45, 50, 52, 53, 88, 103, 106, 133, 135, 146, 147, 150, 154, 160, 169, 173, 177, 189, 202

(C)	express ideas orally based on research and experiences;	24, 26, 30, 31, 33, 34, 35, 36, 37, 38, 39, 40, 42, 44, 45, 49, 50, 51, 53, 56, 59, 60, 64, 67, 69, 71, 74, 77, 79, 80, 82, 84, 86, 89, 90, 93, 97, 98, 99, 100, 101, 103, 104, 105, 106, 109, 110, 112, 113, 114, 118, 119, 121, 122, 124, 125, 128, 129, 132, 133, 134, 135, 138, 139, 140, 142, 143, 145, 146, 149, 150, 151, 153, 154, 155, 158, 161, 163, 164, 165, 167, 168, 171, 172, 176, 179, 180, 181, 184, 185, 187, 190, 191, 195, 200, 201, 203
(D)	create written and visual material such as journal entries, reports, graphic organizers, outlines, and bibliographies; and	25, 27, 30, 31, 33, 34, 35, 37, 39, 40, 41, 44, 45, 50, 51, 52, 55, 57, 60, 61, 64, 65, 70, 71, 74, 75, 79, 80, 81, 82, 85, 87, 89, 90, 91, 94, 95, 100, 101, 104, 105, 109, 110, 111, 112, 115, 117, 120, 121, 124, 125, 130, 131, 134, 135, 137, 140, 141, 142, 150, 151, 154, 155, 157, 159, 160, 161, 164, 165, 170, 171, 172, 175, 180, 181, 184, 185, 190, 191, 192, 194, 195, 200, 201, 202
(E)	use standard grammar, spelling, sentence structure, and punctuation.	43, 45, 181